Wine Tourism Around the World

To the Wandering Islands of Wine

Wine Tourism Around the World

Development, management and markets

Edited by

C. Michael Hall, Liz Sharples,
Brock Cambourne and Niki Macionis

with

Richard Mitchell and Gary Johnson

ELSEVIER
BUTTERWORTH
HEINEMANN

AMSTERDAM BOSTON HEIDELBERG LONDON NEW YORK OXFORD
PARIS SAN DIEGO SAN FRANCISCO SINGAPORE SYDNEY TOKYO

Elsevier Butterworth-Heinemann
Linacre House, Jordan Hill, Oxford OX2 8DP
30 Corporate Drive, Burlington, MA 01803

First published 2000
Paperback edition 2002
Reprinted 2004

British Library Cataloguing in Publication Data
Wine tourism around the world: development management and markets
  1. Tourist trade   2. Wine and wine making   3. Wine industry
  I. Hall, Colin Michael, 1961–
  338.4′791

Library of Congress Cataloguing in Publication Data
Wine tourism around the world: development, management and markets/edited by
C. Michael Hall . . . [et al.]
  p. cm.
  Includes bibliographical references and index.
  ISBN 0 7506 4530 X
  1. Wine and wine making.   2. Tourism.
  I. Hall, Colin, Michael, 1961–
  TP548 . W7725
  641.3′2–dc21   99–086165

ISBN 0 7506 5466 X

For more information on all Butterworth-Heinemann
publications please visit our website at www.bh.com

Composition by Genesis Typesetting, Rochester, Kent
Printed and bound in Great Britain by Biddles Ltd, King's Lynn, Norfolk

Contents

Exhibits

Figures

Tables

Contributors

Brock Cambourne, National Capital Wine Tours, Canberra, ACT, Australia

Tim H. Dodd, Director, Texas Wine Marketing Research Institute, Texas Tech University, USA

Isabelle Frochot, The Scottish Hotel School, University of Strathclyde, Scotland

C. Michael Hall, Centre for Tourism, University of Otago, New Zealand, and School of Food and Leisure Management, Sheffield Hallam University, UK

Michael Howley, Department of Management Studies, University of Surrey, Guildford, UK

Gary Johnson, Tourism Wairapa, Masterton, New Zealand

Anna Marie Longo, 79 Eton Road, Bronxville, New York 10708, USA

Niki Macionis, Centre for Tourism and Leisure Policy Research, University of Canberra, ACT, Australia

Alison McIntosh, Centre for Tourism, University of Otago, New Zealand

Richard Mitchell, Centre for Tourism, University of Otago, New Zealand

Nigel Morpeth, Tourism, The University of Lincolnshire and Humberside, Lincoln, UK

Stephen Page, Centre for Tourism Research, Massey University Albany, Auckland, New Zealand

Robert Preston-Whyte, School of Life and Environmental Sciences, University of Natal, Durban, South Africa

Oliver Richardson, Department of Business and Management, Brunel University, UK

Liz Sharples, School of Leisure and Food Management, Sheffield Hallam University, UK

Angela M. Skinner, Department of Geography, California State University, USA

David J. Telfer, Department of Recreation and Leisure Studies, Brock University, Ontario, Canada

Jetske Van Westering, Department of Management Studies, University of Surrey, Guildford, UK

Michael Whyte, Sales Manager, Vasse Felix Winery, Margaret River, Western Australia, Australia

Preface

This book, like many good wines, has been a long time in development. First discussed between some of the editors in 1994, it has undergone a series of changes in direction until the present outline was established in 1998. Originally envisaged as a book on food, wine and tourism, it is a testament to the growth of wine tourism and the wider recognition of the interconnections between wine and tourism that this book now focuses almost exclusively on wine and tourism. It is also a book which deliberately positions itself as a serious contribution to our understanding of the wine industry. Indeed, it is remarkable that it is only recently that the business aspects of wine have started to be subject to as much scrutiny as viticulture and oenology and the history and romance of wine. Many books have been written on travelling to and within wine regions but, until now, no book has been written on the implications of that travel. However, we would note that this book is only a start in understanding the subject of wine tourism, as there are many regions, as well as many subjects, which require more attention than space allows us to provide here. If the reader will excuse the pun, this book provides only an introductory tasting of the complexities of wine tourism.

This is also a book written by people who are interested and involved in wine from both an academic and a business perspective and the editors and authors clearly hope that this book will be of interest as much to people in the wine and tourism industries as it is to students of the grape. Research on wine tourism is not always as glamorous and attractive as it might seem and, in the same way that one finds occasional corked bottles, so there are also sometimes poor wine tourism experiences. This stated, the editors would like to thank all the wineries, wine-makers and winery personnel who gave so freely of their time and expertise throughout the evolution of this book. We would also like to thank and acknowledge the input of all our contributors, whose knowledge and passion have made this book truly international in scope and focus, as well as the tremendous support provided by our publishers in Oxford.

Several individuals were especially helpful with regard to the provision of information and were always willing to answer questions, including Chris Day, Group Manager, Strategic Planning, BRL Hardy; Gladys Horiuchi, Communications Manager, Wine Institute; Mark Mathewson, Director of Hospitality for Kendall-Jackson and the Artisan & Estate family of wineries; Di Westthorpe, Project Manager, Queensland Wine Industry Project; and Jack Rasterhoff, CEO, Victorian Wineries Tourism Council. To this list we should add a number of people who have contributed to the fieldwork which has led to the development of this book. In particular we would gratefully acknowledge the assistance of Tim Bahaire, Dick and Margaret Butler, Jody Cowper, Dave Crag, Martin Elliott-White, Angela Elvey, Thor Flogenfeldt, Joanna Fountain, Sandra James, John Jenkins, Simon McArthur, Brian McIntosh, Carleen Mitchell, Nigel Morpeth, Meiko Muramaya, Stephen Page, Rachael Parr, Anna Dora Saethorsdottir, and the staff of Munslows who have all contributed to the development of this book in various ways. Finally, we would like to acknowledge the fruit of the vine that provided both inspiration and sustenance throughout the course of this project.

1

Wine tourism: an introduction

C. Michael Hall, Gary Johnson, Brock Cambourne,
Niki Macionis, Richard Mitchell and Liz Sharples

Wine tourism is a significant component of both the wine and tourism industries. Wine and tourism have been intimately connected for many years, but it is only recently that this relationship has come to be explicitly recognized by governments, researchers and by the industries themselves. For the tourism industry, wine is an important component of the attractiveness of a destination and can be a major motivating factor for visitors. For the wine industry, wine tourism is a very important way to build up relationships with customers who can experience first hand the romance of the grape, while for many smaller wineries direct selling to visitors at the cellar door is often essential to their business success. In her standard work on wine, Jancis Robinson (1994: 980) records that

> Wine-related tourism has become increasingly important. For many centuries not even wine merchants travelled, but today

many members of the general public deliberately make forays to explore a wine region or regions. This is partly a reflection of the increased interest in both wine and foreign travel generally, but also because most wine regions and many producers' premises are attractive places. Vineyards tend to be aesthetically pleasing in any case, and the sort of climate in which wine is generally produced is agreeable during most of the year. Getting to grips with this specialist form of agriculture combines urban dwellers' need to commune with nature with acquiring privileged, and generally admired, specialist knowledge. And then there is the possibility of tasting, and buying wines direct from the source, which may involve keen prices and/or acquiring rarities.

Visits to vineyards have been a part of organized travel at least since the time of the Grand Tour, and likely even since the times of ancient Greece and Rome. However, it was not until the mid-nineteenth century that wine began to appear as a specific travel interest. Several factors came together at this time. First, the transport revolution created by the development of the railways enabled greater ease of access. Second, a social revolution occurred in terms of the growth of a new middle class that began to seek quality wine along with the aristocracy. Finally, the publication of the 1855 *Classification of the Wines of the Gironde* for the first time explicitly and officially gave wine, and wine-growing regions, a destinational identity. This classification, which had government sanction, of the wines of Bordeaux, was the result of recommendations made by the Syndicate of Bordeaux Wine-brokers for use during the Paris Exhibition of 1855 (de Blij 1983). The classification served as the basis for the system of appellation control which exists to this day in France, but not only did it reinforce the quality and regional characteristics of Bordeaux wine, it also served to provide a marketing tool for a region and identified specific chateaux as classified growths which in themselves became visitor attractions.

In the modern era wine trails have been a part of the German tourism industry since the 1920s and there is an association of wine trails in Europe which coordinates activities among member countries. According to Johnson (1986: 158) the *Weinlehrpfad* (instructional wine path) 'help to explain and therefore sell German wine, and by the end of the 1970s practically all the eleven wine regions had their own *Weinstraßen* [wine road]'. More recently, Eastern European countries, such as Hungary, have begun to establish wine trails in an effort to attract Western European tourists. For example, Hungary's first wine road, the Villány Siklós Wine Road, was established in Baranya County in 1995 (Tourinform Baranya n.d.). (See Exhibits 2.1, 2.3 and 2.5.)

In the New World wine tourism has also come to be significant. California's Napa Valley is a major drawcard for tourists (see Chapter 15), while the vineyards of New York State and Ontario in Canada have also rapidly become visitor attractions (see Chapter 13). In Australia a number of state governments have developed wine tourism strategies (see Chapter 12), while in both Australia and New Zealand the high profile of their wine in major tourist generating areas in North America and Europe is being used as a marketing tool to attract international visitors (see Chapters 8 and 12). This is then an exciting time for wine tourism. However, it should be noted that the wider benefits and costs of wine tourism are not always appreciated. Similarly, in many parts of the world the interrelationships and synergies that exist between wine and tourism still often go unrecognized.

This book therefore aims to fill these significant gaps in our understanding of the wine tourism phenomenon and the implications for industry, communities and the consumer. The book is international in scope, with selected chapters, case studies and examples being used to illustrate the richness of the subject of wine tourism. This first chapter provides an introduction to some of the key issues which are examined in the book and provides a framework within which wine tourism is examined. It concludes with an overview of the various chapters and case studies. As in all books dealing with a subject for the first time, one of the most important attributes is definition of the field of study, and it is to this subject that this chapter will first turn.

What is wine tourism?

Wine tourism can be defined as: *visitation to vineyards, wineries, wine festivals and wine shows for which grape wine tasting and/or experiencing the attributes of a grape wine region are the prime motivating factors for visitors* (Hall 1996; Macionis 1996). Macionis (1996 1997) proposed a model of wine tourism based around a special interest in wine motivated by the destination (wine region), the activity (wine tasting) or both. Although tourism, including day-tripping and excursions, is important for many wineries in terms of the ability to sell wine either directly to visitors through cellar sales or to place such customers on a direct mail order list, tourism, if mentioned at all, has sometimes been seen in very disparaging terms by some wineries with the implication that those who are seriously interested in wine are not tourists (e.g. Bradley 1982; Hall and Johnson 1997).

The above definition identifies key locations in which wine tourism occurs and clearly distinguishes that visitation may be motivated by 'grape wine' specifically or, more generally, 'the attributes of a grape wine region', sometimes referred to as the 'winescape' (Peters 1997) or 'the wine tourism terroir' (Mitchell, in progress). In the above reference no statement is made as to the length of visitor stay, so 'tourism' here is understood to encompass recreational activity, excursions, day-trips, and overnight stays.

Johnson (1998) raises two issues with the above definition, the first relates to the relevance of the wine region to wine tourism, the second to whether the listed 'motivating factors' result in a too restrictive definition. Johnson validly argues that the attributes of a grape wine region that appeal to those visiting a wine region (such as scenery and open spaces) may be quite unrelated to consuming wine, and raises the question that as grape wine regions are almost always rural areas, at what point does rural tourism become wine tourism? Therefore, at what point does a visitor to a wine region become a wine tourist? Such questions are not merely academic, as the increasing focus on wine and tourism interrelationships by government and industry heightens the need for good data collection on which sound business decisions can be made. Indeed, one of the great problems in tourism is the propensity to overestimate its economic and development benefits in relation to other industries. Nevertheless, as recent research has demonstrated (see Chapter 8) the winescape does provide a set of aesthetic and regional attributes that does appear to be attractive to visitors in its own right. As de Blij (1983: 4–5) observes:

> Surely there are few human pursuits that generate as close a relationship between people and the land they cultivate as does viticulture. The well-tended vineyard is a hillside transformed, the soil turned and aired, the vines trained and pruned, the fields laid out for optimal benefit of sun and shade ... The cultural landscape of viticulture is embellished by the situation, architectural qualities, layout, and general ambience of the towns, villages, chateaux, and more modest wineries that are the foci of viniculture and the wine trade. The tangible attributes of this special cultural landscape are further complemented by a particular atmosphere, an appealing environment that is part of the reason why wine regions the world over attract endless streams of visitors, who come not just to sample the wines.

However, we should note that while much wine tourism occurs in a winescape, some wine-motivated travel, for example, to wine and food festivals and wine shows, will occur in urban areas, while in various parts of the world we also find wineries and even vineyards that have now been surrounded by suburbs and urban sprawl.

Johnson (1998) also argues that the above definition of wine tourism seems to suggest that all visitors to wineries have wine-related motivations, that the scopes of wine tourism and wine tourists are coextensive. However, as various chapters in this book point out, visitors to wineries and wine regions differ in their interest in and expertise on wine. An illustrative example is the story of a church group who booked a tour of a vineyard in Martinborough, New Zealand, only to inform the winery guide on arrival that they did not drink wine, but were nonetheless interested in how it was made (March 1998). Similarly, a more specialist wine tourist may also be motivated by activities other than wine tasting, such as the collection of wine labels (e.g. see Stratemeyer (1998) on the Wine Label Collectors Club of America). Furthermore, as will be readily recognized by many readers, motivations within groups may differ, for example, an avid wine lover whose interest instigated the winery visit, who is accompanied by a friend who does not share the same passion for wine.

From the perspective of his research, Johnson (1998) defined wine tourism as 'visitation to vineyards, wineries, wine festivals and wine shows for the purpose of recreation'. This definition excludes work-related visitation and emphasizes that the activity is recreational. Moreover, it also ignores much of the historical context of wine tourism (e.g. see Johnson 1991). The participant, or wine tourist, was then simply defined as 'one who visits a vineyard, winery, wine festival or wine show for the purpose of recreation'. From the viewpoint of the collection of data such comments are useful. However, from the broader regional perspective such definitions do not adequately convey the romance of the grape, winescapes and wine-producing regions that is so much part of wine and wine tourism around the world.

For those readers unfamiliar with the business of wine, in this book a winery refers to the facility where grapes are made into wine. For the purpose of brevity, winery will be used here to refer to any winery or vineyard complex, with the term vineyard restricted solely to the area where vines are planted. The term wine producer is used here as an all-embracing term for a wine-grower, wine-maker, grape-grower, or the owner or manager of a winery or vineyard.

Wine tourism is a concept and product that is still undergoing substantial development. The term wine tourism embraces two industries which each have substantial implications for regional economies, environments and lifestyles and which have been long entwined. However, the establishment of formal relationships between the two industries has only recently been recognized in some quarters and there remains substantial mistrust and, perhaps more significantly, misuderstandings over how tourism and wine can provide positive contributions to each other and to the regions within which they coexist. It is this series of interrelationships which lies at the core of many of the concepts, issues and cases which are the focus of this book.

A framework for understanding wine tourism

A framework for analysing the nature of wine tourism is provided in Figure 1.1. The model attempts to integrate the demand and supply of the wine tourism experience. The focal point of the model is the wine tourism experience. This is the experience that the consumer, the visitor, has while he or she comes into contact with the elements that comprise the wine tourism product, such as wineries, vineyards, festivals, winescapes and, of course, wine (and, increasingly food – although to quote Oliver Wendell Holmes – Massachusetts Medical Society (circa 1800) – 'wine is a food'). Nevertheless, we should note that the desired experiences or travel outcomes will differ from person to person and from culture to culture. The different components of consumer demand for wine tourism are dealt with in more detail in Chapter 6. However, the next section will briefly cover some of the elements that influence demand for wine tourism.

Demand for wine tourism

Demand comprises the motivations, perceptions, previous experiences and expectations of the wine tourist. There are a number of motivations which influence wine tourism. Few people will actually have the desire to purchase wine as the only reason for visiting a winery. Many will want to learn more about wine in order to improve their knowledge of wines and wine-making – this may be described as an educational motivation. For others, the opportunity to enjoy the social aspects of wine tourism may be a major motivation, while the health aspects of wine may also be emerging as a significant factor in wine consumption and, possibly, wine tourism.

Tourism motivations will not be the same for an individual throughout their life. Motivations will change according to past life experiences and stages in life. In addition, motivations may shift or become greater factors because of promotion campaigns which may create certain perceptions of potential destinations and attractions, such as publicity for a particular vineyard, and which therefore influence recreational travel.

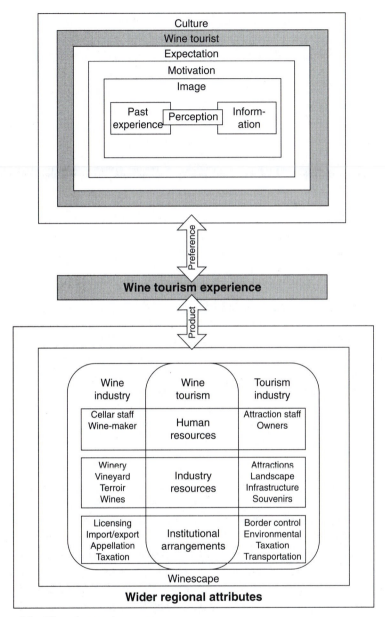

Figure 1.1 The wine tourism system

The perceptions of the traveller comprise three different elements: past experiences, preferences and information. The choice of destinations and visits to attractions will be affected by previous experiences, and their relative enjoyment. For example, if a visitor to a winery has had a poor experience

7

because of poor service then not only may he or she not return to that winery, they may also not purchase that winery's wine at other locations. Preferences refer to individual priorities, often reflecting the individual's personality, in the search for the satisfaction of particular desires or needs (Murphy 1985). Information comes from a variety of sources, some of the most obvious being the food, wine and travel pages in newspapers and magazines, visitor information centres and travel brochures. However, information can also come from novels, guidebooks, the Internet and friends, family and work associates. The work of Longo (1999), related in Chapter 8, for example, noted the importance of word-of-mouth as a factor influencing the decision of travellers as to which vineyard to visit.

Motivations and perceptions combine to construct each individual's image of destinations and attractions and the associated series of expectations regarding the experience at the destination. The image created is of utmost importance because the appeal of attractions arises largely from the image conjured up, partly from direct or related experience and partly from external sources and influences (Hunt 1975). Mental images are the basis for the evaluation and selection of an individual's choice of a destination or attraction. 'This conditions their expectations, setting an aspiration level or evaluative image, against which actual holiday opportunities are compared' (Goodall 1988: 3). According to Murphy (1985: 11), 'This image may be defined as the sum of beliefs, ideas and impressions that a person has regarding a destination. It is a personal composite view of a destination's tourism potential, and where prices are comparable it is often the decisive factor in a tourist's selection process'.

The images are not necessarily the same for each visitor. Nevertheless, image clearly plays a central role in the tourism and wine industries, particularly in terms of selling the romance of wine and wine-making. However, in the promotion of images potential major problems may arise. For example, what if the local people do not like the image that is being created in order to promote their community to tourists? From a long-term perspective on tourism development, an even greater problem may be the disparity between image and reality from the perspective of the visitor (see Chapter 15 on the Napa Valley). If there is a significant divergence, will the tourist have a satisfactory experience that will ensure a return visit or the recommendation of the winery and wine to friends? As Blanton (1981: 121) noted, 'tourist behaviour is often the product of heightened expectations, deflated hopes, exaggerated fears, or frustrated plans. Travellers have special needs and concerns, and the neglect of seemingly small details can sometimes lead to serious consequences'.

The supply of wine tourism

The supply side of wine tourism includes all the resources utilized by tourists for the purpose of wine tourism and the businesses and institutions which transform those resources into a wine tourism product. Resources from the wine industry include wineries, and winery amenities, vineyards, festivals and shows; those from the tourist industry include wine tours, accommodation and associated sectors such as the restaurant, hospitality and catering industries (Macionis and Cambourne, forthcoming). Human resources include wine producers and other viticultural and oenological workers as well as tourist operators. The surrounding environment includes infrastructure, physical environment, scenery, regional cuisine and the social and cultural components of the wine region – the wine tourist terroir. The institutional arrangements which affect wine tourism include not only all levels of government but also legislation, regulations and planning frameworks. In many parts of the world the role of government on wine tourism is substantial in terms of the creation of appellation controls, the establishment of health and safety regulations, planning regulations which affect what can be built and/or grown in certain locations, and the assistance which government may provide to support wine tourism infrastructure and networks.

The wine industry's involvement in tourism is a clear example of what Leiper (1989) refers to as the difference between being in the business and being in the industry of tourism. The business of an organization is defined by the customer groups or functions with which it deals, whereas an industry is a collection of organizations in the same or related line or lines of business and that use common technologies (Leiper 1989). (Examples of tourism 'technologies' include reservation systems, grading systems, industry associations, promotional activity and information exchange.) The concept of partial industrialization is one attempt to describe such difficulties and the consequent problems of coordination, management and strategic development. According to Leiper (1989: 25), partial industrialization refers to the condition

> in which only certain organizations providing goods and services directly to tourists are in the tourism industry. The proportion of (a) goods and services stemming from that industry to (b) total goods and services used by tourists can be termed the index of industrialization, theoretically ranging from 100 per cent (wholly industrialized) to zero (tourists present and spending money, but no tourism industry).

One of the major consequences of the partial industrialization of tourism is its significance for tourism development, marketing and network development. Although we can recognize that many businesses and segments of the economy may benefit from tourism, it is only those organizations with a direct relationship to tourists and/or who actually perceive their customers as tourists that become actively involved in fostering tourism development or tourism marketing. For example, there are many other businesses such as food suppliers, petrol stations, and retailers, sometimes described as 'allied industries', and, in some cases, wineries, which benefit from tourists but which do not readily identify themselves as part of the tourism industry (Hall 1998). Therefore, as Hall *et al.* (1998) noted, in most circumstances, unless there is a direct perceived financial motive for wine businesses to create linkages with tourism businesses, it will often require an external enducement, such as the establishment of linkages by government at no or minimal cost to individual businesses, to create relationships between the wine and tourism industries.

Wine tourism as wine business function/activity

Wine tourism can be the core business for many smaller wineries, especially those who have chosen wine-making as a lifestyle option (Australian Wine Foundation 1996). For other wineries, wine tourism may be a secondary part of their business operation, albeit significant, potentially serving roles as a sales channel, a promotional channel, and/or a means of educating the customer. Wine tourism is therefore an important component of the potential marketing and selling mix of wineries and wine businesses.

Tourism can be such an important factor in the viability of a vineyard that investors will assess a potential site in terms of both viticulture and tourism. As Hooke (1997: 176) remarked of a new winery in Australia: '[they] were knowledgeable enough and smart enough to select a piece of land close to tourist traffic, on a sealed road, on a frost-free slope'.

Many newly established smaller wineries sell most of their wine at the cellar door and develop a mail-order list, and gain an essential source of cash flow in these early stages (Gillion 1998: 13). For established wineries, such as the Brown Brothers in Australia, visitors provide a test-bed for new products: 'We build up the vine numbers till we have just enough to make batches of test wines. We have 100,000 customers visiting the cellar door at Milawa [King Valley, Northeast Victoria] each year, so it's the ideal place to test these varieties on the public' (in Hooke 1997: 85).

Several other advantages, as well as disadvantages, for producers choosing to sell wine at the cellar door have been identified by Dodd and Bigotte

(1995), on the basis of a study of visitors to Texas wineries; these are summarized in Table 1.1 (see also Chapter 7). Dodd and Bigotte present the advantages and disadvantages as they relate to business profitability. For owners who do not depend solely on income from winery sales for their livelihood, the personal enjoyment of hosting visitors may itself provide substantial reward. Indeed, for many smaller 'boutique' wineries which have been established in recent years in Australia, Canada, New Zealand, the United States and even the United Kingdom, lifestyle choice is an important element in developing wineries and vineyards. In these cases business strategies are not geared to increasing volume output but are more

Table 1.1 Advantages and disadvantages of wine tourism for wineries

Advantages

- *Increased consumer exposure* to product and increased opportunities to sample product.
- *Brand awareness and loyalty* built through establishing links between producer and consumer, and purchase of company-branded merchandise.
- *Increased margins* through direct sale to consumer, where the absence of distributor costs is not carried over entirely to the consumer.
- An *additional sales outlet* or, for smaller wine producers who cannot guarantee volume or constancy of supply, the only feasible sales outlet.
- *Marketing intelligence on products.* Wine producers can gain instant and valuable feedback on the consumer reaction to their existing products, and are able to trial new additions to their product range.
- *Marketing intelligence on customers.* Visitors to the winery can be added to a mailing list which can be developed as a customer database to both target and inform customers.
- *Educational opportunities.* Visits to wineries help create awareness and appreciation of wine and the wine industry, the knowledge and interest generated by this can be expected to result in increased consumption.

Disadvantages

- *Increased costs and management time.* The operation of a tasting room may be costly, particularly when it requires paid staff. While the profitability gap is higher on direct sales to the consumer, profit may be reduced if wineries do not charge for tastings.
- *Capital required.* Suitable facilities for hosting visitors may be prohibitively expensive, especially as wine-making is a capital intensive business.
- *Inability to substantially increase sales.* The number of visitors a winery can attract is limited and if a winery cannot sell all of its stock it will eventually need to use other distribution outlets.

Source: After Dodd and Bigotte (1995) and Day (1996)

concentrated on maintaining a level of output that focuses on the production of quality wine at a level which supports desired lifestyle and business attributes. The way in which wine tourism is utilized as a business strategy therefore depends on a mix of factors, including desired economies of scale, business strategies and, for many small owner-operated wineries, lifestyle choice. This is not to say that larger wineries ignore tourism. Far from it. As we shall see throughout the book and the various examples it offers, wine tourism is a significant component of the business strategies of large wine organizations given the opportunities it provides for brand development, providing for positive customer relationships, consumer education and, of course, the search for sales and profits (see Exhibit 1.1)

Exhibit 1.1: Searching for the home of America's favourite Chardonnay

While some researchers (e.g. Beverland 1998) eschew the importance and potential of tourism to wineries, particularly large producers, it is often a crucial component of an integrated business and marketing strategy. Sonoma County based Kendall-Jackson (1999) could be considered one of the success stories of the Californian wine industry. Established in 1974 with some 80 acres of vineyards, the Kendall-Jackson 'Artisans Estates' vineyards now comprises more than 5,000 acres of vines located throughout California, South America and Tuscany in Italy, with their wines being exported to more than 30 countries. Kendall-Jackson produces a range of premium and ultra-premium varietal wines, with their 1982 'Vintners Reserve' Chardonnay being nominated Best American Chardonnay at the American Wine Competition. According to the 1996 *California Wine Winners Book*, for the last three years in a row, Kendall-Jackson has won more gold, silver and bronze medals than any other winery in America, and it was recently nominated the top restaurant wine in America for the last four consecutive years.

According to Kendall-Jackson Director of Hospitality, Mark Mathewson (1998, pers. comm.), while retail room sales volumes are a small proportion of overall sales volume, winery tourism is very important to Kendall-Jackson.

Mathewson notes that while tourism can be critically important for smaller wineries – for major operations such as Kendall-Jackson 'the benefit lies in the opportunity we have to make a lasting impression on a consumer. It is my belief that the positive [wine tourism] experiences in our retail room affects purchase behavior in the marketplace'. To facilitate the delivery of a quality wine tourism experience, Kendall-Jackson operates the California Coast Wine Center in Santa Rosa which incorporates a retail wine tasting facility as well as demonstration vineyards, a self-guided vineyard tour and an interactive culinary garden.

The demonstration vineyard contains some 20 different varieties, ranging from Chardonnay, to California's first domestic hybrid, Symphony. Kendall-Jackson believes that educating the public about wine provides not only a great opportunity for wineries, but is also crucial to retail tasting room success. The 2.5 ha sensory culinary garden, which is planted with hundreds of varieties of fruits, flowers, vegetable and herbs from around the world, simply provides a different hook. According to Kendall-Jackson master gardener, Jeff Dawson 'The idea is to bring people out here and let them taste their wine with matching or even conflicting herbs or foods and take the flavors directly from the garden itself . . . we are trying to give people a physical reference point so that they can feel and taste the flavor component of wine, rather than simply conceptualize a word that describes that taste' (in Cartiere 1997).

Mathewson also says that the utility of the Kendall-Jackson Wine Center is in facilitating consumer visitation as well as hosting trade and hospitality functions and supporting philanthropic activities. He says 'The added experiential elements such as our demonstration vineyards and culinary garden set us apart from others and make us attractive to those looking for something different. They also aid in consumer education, which is big focus in Kendall-Jackson'. Kendall-Jackson also participates in a number of Sonoma County winery events and festivals, which Mathewson states provides substantial public relations rather than revenue benefits to the winery. Indeed, proceeds from events such as the Kendall-Jackson 'Tomato Festival' are directed back into the community.

Winery tourism is obviously an important component of an integrated business strategy at Kendall-Jackson. According to Mathewson 'The prime reason people visit Kendall-Jackson is because they recognize us. Our brand is very well distributed throughout the country and has a consumer following second to none'. Simply put, 'People want to see where America's favorite Chardonnay comes from'.

Brock Cambourne and Niki Macionis

Wine and food festivals also offer similar benefits to those provided by visits to wineries (Campbell 1996: 7; Pratt 1994) (see Exhibit 1.2):

- Wineries gain a cheap (and sometimes profitable) way to promote their brands to new customers.
- Wine regions establish a clearer and stronger identity.
- Wine producers get the opportunity to interact with their customers and gain feedback from them.
- Wine shows, perhaps more than any form of wine tourism, give wine producers access to 'targeted, qualified buyers', or customers with an interest in the products displayed and a desire to purchase them (Snow 1997: 377).

For example, the Exhibition Industry Association of Australia claim that exhibitions and trade fairs are effective in:

- raising profiles
- generating spot, mid- and long-term sales
- providing sales leads and industry contacts
- providing a stage for new product launches (Snow 1997: 377).

Wine exhibitions have a media advantage as a 'critical mass of winemakers is assembled in the one place with a theme, and that creates journalistic interest' (wine show organiser Roy Moorfield, quoted in Snow 1997: 377). For example, the Wine Australia 98 show boasts participation from 42 wine regions and 350 wine companies (WINENZ 1998a,b).

Exhibit 1.2: Fête des Vignerons – 1999 Festival of the Wine-growers

From 29 July to 15 August 1999, the town of Vevey, on the shores of Lake Geneva in Switzerland, played host to the Festival of the Wine-growers. The organization of this event was the responsibility of the

Brotherhood of Wine-growers of Vevey, an established corporation whose roots can be traced back to the beginning of the seventeenth century.

The festival is held in honour of the local wine workers and only occurs five times each century. The last occasion was in 1977. The Brotherhood visits the vineyards under their jurisdiction three times each year to report on the progress of the wine-making.

The 1999 festival was supported by many organizations including Swiss Air, Winterthur, Nestlé, Banque Cantonale Vaudoise, La Poste, TSR, Radio Suisse Romande and 24 Heure Edipresse.

Half a million visitors were expected to attend the 15 open-air performances and four parades which were part of this spectacular event. Five thousand local actors and participants contributed as well as professional singers, dancers, and orchestras (http://www.fetedesvignerons.ch).

Liz Sharples

While this discussion has focused on the effect of wine tourism on wine businesses, the reverse situation can occur, where a tourism business looks to establish a winery to complement its existing attractions. Montgomery (1988) reports on a feasibility study into the effects of adding a winery to Biltmore Estate in Carolina, USA, where the current attractions were the house and gardens. The results allowed management to understand the viability of a winery as a tourist attraction, and to gauge likely customer reaction to the sale of wines on the estate. Furthermore, the development of wineries and vineyards can also substantially affect the nature of tourism in rural areas, providing not only for an increase in visitor numbers but also for changes in the nature of the tourists in terms of their interests, spending patterns and length of stay.

Scale and level of wine tourism

Wine tourism operates on different scales and at various levels. Jack Rasterhoff, Chief Executive of the Victorian Wineries Tourism Council, drew attention to this when he stated:

There are a number of perspectives to wine tourism. For the small wineries it provides cash flow and assists them in achieving a better sales mix at a higher price or yield. It also enables them to successfully brand their product and winery. For larger wineries the effect is different. While wine tourism is an economic necessity for small wineries, large wineries often support cellar door activities as a publicity or public relations commitment. There are also big benefits for the State as a whole, in terms of regional employment and providing a diversity of tourism products to a region (in Fuller 1997: 35).

The tourism and wine industries typically share a structure that combines a small number of very large companies (e.g. airlines and wine corporations) with a very large number of small companies (e.g. tourist operators (see Exhibit 1.3) and boutique wineries). An export focus demands a scale of economy that many individual small wineries cannot hope to achieve, but absorption of smaller wineries through takeovers threatens the independence and innovation of the industry. As BRL Hardy's managing director remarked: 'It is the smaller wineries that add the romance, mystery and magic to the industry' (Day 1996: 27).

Exhibit 1.3: Arblaster and Clarke Wine Tours

Arblaster and Clarke Wine Tours Ltd are based in Hampshire, England, and market themselves as the leading wine tour specialist in the UK. The company was founded by Tim Clarke and Lynette Arblaster in 1986, and since then has experienced steady growth.

The company pride themselves on the high level of personal service that they offer to their clients. All of the staff, from sales team to tour manager, are knowledgeable about both the holiday destinations and the range of wines that will be sampled. Many staff are bilingual. The company organizes tours to all of the major wine-growing areas of the world: the 'classic' destinations of France, Italy, Germany and Spain, and also the 'New World' countries of New Zealand, Australia, California and South Africa. More unusual destinations such as Argentina and Greece are also included in the brochure. Some tours are coach-based, whilst others are based around guided walks. Luxury tours on cruise-liners are also available.

The prices range from £250 for a weekend in the Champagne region of France, to £2,000 for a week-long Greek Wine Odyssey cruise. The company also organizes tailor-made private tours for small groups such as wine clubs and incentive travel for companies who wish to entertain their senior managers/clients. Arblaster and Clarke currently host organized tours for the *Sunday Times* Wine Club, Christie's Wine Education Department, and the British Airways Executive Wine Club.

Many of the wine guides accompanying the tours are Masters of Wine or well-known wine writers/critics, capable of tutoring both beginners and experts. For example, in New Year 2000 the company hosted the Grand Cuvée Millennium Tour to Champagne (Arblaster and Clarke 1999).

Liz Sharples

Boutique wineries are the ones most dependent on cellar door sales as they often do not have sufficient production to distribute through wholesale/retail channels (Australian Wine Foundation 1996). Writing in 1986, Spawton argued that the lack of profit in the wine industry was due to a preoccupation within the industry with 'making and selling rather than applying marketing concepts to winemaking activities' (Spawton 1986b: 89). The failure to apply marketing concepts sometimes extends to wine tourism, in cases where the wine industry and producers do not recognize that visitors to their winery are tourists (Hall 1996; Macionis 1997; Macionis and Cambourne 1998).

If wineries choose to expand and supply exceeds visitor demand, then they will require new customers and alternative distribution channels (Dodd and Bigotte 1995; Gillion 1998). Indeed, larger wine companies negotiating supply contracts with wholesale/retail distributors may be seen as acting in bad faith if cellar door sales substantially undercut retail prices. Wine tourism is then seen as a threat to distributors and, considering the much larger volumes of product involved in wholesale distribution and export orders, of lesser importance. Hence, wine tourism may become a 'publicity or public relations commitment', albeit significant, rather than a core component of the business (Fuller 1997: 35).

Both the wine and tourism industries rely on regional branding for market leverage and promotion (Fuller 1997; Hall and Macionis 1998; Hall *et al.* 1998). Tourism is fundamentally about the difference of place (Relph 1996), while wine is 'one of those rare commodities which is branded on the basis of its geographical origin' (Merret and Whitwell 1994: 174). In describing the importance of tourism place and wine appellation or regions, Hall (1996: 114) argued: 'there is a direct impact on tourism in the identification of wine regions because of the inter-relationships that may exist in the overlap of wine and destination region promotion and the accompanying set of economic and social linkages' (see Exhibit 1.4).

Exhibit 1.4: The vineyards of Vaud

Switzerland is a small country tucked between the mountains of the Jura and the Alps, and surrounded by four major wine-producing nations: France, Germany, Italy and Austria. The country is divided into three language regions of French, German, and Italian and most of the area under vine is located in the French-speaking (Suisse Romande) region. Switzerland has a total area of 15,000 ha under vine, 11,390 ha in the French region, 2,550 ha in the German region, and 930 ha in the Italian region (Swiss Wine Exporters Association 1996).

The wines of Switzerland are not well known throughout the world as the Swiss save most of their wine for the domestic market. Of the 1.2 million hectolitres produced in Switzerland annually only about 1 per cent makes its way to other countries. In fact, with an annual consumption per capita of 50 litres, Switzerland has to import considerable amounts of wine from Italy and France (Kolpan *et al.* 1996). Switzerland's wine output is predominantly white.

Vaud is located in the south-west of the country, close to the Lakes Geneva (Leman), Neuchatel and Morat, and has a deep-rooted tradition of viticulture. The Vaud area is the second largest grape-growing canton in Switzerland and is located in French-speaking Switzerland. Other important wine-producing regions in this area include Valais, Geneva, Neuchatel, all named after their home cantons. The area produces predominantly white wine with about four-fifths of the total wine area of 3,800 ha being planted with the Chasselas grape, although red wine has always been produced in this area using Gamay and Pinot Noir grapes. The demand for this has grown over the last few years.

Cellar door sales have been commonplace in this area for many years, supplying private homes and restaurant owners from the local area, but the area also makes a tourist attraction of its viticulture.

A tourist guide produced by the Office des Vins Vaudois written in several languages is available from local tourist offices, and this is supplemented by leaflets which introduce specific towns/villages in the area, complete with names and contact telephone numbers of vignerons who will organize cellar tastings (Office des Vins Vaudois 1998a). Route maps for walkers giving distances and directions have been set out in collaboration with the Association du Tourisme Piedestre, and these provide full details for walkers who want to explore the area on foot, tasting wine on the way.

The cellars are sometimes located in villages or at growers' premises or occasionally in a chateau. In conjunction with this, the Office des Vins Vaudois also publish a list of recommended inns, 'Pintes Vaudoises', where local food can be sampled, accompanied by local wine. A simple cookery book again produced by the OVV contains recipes of regional specialities such as Gateau aux Raisins (Office des Vins Vaudois 1998b).

Coach tours are also available from certain regional centres. For example, a guided tour is organized from Lausanne through the Lavaux wine-producing area by the Lausanne Tourist Office. The Lauvaux region is famous for its amazing landscape as it lies directly above Lake Geneva (Lac Leman), the vines being planted on thousands of steep terraces supported by substantial stone retaining walls, to prevent erosion and gullying. The strong sunlight combined with the light reflected off the lake and the heat retained by the walls ensures ideal growing conditions. Wine tasting can be organized at numerous cellars within this area where the vignerons will explain the range of wines on offer. The tourist office will also combine a wine tasting at a cellar with a visit to the world-renowned cheesemaking town of Gruyère. A factory visit to look at cheese being made and a meal in a local Swiss restaurant can be included.

Liz Sharples

As Chapter 12 illustrates, in Australia various states and regions are in increasing competition for the wine tourist dollar. The State of Victoria developed the first wine tourism strategy with the Victorian Wineries Tourism Council being established in 1993. In 1995 an equivalent council was established in South Australia, it would appear in reaction to the lead taken by

Victoria. Other state wine tourism bodies have since been established in New South Wales, Queensland, Western Australia and Tasmania, while various regions, such as the Hunter Valley and Margaret River, have also set up their own wine tourism organizations (Hall and Macionis 1998).

At a national level, the Winemakers' Federation of Australia is developing a national wine tourism strategy with funding from the Federal Government's Office of National Tourism (Hall *et al.* 1998). The project objectives include:

- raising the awareness and understanding of tourism in the wine industry
- establishing wine tourism industry standards
- increasing the skill levels of wine tourism practitioners and employees
- fostering links between wine, food and Australian lifestyle (Office of National Tourism 1997 in Hall *et al.* 1998).

The involvement of wineries and wine-grower associations in such initiatives indicates that wine tourism can also be seen as a growth pole for the wine industry as a whole, including a move to quality wine production rather than bulk. For example, the Cyprus wine industry has increasing sales to visitors as an objective in its bid to improve industry performance (Skinner 1993a). Similarly, a large Czechoslovakian wine producer, Vino Mukulov, recognized tourism as a potential sales source and a longer-term stimulus to demand for its products (Jennings and Wood 1992). The company is strategically located near a major road running from Austria to Brno, with the potential to tap into the lucrative Austrian short-break market (Jennings and Wood 1992). In emerging New World wine regions, wine tourism has also assisted wine producers in overcoming scepticism about the potential for quality wine to be produced in non-traditional wine regions and an over-reliance on imported wine (Dodd 1995; Hackett 1997; see also Chapter 13).

However, the importance of wine tourism will also depend on the stage of development that the wine and tourism industries have reached. For example, Desplats (1996) reports on a comparative study of tourism strategies employed by the Armagnac and Cognac industries in Aquitaine. For Cognac, tourism is a very important strategy for industry development and product marketing. The tourist infrastructure is correspondingly developed to a high standard. For Armagnac, tourism is only in the developing stage, there are fewer sales outlets, no coordinated tourism marketing and many producers have little or no contact with tourists. Sales of Armagnac depend mainly on its already-established reputation. Tourism for Armagnac producers is 'seen as a means of supporting a form of local production with an uncertain future' (Desplats 1996).

As this short discussion highlights there are substantial complexities to the development of wine tourism and the various elements of demand and supply which come together to comprise the wine tourism experience. The following chapters and case studies have been brought together to provide the first comprehensive international overview of wine tourism development and management.

Overview of the book

The following chapters are broadly grouped together in terms of wine tourism products and markets (Chapters 2–10) and the interrelationships and linkages between wine, tourism and regional development (Chapters 11–16). Chapter 2 introduces the reader to wine tourism products through an international overview which seeks to provide a flavour of the various ways that wine tourism has developed around the world. As with many chapters throughout the book, various case studies will be provided to illustrate some of the key themes and issues. Chapters 3 to 5 examine wine tourism product development with reference to specific countries. Chapter 3, by Isabelle Frochot, discusses the development of wine tourism in France. In contrast, Chapters 4 and 5 examine wine tourism in New World regions. Chapter 4 by Brock Cambourne and Niki Macionis provides a case study of wine tourism product development in an emerging wine region in Australia, while Chapter 5 by Robert Preston-Whyte discusses the development of wine routes in post-apartheid South Africa.

Chapter 6 by Richard Mitchell, Michael Hall and Alison McIntosh provides an overview of key issues in the relationship between wine tourism and consumer behaviour which details the nature of visitor demands and their demographic and psychographic profiles. This is supported in Chapter 7 by Tim Dodd, which discusses the factors influencing cellar sales with particular reference to the research that he has undertaken at Texan wineries. Chapter 8 by Michael Hall, Anna Marie, Longo, Richard Mitchell and Gary Johnson discusses wine tourism in New Zealand and highlights the results of the different surveys that have been undertaken of winery visitors at both a national and a regional level. Chapter 9 by Michael Howley and Jetske Van Westering discusses wine tourism in England and Wales and notes the difficulties encountered in improving the image of English wine. In contrast, Michael Whyte's case study of winery development at Vasse Felix, one of

Western Australia's most internationally recognized wineries, highlights the positive synergies that can be obtained between wine and tourism at the level of individual wine businesses (Chapter 10).

Chapters 11 to 15 focus on the regional dimensions of wine and tourism relationships. Chapter 11 introduces the way in which wine tourism has become a component of destination marketing, promotion and regional development, and pays special attention to the development of wine tourism networks for the purposes of product development and promotion. This chapter also includes a case study of the way in which wine tourism has become integrated with the Internet. Chapter 12 by Niki Macionis and Brock Cambourne examines wine tourism development strategies in Australia and discusses the development of an Australian national wine tourism plan. This chapter also highlights the critical role which government has played with respect to wine tourism development. In contrast, Chapter 13 by David Telfer highlights the role which free trade and changed government involvement in the wine industry has had on the development of wine tourism in Ontario, Canada, and New York State. The important role of the European Union in wine tourism through its regional development programmes is the subject of a case study by Nigel Morpeth (Chapter 14) when he discusses the relationship between cycle trails and wine tourism in Europe. Chapter 15 by Angela Skinner examines the problems which have emerged in the development of the Napa Valley in California and the lessons which this may provide about the dangers of overdevelopment and the need for more sustainable forms of development in wine regions. The final chapter, Chapter 16, discusses the future of wine tourism and highlights the issues which the wine and tourism industries will need to confront in order to improve not only the benefits of wine tourism but also the level of mutual understanding between the two industries.

Conclusion

Wine tourism is an emerging concept which has become increasingly significant in wine regions throughout the world. As this chapter has demonstrated, wine tourism has a wide range of components which are important for the development of the wine and tourism industries. However, as has also been noted, the extent to which various wineries and wine businesses utilize wine tourism as a strategy for sales, consumer education, brand development and building positive customer relationships will depend on their size, markets, business strategies, and, for many owner-operated wineries, lifestyle choices.

Despite wine tourism's growing economic and social importance there has been relatively little systematic study of its development, the manner in which it is managed and marketed, and the people who visit wine regions and experience the wine tourism product. Such a situation is not just an academic issue as it undermines the basis on which businesses make decisions about their future development and the possibilities which new entrants into the wine and tourism industries identify. We therefore hope that this book will help fill some of this gap and provide a basis from which further work can be undertaken and wine tourism businesses develop on a sound basis. On a more personal note, the authors also trust that this book will convey something of our love of wine, and the enthusiasm with which many visitors come to learn about the grape, wines, wine-making and the social and cultural aspects of wine. For the authors, as well as many of our readers, we can clearly state that every time we pull the cork from a bottle we are all wine tourists. We hope that this book will in some small way help make our future experiences all the more enjoyable as tourists or as suppliers of the experience that is wine.

2

The maturing wine tourism product: an international overview

Brock Cambourne, C. Michael Hall, Gary Johnson, Niki Macionis, Richard Mitchell and Liz Sharples

When Michael Benedict crushed his first batch of grapes 21 years ago, the Santa Ynez Valley was known primarily for its cattle ranches and beet farms. No one thought much about tourism (Sharp 1992).

The last few years have seen an unprecedented interest in the marketing and development of wine tourism in many of the world's wine-producing regions. Indeed, much of the recent resurgence of the wine industry, particularly in the New World, can be attributed to the development of wine tourism, even if many of the wineries concerned have not recognized that they are involved in the tourism industry (e.g. Dodd 1995; Hackett 1997; Macionis 1996; Hall and Johnson 1997; Morris and King 1997a, b; Hall *et al*. 1998; Macionis and Cambourne 1998).

Wine tourism has become big business. For example, the Napa Valley Vintners Association reports that the region's wineries and vineyards attracted some 5.1 million people in 1996, generating some 8,000 tourism jobs and revenues of US$600 million (Napa Valley Vintners Association 1999). In Australia, wine tourism was estimated to account for 5.3 million visits, worth A$428 million in 1995, and is expected to be worth approximately A$1.1 billion by 2025 (Australian Wine Foundation 1996), while the Movimento del Turismo del Vino (MTV) notes that visitors to Italian wineries increased from 400 000 to 2.5 million between 1993 and 1996, resulting in 3000 billion lire in sales (Colombini, pers. comm. 1997).

Clearly, given the space available, this chapter cannot provide a detailed discussion of every wine-producing country in the world. Instead, it aims to provide a broad international overview of the development of wine tourism so as to provide a comparative context for the specific chapters and case studies which follow. It examines the emergence of wine tourism in both 'Old World' European wine regions and 'New World' wine regions (Australia, Canada, Eastern Europe, New Zealand, South Africa, South America and the United States), highlighting catalysts such as rural decline, economic restructuring and industry decline, and changing consumer preferences and industry growth. This chapter also compares the developmental approaches employed in various parts of the world and provides details of various aspects of wine tourism product development, such as winery visits and cellar door sales, guided wine tourism, wine roads and trails, and festivals and events. However, before discussing wine tourism specifically it provides a review of the state of world wine production and wine markets.

The world wine market

Wine is a vast international business, spanning more than half the globe in terms of grape growing and wine production and with followers and markets in almost every country (Johnson 1989). The Office International de la Vigne et du Vin (OIV) reports that world wine production increased by 7.5 per cent in 1996, with the largest wine-producing countries being Italy, France, Spain and Portugal. The OIV also notes that the worldwide area under vines has stabilized after gradually declining since 1980.

In Europe, the area under vines has declined in Italy, France, Moldova and Portugal, while New World wine producers such as the United States, Argentina, Chile and Australia experienced significant increases. Similarly, world wine consumption has also stabilized since a gradual decline in the 1980s and early 1990s. In 1996 the top four wine-consuming nations were France,

Table 2.1 World wine production by country (000 hectolitres and gallons), 1996 compared with 1995 and 1994

Country rank	1996 Hectolitres	1996 Gallons	1995 Hectolitres	1995 Gallons	1994 Hectolitres	1994 Gallons
1. France	59 650	1 575 834	55 610	1 469 105	54 640	1 443 480
2. Italy	58 773	1 552 665	55 702	1 471 535	59 276	1 565 953
3. Spain	32 675	863 208	20 876	551 502	20 995	554 646
4. United States*	17 415	460 062	16 543	437 034	14 994	396 109
5. Argentina	12 681	335 007	16 443	434 391	18 173	480 094
6. South Africa	10 000	264 180	9 660	255 198	9 120	240 932
7. Portugal	9 529	251 737	7 255	191 663	6 521	172 272
8. Germany	8 300	219 269	11 050	291 919	10 180	268 935
9. Romania	7 663	202 441	6 720	177 529	5 370	141 865
10. Australia	6 784	179 220	5 028	132 830	5 874	155 179
11. China	4 300	113 597	4 000	105 672	3 800	100 388
12. Hungary	4 188	110 639	3 289	86 889	3 694	97 588
13. Greece	4 109	108 552	3 841	101 472	3 051	80 601
14. Chile	3 824	101 022	3 167	83 666	3 598	95 052
15. Yugoslavia	3 489	92 172	2 804	74 076	3 058	80 786
16. Russia	2 800	73 970	2 800	73 970	2 960	78 197
17. Brazil	2 320	61 290	3 128	82 636	3 020	79 782
18. Austria	2 110	55 742	2 229	58 886	2 647	69 928
19. Bulgaria	2 000	52 836	2 200	58 120	1 885	49 798
20. Croatia	1 958	51 726	1 785	47 156	1 893	50 009
21. Switzerland	1 304	34 449	1 181	31 200	1 188	31 385
22. Mexico	1 130	29 852	1 480	39 099	2 422	63 984
23. Georgia	1 100	29 060	1 100	29 060	800	21 134
24. Moldova	1 050	27 739	930	24 569	886	23 406
25. Macedonia	1 010	26 682	911	24 067	880	23 248
26. Azerbaijan	1 000	26 418	1 000	26 418	1 000	26 418
27. Uruguay	954	25 203	852	22 508	709	18 730
28. Japan	912	24 093	652	17 225	524	13 843
29. Uzbekistan	900	23 776	900	23 776	1 000	26 418
30. Slovenia	781	20 632	781	20 632	829	21 901

31. Ukraine	763	20 157	1 381	36 483	1 156	30 539
32. Czech Republic	628	16 591	459	12 126	497	13 130
33. New Zealand	573	15 138	564	14 900	410	10 831
34. Cyprus	559	14 768	555	14 662	485	12 813
35. Algeria	392	10 356	571	15 085	500	13 209
36. Slovakia	376	9 933	662	17 489	686	18 123
37. Belarus	350	9 246	350	9 246	500	13 209
38. Lebanon	307	8 110	300	7 925	295	7 793
39. Canada	300	7 925	300	7 925	300	7 925
40. Kazakhstan	300	7 925	300	7 925	150	3 963
41. Morocco	284	7 503	238	6 287	279	7 371
42. Turkey	265	7 001	265	7 001	265	7 001
43. Israel	240	6 340	282	7 450	127	3 355
44. Tunisia	221	5 838	292	7 714	294	7 767
45. Albania	170	4 491	169	4 465	96	2 536
46. Belgium/Lux	–		176	4 650	173	4 570
47. Luxembourg	149	3 936	–		–	
48. Peru	111	2 932	106	2 800	100	2 642
49. Armenia	100	2 642	100	2 642	240	6 340
50. Madagascar	86	2 272	86	2 272	86	2 272
51. Paraguay	77	2 034	77	2 034	74	1 955
52. Bosnia-Herzegovina	54	1 427	34	898	35	925
53. Malta	31	819	31	819	31	819
54. Egypt	25	660	25	660	24	634
55. United Kingdom	24	634	13	343	18	476
56. Bolivia	20	528	20	528	20	528
57. Turkmenistan	16	423	16	423	16	423
58. Belgium	2	53	–		–	
Country total	271 132	7 162 755	251 289	6 638 555	251 844	6 652 210
Other countries	23	608	17	449	22	581
World total	271 155	7 163 363	251 306	6 639 004	251 866	6 652 791

Source: Wine Institute 1998 (http://www.wineinstitute.org/communications/statistics/keyfacts_worldwineproduction.htm) based on data from Office International de la Vigne et du Vin (OIV). Totals may not convert exactly from gallons to hectolitres and vice versa because of rounding.

Notes: * Still wine removed from fermenters. Excludes substandard wine produced as distilling material. Also excludes increases after amelioration, sweetening, and addition of wine spirits.

Table 2.2 World vineyard hectares/acreage by country: raisin, table and winegrape varieties (000 hectares and acres), 1996 compared with 1995 and 1994

| 1996 | 1996 | | 1995 | | 1994 | |
Country rank	Hectares	Acres	Hectares	Acres	Hectares	Acres
1. Spain	1 224	3 025	1 224	3 025	1 235	3 052
2. Italy	922	2 278	927	2 291	956	2 362
3. France	917	2 266	927	2 291	933	2 305
4. Turkey	567	1 401	565	1 396	567	1 401
5. United States	311	768	308	761	308	761
6. Portugal	259	640	261	645	267	660
7. Romania	256	633	253	625	252	623
8. Iran	252	623	245	605	250	618
9. Argentina	211	521	210	519	210	519
10. Moldova	185	457	193	477	193	477
11. China	165	408	152	376	149	368
12. Ukraine	148	366	155	383	162	400
13. Greece	132	326	135	334	136	336
14. Hungary	131	324	131	324	132	326
15. Uzbekistan	125	309	125	309	125	309
16. Chile	116	287	114	282	112	277
17. Bulgaria	109	269	112	277	113	279
18. South Africa	106	262	103	255	103	255
19. Germany	105	259	106	262	106	262
20. Russia	103	255	103	255	103	255
21. Yugoslavia	86	213	87	215	90	222

22. Azerbaijan	85	210	100	247	105	259
23. Georgia	85	210	85	210	90	222
24. Australia	81	200	73	180	67	166
25. Algeria	77	190	85	210	82	203
26. Syria	67	166	68	168	67	166
27. Brazil	61	151	61	151	60	148
28. Croatia	54	133	52	128	53	131
29. Austria	52	128	52	128	57	141
30. Egypt	50	124	49	121	49	121
31. Iraq	50	124	50	124	45	111
32. Morocco	48	119	49	121	51	126
33. Afghanistan	48	119	48	119	48	119
34. Mexico	47	116	46	114	50	124
35. Tajikistan	39	96	39	96	39	96
36. India	37	91	37	91	37	91
37. Tunisia	28	69	28	69	28	69
38. Lebanon	27	67	27	67	26	64
39. Slovakia	27	67	26	64	26	64
40. Macedonia	27	67	29	72	30	74
41. Armenia	24	59	23	57	25	62
42. Japan	23	57	24	59	25	62
43. Slovenia	23	57	23	57	23	57
44. Turkmenistan	22	54	22	54	22	54
45. Korea	21	52	22	54	20	49
46. Yemen	21	52	21	52	21	52
47. Cyprus	20	49	20	49	20	49
48. Kazakhstan	20	49	22	54	20	49
49. Switzerland	15	37	15	37	15	37
50. Czech Republic	13	32	12	30	11	27

1996 Country rank	1996 Hectares	1996 Acres	1995 Hectares	1995 Acres	1994 Hectares	1994 Acres
51. Peru	12	30	12	30	11	27
52. Uruguay	10	25	9	22	9	22
53. Kyrgyzstan	9	22	9	22	9	22
54. Pakistan	8	20	8	20	8	20
55. New Zealand	8	20	8	20	7	17
56. Canada	7	17	7	17	7	17
57. Libya	6	15	6	15	6	15
58. Israel	6	15	6	15	5	12
59. Albania	6	15	6	15	6	15
60. Taiwan	5	12	5	12	5	12
61. Bolivia	4	10	4	10	4	10
62. Bosnia-Herzegovina	3	7	4	10	4	10
63. Madagascar	2	5	2	5	2	5
64. Tanzania	2	5	2	5	2	5
65. Jordan	2	5	2	5	3	7
66. Venezuela	1	2	1	2	1	2
67. Luxembourg	1	2	1	2	1	2
68. Malta	1	2	1	2	1	2
69. United Kingdom	1	2	1	2	1	2
Country total	7 716	19 066	7 738	19 121	7 806	19 284
Other countries	26	64	22	54	21	52
World total	7 742	19 130	7 760	19 175	7 827	19 336

Source: Wine Institute 1999 (http://www.wineinstitute.org/communications/statistics/keyfacts_worldacreage.htm) based on data from Office International de la Vigne et du Vin (OIV).

Italy, the United States and Germany, who between them consume about half of the world's wine. Tables 2.1 and 2.2 detail the major wine-producing regions in terms of total production and percentage of world production, and total area of winegrapes for the period 1994 to 1996. The number of countries which produce wine is quite remarkable, although it should be noted that much of this wine will be for domestic consumption while much will also be for cheaper bulk wines. However, the extent of production does help illustrate the competitive nature of the international wine market. Tables 2.3 and 2.4 indicate the consumption of wine in terms of total and per capita consumption from 1994 to 1996. One of the most interesting aspects of wine consumption in these tables is the extent to which it has fallen on a per capita basis in 'traditional' wine countries of Europe and the Mediterranean, with an increase in newer markets in Asia and North America. Indeed, as will be discussed below, these changing patterns of consumption and their relationship to wine production has had significant impact on the extent to which regions and individual producers have embraced wine tourism.

Wine tourism in Europe

Wine tourism and the active development and marketing of the wine tourism product is a relatively recent phenomenon, even in the European countries with a long established wine-producing history which are usually collectively described as 'Old World' wine regions. While Hall and Macionis (1998) note that visits to vineyards have been part of organized travel since at least the time of the Grand Tour and that wine trails have been a component of the German tourism industry since the 1920s, European wine tourism is essentially still an emerging tourism product (Choisy 1996; Colombini, pers. comm. 1997). Indeed, Mallon (1996) notes that wine tourism only began to gain momentum in France during the 1980s as a result of declining rural economic conditions which led many wine-growers to consider direct sales to tourists in order to expand and diversify farm incomes.

At a pan-European level three key wine tourism organizations exist:

- the European Council of Wine Regions (Assemblia das Regioes Europeias Viticolas);
- RECEVIN, a network of wine-producing towns (based on the Italian 'Citta del Vino' or Cities of Wine concept), which aims to improve the standard of living of residents of wine-producing towns by promotion of wine culture and developing wine-based tourism (Dower n.d.); and
- the Dionysus multimedia network of European wine-producing regions (Hall and Macionis 1998).

Table 2.3 Per capita wine consumption by country (litres and gallons per capita) 1996 compared with 1995 and 1980

1996 Rank per capita	1996 Litres	1996 Gallons	1995 Litres	1995 Gallons	1980 Litres	1980 Gallons
1. France	60.00	15.85	63.00	16.64	90.87	24.01
2. Italy	59.37	15.68	62.00	16.38	79.87	21.10
3. Portugal	58.46	15.44	57.41	15.17	28.84	7.62
4. Luxembourg	50.40	13.31	–	–	–	–
5. Argentina	41.47	10.96	42.32	11.18	76.16	20.12
6. Switzerland	41.17	10.88	41.50	10.96	47.02	12.42
7. Slovenia	38.80	10.25	36.90	9.75	–	–
8. Spain	37.71	9.96	32.90	8.69	59.91	15.83
9. Austria	32.00	8.45	28.80	7.61	35.45	9.37
10. Romania	31.50	8.32	30.93	8.17	–	–
11. Greece	30.93	8.17	30.00	7.93	44.87	11.85
12. Hungary	30.00	7.93	30.70	8.11	34.97	9.24
13. Uruguay	29.45	7.78	25.24	6.67	24.95	6.59
14. Denmark	26.80	7.08	25.50	6.74	12.78	3.38
15. Germany	22.94	6.06	23.36	6.17	25.48	6.73
16. Belgium	20.01	5.29	–	–	–	–
17. Yugoslavia	19.90	5.28	15.10	3.99	17.30	4.57
18. Australia	18.10	4.78	18.30	4.83	17.38	4.59
19. Chile	15.80	4.17	15.00	3.96	50.24	13.27
20. Netherlands	13.30	3.51	14.30	3.78	11.00	2.91
21. Slovakia	13.10	3.46	13.90	3.67	–	–
22. Cyprus	13.10	3.46	13.00	3.43	9.79	2.59
23. Sweden	12.60	3.33	–	–	–	–

24. United Kingdom	12.50	3.30	13.00	3.43	30.13	7.96
25. Czech Republic	11.80	3.12	11.90	3.14	–	–
26. New Zealand	9.90	2.62	8.70	2.30	4.38	1.16
27. South Africa	9.30	2.46	9.63	2.54	9.07	2.40
28. Norway	8.78	2.32	8.78	2.32	1.89	0.50
29. Bulgaria	8.08	2.13	8.08	2.13	21.96	5.80
30. United States	7.27	1.92	6.72	1.78	7.98	2.11
31. Canada	7.08	1.87	6.88	1.82	8.35	2.21
32. Ireland	7.00	1.85	5.25	1.39	3.21	0.85
33. Finland	5.19	1.37	5.51	1.46	4.76	1.26
34. Israel	4.20	1.11	4.00	1.06	4.50	1.19
35. Tunisia	3.09	0.82	2.92	0.77	3.10	0.82
36. Paraguay	2.03	0.54	2.03	0.54	0.98	0.26
37. Macedonia	1.66	0.44	–	–	–	–
38. Brazil	1.58	0.42	1.51	0.40	2.61	0.69
39. Morocco	1.40	0.37	0.80	0.21	11.87	3.14
40. Japan	1.15	0.30	1.14	0.30	0.38	0.10
41. Poland	0.88	0.23	0.88	0.23	69.89	18.46
42. Peru	0.61	0.16	0.68	0.18	9.79	2.59
43. Turkey	0.37	0.10	0.37	0.10	0.60	0.16
44. China	0.33	0.09	0.29	0.08	–	–
45. Mexico	0.28	0.07	0.18	0.05	1.25	0.33
46. Algeria	0.14	0.04	0.18	0.05	1.28	0.34
47. Belgium/Lux.	–	–	20.70	5.47	14.33	3.79
48. Serbia	–	–	25.22	6.66	6.66	–

Source: Wine Institute 1998 (http://www.wineinstitute.org/communications/statistics/keyfacts_worldpercapitaconsumption. htm) based on data from Office International de la Vigne et du Vin (OIV), Gomberg, Frædrikson & Associates and Kristi Ivie.

Note: Based on total resident population.

Table 2.4 World wine consumption by country (000 hectolitres and gallons) 1996 compared with 1995 and 1994

1996 Country rank	1996 Hectolitres	1996 Gallons	1995 Hectolitres	1995 Gallons	1994 Hectolitres	1994 Gallons
1. Italy	35 623	941 088	35 623	941 088	33 025	872 454
2. France	34 795	919 214	36 515	964 653	36 663	968 563
3. United States	19 116	505 000	17 753	469 000	17 375	459 000
4. Germany	18 660	492 960	18 006	475 683	18 196	480 702
5. Spain	14 750	389 666	15 000	396 270	15 336	405 146
6. Argentina	13 551	357 990	13 888	366 893	14 407	380 604
7. Russia	12 500	330 225	12 500	330 225	11 500	303 807
8. Romania	7 252	191 583	6 616	174 781	5 041	133 173
9. United Kingdom	7 243	191 346	7 392	195 282	6 732	177 846
10. Portugal	5 800	153 224	5 695	150 451	5 762	152 221
11. South Africa	4 056	107 151	4 056	107 151	3 649	96 399
12. China	3 941	104 113	3 941	104 113	3 463	91 486
13. Australia	3 297	87 100	3 275	86 519	3 279	86 625
14. Greece	3 200	84 538	3 200	84 538	3 100	81 896
15. Hungary	3 050	80 575	3 087	81 552	3 097	81 817
16. Switzerland	2 915	77 008	2 921	77 167	2 957	78 118
17. Austria	2 640	69 744	2 640	69 744	2 483	65 596
18. Yugoslavia	2 599	68 660	1 823	48 160	3 027	79 967
19. Brazil	2 462	65 041	2 414	63 773	2 816	74 393
20. Croatia	2 300	60 761	2 300	60 761	2 300	60 761
21. Chile	2 291	60 524	2 132	56 323	2 519	66 547
22. Netherlands	2 058	54 368	2 165	57 195	2 009	53 074
23. Belgium*	2 029	53 602	–	–	–	–
24. Canada	1 983	52 387	1 760	46 496	1 841	48 636
25. Japan	1 443	38 121	1 443	38 121	1 434	37 883
26. Denmark	1 414	37 355	1 326	35 030	1 142	30 169

27. Czech Republic	1 182	31 226	1 193	31 517	1 207	31 887
28. Sweden	1 115	29 456	1 148	30 328	1 148	30 328
29. Uruguay	949	25 071	976	25 784	969	25 599
30. Slovenia	796	21 029	796	21 029	800	21 134
31. Bulgaria	709	18 730	709	18 730	709	18 730
32. Slovakia	703	18 572	744	19 655	770	20 342
33. New Zealand	356	9 405	309	8 163	285	7 529
34. Poland	340	8 982	340	8 982	340	8 982
35. Norway	318	8 401	318	8 401	293	7 740
36. Morocco	293	7 740	240	6 340	350	9 246
37. Tunisia	272	7 186	248	6 552	231	6 103
38. Finland	267	7 054	282	7 450	281	7 423
39. Ireland	263	6 948	188	4 967	205	5 416
40. Turkey	233	6 155	233	6 155	234	6 182
41. Luxembourg*	208	5 495	–	–	–	–
42. Israel	180	4 755	160	4 227	107	2 827
43. Peru	146	3 857	141	3 725	121	3 197
44. Mexico	140	3 699	140	3 699	148	3 910
45. Paraguay	109	2 880	109	2 880	109	2 880
46. Cyprus	84	2 219	83	2 193	81	2 140
47. Algeria	39	1 030	57	1 506	50	1 321
48. Bosnia-Herzegovina	32	845	32	845	63	1 664
49. Macedonia	32	845	32	845	42	1 110
50. Belgium/Lux.*	–	–	2 171	57 353	2 224	58 754
Country total	219 734	5 804 926	218 120	5 762 295	213 920	5 651 326
Other countries	2 064	54 527	1 935	51 119	1 334	35 242
World total	221 798	5 859 453	220 055	5 813 414	215 254	5 686 568

Notes: Totals may not exactly convert from hectolitres to gallons and vice versa due to rounding of the multiplier.

*The figures for Belgium and Luxembourg were amagamated until 1996

Source: Wine Institute 1998 (http://www.wineinstitute.org/communications/statistics/keyfacts_worldwineconsumption.htm based on data from Office International de la Vigne et du Vin (OIV) and Gomberg. Fredrickson & Associates.

The European Union has also been involved in wine tourism development at a regional level through the LEADER and Ouverture projects (Nitsch and van Straaten 1995). The activities of the European Union are discussed in more detail in Chapter 11.

Wine tourism in Europe has largely been developed in the form of official wine roads or wine routes. For example, several regions in France, such as Languedoc-Roussillon, have established wine routes linking attractions, regions and wine producers in order to increase the value of viticulture to the economy through tourism (Comité Régional du Tourisme de Languedoc-Roussillon Prodexport 1994). More recently, other European countries such as Hungary, Moldova and Portugal have begun to establish wine routes in an effort to develop related cultural and rural tourism (Hall and Macionis 1998). Many of the wine routes and trails in Europe are being developed with the assistance of the Europäische Weinstrassen (European Council of Wine Roads) based in Bordeaux. The Council encompasses more than 60 wine regions and is supported through the European Council of Wine Regions (Assemblia das Regioes Europeias Viticolas) (Hall and Macionis 1998).

The European Council of Wine Roads has directed its focus in five key developmental areas, including the:

- conduct of an inventory of existing wine roads and trails in Europe;
- development of standardized signposting and pictographic representation of wine roads and their components across countries and regions;
- development of wine road standards and accreditation requirements;
- facilitation of further wine road and trail development;
- marketing of wine tourism via the production of marketing collateral such as wine trail guides and the development of an extensive internet presence, allowing extensive information exchange and networking amongst wine road participants (Assemblia das Regioes Europeias Viticolas 1997) (see Exhibit 2.1).

Exhibit 2.1: Building the wine roads

To facilitate the further development and expansion of wine routes throughout Europe the Assemblia das Regioes Europeias Viticolas (AREV) has developed a *A Methodological Guide to Wine Roads*. Realizing that the success of wine road development is highly dependent upon the management and coordination of a range of participants, the guide aims to provide operational tools that assist individual wine trail 'actors' to maximize their participation. The guide is divided into five sections covering:

Wine Travellers – which identifies the basic features of wine tourists, their motivations and needs, and which provides generic survey instruments to assist wine road participants to further investigate their markets.

Wine Roads – which provides details of minimum requirements or standards expected of wine roads and individual wine road participants. It also discusses successful case studies of wine road development, highlighting complementary product packaging opportunities.

Wine Road Supports – which documents and discusses regulatory requirements involved in rural development, including transport, building, trade, tourism and environmental issues. This section also covers a range of tools that can assist wine tourism participants in developing their activities and businesses, and covers skills such as management, accountancy and marketing, as well as identifying communication and promotional opportunities.

Wine Road Actors – which identifies all the various wine road actors or participants and highlights their roles, responsibilities and training needs as well as assistance available to various sectors. Wine road 'actors' include:

- wineries;
- public bodies;
- agritourist enterprises;
- restaurateurs;
- hoteliers and caterers;
- tour operators and travel agencies;
- speciality product distributors;
- tourist, recreation, cultural, environmental, sports, nature, gastronomy and other associations;
- schools and other teaching establishments;
- complementary service providers.

Marketing – which provides assistance with wine tourism marketing activities and provides details of distribution and communication tools, as well as information relating to marketing strategies and joint or partnership marketing opportunities.

Brock Cambourne and Niki Macionis

The following sections provide a brief discussion of some of the recent wine tourism developments in various European countries.

France

Although wine tourism is said to play a 'growing and fairly significant role in France' (Choisy 1996), its significance to the wine industry is less than in many New World wine regions (Table 2.5). Despite a growing recognition of the potential of wine tourism in France with regard to the diversification of farm economies and regional marketing, researchers such as Choisy (1996), Desplats (1996) and Mallon (1996) note a general lack of participation by wine producers in the tourism sector. However, wine has long been a significant component in the promotion of France as a tourism destination both in terms of image and of the opportunities to experience French cuisine and wines.

Wine tourism began to grow in the 1980s when 'economic constraints led many wine growers to consider direct sales and the development of visitor facilities at many vineyards' (Mallon 1996). Since then there has been a continual increase in the number of vineyards opening to the public, the number of wine routes and the level of tourist infrastructure. This growth has been assisted by large-scale private and public investment as the potential of wine tourism has been acknowledged, but constrained by 'a lack of cooperation between wine producers and tourism developers' (Mallon 1996). Indeed Thèvenin's (1996) examination of wine producers throughout France found that two main types of strategies were favoured in attracting tourists and developing wine tourism infrastructure: substantial investment by individual

Table 2.5 Extent of wine tourism in three wine regions of France

Wine region	Hectares under vine	Wine-growers	Visitor sites	Extent of wine tourism
Alsace	12 000	7 200	185	23% of total wine sales are direct to tourists
Burgundy	21 000	5 000	260	12% of total wine sales are direct to tourists
Bordeaux	115 000	17 800	260	vineyards attract 70 000 visitors per year

Sources: Choisy 1996, Johnson 1991.

producers in tourist infrastructure such as wine museums, research centres, art galleries, exhibition centres, wine routes, restaurants and accommodation; and the formation of informal networks, associations and clubs, such as the Great Wine Club of the Chateaux de Languedoc, or the Association of Young Wine Professionals of Beaune, which work together to develop tourism and jointly market their products to tourists.

As shown in Table 2.5, most French vineyards and wineries are not open to the public and therefore visitation must often be arranged through tour companies or by personal invitation (France in Your Glass 1998). Nevertheless, as Chapter 3 on the development of wine tourism in France by Isabelle Frochot illustrates, wine tourism is expanding substantially.

Italy

> To be sure it is a great resource. But today it is viewed from the tourist standpoint. We are speaking of wine, a drink famed through the centuries, which has caused thousands and thousands of verses and pages of prose to be written, which is an irreplaceable, noble food, a pleasure for the palate, and contributes towards the economic well-being of many. But which can also be a tourist attraction. (Mollo 1999)

Italy is the world's largest producer of wine, yet formal wine tourism is a relatively recent phenomenom in Italy. Prior to 1993 the majority of Italian wine producers failed to realize, or ignored, the tourism potential of the wine industry. In addition, the Italian public did not consider wineries as tourist attractions (Colombini, pers. comm. 1997). However, in 1993 the Movimento del Turismo del Vino (Italian Wine Tourism Association) was founded with the aim of increasing visitation to wine-producing areas utilizing the slogan 'see what you drink' and with 'the strong belief that wine cellars can attract visitors like a museum or resort'. The Movimento del Turismo del Vino (MTV) is a non-profit association comprising 600 members including wine producers, oenologists, restaurateurs, travel agents, media and wine experts, and which has established regional delegations charged with the promotion and organization of local events (Pavan 1994a, b). The activities of the MTV are primarily marketing focused and include:

- the organization of the Open Cellars Festival (reported to be the largest wine festival in the world, where Italian wineries open to the public en masse);
- the production of marketing collateral (including regional, national and Internet catalogues of Italian wineries);

- the development of wine roads;
- research;
- the development of 'merit requirements' for cellar door operations.

Despite an increase of visitors to Italian wineries from 400 000 to 2.5 million (resulting in 3000 billion lire in sales) between 1993 and 1996, the MTV notes that the prime obstacle to wine tourism development in Italy is ensuring supply by convincing wine producers to open permanently to the public. In fact, of the MTV's 600 members, only 392 are wine producers, of which only 23 per cent accept private visitors without a telephone booking. Furthermore, in 1997 only 3.2 per cent of Italian wine producers were reported as participating in wine tourism (Colombini, pers. comm. 1997).

Figure 2.1 Cooperative winery in Italy.

The catalyst for MTV's foundation was a study by Professor Corigliano of the Bocconi University, Milan, that identified the importance of wine in making leisure choices (Pavan 1994a: 6). The non-profit organization has introduced a number of initiatives that include environmental protection measures, the development of wine routes and the Cantine Aperte (Open Cellars) programme.

The MTV notes that wine tourism can be a powerful instrument for diversifying regional economies, and increasing the reputation, image and marketing of wine regions and regional wines. Specifically, wine tourism:

- increases the prestige and image of wine, especially those of high quality;
- provides the opportunity to increase a consumer's (or potential consumer's) understanding of wine, thus establishing trust in the product and encouraging more responsible use [sic] of wine;
- increases the commercial possibilities of wineries through both direct sales and other distribution channels (associated hospitality sectors such as restaurants);
- adds value to regional landscapes, foods and cultures (Colombini, pers. comm. 1997)

Due to the seeming lack of recognition of wine as tourist product, it is important to note that the MTV has actively sought to develop and market the wine tourism product and wine roads in conjunction with complementary and recognized tourism products, such as historic and artistic centres and archaeological sites. It has also introduced a number of initiatives that include environmental protection measures and the enhancement of wine routes by developing standardized signposting and wine road pictographs to facilitate the cross cultural/border flow of tourists (see Exhibit 2.2). In fact the Assemblia das Regioes Europeias Viticolas now models much of its activities in this area on the MTV's initiatives (Assemblia das Regioes Europeias Viticolas 1997). Several of the MTV's marketing activities have also been extremely successful, especially the Cantine Aperte (Open Cellars) programme. This began in 1993, with 100 Tuscan wine producers opening to the public on 9 May. By 1995, Cantine Aperte had grown to 595 wine producers opening their doors to some 400 000 tourists in a single weekend in May (MTV 1995); by 1996 this number had grown to more than 700 wine producers, while in 1998 more than 1000 wineries participated, receiving more than 1 million visitors (MTV 1999; see also Mollo 1999). It is claimed that Cantine Aperte is now the largest wine festival in the world.

Exhibit 2.2: Wine cellars and the Strade del Vino

Chair of the Movimento del Turismo del Vino, Donatella Cinelli Colombini, notes that the demand for wine tourism in Italy far exceeds the supply of the wine tourism product. Of the MTV's 392 vineyard membership, only 23 per cent accept private visitors without a telephone booking. This says Cinelli Colombini (1997) 'is very sad considering the enormous potential of Italian wine cellars'. Cinelli Colombini also notes that Italian wine cellars are extremely diverse and that 'those who venture into them believing that they will find many similar cellars will be surprised to find them all different'. The characteristics of the MTV's vineyard members are:

- 89 per cent offer free wine tastings;
- all but five also include a farm producing other products such as olive oil or fruit;
- in all cellars there is at least one person who speaks a foreign language, the most prevalent being English (83 per cent);
- tasting rooms are present in 241 (61 per cent) of wine cellars, 68 cellars admit to having poor facilities, while 29 per cent of wine cellars host tastings in the producers' homes;
- 33 per cent of wine cellars have facilities for serving food (usually an open air restaurant);
- most premises have some historical value: for example, 93 are located in an ancient or rural village; 24 in a castle; 79 in a villa and 98 in an old colonial house.

Donatella Cinelli Colombini also notes that in order for Italian wine tourism to compete with other European nations wine tourism product development must create a superior offering. To facilitate this the MTV has implemented a cellar door certification or accreditation scheme that wine producers must adhere to in order to participate in the *Strade del Vino* or Wine Roads. Cinelli Colombini notes that the wine cellars 'become a sort of flag carrier for the whole area and as such it becomes necessary to impose a number of prerequisites'. These prerequisites or 'merit requirements' revolve around:

- *the quality of the wine produced* – the cellar's wine must be the qualified extension of its brand name; they must sell primarily bottled wine; there should be no leaking barrels, wine smells etc. evident in the cellar; and the cellar should avail itself of the expertise of an oenologist;
- *accessibility of the cellar* – the cellar must be accessible to the tourist; access roads should be improved; car parks (which do not offend the beauty of the area) must be established close to

the cellars; and the least accessible cellars should be accessible from the wine road via four-wheel drive minibuses;

- *hospitality* – welcome to the winery must be warm and courteous. Hospitality is a qualifying factor of the relationship with the tourist. To accomplish this signs noting opening times and languages spoken should be provided; staff should be both organized and smiling; brochures promoting the entire region should be available; and disabled facilities should be provided;
- *wine tasting* – if a separate tasting room is not provided, wine producers should take tourists to their home (while some privacy may be lost, the wine cellar will gain loyal customers); and wine should be served at the correct temperature;
- *sale of wine* – wine should be available for sale, but should not be imposed on the tourist;
- *opening hours* – the wine cellar should be open for a minimum of 30 hours per week and during public holidays.

Brock Cambourne and Niki Macionis

Undoubtedly, wine tourism is going to be an area of growing significance to the Italian wine and tourism industries with a business turnover estimated at 3000 billion lire in 1998 and an 8 per cent increase in 1999 (*Wine News* 1999). According to *Wine News*, 'Wine tourism may well become in the course of the next 3–5 years not only an essential element in safeguarding the environment and rural lifestyles but also a genuine opportunity for employment and enterprise, with investments of 500 billion lire and 10 000 new jobs (both new trades and small business launches)'. The Italian government in conjunction with MTV supported research presented during Vinitaly '99 of the 50 leading wine tourism areas in Italy, indicating potential for development and growth in terms of both investments and employment. As in the case of France, emphasis is being laid on the contribution that wine tourism can make to regional development and the stimulation of employment and business development opportunities in wine regions that have been affected by rural economic restructuring. According to *Wine News* (1999), such developments, 'may be found in the promotion of hospitality facilities and gastronomy, local events, specific products for this kind of tourism (of some status and not exclusively wine-oriented), permanent training of operators, the care and visibility of places, vineyards, cellars and landscapes, the enhancement of historical, cultural and artistic resources, and monitoring of the preferences of "wine" tourists'.

The Iberian Peninsula: Portugal and Spain

Portugal is a country which by virtue of its ancient trade links with Britain has long used wine as a means to link wine regions with tourism. The city of Oporto in northern Portugal uses the port wine connection extensively in its promotion as well as in the hosting of events and festivals. From the perspective of local politicians and government officials such relationships create the opportunity for long-term loyalty from visitors to the region in terms of their wine purchasing behaviour. However, while port has a high profile, particularly in the British market, it has diminished in popularity as consumers have focused on lighter, fruitier styles of wine for immediate drinking.

Mayson (1997) describes his travels to the port houses of the Douro Valley, Portugal. Set amidst rugged and breath-taking scenery, the tourist infrastructure is relatively under-developed with accommodation scarce and only restricted car access. The port houses have only recently begun to open to tourists, and previously were relatively unreceptive (Mayson 1997). Nevertheless, market awareness of port has provided an opportunity for Portugal to promote its other red and white wines (Mayson 1998), particularly from the Duoro valley, which is the site of the port grape vineyards.

The Alto Minho region in northern Portugal, which is best known in wine terms for production of Vinho Verde, has also been attempting to develop linkages between wine and tourism. The Vinho Verde DOC region is Portugal's largest demarcated wine region. The Alto Minho region has received substantial EU funding through various regional and rural develop-ment programmes, such as Leader, to improve tourism product development and promotion, including wine tourism (see Exhibit 2.3). Interestingly, the region's wine tourism product has mainly been aimed at international and domestic tourists who have already arrived in the region to see its culture and heritage, rather than specifically using the region's wine as a branding tool to attract tourists. Wine tourism related development has included the creation of wine routes, provision of homestay accommodation and guides to the gastronomic opportunities in the region (AREV 1997). However, as in Italy, much of the information and promotional material pertaining to wineries and wine routes appears to have been published with inadequate attention to the ability of wineries to cater for visitors, especially inter-national tourists, to provide tasting rooms, and to understand the interests and needs of the market.

Exhibit 2.3: The Dão Wine Route

'*The historic vines of Portugal, long dormant, enter a new age.*'

(Greene 1999)

Historically, Portugal has had a relaxed attitude to its wine production, with a huge array of different grape types being cultivated on hundreds of small farms, often with other crops in the same field (Kolpan *et al*. 1996). The result has been a host of interesting and complex wines that certainly had a strong local identity, but were only enjoyed by a limited number of educated consumers throughout the world (Kolpan *et al*. 1996). Portugal's farmers have clung fiercely to this centuries-old traditional form of cultivation, but this unwillingness to move with the times, combined with often complex politics, prevented Portugal from becoming a serious player in the modern global wine market (Greene 1999). Times are changing, however. Farmers are now being encouraged to update their wine-making practices and premiums are being paid to the producers who can bring in high quality grapes from designated plots. The government is keen to put Portugal firmly on the international map and is working closely with producers in an attempt to promote their wines more successfully.

Figure 2.2 The winescape of northern Portugal.

One region keen to attract attention is the Dão area situated in the middle of Northern Portugal in the province of Beira Alta. The region has a contrasting topography, mountainous in the north, but flatter in the south, and a climate that, although mild, can be cold and rainy in the winter but very hot and dry in the summer.

Vines are planted as high as 800 metres, but the majority of them are grown for DOC (Denominaçãe di Origem, Controladad). Dão wines are planted between 400–500 metres.

The Dão region covers a geographical area of 376,000 ha with about 20,000 ha devoted to vine growing. The 'vineyard parcelling' that exists in much of Portugal still means that 100,000 different landowners are responsible for more than 50 per cent of the region's total wine production but, at the same time, medium- and large-sized private wine-makers have now started to manage and create their own individual wines on the rest of the land (Comissio Vitivinicola Regional do Dão 1999).

The region produces an average of 500,000 hectolitres of wine each year, primarily from cooperatives and wine-making centres, but individual wine-makers are now making an impact. Innovative technology has now combined with local knowledge in this region to produce some outstanding wines that have started to impress the world stage.

The Dão region is keen to attract visitors to the area as part of this development process, and the creation of 'The Dão Wine Route' is a positive step in the right direction. This venture is a result of the combined efforts of the Gabinete da Rota do Vinho do Dão, and three local tourism associations. The initiative is also supported by the Regional Vitiviniculatural Commission of Dão, an inter-professional body whose aim is to represent the interests of the professions involved in the production and trade of Dão wines, and to defend the national and regional heritage from which the vinicultural products can benefit. The Dão Wine Route is published on a map available from local tourist offices and vineyards and outlines details of 17 wine-producing *quintas* or *casas* that can be visited for wine tasting (Graca 1999). Symbols provide details of the facilities available at each destination. At the centre of the tour is Viseu, the beautiful capital city of this region, which is also home to the Regional Vitiviniculatural Commission of Dão.

Liz Sharples

Despite Spain being one of the largest wine producers in the world, wine tourism is relatively underdeveloped there. Tourism has, however, been acknowledged as one method of revitalizing rural areas, improving regional economies and preserving the natural and cultural heritage of viticultural areas, while Spain is also increasingly utilizing the large number of tourists it receives as a means to promote its wine regions and wine types. For example, sherry is undergoing a revival (Broom 1998a) while regions such as Rioja in northern Spain have established an export department which coordinates the activities of the various bodegas in the area and which utilizes the links between wine and tourism as a major promotional tool (*Decanter* 1997). Investment in modernizing the Spanish wine industry has come from the private sector rather than through the conservative cooperative system (Broom 1998b). Interestingly, it is also the private sector which has been the most enthusiastic about wine tourism, although some government and EU funding has been put into rural tourism development in the wine regions.

Gilbert (1992: 27) noted that increasing interest in 'active holidays and participative activities' as well as a rising level of demand for tourist products with a cultural aspect 'provides a major opportunity for the viticultural sector' in Spain. Indeed, a 1992 analysis of the tourism potential of the Rioja region in Spain identified wine and gastronomy as having outstanding tourism potential. This analysis also proposed an action plan for the development of wine tourism in Rioja which included:

- an inventory and classification of wine-producing bodegas according to availability and suitability of tourist services, the supply of supplementary products such as catering and craft work, and the historical interest of the facility;
- the renovation of some bodegas to increase tourist readiness;
- the provision of tourism training for wine producers and vineyard staff;
- the selection of the most accessible and interesting vineyards for inclusion in tourism programmes;
- the establishment of strategic relationships and marketing partnerships with complementary hospitality sectors such as restaurants;
- the creation of a centrally located wine museum which would contain 'elaborate information about wine, their history etc.' (Gilbert 1992: 31).

Spanish wine tourism development efforts have obviously been successful to date. Indeed, a European Union ECOS-OUVERTURE project, aimed at integrating Moldavia in the rural tourism network of European wine-producing regions, notes that the Rioja region as a partner in the project brings 'real expertise in the field of integrated rural [tourism] development', particularly with regard to the Rioja Wine Route (ECOS-OUVERTURE 1998) (see Chapter 14).

Germany and Austria

How best, then, is the huge range of Germany's production to be explored, and how is it to be enjoyed? The ideal way, without a doubt, is to set off on a leisurely tour, preferably walking, with this Atlas in your pack. The short distances between villages would only lend vigour to the thirst, and zest to the appetite. A month could be spent exploring the Mosel in this way; another month the Rheingau . . . a lifetime of summer holidays could go by without exhausting the variety of every Gemeinde in every Gebiet.

Lacking the leisure to drink in Germany this way, we can quite easily arrange an armchair tour, either in macro-focus, ranging from wines of contrasting regions, grapes, categories and ages, or micro-focus, contrasting even on one village, or one producer, and tasting for smaller and more subtle distinctions. Either course will reveal at once how German wine is infinitely various; a unique cultural heritage worth a lifetime of study (Johnson 1986: 19).

Germany and Austria have a long history of formal wine tourism. As noted in the first chapter, Germany has had an official series of wine roads since the 1920s, with the first *Weinlehrpfad* (instructional wine path) being established at Schweigen. Such wine paths are well signposted and contain information on interpretive panels on viticulture, wine and culture. Some of the earliest available research on the relationship between wine and tourism was conducted in Mainfranken, Bavaria (IGUW and GGW 1984). The centre of Franconian wine production is Würzburg where three of the 'oldest, biggest and best wine estates in Germany' are to be found, all of which offer vineyard cafés (Johnson 1991: 280–1). Wine tourism has played an important role in maintaining wine sales in an increasingly competitive wine market. According to Johnson (1986: 158): 'Efforts to build up a clear identity for the wine growing regions have been linked with the reconstruction (*Flurbereinigung*) of the vineyards, and the value of tourism has not been forgotten. The new *Weinlehrpfad* help to explain and therefore to sell

German wine, and by the end of the 1970s practically all the eleven wine regions had their own *Weinstraßen'*.

The promotion of wine tourism in Germany's wine regions has continued following the reunification of Germany. For example, the German Wine Institute produce a guide (Deutsches Weininstitut 1996/97) on 'Vintners to Visit/*Resen zum Winzer'* primarily in English and German but which also contains information in French, Spanish, Dutch and Italian. The brochure provides information on 'visitor-friendly wine estates, wineries and cooper-atives', the languages they speak, availability of wine tastings, cellar tours and vineyard tours, whether or not there is a restaurant (*Gutsausschank/ Gutsschänke*), wine pub (*Strausswirtschaft/Besenwirtschaft*) and/or guest rooms, and the size of the group each can accommodate. The provision of such a detailed brochure is a measure which many other wine regions could hope to emulate. In addition, the German Wine Institute produces a brochure on German wine festivals. The 1999 brochure listed over 500 wine festivals to which visitors were invited (Deutsches Weininstitut. 1999).

More recently, the linkages between wine and tourism have become even more formalized through the development of the 'Culinary Germany' marketing concept. Under the 'Culinary Germany' brand the German National Tourist Board (DZT) is aiming to position Germany as an attractive travel destination combining culture and wine and food. The DZT's own research indicates that 'wining and dining' is the second most important holiday activity for German holidaymakers and the third most important for Europeans. A Black Forest Route is being used as a pilot project for the programme which consists of public–private partnerships between local government marketing associations, the hospitality industry and wine-growers' organizations (German National Tourist Board 1999).

Tourism is also contributing to the economies of many of Austria's wine regions (Baranyi 1990). Tourism has also been important in restoring the perception of the quality of Austrian wines following the 'Austrian wine scandal' of 1985 'in which a few idle and dishonest (not to say criminal) growers and merchants were caught adding diethylene glycol to their wines to give them more body' (Johnson 1994: 222). Many of Austria's principal vineyards are a comfortable day-trip from Vienna. As in Germany, small wine producers gain supplementary income through the provision of tourist accommodation as well as direct sales (Ranner 1997). For example, wine tourism is a considerable attraction in Burgenland, where smallholdings predominate (38 per cent of the 4804 vineyards are less than a hectare) (Ranner 1997).

The rebirth of the wines of Eastern Europe

The collapse of the state communist countries of Eastern Europe in the late 1980s and early 1990s led to a revolution that was viticultural as much as economic and political. After years of collectively-produced wine that robbed vineyards, varieties and even regions of much individual expressions of terroir, recent years have seen a dramatic growth of replanting and reinvestment in the newly privatized vineyards of Bulgaria, the Czech Republic, Hungary, Moldova, Romania, the Slovak Republic, Slovenia and the Ukraine (Johnson 1994; Kolpan *et al.* 1996). The privatization of the former collective vineyards and the opportunity to produce quality bulk wine at low cost has attracted substantial investment from Western European wine and food companies, including the British supermarket chain Sainsbury's. Investment in the vineyards has gone hand-in-hand with foreign investment in other industries including tourism, along with substantial aid and loans from the European Union.

As in Western Europe, much of wine tourism related development has been characterized by the creation of wine roads, often with European Union assistance and funding. For example, effective advertising is beyond the finances of most small wine producers in Slovenia so the 20 official Wine Routes (*Vinske ceste*) in Slovenia provide an important means of attracting visitors (Alkalaj 1996). Every wine region has at least one wine route. Routes are included on most tourist maps and a viticultural map of Slovenia has been produced with information on wineries and their wines. Similarly, wine road development is being undertaken in Hungary (e.g. Tourinform Baranya n.d.) and Moldova (see Chapter 11), in an effort to attract Western European tourists. The development of wine tourism in Hungry is symptomatic of what is occuring in the region.

Hungary

The history of wine production in Hungary has been long and eventful, with evidence of vines being grown and wine being made as early as the 5th century AD (Johnson 1994). The last ten years have been particularly exciting as the country has made the bold change from state-operated monopolies to private enterprise, but the wine industry appears to have embraced the change positively.

A major investment programme has been underway and, with the guidance of influential wine professionals from both the UK and Australia, the industry has developed substantially. Vineyards have been improved, top quality rootstocks have been selected and planted, and state-of-the-art production facilities have been installed.

Hungary has demonstrated that it has a commitment to improve both the output, and the quality of the wine it produces, in order to compete successfully on the world market. It also wants to ensure that international investment will continue in the future.

Hungary is now the world's eleventh largest wine-producing nation and it exports more than half of its 115 million gallon/4.6 million hectolitre production each year (Kolpan *et al.* 1996).

The country has much to offer in terms of quality wine. The industry can now offer a remarkable fusion of both Old and New World wines to the consumer, ranging from the world famous Tokaji dessert wines, made since the early 1700s, to the full-bodied red Eger's Bikavér, better known in the west as 'Bull's Blood', made from grapes grown on the foothills of the Bükk Mountains.

Wine tourism is an important element of this metamorphosis (see Exhibit 2.4). A comprehensive book published by the Hungarian Collective Agricultural Marketing Centre (AMC 1999) provides detailed information about each of the 22 wine-producing regions, as well as providing general information about the industry in general. Each region is depicted in terms of its size, climate, soil type, and grape varieties grown, and the wine cellars, taverns, accommodation, restaurants, tourist attractions and festivals in each area are listed. A useful map is also included to help visitors plan their route.

Exhibit 2.4: Hilltop Vineyards

One venture that has embraced the concept of wine tourism is the Hilltop Vineyard in the Åszár-Neszmély region, 75 km north-west of Budapest. The vineyard was founded in 1990 by the four owners and directors: Eva Keresztury, formerly a wine merchant, Imre Trák, formerly a banker, Judit Storcz, previously a wine merchant, and Akos Kamocsay, a renowned wine-maker.

The vineyard has seen steady growth since its opening, now exporting 8 million bottles a year (1998 figure) representing about 35 per cent/65 per cent of the total export volume/value respectively of the country. The UK is their main market, taking 95 per cent of their exports (Hungarian Food and Wine Bureau 1999). The company owns wineries at Neszmély and at Czászár (about 30 km away) and 450 ha of vineyards surrounding these sites. A major extension and refurbishment programme in 1994–98 costing US$6 m has ensured that the company is now operating with state-of-the-art facilities, employing 80 well-qualified staff.

The vineyard produces a varied range of wines, currently with the emphasis on white wines, but work is now in progress to develop the red wine range that they offer.

In 1997, Akos Kamocsay was chosen as 'Wine-maker of the Year' by *Grapevine*, London, and in 1998 the wines won numerous medals in the UK, Belgium, and Hungary at various wine festivals, including 'White Wine of the Year' at the International Wine Challenge, London.

The vineyard is situated on a hillside overlooking the Danube, and regularly organizes winery tours with tutored tastings. A 'wine hotel' and restaurant on site offer accommodation and gourmet meals produced by one of Budapest's top chefs, András Szèkelyi. The restaurant offers traditional Hungarian specialities and an unparalleled view of the Danube, the surrounding hills and the well-managed vineyards. The area also offers other attractions for hotel guests, an international cycling path leading between the Neszmély Hills, a swimming pool and thermal pool at the town of Tata nearby, horse-riding and hunting in the nearby forests, and watersports on the Danube, only 2 km away (Hilltop Neszmély Ltd 1999).

Liz Sharples

The Eastern Mediterranean

Greece and the surrounding Eastern Mediterranean countries have an ancient wine-making history. There is evidence of vines being grown and wine being made in this area for at least 4000 years (Kolpan *et al.* 1996). Progress, however, has not always been easy. The rise of the Ottoman Empire prevented the development of the wine culture in Greece as many vineyards were destroyed and the land used for other purposes such as grazing and growing of other crops (Kolpan *et al.* 1996). While the wine-making continued (especially in Greece's many monasteries), quality had been compromised – until '1969 with the revision of wine-legislation: Greece wanted to conform to EU standards – wine production included, in order to apply for future membership' (Cruise Club Holidays n.d.). Neighbouring Turkey is one of the world's largest producers of grapes but, for religious reasons (99 per cent of the country is Muslim), domestic consumption and production has remained at low levels (Bassler 1998), although the growth of international tourism to Turkey has led to greater exposure for its wines.

Over the last twenty years, the European Union has done much to raise the standards of Greek wine. Wine production in Greece has moved from primitive to modern wine-making techniques and has implemented an appellation control system, with about 12 per cent of Greek wines qualifying for appellation status from twenty-six wine regions. Growing interest in the Greek wine industry led to the organization of the first Thessaloniki International Wine competition in March 1999, when 262 samples from seven countries were judged in accordance with international rules. Greece's main wine-producing regions are Peloponnisos, Altica, Macedonia, Sanos, Santorini and Crete (Johnson 1994).

In Greece, where the first VQPRD (vin de qualité produit dans une région déterminée) wines in history were produced (Focus Multimedia 1997), the tax regimes of the Ottoman occupation led to the demise of a wine-making tradition that began 4000 years ago. Today, Greece and, to some extent, Israel and the Lebanon, are experiencing a resurgence of their ancient traditions of wine-making. For Greece this has also seen the establishment of appellation regulations in line with EU standards (Seferiades 1998). This resurgence has led to the development of wine tourism products and the use of local wine and cuisine in generic tourism promotion. For Greece this has seen the development of cruise packages (e.g. Cruise Club Holidays n.d.), World Wide Web sites promoting wine tourism (e.g. Seferiades 1998), wine roads (e.g. Wright 1996a) (see Exhibit 2.5) and the promotion of Greek wine at international resorts (e.g. Grecotel n.d.). Greek wineries are present throughout the country and, because of its geography, are generally some distance apart, making wine touring difficult in comparison to other wine regions such as Burgundy or Napa (Wright 1996a).

Exhibit 2.5: The wine roads of Macedonia

The province of Macedonia situated in the far north of Greece is well known for its red wine production using the Xynomavro grape. A recent initiative in this area has been the setting up of a pioneer tourist programme called the 'Wine Routes of Macedonia' developed by the united efforts of the Wine Producers' Association of Macedonian Vineyards members (Wine Producers' Association 1999).

Nineteen wine producers have worked together to create four wine routes linking vineyards with other important tourist attractions in the area. The wine roads are named; The Wine Road of the Olympian Gods, The Wine Road of the Macedonian Kings, The Wine Road of Hallikidiki, and The Wine Road of Dionysus.

The maps available pinpoint the wineries and give full details of the producers, their contact numbers and their opening hours.

Important archaeological sites and sites of outstanding natural beauty are also highlighted, as well as overnight accommodation details, and restaurant facilities. The vineyards that are open to the public carry out wine tasting as well as offering wine sales and the opportunity to buy wine books and accessories. The tourist initiative is fully supported by an EU funding initiative, LEADER II, which is designed to help the promotion of tourism in rural areas.

Liz Sharples

Wine tourism in Israel

The eastern shores of the Mediterranean, and in particular Israel, are known as the birthplace of wine, with archaeological evidence proving 'the existence of wine in Palestine society, over 4,300 years ago' (Leibowitz 1998). Despite these ancient beginnings there have been long periods when Greek, Turkish and Israeli wine production has been sadly lacking in quality. In fact, the Israeli wine industry all but disappeared for a period of 1600 years and were it not for the generosity of Baron Edmond de Rothschild in 1882 in establishing wineries at Rishon-le-Zion and Zichron-Yaacov Israeli wine might not exist today.

In Israel, wine, while having a growing domestic culture, is generally considered an incidental part of tourism, although there is an increasing focus on its wineries and wine regions (Marcus 1999). Several districts of Israel have wineries with developing tourist visitation (e.g. the Negev, the Haifa–Jerusalem coast, the Golan Heights and Upper Galilee). Several of these wineries also have visitor facilities ranging from tasting rooms to picnic areas and winery tours, with many also selling a range of other locally made products (e.g. olive oil, cheese, confectionery and breads) from the cellar door (Kosher Wines 1997).

Traditionally, Israeli wine production consisted of sweet, kosher wine (Walton 1996); however, since the emergence of the Golan Heights Winery as a world class wine producer, the profile of Israel's wine industry has increased markedly (Montefiore, pers. comm. 1999). Since 1990, six boutique wineries have opened in Israel riding a 'wave of Israeli interest in wine' (Rogov 1995; Sher 1997: 36). Consumption has increased from under four litres per capita in 1993 to nearly five litres in 1996 (Sher 1997). The Israeli Ministry of Tourism database (Infotour 1997) lists three wineries open to the public in Galilee, Mount Carmel and in the Golan Heights. Wine tourism development in Israel has been largely facilitated by the wineries themselves, with little or no government assistance or coordination.

According to Adam Montefiore, International Marketing Manager for Golan Heights Winery, visitors come to the Golan Heights Winery primarily because of an interest in wine and because the winery is well positioned on the general tourism route in the region. He notes that the winery now receives around 100,000 visitors a year and says that 'the main benefits of tourism to the winery are educational', in that it creates new markets by 'introducing people without a strong wine culture to quality wine'. Specific wine tourism activities at the Golan Heights Winery focus on enhancing the educational aspect of the winery experience and include:

- guided tours;
- an 'Academy of Wine', offering formal wine education and training opportunities; and
- a wine and gastronomy festival called the 'Golan Vintage – Wine and Culinary Festival', which promotes and emphasizes the entire region (Montefiore, pers. comm. 1999).

New World wine tourism

In the 'Old World' rural economic restructuring and changed consumer preferences have been a major factor in encouraging the development of wine tourism. However, in the 'New World' countries, especially the United States, Canada and Australia, consumer preferences have been towards greater wine consumption, and of a higher quality. The development of wine tourism has received explicit government assistance in the form of facilitating legislation, as in the United States and Canada (see Chapter 13), often in conjunction with network development and funding, as in the case of Australia (see Chapter 12).

In contrast to Europe, New World wine-producing countries such as the United States, New Zealand and Australia also exhibit high levels of wine tourism participation. For example, while Choisy (1996) and Mallon (1996) note that only around 5 per cent of wine producers in Burgundy are involved with tourism, and the Movimento del Turismo del Vino reports that only 3.2 per cent of Italian wine producers actively participate in tourism, Macionis (1997) notes that almost 90 per cent of Australian wine producers provide cellar door tasting facilities, while 60 per cent of New Zealand wineries offered cellar door sales in 1995 (Hall 1996).

Wine tourism in the Americas

Amongst the New World wine regions, California, and the Napa Valley in particular, has one of the highest profiles and a strong tourism focus (Johnson 1991; Hall and Macionis 1998; Yates 1997). California is also one of the world's largest wine regions with 700 wineries and over 121,000 ha under vine in 1990 (Johnson 1991). At the other extreme, Indiana had only 18 wineries in 1995 (Indiana Wine Grape Council (IWGC) 1998b). Despite this small number, the Indiana Wine Grape Council reported US$1.8 million in wine sales to tourists (Hall and Macionis 1998). The Council was established in 1989 (IWGC 1998a) by the Indiana General Assembly with the mission to 'enhance the Indiana economy by establishing a successful wine grape industry through grape and wine research and market development. The effort focuses on improving the quality of Indiana wines, matching grape and fruit cultivars to Indiana soils and climate, and promoting Indiana wineries to consumers and tourists' (IWGC 1998b).

The value of the wine industry to regional economies and its interdependence with the tourism sector has also been recognized in the United States. Brown (1981) reports that the vineyards of the Napa Valley, California, are the second most visited tourist attractions in that State after Disneyland (see also Chapter 15). The wine industry is reported to inject over US$30 million dollars into the local economy in Long Island, New York, with 'the thousands of visitors and guests who flock to the wineries each week providing the most significant part of the wineries' sales' (Moynahan 1995), while in Oregon, the Oregon Wine Advisory Board (1995) estimates that the wine industry contributes US$75 million per annum to that state's economy.

While most wine tourism development focuses on the supply side, the Indiana Wine Grape Council has also acted to educate the customer. Under the title 'Seven Tips for Touring Indiana Wineries', the Council has published a 'code of conduct' of the sort more commonly associated with ecotourism (IWGC 1998c). The guidelines are a mixture of customer etiquette and host responsibility. They are reproduced here in full as an example of a code of conduct at wineries that can help clarify the expectations, responsibilities and rights of visitors and hosts alike (Table 2.6).

Despite the previously noted impressive statistics regarding the economic value of wine tourism in the United States, and the fact that the resurgence of the wine industry in many parts of the United States 'can be attributed to winery tourism' (Dodd and Bigotte 1995), it is surprising that the California Trade and Commerce Agency does not yet recognize the concept of 'wine tourism', (Hook, pers. comm. 1996), while other US wine regions are only

Table 2.6 Seven tips for touring Indiana wineries

Call	Check directions, business hours, area lodging, and tour schedules. Some wineries are in the Eastern time zone, some in Central. Most are open Sundays for tasting and carry-out sales!
Learn	Wineries are the best place to learn about winemaking and wine tasting. Ask questions.
Ask	If a member of your touring party is physically challenged, call in advance to find out if the winery is accessible. Many have alternative entrances for visitors with limited mobility.
Dump	Don't feel obligated to finish a sample. Most wineries have dump buckets on or under the counter; if those are not visible, ask the server to pour out the wine.
Spit	If you're planning to visit several wineries in a day, you may wish to spit out the samples you're tasting rather than swallow them. That's how professional wine judges keep their senses while tasting several hundred wines!
Eat	Enjoy a sandwich or a cheese tray at the wineries that serve food. Food slows the rate of absorption of alcohol, thereby decreasing the effects.
Kids	Children are allowed in every Indiana winery. However, there's limited entertainment for them at some, so bring a book to occupy them while you taste the wine. And remember to watch them carefully around equipment and glassware.

Source: Indiana Wine Grape Council 1998c.

now beginning to consider wine tourism development and strategies (Chandler, pers. comm. 1997; Byrne, pers. comm. 1997). Such comments illustrate the immaturity of wine tourism as a distinct tourism product.

Nonetheless, a number of American states and regions have established wine industry promotion and marketing organizations, such as the Oregon Wine Advisory Board, the Texas Wine Marketing Institute, the New York Wine and Grape Foundation, the Colorado Wine Industry Development Board, the Lodi-Woodbridge Winegrape Commission and Virginia Wine Marketing Office. These organizations are primarily government funded and, while their general brief is to foster the economic growth and development of wine and winegrape industries in these states, several explicitly pursue the development and marketing of wine tourism. For example, Colorado State Statute 35–29.5–103 regarding the establishment of the Colorado Wine Industry Development Board, lists the promotion 'and integration of the Colorado wine industry as a component of the State's tourism program' as one of the prime objectives of the Board (http://www.ppld/CoStatutes/T350/T350029501030.html), while the Virginia Wine Marketing Office states that its prime marketing strategy is 'to encourage and promote wine tourism, visits to wine country and wine festivals', through the production and distribution of wine region maps and festival and tour guides (Macionis 1997). In New York State, the New York Wine and Grape Foundation has funded and established a number of regional wine associations to cooperatively promote member wineries and wines. These associations engage in a number of joint activities such as the production and distribution of brochures, the erection of roadway signs and joint wine tastings (Henehan and White 1990).

Although not traditionally associated with fine wine, Canada has also undergone a revolution in wine production in recent years. The Niagara region of Ontario and the Okanagan Valley of British Columbia have both developed as areas in which quality wine is produced and which rely substantially on visitors for winery sales. Wine tourism development in Ontario and New York State is discussed further in Chapter 13 by David Telfer. However, wine tourism is also significant to wineries in the Okanagan. According to Senese (1999), the dramatic expansion of quality vines and wines of VQA standard in the Okanagan is a very recent phenomenon, bringing with it an equally spectacular expansion of wine tourism services, facilities and events, and observes that,

> Despite the apparent youth of the wine industry in the Okanagan, its ancillary industry, wine tourism relies heavily upon the appeal, image,

and history of 'old world' European wines to attract and entertain the tourist. The result: 'new world wines' with 'old world images' and a dramatically altered and expanded cultural landscape of tourism in the Okanagan (Senese 1999).

Tourism is also gradually becoming important for wine in South America. Although South American wineries make almost 10 per cent of the world's wine it has been little known outside the region until recently, primarily because the vast bulk of the wine has been produced for domestic consumption. In addition, the industry has historically been organized on a mass production basis with less than a hundred of the 1800 wineries on the continent aiming to produce wine of an international quality (Johnson 1994).

However, following a decline in the levels of domestic consumption, many wineries are now undergoing substantial change as they seek to improve the quality and consistency of their wines for the export market, particularly to Europe and North America (Weston 1999) (See Exhibit 2.6). The degree to which such changes are occuring was described on the front cover of the May 1999 issue of *Decanter* as a 'revolution'. Tourism has started to assume a degree of importance for the export market because of the role of international tourism in creating brand awareness and market exposure, often through cooperative relationships with national airlines, such as Aerolinas Argentinas. In addition, tourism brochures and promotions for Argentina and Chile are starting to feature images of vineyards, particularly as their wines become better known in markets such as the UK.

Exhibit 2.6: Malmann in Mendoza

The name 'Malmann' is well known in Argentina. For over ten years he appeared in a regular cookery series on television and he now owns a chain of coffee shops (Los Classicos) in Buenos Aires, and five restaurants in Mendoza, Bariloche, Buenos Aires and Uruguay (Whitaker 1999).

The Mendoza restaurant is set in the heart of the Argentinian winelands within the grounds of Bodegas Escorihuela, a working winery owned by wine expert Nicolas Catena. The restaurant is called '1884', aptly named after the year that the winery was founded, and has a menu designed to celebrate the marrying of regional wines with traditional dishes such as Empanadas, a spicy baked meat-filled pasty. Whitaker (1999) reports that Malmann supports the economy of the area by buying as much produce as possible from local suppliers. The restaurant demonstrates one way in which visitors can be attracted to a local winery.

Liz Sharples

Wine tourism in Australia and New Zealand

The potential value of special interest tourism products, such as wine tourism, has not gone unrecognized in Australia (see Exhibit 2.7). Indeed, Australia is unique in its approach to wine tourism development in that several state governments have formally established organizational structures to facilitate the development of wine tourism.

For example, in 1993, the Victoria State Government established the Victorian Wineries Tourism Council (VWTC), to take advantage of Victoria's growing reputation as a wine tourism destination. With wine becoming one of the main foci of the tourism drive in South Australia, the SA Government has followed suit with the formation of the South Australian Wine Tourism Council (SAWTC) in 1996. According to the former South Australian Premier, Mr Dean Brown, 'wine tourism is there to be developed' (*The Australian* 1995: 4) and 'is going to be a big money earner for South Australia' (*Weekly Times* 1995: 22). The former South Australian Premier's support for wine tourism is reflected in that state's tourism marketing and promotion. Indeed, the Chief Executive of the South Australian Tourism Commission, Mr Michael Gleeson (in Innes 1995: 5), stated that 'we're so good at wine tourism we have made it the single most important focus for tourism in our marketing for the next two years'.

On a regional basis, the Federal Government has funded a number of wine tourism related initiatives and developments, under both the Rural and Regional Tourism Development Programmes, including the development of regional tourism marketing strategies, wine trails, vineyard signage systems and wine region visitor centres (Macionis 1997). In addition, in 1997 the Office of National Tourism (ONT – formerly the Department of Tourism, DOT) awarded a grant of A$70,000 to the Winemakers' Federation of Australia to develop a national wine tourism strategy. Further details of the development of the national wine strategy are discussed in Chapter 12.

Figure 2.3   Hillstowe Winery tasting rooms, Adelaide Hills, South Australia.

Exhibit 2.7: Australia's boutique boom

The emergence of wine tourism in Australia is the result of several catalysts, which significantly increased the accessibility and appeal of wine to the Australian public. Cultural factors, such as post-war immigration and a subsequent greater influence of European values and lifestyles, broadened the appeal of wine as a lifestyle product. In addition, marketing and technological innovations, such as the 'bag in the box' or wine cask and a generally increasing level of affluence in Australian society, made wine more accessible to the Australian public (Macionis 1997).

The most influential catalyst was however the 'boutique boom' of the early 1970s which saw the emergence of many small, boutique or farm wineries all across Australia. Without extensive distribution networks these small wineries depended substantially upon direct sales via the cellar door for their economic viability, which is directly linked to the growth of wine tourism.

It is interesting to note that Australia's Hunter Valley as it exists today, with its 70 plus wineries, conference centres and resorts and which attracts in excess of one million visitors per year, did not exist in the 1960s. Indeed, in the 1960s and early 1970s there were only the most rudimentary facilities, and sales outlets existed at very few wineries, with just Elliots, Tulloch, Drayton's Bellvue and Drayton's Happy Valley offering cellar door access and facilities. In addition, there were no restaurants, and merely two small hotels on the outskirts of Cessnock (Halliday 1994).

In the 1960s, the majority of wine was sold in bulk to breweries and wine and spirit merchants for distribution, thus somewhat negating the need for cellar door outlets. Murray Tyrell, Chairman of Tyrell's Wines, recalls: 'wine was still sold mostly in bulk . . . there was no need to get out and promote wine in bottles, because it was all sold anyhow, and we made enough money to exist' (*Weekend Australian* 1996: 28). As a consequence, Tyrell's did not even start selling wine under its own label until 1962 (Halliday 1994). Bruce Tyrell, Managing Director of Tyrell's Vineyard, recounted that 'the growth of the place [Hunter Valley] has only happened in recent times. In the 1960s business was pretty slow, and you could literally stop ploughing to serve a customer, we weren't exactly rushed off our feet. Then in 1967 the place began to go. I guess it was all part of the wine boom' (*Weekend Australian* 1996: 28).

While South Australia was well endowed with wineries throughout the Southern Vales, and the Clare and Barossa Valleys, there was little or no tourist infrastructure or accommodation. Coonawarra had nothing for the visitor unless 'one had a personal invitation', and Padthaway barely existed (Halliday 1994: 55). The situation was similar in Western Australia, with the Swan Valley region in decline, in part due to urban pressures, and the Margaret River and Mt Barker regions only just beginning to develop in the mid-1970s.

In 1963, Max Lake established his Lake's Folly Winery in the Hunter Valley, the first new winery in the region since the Second World War. He thus became the first of many hundreds of what James Halliday refers to as 'weekend winemakers', who established their own vineyards and wineries for lifestyle reasons above economics. These adventurous new wine-growers, growing grapes and making and selling wines on a small scale, and with a personal touch and flair, heralded and, ultimately, constituted the 'boutique boom' (Rankine 1989).

The significance of Max Lake's vision cannot be overstated. With the production of his first foot-trodden wine in 1966, and then his first commercial vintage in 1967, he showed that even a rank amateur could establish a winery and produce a reasonable wine. In the words of James Halliday, Max Lake 'had not so much rubbed Aladdin's lamp, he had opened Pandora's box' (Halliday 1995: 26).

The 'boutique boom' was not restricted to the Hunter region, which, following the success of Lake's Folly, also saw the establishment of small enterprises such as Marsh Estate, and large syndicates like Rothbury Estate and Hungerford Hill. All over the country there was a proliferation of small 'boutique' wineries. It was almost as if every prosperous person who had ever sipped a glass of wine wanted their own vineyard (Beeston 1994). For instance, in the 1960s, in Victoria, Reg Egan established Wantrina, in what is now the Yarra Valley. Balgownie Winery was developed near Bendigo, and the Seftons established their Idyll Vineyard near Geelong. A new wave of boutique wine-makers was also emerging in South Australia, with the first Redmans of Coonawarra vintage in 1966, St Halletts in the Barossa Valley in 1967, and the establishment of wineries such as Wirra Wirra in McLaren Vale in 1968. At the same time, names such as Vasse Felix, Moss Wood and Plantagenet were emerging in Western Australia (Halliday 1994).

The 1970s witnessed the continued growth of the boutique winery phenomenon. Victoria continued its winery resurgence with the establishment of the Goulburn Valley, the Pyrenees and the Mornington Peninsula regions as wine-producing districts, and the rejuvenation of the north-eastern region around Rutherglen. New South Wales saw the rebirth of the Mudgee region with the establishment of wineries such as Botobolar and Montrose, as well as the first plantings in the Hilltops region around Young (Barwang and Nioka Ridge wineries). Canberra, the nation's capital, was also caught up in this boutique boom with the establishment of Dr Edgar Riek's Lake George Vineyard, and Dr John Kirk's Clonakilla Winery in 1971. In 1972, the emergence of the boutique wine industry spread to Tasmania when Andrew Pirie established Piper's Brook.

The Lake's Folly phenomenon extolled confidence in small wineries. These boutique wineries appealed to the Australian public because they presented the small wine-maker as an underdog, competing against the anonymous face of large wine-making organizations. To the weekend visitor and tourist, the local wineries of large, national wine-makers were often closed. The small boutique winery was wine-making with a human face (Beeston 1994).

Despite the opinions of industry leaders of the time, who dismissed the boutique boom as 'distracting the wine buying public from the major producers' (Beeston 1994: 236), it is these small wineries involved in growing grapes and making and selling wines with a personal touch and flair, that are the driving force behind the burgeoning wine tourism industry in Australia. Their approach and existence finds considerable sympathy with consumers who can relate to an individual wine-maker in a small winery. Put simply, the small, 'boutique' wineries have achieved an importance in the industry far out of proportion to the volume of wine which they produce (Rankine 1989; Halliday 1995).

In recent years, there has been a doubling in the number of small boutique wineries, which produce small amounts of quality bottled wines (Committee of Inquiry into the Winegrape and Wine Industry in Australia 1995). Although these small boutique wineries account for only a tiny percentage of the national crush (3 per cent in 1989), they are nevertheless important in adding individuality to the industry (Rankine 1989).

Niki Macionis

Wine tourism, although still in its infancy in New Zealand, is a growing tourist attraction. As in Australia, the boutique winery has became the 'human face' of wine-making in New Zealand, providing personal touches and personality and deliberately attracting visitors while, until recently, the larger wineries have tended to focus on a less personal approach to sales. Nevertheless, despite the lack of substantial government funding for the development of wine tourism strategies in New Zealand, several regions have shown considerable initiative in developing wine routes and providing information for visitors. At the national level, the New Zealand Tourism Board has also started to develop strategic marketing alliances with the New Zealand Wine Institute and regional wine and tourism organizations, including Marlborough and Martinborough. The development of wine tourism in New Zealand is discussed in greater depth in Chapter 8.

South Africa

South Africa is one of Australia and New Zealand's major competitors for export sales to Europe. After many years of trade embargoes because of the state's previous apartheid policies, the South African wine industry has now begun to modernize as it competes for the export market, including vinifying wines according to individual vineyard blocks to allow for a better quality selection process. South Africa's major competitive advantage lies in its relative proximity to the UK market, which currently accounts for 40 per cent of local wine exports. It is just 15 shipping days away, as opposed to the several weeks entailed for producers from Australia and New Zealand. According to Green (1999), 'Initially South Africa made its mark at the lower end of the British market and we are working hard to dispel the image of being a producer of only mass volume wines. Fortunately, increasing exports from top level producers are proving to more sophisticated consumers that the country is able to offer an interesting array of quality New World style products.'

The South African wine industry also views wine tourism as another key growth area in the British market because of the exposure it gives visitors to South African wines. Chapter 5 by Robert Preston-Whyte discusses the development of wine routes in South Africa. According to Green (1999) 'The Western Cape is already a destination of choice for the British travel market given the favourable exchange rate. Through promotional activity designed to encourage the sampling of our wines, we can grow the loyalties of British consumers at this end. Once they return home they will be more inclined to buy South African products'.

Conclusions

As this chapter has indicated, wine tourism is an increasingly important component of regional development strategies and individual wine business decisions. However, this chapter has just touched the surface of the many issues which emerge in examining the development of wine tourism around the world. Clearly, it is impossible to cover every wine region in the world in depth in terms of wine tourism. Instead, the remainder of the book will provide a guide to some of the key issues which emerge in its management, marketing and development in terms of both themes (such as ensuring we understand the consumer), and regional case studies (for example, of Australia, Canada and the United States), which can indicate to the reader how different places are responding to the challenge of developing quality wine tourism products.

3

Wine tourism in France: a paradox?

Isabelle Frochot

There is no doubt that France, the world's premier destination in terms of international visitor arrivals, is characterized by strong and powerful images linked to its cultural and gastronomic heritage. However, despite French wines having a strong and established reputation around the world, France has been increasingly facing tough competition from emerging wine-producing regions, particularly in the New World (*Geographical* 1994). Furthermore, in recent years, wine consumption in France has steadily decreased (from 90.87 litres/head/year in 1980 to 60.00 litres/head/year in 1996). Nevertheless, this has been offset by an increase in the consumption of quality wines, with more AOC wines being drunk than ever. Consumer interest in wine, particularly quality wine, has also been aroused by the so-called 'French paradox', whereby a variety of health benefits have been attributed to moderate wine consumption.

In terms of the supply of wine tourism products and opportunities, wine-makers, suffering economic decline in the early 1980s and tougher limitations on alcohol advertising, have also realized the advantages of selling their wines directly to consumers and have gradually opened their cellars to visitors. More than 20 per cent of Burgundy wines and 23 per cent of Alsace wines are now being sold direct to tourists from the cellar door. Consequently, there has been a growing interest in the French wine industry which has assisted in its development as a tourism asset.

This chapter will review how wine tourism has evolved across different French regions. The chapter will discuss the range and types of wine attractions which have been developed in France; the importance of wine routes; the establishment of wine events; the structure of the market in terms of individual and packaged products; and concludes with an analysis of wine tourist motivations and behaviours in France

Wine attractions in France

Opening the cellars for business – tasting rooms and visitor centres

Recognizing the need to make the wine world more accessible and understandable to a wider audience, wine-makers and tourism organizations have developed a varied range of attractions based on the wine theme in an attempt to encourage visitors' access to cellars/wineries. In some regions the vast majority of properties open to the public are small businesses in which services are usually provided by the winery owners themselves. For example, in Burgundy 37 per cent of wine-makers welcome up to 1000 visitors per year and 40 per cent between 1000 and 3000 visitors (Comité Régional du Tourisme de Bourgogne 1997). Visits to smaller cellars/wineries are usually free of charge, although some wine-makers charge a fee for tasting wine if the visitors have no intention to purchase. Because of their small size and fragmented nature, wine tourism marketing and promotion of these smaller cellars is usually limited to the display of a sign outside their buildings (see Figure 3.1), participation in a wine-maker's charter, and a listing in a wine guide (the Hachette guide being the most popular). Wine tourism participation is not, however, limited to these smaller cellars. In a number of French wine regions some larger producers have also made tourism one of their major activities, developing their wineries into very professional, commercially run and popular tourist attractions. For example, in Burgundy the cellar of La Reine Pédauque in Beaune welcomed 130,000 visitors in 1997, Les Caves de Bailly 90,000 visitors, while the cellars of both the Patriarche (the largest in the region) and the Meursault Castle welcomed 40,000 visitors each (Comité Régional du Tourisme de Bourgogne 1997). These larger cellars/wineries

Figure 3.1   An example of an individual wine-maker's promotion.

usually provide guided visits in both French and various foreign languages, a visitor centre and a shop, and usually charge an entrance fee. A study conducted among Burgundian wine-makers in 1997 (Comité Régional du Tourisme de Bourgogne 1997) indicated that visitors spend on average FF520 per visit with a tendency to buy wines of superior quality (44 per cent of purchases concern premier crus).

Similarly, the Bordeaux region has seen the development of popular wineries with some chateaux in the Medoc region opening all year round and welcoming as many as 70,000 visitors annually. Major Bordeaux producers also provide tasting rooms and trained personnel in an effort to attract more visitors to their chateaux. Although such improvements and value added services might represent a substantial investment for the wine properties, a survey of Bordeaux chateaux which have undertaken such developments showed that the benefits gained from the direct sales to visitors and from the wine tasting fee more or less covered the initial investment within the first year of operations (Chambre de Commerce et d'Industrie de Bordeaux 1992). Furthermore, in order to widen their general tourism appeal, the chateaux in the Bordeaux region have associated their wine production and image with other destinational attractions and products, such as sports (polo), painting exhibitions and various artistic themes and events.

Another interesting example of wine tourism development can be found in the Cognac region where several major companies have invested heavily in the provision of visitor centres in order to attract visitors, in addition to the traditional visits and tasting activity already available. The value of these developments, beyond the financial gains of the direct sales they encourage, is mostly promotional in that they contribute to developing a strong winery image and familiarize consumers with the brands involved. Given that 80 per cent of their production is exported, Cognac makers consider the image of their product amongst tourists as being particularly important. This kind of promotion (i.e. tourism) is also seen by some companies as a way of circumventing strong restrictions imposed on them by the 'Evin law', which drastically limits the content of the promotional message and advertising of alcohol. These visitor centres are usually located on the premises and most often include slide shows, exhibitions, tasting rooms, and bilingual guides. Each company offers a themed visit, which is usually free of charge, and a free tasting or a free sample of the product is normally provided. It should, however, be noted that not all wine companies can match the extent of the development services provided by the Cognac producers – which are based on a prestigious product of international recognition (and little competition) and which are often regarded as benefiting the whole region.

Wine museums

Beyond the actual cellars and wine-producing companies and their direct contacts with visitors, several other attractions linked to the wine theme have been developed in different regions. One of the most common attractions encountered is the wine museum, present in most French wine regions. These are often the result of the enthusiastic actions of local individuals supported by some type of public funding (the wine route in Alsace alone links twelve wine museums). Wine museums usually present a history of the wines in the region concerned, a detailed explanation of wine-making processes and the various local traditions associated with wine.

Another attraction of interest is the *Maison des Vins*, which are usually linked with wine visitor centres and which usually provide information on a specific wine region or delimited wine-producing area. These centres provide visitors with exhibits and general information about the characteristics of the wines and vineyards from the region, wine-making processes, basic wine tasting principles, and visitors are usually offered a choice of wines to taste. In the Bordeaux region, the Maison des Vins de Bordeaux offers an audio-visual presentation, permanent tasting, shops and information, and welcomes 50,000 visitors every year, half of whom are foreigners. This region also has another four Maisons des Vins located in different areas of the Bordeaux region, one of which, at St Emilion, welcomes as many as 70,000 visitors a year.

Other attractions also based on the wine theme include the Marché aux Vins (the wine market) located in Beaune, Burgundy, which offers visitors a range of 18 different wines for tasting at an entrance price of FF50 and welcomed 44,000 visitors in 1998. More unusual attractions based around the wine theme include the Château de Tourelles (Nîmes–Vard), which was developed by a wine-maker and an archaeologist whose combined expertise led to the creation of wines based on Roman recipes from the 1st century BC (wines flavoured with different types of dried flowers, fruit stones and spices). Locally produced wines can be tasted along with the Roman wines and this attraction received 11,000 visitors in 1994. In the Beaujolais region, Le Hameau du Vin (the wine hamlet) offers a unique tasting centre located in an old train station. The history of the transport of wine, wine-making, a vast wine cellar, several audio presentations and wine tastings are included in the visit (for a price per person of FF65) with the site

Figure 3.2   Les Chevaliers du Tastevin.

attracting 102,000 visitors in 1997. In Burgundy, the Châteaux du Clos de Vougeot, which is located in the middle of the region, charges for a visit of its buildings which include gigantic wine presses, massive wine storage and an exhibition and display of elements related to the wine-making process. Although the chateau does not offer tasting opportunities, it receives more than 80,000 visitors every year, a success which is also partly due to its role as the head office of the Confrérie des Chevaliers du Tastevin, a well-known wine-makers' fraternity (see Figure 3.2).

Heritage attractions

Heritage attractions which are within close proximity of a wine region also benefit from this locational advantage, regardless of whether they are directly or indirectly related to wine. For example, in Beaune, Les Hospices de Beaune (an old charitable hospital), which is located in the town centre, welcomes over 400,000 visitors a year, with the visit concentrating only on its heritage components despite this being the most important vineyard owner in the region. If wine regions include a wide choice of opportunities for wine tasting and visiting various attractions, then the link between all these actors or stakeholders will be the wine routes, which facilitate and direct visitors across regional networks, and it is to this that the chapter will now turn.

The importance of wine routes

The development of tourist routes has become increasingly popular as a tourism promotional tool in France since the mid-1980s, with 270 being recorded across the country in 1997 (Jaladis and Facomprez 1997). These tourist routes, which suggest and package itineraries across French regions, have been very popular and successful for special-interest tourism products, such as the gastronomic routes (e.g. the olive route in Provence or the cheese route in Auvergne). They have also been associated with other themes (a traditional craft-skills route in Morvan, for instance). Wine is a subject for which such tourist routes are particularly relevant and many have been very successfully developed. In some regions, such as Burgundy, the wine routes are usually very familiar to tourists since the names of the villages often represent the actual names of wines. Similarly, in the Bordeaux region, the wine routes often take visitors to the main chateaux which are equally well known to tourists.

Usually a wine route consists of a designated itinerary (or several) through the wine region (see Figure 3.3) which is thematically signposted as well as

Figure 3.3 Wine routes: a mix of wine and heritage.

being marketed and interpreted via a free leaflet and map, which notes the different vineyards and wine-makers and provides information on sites of historical and other interest. Beyond the production of a leaflet to guide and inform visitors along the route, pictographic road signs are also created which utilize specific logos to guide visitors (for instance, stylized champagne bubbles with blue and yellow colours are used in the Champagne region). A tourist route targeted at a specific and restricted topic, such as wine, will not appeal to all visitors, and therefore some wine routes are combined with other attractions and products to form diversified tourist routes. For example, in Alsace, the wine route is combined with the historic castle route. Some wine routes, however, such as the ones developed in the Rhône valley (which includes seven itineraries), provide information solely in relation to wine and their aim remains principally to promote and sell the wines.

The logistics of wine route development are relatively complex and often involve several partners. Such partnerships are traditionally the result of cooperation between tourism organizations who want to promote their region (e.g. information centres, departmental and regional tourism organizations) and wine businesses (e.g. syndicates, associations, wine visitor centres and wine-makers) who have a commercial interest in promoting their wine (Jaladis and Facomprez 1997).

The wine routes encountered in France can be quite varied: in the case of Alsace (which has 12,000 ha of vineyards), visitors have the opportunity to visit more than 185 wine-makers and twelve wine museums. The creation of the wine route has been very successful and since its inception has witnessed an increase in tourist arrivals of 8.8 per cent compared with the average regional increase of 2.2 per cent (Choisy 1996).

In Burgundy (which has 21,000 ha of vineyards), the regional tourism committee has persuaded 200 wine-makers and wine tourism-related operators to sign a welcome charter named *Bourgogne découverte: de vignes en caves* (Discovery of Burgundy: from vines to cellars) and provides them with customer care training courses. Created in 1991, this scheme is promoted via a free guide which lists the addresses of the wine-makers and the types of wines which can be bought. The wine-makers joining the charter undertake to provide a warm and personalized welcome to visitors, adhere to the opening times which have been indicated, improve their foreign languages skills and offer at least one wine for tasting free of charge. Each wine-maker also displays and provides information on the Burgundy region as well as offering a guided visit of their cellar/winery if requested. This Burgundy wine route has been organized by the Chambre de Commerce de Dijon in cooperation with corporate sponsors such as EDF and GDF (the national electricity and gas organizations), while a European Union grant has provided further funding. The first step in organizing the wine route was the design and deployment of road signs (see Figure 3.4). In the longer term it is planned to illuminate monuments (with the help of EDF) and create self-guided information panels in participating vineyards. The *Bourgogne découverte: de vignes en caves* route has also been promoted via the staging of a marathon in the vineyards, the Marathon des Grands Crus, in the autumn every year. The local villages located along the wine (and marathon) route contribute by improving the appearance of their village including providing flowers, making the local population aware of the project and providing lighting in the evening.

Figure 3.4 Wine route sign in Burgundy.

In Bordeaux, the largest French wine region (with 115,000 ha of vineyards), wine tourism is also booming. Of all French regions, Bordeaux, with its world-renowned chateaux, remains one of the most popular destinations for wine travellers because of the reputation of its wines and its close proximity to the sandy Atlantic beaches. The Loire Valley is also well known due to the extent of its vineyards and its vast range of impressive historical chateaux. The synergy that exists between these assets contributes substantially to the region's success in the tourism market. It is also interesting to note that the simplicity of some of its wines can also represent another recognized strength: 'There are few visitors who can resist its charms: fairy-tale castles, lazy rivers and woodlands, a classic yet sublimely simple regional kitchen and [mainly] abundant uncomplicated wines' (Millon 1989: 122) (see Chapter 6).

Champagne has four different wine routes of between 70 and 120 km. These routes are detailed in a leaflet which, beyond the wine-related information, also notes all the historical and natural sites of the region, as well as numerous cultural events, national parks and footpaths. The champagne route groups 75 wine-makers who, like Burgundy producers, subscribe to a welcome charter, and compete for the award of the Bouchon d'Or (the golden cork). This is awarded to properties with outstanding hospitality skills, well-maintained buildings, and which incorporate educational qualities in their wine tourism product. It should also be noted that the larger Champagne businesses (Les Grandes Maisons) have developed their properties to offer well-organized visits and very professional services which obtain high satisfaction levels among visitors.

Wine events

France has a long tradition of gastronomic and wine-related events with local *fêtes* usually held on an annual basis to promote specific culinary products. While such *fêtes* may be of appeal to tourists during the summer tourist season, their promotional efforts and organization are often geared towards the local and domestic markets. In regard to wine, while these *fêtes* often coincide with different stages of the wine-making process (e.g. grape harvest, vin nouveau), they can also correspond to the celebration of patron saints. For example, in Burgundy the Confrérie des Chevaliers du Tastevin celebrates the patron saint of wine-growers, St Vincent. This event, which is staged on the fourth weekend of January each year, attracts between 100,000 and 130,000 visitors (primarily from the local or domestic market). The event involves a mass on the Saturday morning followed by a procession through the village (see Figure 3.5), with each participating wine-making village displaying their own representation of St Vincent. Each year a different village of the wine coast hosts the event, making a special effort to decorate the streets and buildings (preparations start at least a year ahead), and wine-makers make one or two collective wines in the preceding years. Visitors can buy a glass and 'neck-glass' holder for a modest sum of FF20, which then allows them to drink as much as they wish of the collective wines from the different cellars/wineries open through the village during the two days of the festival. Obviously, the success of the operation needs careful planning as crowding in such small villages is often a problem. The opening times and number of cellars open to the public have been restricted in recent years in order to limit excessive alcohol consumption. Burgundy also stages a prestigious and popular annual event, the Vente des Vins des Hospices de Beaune, which is the biggest annual charity sale in the wine world. The Vente des Vins des Hospices de Beaune is held on the third weekend of November each year, usually supported by a famous artist, and includes two festive dinners. The local attractions and the entire region benefit from an influx of more than 2000 visitors over the weekend.

Figure 3.5 St Vincent Tournante event.

The Alsace region also has well-developed events along its wine route. Like other French wine regions, Alsace is known for the quality of its hospitality. The number of its local wine festivals and the quality of Alsace wine has become very popular with German and Belgian tourists. While the Alsace region appears to have successfully developed various events for tourists, it should be remembered, as noted previously, that across France the variety of wine-related events have been, and remain very much targeted towards the local and domestic markets, often occurring outside the main tourism season.

The packaging of wine tourism

Despite the obviously increasing value of wine tourism in France, it is important to recognize that wine is rarely the sole theme of a package tour. While it may represent an important aspect, wine is often linked with other historical and cultural characteristics of the region. Historically, package tour products in France have been developed more for the group market (often pensioners or associations) and foreign visitors (Charvet and Desplats 1995) and, while there are very few statistics available on this market, it would appear to be fairly limited. For example, package tours to Burgundy comprise at the most 20 per cent of the total visitor market. Recently, some new products combining wine and other complementary activities – wine/

gastronomy and architecture, wine and mountain biking, wine and boat cruising, wine and golf – began to appear in the marketplace. The advantage of these types of products is their flexibility and their appeal to a wider audience, but it is too early yet to judge their success. Therefore, because of the limited market, travel agencies tend to tailor wine tourism packages for individual tourists, rather than develop more standard wine-orientated package tours. Domestically, package holidays are not common in the French domestic travel market, with most French tourists preferring to organize their holidays themselves by collecting information on the various products and attractions on offer. They tend to travel independently, using their own vehicles, and to this extent wine routes are an attractive and flexible way to visit the vineyards.

Those packaged products which are centred solely on the wine theme tend to be marketed as short breaks (two or three days), appeal mainly to the connoisseur market, and to attract higher spenders. These packaged wine tourism products can offer services directly related to wine such as wine tasting skills and include wine tastings at several chateaux. If visitors want to gain an in-depth knowledge of the complexity of wines and wine tasting processes, local professional associations offer a variety of wine courses but these are quite expensive. For instance, the CIVB (Interprofessional Committee of Bordeaux Wines) provides classes on wine in French, English, German and even Chinese and Japanese; however, its student numbers for 1997 totalled only 600.

The demand for wine tourism in France

Despite the significance of wine tourism little research has been conducted on wine tourist motivations and behaviour. With regard to tourist motivations, there is little doubt that French gastronomy has always represented an important tourism asset. Indeed, a study on rural tourism across France indicated that for 80 per cent of all tourists (domestic and foreign) the main focus of their holiday is 'culture, history and architecture', the next reasons being gastronomy and oenology (60 per cent) and outdoor activities (40 per cent) (Daniel 1994). Similarly, studies conducted in French wine regions also attest to the importance of wine and gastronomy as key attractions. For example, French tourists surveyed in Burgundy associated this region with its wines and vineyards above any other aspects such as heritage – which ranked fourth in regional destination association (Comité Régional du Tourisme de Bourgogne 1997). It is, however, paradoxical to note that, at the same time, visiting wine cellars/wineries and vineyards is not the most common visitor activity. In fact, in this same study, visiting wine cellars/wineries was ranked fourth, with 80 per cent visiting heritage sites, 72 per cent simply travelling through the region, 52 per cent eating in restaurants and only 40 per cent visiting wine cellars. A similar study conducted in 1991 on tourist motivation in Dijon, the capital of Burgundy (Frochot 1991), reported similar results which indicated that, while Burgundy's image was strongly associated with gastronomy and wine, heritage was by far the most important reason for holidaying in the region, and wine-related visits were not the prime activity. This latest study suggested that wine seemed to have a greater importance for foreign tourists, particularly for American and British visitors, a result which should deserve further attention. However, such a situation is similar to the observations of Donatella Cinelli Colombini of the Movimento del Turismo del Vino recorded in Chapter 2, that one of the most significant obstacles to the development of wine tourism, in a country with a historical wine culture, is getting the domestic population to acknowledge wine tourism as a legitimate form of recreation and tourism activity.

The situation would appear to be similar in Bordeaux where, despite an established and strong reputation for quality wine production, wine and gastronomy is ranked only fourth as a tourist motivation for visiting the region, while seaside recreation and visiting the Atlantic coast are ranked as primary tourist activities. In examining French wine tourism popularity and demand, it should be noted, however, that a major drawback to the existing data is their lack of differentiation of the types of sites visited. For instance, it is not possible to separate wine-related attractions visited from traditional heritage attractions. Limiting an analysis of the wine tourism market to the visits of wine cellars and vineyards would be too restrictive since the annual numbers of visitors to wine-related attractions certainly attest that the wine theme constitutes a strong tourism asset.

The French wine tourism market is characterized by a relatively short length of stay. For example, in Alsace most holidaymakers stay four nights or less, while in Burgundy the average stay is 1.3 nights. It is interesting to note that the wine tourism market does not necessarily follow the seasonal trends of traditional tourism markets in these regions. Arrival statistics for Burgundy show an increase in winter months while the summer season (May to September) observes lower frequency rates. Indeed, wine tourism seems more able, particularly for the domestic market, to accommodate short-term holidays (weekend breaks, short breaks) out of the main summer season, while the summer season appears more able to accommodate longer holidays, mixing wine with other aspects of interest, an option particularly popular with foreign tourists (Chambre de Commerce et d'Industrie de Bordeaux 1992).

Conclusion

This review supports the notion that wine is a strong destinational asset which attracts tourists to France. Indeed, rural economic restructuring, and a realization by wine-makers of the economic benefits of wine tourism, has led to an increasing number of producers embracing tourism and the development of a diverse range of wine tourism products and practices. Wine-related tourism attractions in France range from small, family-operated concerns, offering little more than tasting and rustic ambience to major, well-organized and tourist-orientated chateaux, as well as wine museums and cultural festivals. Despite the absence of precise statistics, the success of wine-related tourist attractions and events highlights an obviously important, if somewhat untapped, tourist market. Although France and French regions benefit from the strong image associated with their wine and gastronomy, it does not necessarily translate into active wine tourism once the visitors are in the region. Indeed, other destinational attributes such as heritage and culture dominate tourist motivations. It would seem at present that the package tour market which is interested solely in wine is restricted to a smaller number of passionate connoisseurs or groups. However, the short-stay and weekend market exhibits considerable potential to attract large numbers of domestic visitors. Whether wine tourism could exist independently from French tourism's main strengths is debatable, but, nevertheless, it attests to the powerful synergy which exists between wine and France's more general tourism assets.

4

Meeting the wine-maker: wine tourism product development in an emerging wine region

Brock Cambourne and Niki Macionis

Wine tourism, or more simply cellar door visitation, is an essential component in the growth and success of many small wineries (Henehan and White 1990; Bracken 1994; Golledge and Maddern 1994; Dodd 1995; Hackett 1997; Morris and King 1997a, b; Macionis 1997; Hall and Macionis 1998). The Winemakers' Federation of Australia *Strategy 2025* states that 'For many small wineries, especially those with a strong lifestyle business motivation, wine tourism [cellar door visitation] can be the core business function' (Australian Wine Foundation 1996: 7). For small wineries, particularly in emerging or non-traditional wine producing regions, wine tourism is often an economic necessity, providing cash flow and assisting them to achieve a better sales mix at a higher yield, while at the same time providing opportunities to brand their product and winery successfully.

This chapter examines the emergence and growth of wine tourism in the developing cool climate Canberra District wine industry, surrounding Australia's national capital. The chapter discusses issues and challenges encountered in a developing wine region; examines the region's wine tourism market and their motivations; and details the wine tourism product development and marketing activities employed in the region, including the establishment of guided tours and special events, as well as the role of tourism organizations in the development and promotion of wine tourism in the Canberra region.

Background

In 1997, there were nineteen wine producers in the Canberra District producing approximately 30,000 dozen bottles of wine, from an estimated 500–600 tonnes of grapes (Helm, pers. comm. 1997). This level of production accounts for approximately 0.05 per cent of national production (Deves 1996). The Canberra District wineries are distributed within three distinct sub-regions. The majority are in the Murrumbateman/Yass region, with a sub-district in the Hall area and another in the Bungendore/Lake George area. The distribution of wineries in the Canberra District is shown in Figure 4.1. There are also some thirty-five additional vineyards in the region totalling approximately 500 acres, of which 325 acres are currently in production (Joshua, pers. comm. 1997).

The Canberra District wine industry can be seen as exemplifying many of the younger Australian wine regions which developed as a result of the 'boutique boom' in the 1970s and 1980s (Rankine 1989; Halliday 1995; Macionis 1996, 1997). The region's wineries are typically family run and most crush less than fifty tonnes of grapes (Deves 1996). The average crush in the region is approximately thirty-two tonnes, with the largest of the Canberra District wineries processing around fifty to one hundred tonnes of fruit, and some as little as two tonnes. Currently, the largest producers are Doonkuna Estate, Helm Wines, Lark Hill, Jeir Creek, Brindabella Hills and Madew Wines (Centre for Tourism and Leisure Policy Research 1998). Like many other developing Australian wine regions, cellar door sales are extremely important to Canberra District wine-makers. Macionis (1997) reports that in 1996 cellar door sales, on average, accounted for around 47 per cent of all wine sales, with approximately another 20 per cent of total regional production distributed via other associated tourism and hospitality sectors, such as hotels and restaurants.

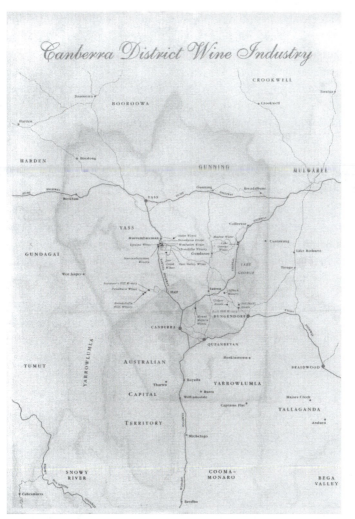

Figure 4.1 Distribution of wineries in the Canberra District. Designed by MA@D Communications, Canberra. Reproduced with permission of the ACT Chief Minister's Department.

With access to more substantial quantities of quality fruit, the Canberra District wineries have, in recent years, begun to shed their novice image and now consistently produce high quality table wines of a classic 'cool climate' style (Macionis 1997). These developments have led to a greater acceptance by associated hospitality and tourism industries, such as hotels, restaurants and tour operators. With higher volumes of production and a subsequent increased interest and demand for their primary product, the Canberra District vignerons have found themselves being rapidly propelled, if they are not already involved, into the tourism industry. Indeed, cellar door visitation in the Canberra District has more than doubled over the last three years, with active wine tourism practitioners reporting increased cellar door sales ranging from 30 per cent to more than 100 per cent as a result of tourism (Centre for Tourism and Leisure Policy Research 1998). However, before examining Canberra region's wine tourism development strategies, it is helpful to understand some of the challenges faced by an emerging wine region and also some characteristics of the area's wine tourism market.

Canberra District wine tourism challenges

Macionis (1997) notes that, until recently, the Canberra District wine industry (like many other developing regions in Australia) operated largely outside the main tourism infrastructure. This lack of inter-industry integration has resulted in a number of critical wine tourism developmental issues, the most notable of which, in the context of an emerging wine region, are:

- a lack of tourism understanding by the wine industry (and vice versa); and
- an absence of effective inter-sectoral linkages and relationships, resulting in a subsequent lack of awareness of the region as a wine tourism destination.

Macionis (1997) reports that a substantial proportion of Canberra District winery owners/wine-makers do not consider themselves part of the tourism sector, despite the reluctant admission of many to needing tourism in order to make their businesses profitable. During interviews with Canberra District winery owners/wine-makers Macionis recorded comments such as:

- 'tourism does not attract the kind of visitors I want to my winery';
- '[tourism] questions not applicable';
- 'tourists taste wines and demand vineyard tours, but are rarely interested in buying the wines themselves'.

With specific regard to the Canberra District's wine tourism profile, Macionis (1994) reported that Canberra consistently rated last, if at all, as a wine tourism destination among a survey of Sydney travel agents, and that approximately 80 per cent actually had no prior knowledge of the existence of the Canberra District wine industry. Furthermore, she reported that there was also an overall lack of awareness and poor positioning of the Canberra District wine industry among local and other domestic tourism sectors (Macionis 1997). Indeed, until recent years, the traditional focus on Canberra's national capital status and national icons did little to encourage inter-sectoral integration of the wine and tourism sectors. However, in response to the findings of several market research reports which noted that 'new and surprising' cultural tourism products such as visiting wineries had strong market appeal (Scott *et al.* 1994; Market Attitude Research [MARS] 1996), the Canberra Tourism and Events Corporation (CTEC) has begun to broaden its destinational and marketing approach and activities. Even so, it was not until 1996 that the ACT Tourism Development Strategy for the first time explicitly identified the Canberra District wineries as a component of the ACT's attraction base, stating that: 'the surrounding region also provides a diverse range of natural and built attractions. Of particular note is the Canberra District Wine Industry which is within one hour of Canberra City and is an internationally recognized geographic "appellation" zone – much the same as the more well known Barossa and Hunter Valley areas' (Canberra Tourism 1996: 48). Such explicit acknowledgment of the Canberra District wine industry's place in the ACT and region's attraction base is indicative of an increasing recognition of its positioning within the regional tourism portfolio by public and private tourism interests.

Canberra District wine tourism

A number of researchers have attempted to categorize or segment winery visitors based upon a number of demographic or behavioural characteristics. However, such categorizations have often resulted in very narrowly-defined wine tourism target markets. For example, Edwards (1989) believes that educated and sophisticated individuals or 'wine connoisseurs' are the most likely market segment to engage in wine tourism. With specific regard to the Canberra District, Macionis (1994 1997) reports that cellar door visitors could be classified as:

- indulgers: 20–49 years of age;
- engaged in full-time employment;
- regular consumers (drinking wine at least once a week);
- having a basic to intermediate knowledge about wine;
- coming from the local catchment area (Canberra Region) and Sydney.

While such categorizations provide valuable insights into the broad characteristics of winery visitors, it is important to realize that they are only indicative and can be somewhat exclusive. To maximize the value of such wine tourist profiles it is helpful to acknowledge and understand the variety of wine tourism motivations and how they relate to both existing and potential wine tourism markets.

Wine tourism motivations

While the primary motivations for winery tourists/visitors are wine related, that is, sampling or buying wines, a number of secondary or peripheral motivations that are integral to the total wine experience have been identified (Maddern and Golledge 1996; Macionis 1997; Hall and Macionis 1998) (see also Chapter 6). These include:

- wine related (sampling, buying, quality);
- attending wine-related festivals or events;
- socializing with friends/enjoying a day out;
- enjoying the country setting or vineyard destination;
- meeting the wine-maker;
- learning about wine/wine-making (education);
- eating at winery restaurant/picnic/ BBQ (food and wine link);
- tour of a winery (education);
- visiting or experiencing other attractions and activities;
- entertainment (Macionis 1994; Maddern and Golledge 1996; South Australian Tourism Commission 1996).

By recognizing and addressing the broad and multi-faceted nature of these motivations, regional marketing agencies and individual wine tourism practitioners are better able to both develop their wine tourism product and ensure visitor satisfaction with the product (see Exhibit 4.1). Another way of examining a region's wine tourism market is to examine the entire market portfolio, which includes primary, secondary and potential wine tourism market segments.

Exhibit 4.1: Meeting the wine-maker

At an individual enterprise level, the Canberra District wineries that realize the greatest benefits from wine tourism are those that have actively sought to understand and provide for the needs and motivations of winery tourists. Indeed, the wineries exhibiting the highest levels of cellar door visitation are those that service the peripheral or secondary wine tourism motivations, including:

- the staging of winery festivals and events;
- the provison of picnic facilities and the opportunity of eating at the winery;
- offering tours of the winery;

- providing opportunities to learn about wine/wine-making and meet the wine-maker (Centre for Tourism and Leisure Policy Research 1998).

One of the most successful wine tourism practitioners in the region is Ken Helm of Helm Wines at Murrumbateman. A state tourism award winner, and national tourism award finalist, Helm Wines has been described by Australian Master of Wine (MW) Rob Geddes as one the best cellar door experiences in Australia. Helm is a firm

Figure 4.2 Meeting the wine-maker: Ken Helm of Helm's Wines.

believer that 'to be successful and to continue growing in the market, wine-makers must realize that they have to do more than just pour booze'. People visit wineries he says 'for the total wine experience. Gone are the days when a wine-maker can just sit back and pour a glass of wine to prospective customers – if that's all people want they can just buy a bottle at their local retailer and drink it at home!' According to Helm, wine tasting and the winery experience are proactive, not passive activities (Figure 4.2):

> I try make sure that cellar door visitors at Helm Wines get to experience my wines, my winery and myself with all their senses – they can taste, see and smell the wine – during Spring when the winery begins to warm up and the wine begins its secondary fermentation, visitors can even hear the wine if they put their ear to a barrel. They can also see, smell and touch things in the winery itself. I offer guided, behind the scenes tours of the winery to help put everything into context, and provide the opportunity for winery tourists to learn a little bit more about wine and wine-making.

According to Helm, it is a combination of all these things, as well as interacting with the wine-maker and 'hearing from someone with a passion about their product, straight from the horse's mouth, if you like, that contributes to the total winery experience'. This, he notes, has helped him to develop new markets and considerable consumer and community loyalty, 'by personalizing the winery experience, people learn a little bit more about my wines and myself', which he believes helps develop trust in the product.

Such an approach has obvious benefits. Macionis (1997) reports that Helm Wines exhibits the highest volume of cellar door visitors per annum of all the Canberra District wineries, while National Capital Wine Tours' guides and internal figures note that Helm Wines achieves the highest yield per winery visitor on organized wine tours.

Brock Cambourne and Niki Macionis

A wine tourism market portfolio

To develop a wine tourism market portfolio we have used data from the Roy Morgan (1996) Holiday Tracking Survey, which measures travel intentions and behaviour, based on 16,000 interviews nationally. By utilizing both demographic (e.g. age, sex, socio-economic background) and psychographic (e.g. tastes, beliefs, values, attitudes and opinions) data a series of life-cycle 'value segments' are described which group people sharing similar character-istics. A summary of these 'value segments' is provided in Table 4.1.

By then examining the percentage of these 'value segments' that visit wineries a market portfolio for wine tourists is developed. Table 4.2 details a market portfolio for winery visitors in Australia generally; for long-established and well-known regions such as the Hunter Valley region in New South Wales and the Barossa Valley region in South Australia; and for visitors to developing Canberra District wineries.

In general those groups categorized as 'Visible Achievers', 'Socially Aware', 'Traditional Family Life' and 'Young Optimists' comprise the majority of winery visitors, and would thus appear to be the most appropriate target markets for wine tourism marketers and practitioners.

It should be noted that the Roy Morgan (1996) Holiday Tracking Survey data is based upon behaviour relating to trips of three days or more and thus removes bias which may arise from winery visitation within the immediate regional catchment area. It is important to recognize that a variety of value/market segments with a range of wine tourism motivations visit wineries, as opposed to the narrowly defined '30–50-year-old, tertiary educated, high income earners' previously described. It is also important to note that the relative proportions and rankings of each of these market or 'value segments' varies for each region, reflecting both the product and market life cycles.

Nationally, and in more established high profile regions such as the Hunter and Barossa Valleys, the 'Visible Achievers' value segment represents the highest ranking wine tourism market segment. This value segment, which is characterized by ego enhancement and the need for recognition of their achievement or visible evidence of success, could be expected to be one of the first groups to embrace fashionable new tourism and aspirational lifestyle trends such as wine tourism but, being somewhat traditional, may be cautious of the emerging, relatively-unknown regions such as the Canberra District. On the other hand, the 'Socially Aware' value segment comprise the highest ranking wine tourism market segment in the Canberra District. This group, which is characterized by the pursuit of a stimulating and experiential lifestyle, and are perhaps a little more innovative, may find an emerging wine region more appealing.

Given the relative youth of wine tourism these top ranking market segments could be considered 'mature' markets, whereas less developed and represented

Table 4.1 Roy Morgan 'Value Segments' and characteristics

Value Segment (% of population)	*Characteristics*
Conventional Family Life (11.2%)	**Middle Australia, people whose life is centred around their family**: skilled tradesmen or middle office workers, with mortgages and superannuation, small savers; around 38 years of age, on average incomes, they struggle to give their children better opportunities than they had; not ambitious and prefer to spend spare time with the family and at home; respond to familiar and conventional advertising, which emphasizes product benefit, influenced by pre-existing attitudes to brand.
Look at Me (14.1%)	**Young people seeking an exciting life and a fun time**: living for today – tomorrow will take care of itself; fashion and trend conscious, wishing to be seen as different from their family but similar to their peers; active socially, enjoy both watching and taking part in sport and lifestyle activity; respond to visually dramatic, exciting or humorous advertising approaches, sensitive to cues which denote understanding of the young person's world.
Traditional Family Life (17.8%)	**The over 50, empty nest and mostly retired version of Middle Australia**: strong commitment to traditional roles and values, cautious of new things; time for new interests and to get away to nice places; concerned about their health and religion plays a strong part in their life; respond to practical advertising ideas and clear communication.
Something Better (9.0%)	**Upwardly mobile younger couples, building up their business, career driven**: both earning good incomes, but borrow a lot to fund lifestyle, confident, ambitious and aggressive; respond to clever, unusual and special advertising or marketing appeals, aspirational lifestyle must be considered.
Visible Achievers (14.6%)	**Around 40 years old, this group are the wealth creators of Australia**: work for financial reward and job stimulation, seek recognition and status for themselves and their families; world of 'good living', travel, recreation, other evidence of success; respond to clever, unusual and special advertising or marketing appeals, aspirational lifestyle should be considered, sceptical about claims or offers.

Value Segment (% of population)	Characteristics
Young Optimist (7.0%)	**The student generation, active, trendy, outgoing**: often the children of Visible Achievers or Socially Aware, see themselves as very progressive; young singles or couples, living together, at uni or just started a profession, relatively well off, they collect new experiences, ideas and relationships; trend setters, ambitious and very career orientated, by far the most dynamic and active group; respond to the most intelligent and creative appeals, but generally scornful of advertising.
Socially Aware (9.9%)	**Tertiary educated people in top jobs, the most educated segment of the community**: avid arts goers, with no real money worries, tend to be wealth managers; experiential tourists who pursue a stimulating lifestyle, both in their homes and leisure activities, very green and progressive; respond to stylish, tasteful and intelligent marketing appeals, concepts and ideas are important, they reject hype.
A Fairer Deal (7.0%)	**Working class and blue collar**: around 30, low incomes and struggling to make ends meet; not at all active in leisure pursuits, tend to be home-bound and watch TV.
Real Conservatism (5.3%)	**Observers of society, rather than active participants**: very traditional, religion plays a big part in their lives, more likely to be found on the land or in quiet suburbia; financially well off, hoarders rather than spenders; traditional holidays such as camping and fishing are popular, very cautious about new products and ideas.
Basic Need (4.1%)	**Older retired workers and widows living (often alone) on a pension**: very traditional views with a strong Christian ethic; follow a survival lifestyle.

Source: Adapted from Roy Morgan (1996) Holiday Tracking Survey

Table 4.2   Percentage and rank of Roy Morgan Value Segments that visit wineries

| Value Segment | Percentage of each Value Segment visiting wineries (rank) | | | |
	Nationally	Hunter Valley	Barossa Valley	Canberra District
Conventional Family Life	6.0 (7)	3.0 (9)	9.0 (5)	6.6 (6)
Look at Me	7.0 (5)	11.6 (5)	9.5 (4)	0 (9)
Traditional Family Life	17.9 (3)	12.5 (3)	7.0 (6)	24.3 (2)
Something Better	6.3 (6)	11.8 (4)	5.1 (7)	10.2 (4)
Visible Achievers	25.8 (1)	19.1 (1)	27.6 (1)	17.7 (3)
Young Optimist	9.4 (4)	10.7 (6)	16.8 (2)	1.6 (8)
Socially Aware	20.7 (2)	18.8 (2)	15.3 (3)	27.7 (1)
A Fairer Deal	1.6 (10)	2.8 (10)	3.4 (9)	2.3 (7)
Real Conservatism	2.7 (8)	6.1 (7)	3.1 (8)	8.2 (5)
Basic Need	2.5 (9)	3.7 (8)	3.1 (8)	0 (10)

Notes: The Roy Morgan (1996) Holiday Tracking Survey data is based upon behaviour relating to trips of three days or more, thus removing bias which may arise from winery visitation within the immediate regional catchment area.

markets, such as the 'Young Optimist' or 'Something Better' value segments, could be considered new or developing markets. Thus, the strategic marketing and wine tourism product development challenge lies in implementing strategies that encourage the growth of these new market segments, while retarding the decline of more mature segments as each goes through their own life cycle. The following section examines how an understanding of development issues and markets have contributed to wine tourism development in the Canberra region.

Canberra District wine tourism development

Unlike several Australian states with a longer, more continuous wine industry history such as Victoria, South Australia, NSW and Western Australia, the ACT does not possess a specific wine tourism body (these wine tourism development organizations will be examined in detail in Chapter 12). Rather, the development of wine tourism in the region has been largely dependent upon a few active wine tourism practitioners, facilitated and assisted by the region's prime destinational marketing organization, the Canberra Tourism and Events Corporation (CTEC). With limited resources available, Canberra

District wine tourism development initiatives have been focused in three primary areas, including:

- industry integration;
- festival and event development;
- public relations.

Industry integration

Perhaps the most significant developmental issue facing wine tourism in general is the absence of effective inter-industry linkages and inter-organizational cohesion and cooperation. Wine tourism represents a form of diversification for wine-makers, from agricultural production to the provision of value added services and experiences, and despite the often economic necessity of tourism to many small producers, there is generally a lack of tourism understanding and formal tourism participation by the wine industry (Macionis 1997; Renwick 1977).

This was indeed the case in the Canberra District in the early 1990s. Prior to the establishment of National Capital Wine Tours, the ACT's first specialized wine tourism operator, in 1993, the Canberra District wine industry had no explicit position within, or relationship to, the regional tourism sector. At the time of its establishment, National Capital Wine Tours encountered an industry that was, to say the least, circumspect with regard to involvement in the tourism sector. In addition, a general lack of understanding about tourism and how it can benefit wineries resulted in lack of intra-sectoral cooperation. While some wineries firmly believed that they could gain considerable advantage via tourism involvement, others were less sure. Exemplifying such intra-industry conflict, Macionis (1997: 70) recorded comments such as 'I also believe that while tourism will become an increasingly important part of our District, we must not lose sight of the fact that we are wine makers, and must be judged first and foremost on the quality of our products'. Such dichotomies in individual wineries' approaches to tourism involvement has made the articulation of a cohesive and attractive regional image a difficult and protracted process.

As a 'fully industrialized' wine tourism practitioner (see Chapter 1), National Capital Wine Tours provided the first explicit wine tourism linkage for the Canberra District wine industry. As the 'industrialized' component of the regional wine tourism sector, National Capital Wine Tours also places considerable emphasis on the role of the tour operation as a 'culture broker' or mediator. By structuring and designing tours with a substantial educative component and acknowledging wine tourism motivations such as the desire to meet the wine-maker, the tour operation mediates the interaction between wine tourists and wineries. In doing so, the wineries' perception of tourism exploitation is minimized, while at the same time enriching the overall wine tourism experience (Cambourne 1999).

Considerable advances in wine industry and tourism sector integration have also been achieved via proactive participation and representation in tourism sector organizations. The Canberra District wine industry is now represented on the Board of Directors of Tourism Council Australia, Canberra Region Branch and the Canberra Convention Bureau as well as CTEC's Events Funding Assessment Committee and the ACT Festivals Working Party.

These forums provide a basis for increasing the profile and position of the wine industry within the tourism sector, developing inter-industry linkages and facilitating inter-industry understanding and integration. As a consequence of such interaction, a visible tourism presence and constant lobbying, the Canberra District Wine Industry's tourism profile and potential has dramatically increased. The increasing importance and positioning of the Canberra District Wine Industry within the regional tourism portfolio is evidenced by an increasingly obvious utilization of wine industry imagery in a range of destinational marketing collateral such as:

- CTEC's primary print marketing tool, the *Canberra Holiday Planner*;
- the Canberra Convention Bureau's principal marketing tool, the *Meeting Planner's Guide* and in their 'Hop, Skip and Jump' international incentive programme;
- a national television and cinema advertising campaign.

A higher degree of 'tourism industrialization' and integration is also evidenced by:

- the inclusion of the Canberra Vintage Festival as a major component of CTEC's Autumnfest campaign;
- the implementation of a wineries category in the state tourism awards structure (the ACT became only the second state or territory in Australia, after Victoria, to explicitly acknowledge the wine industry's contribution to and involvement in the tourism industry, through the tourism awards structure;
- the development and marketing of wine tourism packages with various accommodation establishments (Cambourne 1999).

CTEC has also been proactive in fostering inter-sectoral integration and the development of regional wine tourism through the appointment of a Wine Industry Tourism Development Executive, charged with fostering productive linkages and interaction between the wine and tourism sectors, as well as assisting and facilitating wine tourism product development. CTEC has also provided considerable marketing assistance to the Canberra District wine industry by facilitating and partially funding a regional wineries brochure, and by ensuring that brochure's distribution and exposure through consumer travel shows and regional tourism offices.

Festival and event development

The impact of winery-related festivals and events on winery visitation can sometimes be substantial and dramatic (Golledge and Maddern 1994). Until 1995, the Canberra District wine industry boasted only one regional event, The Days of Wine and Roses, held in October each year, in which a number of the region's wineries host local restaurateurs and regional new-release wines are featured. Noting the marketing success of the Victorian Wineries Tourism Council's events-driven strategies, National Capital Wine Tours has developed and implemented several new regional events, including:

- Jazz in the Vines in February (where bands from the nationally acclaimed St Valentine's Day Jazz Festival are booked to play over a weekend at a number of Canberra District wineries);
- the Canberra District Vintage Festival, a six-week celebration of the vintage period in April and May.

CTEC has provided substantial support for the marketing and promotion of these events through their Visiting Journalist Program (VJP), the production of marketing collateral and the packaging of the Canberra District Vintage Festival. These events provide not only substantial public relations value to the winery participants, but also develop new markets by attracting a greater range of visitors and generate significant cellar door sales. Indeed, both Jazz in the Vines and components of the Canberra District Vintage Festival have generated the highest level of cellar door sales in the participating wineries' history. Additionally, monthly visitation to the Canberra District wineries peak in February (Jazz in the Vines), April (Canberra District Vintage Festival), and October (Days of Wine and Roses). In fact, when data from these three festivals is discounted, average visitation at the Canberra District wineries exhibits a reversal during these three months, going from peak levels of visitation to the lowest recorded levels (Macionis 1997). As well as stimulating visitation, if well structured and conceived, these events also have long-term effects with visitors developing brand loyalty and a relationship with the winery.

Given the limited resources available for the implementation of new events in an emerging wine region, both Jazz in the Vines and the Canberra District Vintage Festival were conceptualized and developed so that they could be 'piggybacked' onto existing successful regional events, thus increasing the opportunities for success and minimizing the financial input required. In the case of Jazz in the Vines, the long-running and nationally acclaimed St Valentine's Day Jazz Festival, provided a perfect synergy for wine industry integration in the regional festivals' portfolio, while CTEC's Autumnfest, Canberra's Season of Festivals, presented another 'piggyback' opportunity for the Canberra District Vintage Festival.

These events are also structured and marketed to ensure success for participating wineries. Macionis (1997) notes that tourism promotions and activities that are perceived by wine-makers in the Canberra District to be successful in attracting visitors to their wineries have several characteristics including:

- they demonstrate a tangible, short-term (if not immediate) economic return to participants;
- they are familiar and thus tangible to participants and perhaps exhibit a strong internal product focus (e.g. wine exhibitions/shows, public tastings).

As such, individual festival events are scheduled and structured not only to maximize visitation, but also to achieve the above objectives. For example, in the case of Jazz in the Vines the nature and structure of the event (four to five hours of performances at several wineries) encourages patrons to stay at the wineries for an extended period of time, thus maximizing the opportunities for expenditure. Ensuring a variety of performances, including Dixieland, traditional jazz, modern jazz and even blues, at the various venues also attracts a wider market base, with different needs and motivations.

Vintage festival events are also themed within the capabilities and 'comfort zone' of the participating wineries. For example, wineries with limited tourism experience have been encouraged to develop and implement highly structured, internally or product-focused activities and events such as tutored or vertical tastings for inclusion in the Vintage Festival. To facilitate winery visitation by a wider range of wine tourism markets, the Canberra District

Vintage Festival now comprises a range of themed events, designed to appeal to a range of motivations (and 'value segments'), such as:

- education/learning about wine/meeting the wine-maker (tutored/ vertical tastings; behind the scenes tours and hands-on wine-making tours such as those conducted by National Capital Wine Tours);
- socializing/day out (food, wine, jazz, 'Grape Stomping' staged by Helm Wines and Jeir Creek Winery);
- entertainment (musical events such as 'Haydn in the Winery' held by Yass Valley Wines);
- food and wine link (gourmet food and wine tastings/pairings).

With almost 50 per cent of Canberra District winery visitors originating from the ACT and surrounding region (Macionis 1994 1997), the marketing and delivery of these festivals and events is deliberately locally-directed in order to ensure visitation and subsequent cellar door sales. They are, however, linked to the region's nationally and interstate directed activities, such as Autumnfest, to facilitate wider destinational exposure and encourage interstate visitation. Including statements from participating wineries such as 'this event is our way of saying thanks to all our regular customers and the community for their support over the last year' in all press releases and public relations material also fosters and develops the regional community's feeling of pride and 'ownership' of the local wine industry and individual wineries.

Public relations

Welsh (1994), in an analysis of marketing factors contributing to success among small businesses in the Australian wine industry, reported that wine-makers utilized various print media, but without commitment. With specific reference to tourism publications, he noted that 71.7 per cent of his respondents agreed or strongly agreed with the statement that 'I am not convinced that advertising in tourist magazines actually attracts any custom' (Welsh 1994: 213). He also notes that wine-makers in his study expressed a degree of reluctance and suspicion in relation to hosting journalists and the use of media in public relations activities. In a similar agri/rural tourism context, Clarke (1996) reported little recognition of alternative marketing and communications techniques among farm accommodation providers in the UK. Furthermore, she noted that public relations activities were pursued with seeming reluctance and that media familiarizations were viewed as controversial, with feelings of exploitation expressed.

In contrast, media familiarizations for wine, lifestyle, travel, business and meetings, industry publications have been utilized extensively and very successfully as a wine tourism public relations vehicle in the Canberra District. With an increasing consumer interest in wine tourism, CTEC has sought actively to involve the Canberra District wine industry in their Visiting Journalist Programme. This programme has yielded considerable results, generating media coverage with an advertising value in excess of A$491,000 during 1996/7.

The cool climate wine capital's tourism future

The Canberra District's wine tourism future would seem to be assured. The region's national capital status, as well as an existing high quality tourism and cultural infrastructure, makes its wine tourism product and positioning unique, both within Australia and internationally. The activities and initiatives implemented in the last few years by agencies such as the Canberra Tourism and Events Corporation and proactive regional stakeholders, have developed a strong wine tourism product and market base. Indeed, in contrast to the Canberra wine industry's historically low profile, recent research conducted by the ACT Cultural Facilities Corporation reports that visiting wineries was the second most popular reason for visiting Canberra (Market Attitude Research Services [MARS] 1999). However, the most significant catalyst in the evolution of wine tourism in the Canberra District is the entry of Australia's second largest wine producer, BRL Hardy, to the region. In addition to planting approximately 250 ha of vineyards in and around the ACT and building a 4,000 tonne winery, BRL Hardy's activities include significant investment in a regional wine tourism and interpretive centre (see Exhibit 4.2)

Exhibit 4.2: Coonawara in Canberra!

According to BRL Hardy chairman, John Pendrigh, the Canberra wine-making region could become as well known, both nationally and internationally, as the famous Coonawara region in South Australia (Schroder 1997). Indeed, the decision of one of Australia's and the world's largest wine producers, BRL Hardy, to plant some 250 ha of premium grape varieties in and around the ACT and develop a world class wine, tourism and cellar door facility as a focal point of the local wine industry will both reinforce the region's stature as a premium wine-producing area, and significantly increase the domestic and international availability of Canberra wines. In fact, within seven to ten years it is anticipated that BRL Hardy winery will be producing around 100,000 cases of Canberra wine, approximately 2.5 times the volume currently produced by existing wineries (Day, pers. comm. 1997; Smith Kostryko Cohen 1998).

Central to the BRL Hardy proposal is a wine tourism complex and regional wine industry interpretive centre, which will be a 'flagship for the local wine industry and a natural starting point to experience the wineries and vignerons of the region' (Smith Kostryko Cohen 1998: 1). This major development is scheduled to occur in three phases, beginning with the development of the wine tourism centre in 1999. This first stage comprises a regional interpretive centre, cellar door and wine tasting facility, a 100-seat café/bistro; landscaped grounds, including a picnic and concert area and Stage 1 of the wine-processing plant, which will be ready to process fruit from the 2001 vintage (see Figure 4.3).

Stage 2 of the development, due for completion in 2004, will include a 150-seat capacity fine dining restaurant (specializing in BRL Hardy and Canberra District wines), a VIP centre and a winery fermentation facility. The final stage of this development, beyond 2004, will see the completion of a fully integrated winery facility, including a wine maturation facility and cask room. A possible further development may see the establishment of a vineyard and winery operations training centre (Smith Kostryko Cohen 1998).

By 2004 the winery will have the capacity to process up to 4000 tonnes of fruit and, according to BRL Hardy's Chris Day, it will be the fruit processing centre for the entire southern New South Wales area, processing fruit from Tumbarumba, Young, Mudgee and the Canberra region. He notes that several factors attracted BRL Hardy to the Canberra region, including the ability of the area to produce extremely high quality wine and 'the opportunity to make BRL Hardy's name synonymous with the [Australia's] national capital'. The region's national capital status is, in fact, seen by BRL Hardy as one of the region's great marketing strengths.

BRL Hardy's presence in the Canberra region will undoubtedly enhance both the general and wine tourism prospects for the area.

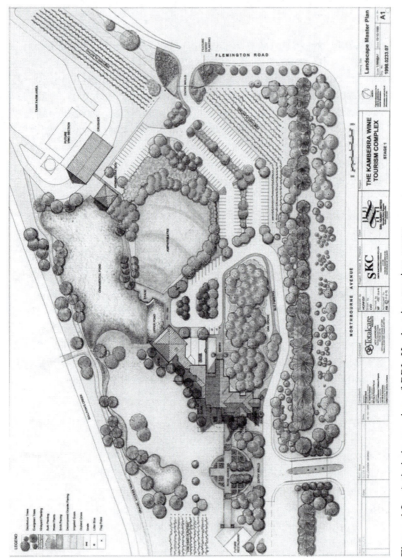

Figure 4.3 Artist's impression of BRL Hardy wine tourism centre.

Chris Day believes that the BRL Hardy development will become an 'integral component of the regional wine tourism experience, and with twenty or so producers in the area now, increasingly people will come to Canberra specifically to visit the wineries. With such a number of wine producers, it will be impossible for people to visit all the wineries in one day – thus they will need to extend their stay for two to three days – staying in hotels, eating in restaurants, shopping, buying wines', and taking their memories home in a bottle.

Brock Cambourne and Niki Macionis

Realizing that the presence of a global wine company, such as BRL Hardy, will dramatically change the structure and image of the previously exclusively boutique Canberra wine industry, existing stakeholders, in conjunction with the ACT Government, are developing a 'Canberra District Wine Industry Development Plan', including a regional wine tourism strategy. The challenge therein will be to optimize the aspirations of all stakeholders, both multinational and boutique, while still providing the opportunity to meet the wine-maker.

Wine routes in South Africa

Robert Preston-Whyte

In his 1999 guide to South African wines, John Platter (1999) is upbeat about the future of the wine industry. His confidence is based on the 'newness' of everything: new regions, new investors, new winemakers, 'new' grape varieties, new export markets:

> One minute it seemed the wine industry's governing fathers still had all their crazy quota and area restrictions and pricing privileges in place, a farrago of nonsense consonant with the old South Africa. Now people of all races are allowed to grow anything, anywhere, sell at prices they think the market will stand; and unions, farm owners, MPs, consumers, sociologists and all-comers are 'interfering' in the reassuringly unsettling ways of a democracy. (Platter 1999: 4)

This new found ebullience has not escaped the tourist, nor have the potential benefits to be gained from tourists escaped the wine producers. One product of this mutual awareness is the wine route.

In 1971 the first wine route was opened in Stellenbosch. The success of this venture coupled with the importance of projecting a marketing image prompted the development of other routes. Now there are fourteen wine routes in the south-west Cape, most within 100 km of Cape Town, and one along the Orange River. Their history has not been uneventful and the first part of the chapter comments on some of the issues that influenced their development. It then makes sense to separate the supply aspirations of the wine producers from the consumption demands of tourists. Thus the second part discusses the location of the wine producers in the bounded spatial entities defined by wine route associations. Here they owe allegiance to the economic and ecological forces that sustain the production of grapes. Tourism is one way in which the product of their labour can be tested, advertised, distributed and sold. The final part recognizes the tourist perspective. Wine estates are cultural spaces. They embody the ritual and mystique that surrounds the creation of wines. They celebrate the conquest of nature by contrasting the bucolic serenity of vineyards with stark surrounding mountains. They emphasize a cultural heritage with European roots yet with strong local traditions. All combine to produce the cultural experiences that are valued for their range and diversity.

Change and the South African wine industry

The emergence of wine routes over the last three decades has taken place against a background of social and political change in the country. Given the complexity of factors that influence change it is difficult, if not impossible, to attribute causation to specific events. However, it may be possible to recognize the influence of some actions or events that either encourage or discourage the energetic innovation necessary for the successful development of a wine route. This energy can be repressed by stifling regulations. On the other hand, benign political change and exposure to globalizing influences may release it.

The South African wine industry is no stranger to regulation. Having recovered from the 1885 devastation of the wine lands by the phylloxera louse, by 1918 wine overproduction appeared to be a problem. This led to the formation of De Ko-operatieve Wijnbouwers Vereniging van Zuid Afrika Beperkt (KWV) 'To control the sale and disposal of products of its members in such a way that they will always be assured of an adequate income for such products' (Hands and Hughes 1997: 14). The influence of the KWV grew further in 1924 when the Wine and Spirit Control Act No. 5 required all producers to join the organization and empowered them to set minimum prices for wine for distillation. In 1940 the KWV were further empowered by the Wine and Spirit Control Act No. 23. Wine production now required a permit obtained from the KWV and all transactions between producers and sellers had to be sanctioned by them. Further legislation in 1956 allowed the KWV to impose a quota system on vineyards limiting the number of vines that could be planted. Only vineyards with quota could produce grapes for wine-making. In 1973 the government introduced further legislation designed to introduce quality control via the Wine and Spirit Board through authenticating the claims on the wine label as to the vintage, area of origin and cultivar.

While the objective of controlling overproduction was doubtless well intentioned, the monopolistic power of the KWV did not encourage entrepreneurial innovation in the wine industry which, until the early 1990s, 'dozed happily in isolation' in a state of 'subsidized slumber' (Platter 1997: 7). It took the collapse of apartheid to liberate the industry from the mindset of state protection. The years since then have seen feverish efforts to undo the damage of the past. In 1992 quotas were eliminated. Wine producers responded by entering the market. Between 1992 and 1999 the number of wine producing cellars grew by 52 per cent (Figure 5.1).

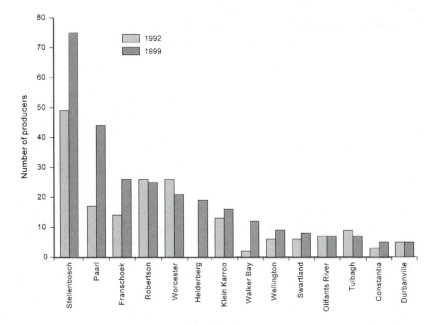

Figure 5.1 Change in the number of wine producers by wine routes between 1992 and 1999 (data after Platter, 1992; 1999).

Data on wine production is not available as wines are aggregated under the title of 'beverages' by the state Central Statistical Services. However, data on trade in wine is available through the Southern African Customs Union (SACU). Although the union includes South Africa, Swaziland, Lesotho, Botswana and Namibia, effectively the wine is produced in the south-western Cape. The value of wine exports is shown to surge in 1995 (Figure 5.2). Although this increase was a response to the lifting of sanctions it may include evidence of a growth in total wine production. The general lack of data on the wine industry is distressing. However, there is a growing awareness of this deficiency and a detailed investigation will soon be started by the Industrial Development Corporation.

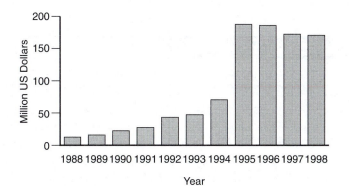

Figure 5.2 Value of exports through the South African Customs Union, 1988–98 (Industrial Development Cororation databank). Export values are given in US dollars to accommodate the depreciation of the rand.

The wine producers fall into three groups. Estate wineries make wine from grapes grown on the estate; cooperatives turn into wine the grapes grown by cooperative members; independent cellars buy in both grapes and wine and make wine for bottling under their brand name. Previously it was the required practice to sell grapes to a cooperative that would in turn sell in bulk to a large wholesaler who would then bottle the wine under one of their brand names. This practice is rapidly on the decline. Instead there is now a proliferation of labels as cooperatives do their own bottling and growers begin their own cellars and bottling under their own name.

The most dramatic increase in the number of wine producers has been in the Stellenbosch, Franschhoek, Paarl, Helderberg and Walker Bay districts. Labels have proliferated as each producer strives to establish a niche in the market. This provides a wonderful opportunity for the inquisitive tourist with a palate that thrives on variety.

The collapse of apartheid had other consequences. It signalled the start of a process by which South Africa joined the global community. Through their visitors, and increasingly through the Internet, wine estates are linked to the transnational dynamics of consumerism and concomitant convergent metro-politan lifestyles that appear to accommodate both cultural homogenization and proliferation. At the same time global sameness is constantly reworked into local contexts (Robertson 1995). One of the primary attractions of wine estates is to taste and evaluate the local wine. The changes that manifest themselves in the production and marketing of wine and wine regions chronicle the shift in tastes, behaviour and cultural interaction in a continually evolving social domain.

The 'production' of wine routes

During 1659 Jan van Riebeeck, sent by the Dutch East India Company to establish a victualling stop for merchantmen en route to the East Indies, noted in his diary 'Today, praise be to God, wine was made for the first time from the Cape grape' (Hands and Hughes 1997: 24). Since then vineyards have been planted throughout the Western Cape province as wine producers take advantage of the varied terroir. Rainfall and temperature conditions that are characteristic of the coastal areas are modified by the complex mountain terrain further inland. These areas also contrast with the hot and dry conditions that prevail in the Olifants River area in the north and the Klien Karroo in the east. Embedded in the consciousness of those who inhabit these varied environments are feelings of regional pride for the wines that are produced. Wine routes are a production of this local patriotism (Figure 5.3).

The development of the first wine route in the Stellenbosch area in 1971 was the product of leadership, determination and endurance in the face of obdurate bureaucracy. The initial idea of establishing wine routes was conceived by Frans Malan of the Simonsig Estate during a tour of the Route de Vins at Morey St Denis in Burgundy (Stellenbosch Wine Route 1992). Assisted by Neil Joubert of the Spier Estate and Spatz Sperling of Delheim Estate, the group soon to be known as 'The Three Angry Men with a Cause' (Stellenbosch Wine Route 1992) took on the government to fight for changes in the liquor law to facilitate the tasting of wines on estates. The prolonged negotiation with government agencies over revisions in the liquor law to permit such tasting indicates that the diffusion of new ideas and practices across cultural and national boundaries can be a complex matter. However,

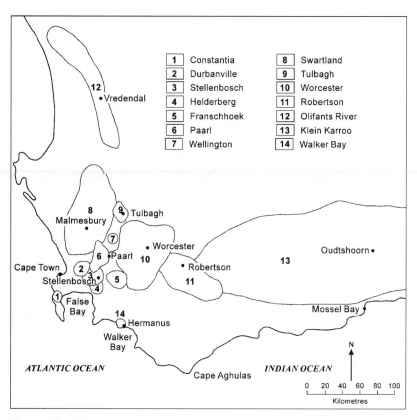

Figure 5.3 Wine routes of the Cape.

once established the success of the Stellenbosch Wine Route led to the development of adjoining wine routes as wine producers beyond the Stellenbosch area soon began to recognize the potential benefits of wine route tourism.

The concept of a bounded space is vital to the idea of a wine route since it defines for its wine-producing members an identity that proclaims unique attributes for their wines and cultural heritage. This enables them to participate in political and economic activities in the competitive drive for visitors. In order to stress the attributes that distinguish them from their competitors, wine route associations tend to employ a rhetoric that stresses the nature of the grapes and the wines they produce, the soils and climate that give them their distinctive character and the cultural heritage that nurtured them. Each route seeks to articulate a distinctive set of attributes that endows it with a distinctive 'trademark' (Moran 1993) or that enables them to claim some unique feature.

Wine tasting is, of course, a primary objective so that the number of wine prizes secured in the district becomes a widely advertised fact. For example, the Stellenbosch Wine Route (1996) proudly proclaims that 'Amongst the wines sold on the Stellenbosch Wine Route, 13 received double gold and 63 gold Veritas Awards, the highest honour for excellence in wine-making in this country. Considering the total of 51 double gold and 185 gold awards, it means that a quarter of the double gold and a third of the gold medals were awarded to members of the Stellenbosch Wine Route'. If a wine route is forced to take a back seat on grounds of wine quality then other attractions are found to lure the visitor. These may include racehorse breeding, rose and fruit growing, trout fishing, river rafting and cheese production. The search for distinctive features is not difficult in a region so richly endowed with natural beauty, cultural heritage and a range of products additional to wine.

The mix of environmental, cultural and social features that convey a distinctive character to each wine route is usually perceptible. The tourist is expected to recognize and value the difference in the landscape when moving between wine routes. If not, markers provided by the wine route associations will certainly draw them to the attention of tourists. A thumbnail sketch of each wine route illustrates these features.

Constantia

This wine route encompasses five estates that cling to the picturesque east-facing slopes of the Constantiaberg that is an extension of Table Mountain. Environmentally the area is well watered in winter by orographic rainfall over Table Mountain, cooled by summer sea breezes from nearby False Bay, shaded from the fierce westering sun by the mountain and blessed with excellent soils. Three of the wine estates are part of the original farm called Constantia that was granted in 1685 to Simon van der Stel, first Dutch Governor of the Cape. Simon van der Stel's homestead at Groot Constantia provides an excellent example of Cape Dutch architecture and is the location of South Africa's first vineyard. The position of these estates within Cape Town's southern suburbs, the superior quality of the wines and the surrounding aura of bucolic maturity combine to make these vineyards amongst Cape Town's most visited tourist sites.

Durbanville

Also close to Cape Town, this area has been notable over three centuries, first as the producer of quality fresh produce and now from the character and stature of winegrapes. The cool sea breezes that blow onshore from the adjacent Atlantic Ocean and the heavy local dews caused by nocturnal cooling of moist maritime air are seen as uniquely important features. The quality and range of wines from red and white noble cultivars to cellar blends is attributed to the wide selection of slope aspects and the rich, deep, well-drained red soils with good water retaining quality that allow cultivation without irrigation despite an average annual rainfall of only 550 mm.

Stellenbosch

This route takes its name from the historic and architecturally renowned Afrikaans university town of Stellenbosch, with its oak-lined streets, that was founded in 1679. Vineyards that extend in all directions make use of sandy alluvial soils in valley bottoms and acidic decomposed granitic soils on the surrounding mountain slopes, while the heat load on the vines varies with changing aspect. Like other wine routes that have a local town as the focal point, all roads converge on Stellenbosch. Wine producers that are part of the wine route are located along these roads. They are well advertised by roadside signs, provide adequate parking for visitors, encourage the tasting and purchase of their wines, offer teas and lunch and never fail to advertise their historical heritage. If choices must be made concerning which wine producer to visit, an informative brochure details the attributes of each. In addition to mandatory wine tasting, these may include cellar tours, wine sales, 'coachman' lunches, coach rides, and a local museum featuring Cape furniture and other items used by the Dutch in the creation of a cultural space.

Helderberg

Until recently this wine route, bordering on False Bay between Cape Town and Stellenbosch, was regarded as belonging to the Stellenbosch wine route. In an intriguing example of wine route politics, separation from the mother route has occurred. The nearby maritime influence and mountainside elevations are cited as features that make it different from Stellenbosch. The number of reputable wine producers, the proximity to Cape Town and access to a range of accommodation make the Helderberg wine route a new and formidable competitor.

Franschhoek

The wine route lies in the Franschhoek valley immediately west of Stellenbosch. Its suitability for wine production was recognized some 300 years ago when the Huguenots settled there. Members of the Vignerons de Franschhoek maintain the distinctive French signature. Mountains enclose the valley on all sides. The valley floor and lower mountain slopes contain tidy rows of vines that surround wine estates. Twenty-six wine producers offer wines from all noble cultivars and classic styles. The celebration of the conquest of culture over nature does not stop there. The French reputation for fine food is everywhere in evidence with acclaimed restaurants that offer everything from Cape country fare to French cuisine. The impressive Huguenot monument and museum at the head of the valley firmly underlines the cultural origins of the area.

Paarl

Also located in a river valley, the Paarl wine route has a complement of 35 wine producers. An imposing monument to the Afrikaans language set atop a granite dome that rises above the nearby town is a noteworthy feature of the route. The monument serves the same purpose as the one at Franschhoek but in this case features the cultural roots of Afrikaners. Attractions do not stop there. There is the Nouveau Wine Festival in April and the Sparkling Wine Festival in September. In March there is trout fishing with the wine-makers. From June to August river rafting with the wine-makers on the Doorn River is also on offer. Mountain biking can be enjoyed from October to April.

Wellington

This is a small wine route in close proximity to Paarl. Its larger neighbour easily could accommodate it. However, the close proximity of the nine wine producers and the presence of the nearby town of Wellington nestling in the foothills of the Hawekwa mountains provides a territorial identity for the route.

Swartland

This is an agricultural landscape set in rolling wheat lands. The cooling effect of the sea breezes that blow off the Atlantic Ocean coupled with low rainfall and a warm summer climate combine to produce wines that win national prizes as well as a range of affordable white and red wines.

Tulbagh

In addition to its wines, this small wine route can offer curiosities drawn from both the natural and the cultural landscape. Some years ago an earthquake devastated much of the town. This focused attention on the architectural heritage and all notable buildings have been restored. Both the fact of the earthquake and resultant restoration now provide a focus for this wine route.

Worcester

This warm, dry inland wine route produces about 20 per cent of the national crop (Platter 1999). Its distinctive feature, apart from drinkable dessert wines and a range of classic varieties that have won medals at national wine shows, is the spectacular mountain and valley terrain.

Robertson

Located in the Breede River valley, this wine route is typically hot and dry. It is noted for its white wines. However, other activities are also advertised. These include the production of champion horses, roses, and the annual double canoe marathon on the Breede River.

Walker Bay

The wine producers in this wine route are pioneers. This is the most southerly location of all wine producers. The presence of the vineyards on cool coastal southerly uplands adds a new dimension to the Cape wines and a fresh perspective for the wine tourist. The coastal town of Hermanus is noted for its whale spotting.

Klein Karroo

The wine route is noted for its sparse rainfall and hot summers. It is also extensive. A visit to each wine producer would require a journey of some 300 km. Although small in production the route is environmentally distinctive. Bordered in winter by snow-topped mountains 'this is a place of fabulous flora, where the shy lynx rules and the black eagle swoops gloriously' (*South African Wine Directory* 1999). The wine route association actively markets the limestone Cango caves, its ostrich farms and superb mountain passes. It is also distinctive for the quality of its dessert wines, its cheeses and fruit.

Olifants River

While most routes are characterized by some distinctive environmental or cultural features, the Olifants wine route stretches over 200 km through a landscape notable for its diversity. The cool marine environment of the West Coast leads to the hot Namaqualand Plain that, in turn, is backed by the imposing Cederberg Mountains. After the first spring rains the harsh landscape is softened by a multicoloured carpet of spring flowers which is a major tourist attraction. However, this is mainly a bulk wine-growing area.

The broader perspective

The 'supply' of wine routes through the participation of wine producers and the orchestration of wine route associations is to meet what appears to be a growing demand for wine tourism. The success of a route is a measure of the way in which this demand is accommodated. Although the tasting of wine is the *raison d'être* of any route, this feature alone is unlikely to sustain tourist growth. It is worth reflecting on some of the other factors that widen the scope of the wine route experience.

Tourists on wine routes tend to travel in groups. Wine producers are aware of this and consciously create spaces where people can communicate while engaged in the ritual of wine tasting. The public expression of attitudes, beliefs, opinions and values that are encouraged in these places makes them into a form of public space. Although the notion of public space often is deeply ambiguous, sometimes controversial and frequently contested (Habermas 1962; Zukin 1995; Bell and Valentine 1997), wine estates share with other forms of public spaces their ability to be many things: 'a place, an idea, an ideal, a contested concept' (Mitchell 1996: 128). This notion of space provides a convenient window through which to view the mystique and intrigue of wine route constructions. As a form of cultural consumption they provide spaces in which the pleasures of tasting, eating, and gazing on heritage landscapes can be experienced and valued. In this role they become part of a collection of symbols, signs and sights that contribute towards the cultural richness of the wine lands.

The 'idea' of a wine route also incorporates images that sustain the notion of exploration and discovery. It requires a journey during which a range of unanticipated experiences may be encountered. This expectation is encouraged by the claims of distinctive attributes that are peculiar to the route. The quality of the wine, the beauty of the landscape, the friendliness of the inhabitants, the matchless quality of Cape cuisine and the elegance of the architecture are all claimed. These assertions must be assessed and judged by the tourist as part of the ritual that engages its own ceremonial agendas and obligatory rites in the tasting of wines, the appreciation of architectural merit or the recognition of natural beauty.

Many writers (e.g. Shields 1981; Giddens 1984; Harvey 1989; Soja 1989; Lefebvre 1991; Massey 1994) have discussed how space is presented as a dimension of social life. Their argument is pertinent to the Cape wine estates as the country engages in the complex process of change. This is a society in transformation that demands recognition through the symbols that represent freedom from all forms of discrimination. This includes experiments between estate owners and their labour in the ownership of the land and its resources. Wine producers are beginning to emerge from the ranks of those previously disadvantaged by the apartheid regime. This leads to an awareness of the moral involvement that accompanies the tourist engagement with the route (MacCannell 1989). It raises questions about the nature of boundaries between public and private space, and between those that are culturally and socially identified, constructed, controlled, contested and regulated. All this provides an intriguing setting that demands exploration by an organized tour or the unfettered freedom of a hired car and a map of the wine route.

Finally, a wine route allows the tourist to engage with the diversity of the cultural and natural features of the landscape. The spirit of Simon van der Stel still broods over Groot Constantia where in 1685 he is reputed to have planted 100,000 vines. The homes at Tulbagh suddenly acquire a new interest having been rescued from earthquake destruction. Now it is possible to agree with Jan Smuts that 'In a country where, as a rule, Nature is everything and Art literally nowhere, our old Dutch houses form an exception to the rule' (Hands and Hughes 1997: 23). Restaurants abound. Even the most humble restaurant is able to benefit from the atmosphere of authenticity that pervades the oak-lined streets and the simple elegance of the Dutch façades in many towns. It is an environment in which the visitor finds little difficulty in lingering – for days if possible. And so accommodation has emerged that ranges from the luxury hotel to country inns and bed and breakfasts to meet this emerging need.

Concluding comments

Tourists on their first visit to Cape Town are likely to rank two objectives highly. The first is to ride the cable car to the top of Table Mountain. This 1000 m vantage point enables tourists to identify many points of interest. Robben Island, the notorious political prison where Nelson Mandela languished for 28 years, squats in Table Bay. White sandy beaches in an indented cove and headland coastline lie at the interface between upmarket homes that hug the slopes of the mountain and the cold blue sea. Highly frequented tourist locations such as the Waterfront and Parliament are clearly visible. When the tourist turns to gaze north and east the second objective appears. This is the wineland area that lies seductively in the foothills and valleys of the surrounding mountains. Tourist brochures tell the tale. In the Western Cape, wine defines the place. The consumption of all that is offered by a visit to a wine route becomes virtually mandatory.

In the unlikely event that a tourist may require further confirmation of the importance of wine in the region, any doubt would be removed by a stroll along the wine shelves in most supermarkets. A profusion of local wines, displayed in bewildering variety, invites consumption. Imported wines accompany them from regions as far removed as Chile, Argentina, Australia and Europe. The opportunity to compare local with imported wines sets the mood. The availability of wine routes within easy access of Cape Town, even within the suburbs in the case of Constantia, provides an enticement that is hard to resist.

In the last few years the Cape wine routes have begun to project themselves as much more than the tasting of wines at selected wine producers. There is now more of a holistic vision that includes the consumption of nature and heritage with the concomitant provision of accommodation and restaurants. But the vision is wider still. When workers on the wine estates are able to produce and market their own wines, a wind of change is blowing. Appreciation of the social and economic transformation of the winelands is also on the tourist agenda. However, wine and its consumption remain the focus. Platter (1999: 4) has the last words: 'How enjoyable and thirst-making to be able to say as you twirl a bottle: "The woman who produces this jumps out of aeroplanes for fun and has a weakness for Italian ski instructors". You cannot make great wine without passion – and nor should we drink it without it'.

6

Wine tourism and consumer behaviour

Richard Mitchell, C. Michael Hall and Alison McIntosh

An understanding of consumer behaviour is critical to understanding all marketing activity which aims to develop, promote and sell products. By understanding how consumers make their decisions to purchase and/or consume products we are able to gain a better understanding of when we need to intervene in their decision-making process. Appropriate intervention can, in turn, be used to persuade them to purchase 'our' product. As Swarbrooke and Horner (1999: 3) argue, 'We will know who to target at a particular time with a particular . . . product. More importantly, we will know how to persuade them to choose certain products which we will have designed more effectively to meet their particular needs and wants. An understanding of consumer behaviour is therefore crucial to make marketing activity more successful'.

Consumer behaviour is 'the behaviour that consumers display in searching for, purchasing, using, evaluating, and disposing of products,

Table 6.1 Summary of research into wine tourists

Researcher	Year	Summary of research	Focus
Paradice and Krumpe (* HVRF)	1989	Research into the characteristics of day visitors to the Hunter Valley wine region (Macionis 1997).	Demand
Corigliano (Movimento del Turismo del Vino)	1993	Research into people who consider wine to be an important aspect of their holiday (MTV 1995).	Demand
Golledge and Maddern (†VWTC)	1994	Attempts to provide a better understanding of the profile of Victorian wineries and their visitors.	Supply
Dodd	1995	Opportunities and pitfalls of tourism for the wine industry.	Demand
Dodd and Bigotte	1995	Study of visitors to Texan wineries that examines perceptions and behaviour, also demographic segmentation.	Demand
Hall	1996	Wine tourism in New Zealand. Examination of demand on the basis of industry. Definition of wine tourism.	Supply
Maddern and Gollege (†VWTC)	1996	A cellar door survey that attempts to gain a greater understanding of the Victorian winery market.	Demand
Macionis	1996	Nature and potential of wine tourism in Australia. Inferences made about wine tourists.	Supply
Dodd and Gustafson	1997	The effect of product attributes, setting and service on attitudes and behaviour at wineries.	Demand
Morris and King	1997	A study of the decision-making process of winery visitors.	Demand
Johnson	1998	New Zealand national winery survey (tourism/wine linkage and attitudes to tourism. Inferences made about wine tourists on the basis of questioning of wineries.	Supply

Author	Year	Description	Classification
Hall and Macionis	1998	The development of wine tourism in Australia and New Zealand. Inferences made about wine tourists.	Supply
Beverland, James, James, Porter and Stace	1998	A study of wine tourists to West Auckland (New Zealand), replication of Morris and King 1997.	Demand
Ali-Knight and Charters	1999	A study of the importance of wine education to West Australian wineries. Some inferences made.	Supply
Carlsen, Getz and Dowling	1999	A summary of all papers presented at the 1st Australian Wine Tourism Conference 1999, including commentary on the motivations and behaviour of wine tourists.	Supply
Longo	1999	An investigation of the winery visitor at a selected number of wineries.	Demand
King and Morris	1999	Results of 1996 study of Margaret River winery visitors that tracks their post-visit behaviour.	Supply
Mitchell and McIntosh	1999	A framework for the study of the New Zealand winery visitor.	Demand
Morris and King	1999	A wine tourism product model drawn from research into the Margaret River winery visitor.	
Nixon	1999	A tour operator's perspective on profiles of winery tourists.	
Robins	1999	Potential areas of research drawn from the Australian national and international visitors' surveys.	Supply
Williams and Young	1999	A case study that examines the influence of wine club membership on winery visitation.	
Mitchell	in progress	A nationwide survey of winery visitors, their on-site experiences and future behaviour.	Demand

Key: * Hunter Valley Research Foundation. † Victorian Wine Tourism Council services and ideas which they expect will satisfy their needs' (Schiffman and Kanuk 1987: 6). Consumers are influenced in their decision-making processes by many internal and external motivators and determinants when they choose products. Consumer behaviour research is the study of why people, either individually or in groups, buy the product they do and how they make their decision (Swarbrooke and Horner 1999). Such research therefore examines a range of internal (e.g. motivation, attitudes and beliefs, learning, lifestyles and personality) and external (e.g. demographics, reference groups and culture) influences on decision-making (e.g. purchase decision, choice, brand awareness and loyalty, evaluation and post-purchase decisions). Perhaps not surprisingly, given the scope of the subject area, research on consumer behaviour is interdisciplinary, drawing on concepts and theories from such disciplines as psychology, sociology, social psychology, marketing, cultural anthropology and economics.

Consumer behaviour research is important for stakeholders in wine tourism because it can help provide important insights into who the wine tourist is, what motivates them to visit a winery, take a guided tour, attend a wine festival or purchase wine and why, thus allowing marketers and managers to effectively target and develop markets. Although there has been substantial growth of research into the wine tourist in recent years, the amount of research is extremely small compared to research on other service industries, and an examination of this literature suggests that much of the information on winery visitors has been inferred from the wineries' perspective (i.e. supply-side research) rather than from the visitors themselves (demand-side).

Supply-side perspectives have made several useful observations relating to definitions and typologies of wine tourism and wine tourists (e.g. Hall 1996; Macionis 1996; Hall and Macionis 1998), visitor demographics (e.g. Golledge and Maddern 1994; Macionis 1996; Johnson 1998) and wine tourist motivations (e.g. Hall 1996; Macionis 1997; Johnson 1998; Ali-Knight and Charters 1999). However, as these perspectives are drawn from the estimates and perceptions of wineries and an examination of existing tourism literature and are not based on empirical evidence drawn directly from the consumer (the visitor), the inferences made regarding consumer behaviour must be treated with a degree of caution.

Recently, however, research has begun to focus directly on the consumer (the wine tourist) as the need for an understanding of wine tourists and their behaviour is increasingly recognized by the industry. In an attempt to provide empirical data on the wine tourist, researchers have begun to examine wine tourism from the tourists' perspective (Dodd 1997; Dodd and Bigotte 1997;

Dodd and Gustafson 1997; Morris and King 1997a, b; Beverland *et al.* 1998a, b; Longo 1999; Mitchell and McIntosh 1999). Industry research has also begun to gather information on wine tourists in some areas (e.g. Paradice and Krumpe 1989; Movimento del Turismo del Vino (MTV) 1995; Maddern and Golledge 1996). Much of this research has sought information on visitor demographics, purchasing behaviour, decision-making processes, and linkages with other activities in the wine region.

When combined, the existing research into the wine tourist provides a useful, albeit incomplete, picture of wine tourist consumer behaviour. Table 6.1 provides a summary of the studies to date that have provided an insight into the wine tourist and their behaviour (from both a supply and a demand perspective). This chapter will draw on these studies in order to provide an insight into the characteristics of the wine tourist, their behaviour, motivations and experiences. The chapter provides a summary of research into the wine tourist and their behaviour and draws a picture of the winery visitor (albeit a sketchy one), providing demographic profiles, lifestyle information and describing some of the motives for their visits. Drawing on literature which focuses on the range of experiences of wine tourists, the chapter concludes by proposing a framework that will allow researchers and managers to develop a clearer understanding of winery visitors and their behaviour.

Who is the wine tourist?

Chapter 1 provided various definitions of wine tourism and the wine tourist. For example, Johnson (1998: 15) put forward a definition of the wine tourist as 'visitors to vineyards, wineries, wine festivals, and wine shows for the purpose of recreation'. However, such a definition tells us little about who the wine tourist is, what they do and why.

In order to understand the phenomenon of wine tourism it is important that a profile of the consumer (wine tourist) is developed. However, as Johnson (1998: 28 after Macionis 1997: 28–32) points out, 'there is little published research on the characteristics of wine consumers, let alone wine tourists'. Johnson continues, 'the available market segmentations tend to be product-focused . . . [ignoring] the experiential and recreational motivations that may be of importance to wine consumers, and more particularly to winery visitors/ tourists' (Johnson 1998: 28 after Macionis 1997: 31) – a point that this chapter will discuss in more detail later. Johnson (1998: 29) also suggests that an 'understanding [of] why someone does not, or cannot, visit is obviously of equal if not greater interest to wine producers', yet we know little about these

Figure 6.1 Wine tasting at Grant Burge Wines in the Barossa Valley, South Australia.

people either. Despite this lack of information on the wine tourist, some demographic and psychographic details of the wine tourist can be drawn from the literature.

Early 'stereotypical' descriptions of winery visitors ranged from 'wine connoisseurs' (Edwards 1989), to 'the passing tourist trade who thinks a "winery crawl" is just a good holiday' (McKinna 1987: 85) to 'mobile drunks' (Spawton 1986a: 57) (all examples cited in Macionis and Cambourne 1998). It is uncertain whether these descriptions are a reflection of the consumer of the time or just observations of the extremes. However, one thing is certain: recent research into the wine tourist is able to provide more detailed

Figure 6.2   Tour group in the wine cave, Gibbston Valley, New Zealand.

descriptions of the wine tourist based on empirical data, perhaps dispelling the myths of the 'connoisseur' and the 'drunkard'.

Demographic profile

A number of recent studies, conducted mainly since 1995, have been able to provide demographic profiles of the wine tourist (see Table 6.2). Details such as gender, age, income and origin all provide a useful insight into who the wine tourist is. This information has been gathered for a relatively small number of wine regions, mainly from Australasia, and is usually of limited geographical extent and with relatively small sample sizes. However, there does appear to be a degree of consistency across all of the studies, which allows for some generalizations to be made although each region, winery and festival will have its own particular set of visitor characteristics.

Table 6.2 shows that the 'wine tourist' is usually 30–50 years of age, in the moderate to high income bracket and comes from within or in close proximity to the wine region itself. Similar profiles have been put forward by Johnson (1998) and Macionis and Cambourne (1998), while Folwell and Grassel (1995:14) also assert that the Washington state winery visitor of the late 1980s was someone 'who is middle-aged with an above average income'. Such information provides a useful basis for marketers and winery managers to

Table 6.2 Comparisons of visitor demographics

Visitors at	Male %	Female %	Mid-age %	Upper income %	Within region %	Out of region %	International %
Texas wineries	46	54	49	40	85	15	n/a
Victoria wineries	48	52	39	67	79	21	3
Canberra wineries	53	47	56	22	76	24	4
Augusta-Margaret River wineries	52	48	29	67	62	38	9
Barossa Festival	49	51	51	21	78	22	7
New Zealand wineries (supply)	50	50	24	n/a	n/a	n/a	18
New Zealand wineries (demand)	46	54	46	41	38	62	26
West Auckland wineries	n/a	n/a	41	66	80	20	8

Sources: Adapted from Johnson (1998: 30). *Texas wineries*: Dodd 1995; Dodd and Bigotte 1995, 1997; *Victoria wineries*: Maddem and Golledge 1996; *Canberra wineries*: Macionis 1997; *Barossa Festival*: Tourism South Australia 1991; *Augusta-Margaret River wineries*: Morris and King 1997a; *New Zealand wineries (supply)*: Johnson 1998; *New Zealand wineries (demand)*: Longo 1999; *West Auckland wineries*: Beverland, *et al.* 1998a, b.

Notes: All figures are percentages. Figures for *Canberra wineries* and *New Zealand wineries (supply)* are based on wine-producers' perspectives. *Mid-age* is the percentage of visitors 30/31–49/50, except *Victoria* where it is 35–54. *Upper income* is the percentage of visitors in top third of income or occupation brackets. *Within region* is visitors from within the region, *Out of region* is visitors outside the region or state (including overseas), *International* is international visitors only. For *Barossa Festival*, the region is South Australia, for *Canberra wineries* the region is Australian Capital Territory and New South Wales and for *West Auckland* the region is Auckland. *New Zealand wineries (supply)* figures only distinguish between domestic (18.1%) and international (81.9%). *West Auckland wineries* income inferred from occupational status (66% professionals and managers).

more effectively target potential visitors and wine consumers. However, as Johnson (1998: 31) suggests, 'we do not know whether the tourist characteristics and market segments described ... are accurate and homogeneous and whether they are comparable between countries. Further visitor market research is required to establish a detailed profile of wine tourists and wine tourist segments, and to ascertain how wine tourism relates to other forms of tourist activity'. Indeed, recent research by Longo (1999) and Mitchell (in progress) (see Chapter 8) in New Zealand indicates that there are significant differences in winery visitors between regions let alone between countries. Such an observation is extremely important as it highlights the fact that profiles of wine tourists in one region should not automatically be assumed to be the same as in another, or even from one winery to another.

Psychographic profile

While demographics can provide the basis for simple segmentation of wine tourist markets, psychographic data (such as motives, lifestyles, interests, attitudes and values) allow the researcher to add '... vitality to consumer [wine tourist] profiles that cannot easily be captured by demographics' (Schiffman and Kanuk 1987: 141). In the absence of any research dedicated to identifying the psychographic profile of wine tourists, data relating specifically to wine tourists is once again relatively scarce. A search of the existing literature, however, allows an albeit fragmentary picture to emerge of some of the lifestyles, interests and motivations of wine tourists.

Wine lifestyle

Most obviously, it is possible to gain an insight into the wine interests of the winery visitor. Information gathered on their previous experience with wine (for example in studies by Pavan 1993; Dodd and Bigotte 1995; Maddern and Golledge 1996; Morris and King 1997a; Beverland et al. 1998a; Longo 1999) reveals that typically (and perhaps not surprisingly) winery visitors are 'regular consumers of wine, have an intermediate to advanced knowledge of wine and visit wineries or wine regions several times a year' (Johnson 1998: 29 after Macionis and Cambourne 1998).

An examination of some of the data pertaining to wine consumption habits reveals an average of three to four visits to wineries per annum and the purchase of between three and eight bottles per month (Dodd and Bigotte 1995; Beverland et al. 1998a, b; Longo 1999). A study of winery visitors in Texas, for example, found that visitors bought an average of 3.35 bottles per month with 25 per cent of respondents having previously visited a winery at least once

(Dodd and Bigotte 1995). Longo (1999) found that, on average, New Zealand winery visitors made between three and four visits per annum and purchased around two bottles per week, spending between $NZ21–30 on wine.

Empirical evidence relating to the wine knowledge of winery visitors is, perhaps, less conclusive. Around half of the visitors to Victorian (55 per cent) (Maddern and Golledge 1996) and New Zealand (50.5 per cent) (Longo 1999) wineries reported that they had an intermediate knowledge of wine, 40 per cent basic knowledge and less than 10 per cent advanced knowledge. Wineries' perceptions of the visitors' knowledge, however, were less flattering with Canberra wineries ascribing basic knowledge to 62 per cent, intermediate to 31 per cent and only 7 per cent advanced (Macionis 1996), while New Zealand wineries ascribed 27 per cent, 80 per cent and 17 per cent respectively (Johnson 1998). King and Morris (1997), in a study of winery visitors in the Margaret River region of Western Australia, reported that 52 per cent of respondents rated themselves knowledgeable/highly knowledgeable in wines.

Establishing the level of interest in wine of winery visitors is extremely important in terms of educating the consumer. Wine tastings, wine festivals, guided tours and visits to the cellar door are all part of the means by which people encounter and learn about wine. In many New World countries, such as Australia, New Zealand and the United States, where wine drinking is not an established part of the way of life, wine tourism may serve a very important role in introducing customers to wine tasting and the development of their wine knowledge in a friendly, social and unthreatening atmosphere. For example, research by Longo (1999) and Mitchell (in progress) in New Zealand reinforces the extent to which the desire to learn about wine motivates the wine tourist. Moreover, from an industry perspective, 'wine education plays a fundamantal role in the growth of the wine industry. An educated and well informed marketplace translates to better sales of premium wine' (Hills 1998).

Wine clearly plays an important part in consumer lifestyles. In Australia this has been recognized in the wine industry's *Strategy 2025* document which had the vision 'that by the year 2025 the Australian wine industry will achieve $4.5 billion in annual sales by being the world's most influential and profitable supplier of branded wines, pioneering wine as a universal first choice lifestyle beverage' (Winemakers, Federation of Australia 1996: 200). Indeed, *Strategy 2025* emphasizes that wine is 'the late 20th century lifestyle beverage of moderation. It is more than just a beverage, it has become a lifestyle product with a high degree of complementarity with food, hospitality, entertainment, the arts and tourism' (Winemakers' Federation of Australia 1996: 197). Although Clancy (1998: 4) has noted that one of the impediments to attaining this vision will be the need to keep Australian wine accessible and affordable to Australian domestic consumers, the basic observation that wine is part of various consumers' lifestyles holds true. Similarly, Winegrowers of New Zealand in their Scenario 2010 for the New Zealand wine industry also emphasize the lifestyle dimensions of wine noting that 'As a high added value, innovative product New Zealand wine is marketed and sold to appeal to fashion leaders, opinion leaders, consumers with high disposable income, new age wine connoisseurs, the new generation, 18–30-year-old women, and the health conscious' (*New Zealand Wine Grower* 1999: 8).

In an attempt to understand more about the values and lifestyles of Australian winery visitors, Macionis and Cambourne (1998: 44–5) have used data from the Roy Morgan (1996) Holiday Tracking Survey to develop a 'wine tourism market portfolio' '. . . which measures travel intentions and behaviour and is based on 16,000 interviews nationally'. This approach combines demographic (e.g. age, sex, socio-economic background) and psychographic (e.g. tastes, beliefs, values, attitudes and opinions) data to develop 'Value Segments' which group people sharing similar characteristics (See Chapter 4 for more detail).

A lifestyle approach to wine tourism consumers has also been adopted in Italy. According to the Movimento del Turismo del Vino, there are four types of wine tourist :

- *The Professional:* 30 – 45 years old, knows wines and the wine world, can discuss the fine points of the wines with the wine-maker, and can competently judge a wine's virtues and faults. Always interested in new things, and willing to devote considerable time and energy to their discovery.
- *The Impassioned Neophyte:* 25–30 years old, well off, likes wines and sees them as a vehicle through which to cement friendships, enjoy foods, and explore the countryside. Generally travels with friends, some of whom may be Professionals, and always has a wine guide handy. Eager to learn, but less serious about wine than the Professional.
- *The Hanger-On:* 40–50 years old, wealthy, attracted to wines because knowing something about them is a mark of distinction. Is satisfied with a knowledge of just the basics, and is more easily swayed by the comments of others than those belonging to the previous categories. Is also drawn to famous names, and more easily impressed by appearances. Sometimes asks for a discount.

- *The Drinker:* 50–60 years old, visits wineries as part of a group on Sundays, treating them as an alternative to a bar, gulps the wine and asks for more, also asks to buy in bulk, sometimes pulling a tank or demijohn from the back of the car (Corigliano 1996).

Another way to learn about the lifestyle choices of winery visitors and, in particular, their interests and hobbies is to examine the type of popular literature (e.g. newspapers and magazines) that they regularly read. To this end, two recent studies (Maddern and Golledge 1996; Longo 1999) have provided data that permit some, albeit tentative, inferences along these lines (see Chapter 8). Not surprisingly, epicure, cuisine and wine literature is prominent; however, travel and entertainment magazines are also significant. This suggests that experiential aspects of lifestyle (e.g. socializing, travel, entertaining and dining out) are likely to be significant and that materialistic aspects might be less important.

Motivation

According to Iso-Ahola (1980: 230 in Crompton and Mackay 1997: 425) 'a motive is an internal factor that arouses, directs, and integrates a person's behavior'. Table 6.3 summarizes the motivations that have been identified in four Australasian studies. External motives (or 'pull-factors') are those that draw the winery visitor to the winery and are in general characteristics or activities of the winery (e.g. tasting and buying wine, tours and dining services) and, as the most easily elicited motives, are those most often cited. However, according to Johnson (1998: 34), the study of

> . . . internal motivations in addition to pull factors . . . allows operators to identify new products that can fulfil the same basic needs. [A] level of abstraction also allows us to compare tourist motivation across a wide range of tourism types and to better understand tourist demand. The study of internal motivations would reveal the similarities in and differences between wine tourist demand and general tourist demand, within different wine tourism market segments.

Several of the internal motives identified in Table 6.4 can be analysed to reveal motivations that are rooted more deeply in the values, beliefs and attitudes of the visitor. Qualitative data from a study of Central Otago (New Zealand) winery visitors (Mitchell forthcoming) suggests that for many, *tasting* and *learning about wine/winemaking* is a way to 'minimize risk' when purchasing wine (i.e. by increasing their experience and knowledge they are

Table 6.3 Ranking of motivations for those visiting wineries

	Victoria (n = 1552)	*Canberra (n = 85)*	Canberra (n = 13)	New Zealand (n = 82)	Internal/ External
Tasting wine	1	1	1=	1	External
Buying wine	2	2	1=	2	External
A day out	–	3	7	3	–
Socializing	3	–	6	7	Internal
Learning about wine	4	6	5	4	Internal
Relaxation	–	–	3	5	Internal
Winery tour	6	–	9	6	External
Meeting wine-maker	7	5	4	8	Internal
Eating at winery	5	–	–	11	External
Picnic/BBQ	9	–	10	10	External
Entertaining	8	–	–	–	–
Rural setting	–	4	–	–	External

Sources: Victoria: Maddern and Golledge 1996; Canberra: Macionis 1994, 1996; New Zealand: Johnson 1998.

Notes: *Victoria and *Canberra based on visitors' self-reported motivations. Canberra and New Zealand based on wineries' perception of motivation.

able to make more informed decisions about wine). Similarly, further examination of a *day-out* and *relaxation* as motives reveals a need for *escape* from city life. Visitors who were motivated by *meeting the wine-maker or owner*, were concerned with such things as the *believability* and *passion* associated with the wine interpretation and therefore raise issues of *authenticity* (Cohen 1983).

Johnson (1998: 15) proposes perhaps one of the most elementary typologies, on the basis of motivation: that of *specialist* versus *general* wine tourist. While the general wine tourist is 'one who visits a vineyard, winery, wine festival or wine show for the purpose of recreation', Johnson suggests that the specialist wine tourist is 'one who visits a vineyard, winery, wine festival or wine show for the purpose of recreation and whose primary motivation is a specific interest in grape wine or grape wine-related phenomena'. This definition therefore excludes the tour party whose key motivation was certainly not wine per se, but the desire to have a relaxing day out (Johnson 1998: 15). However, this typology is largely untested and the relative size of the specialist/generalist market is unknown. The earlier discussion relating to the knowledge of wine suggests that the number will be

Table 6.4 Stage of travel experience

Stage of travel experience	Wine experience	Opportunities
Pre-visit (anticipation)	Wine from destination/winery at home, restaurant or wine club.	Distribution in main origin areas for regional tourism.
	Previous experience at winery/wine region. Previous experience of other wineries.	Positive on-site experiences (past). Promotional material that uses place attributes as well as wine attributes.
	Promotional material and advertising for winery/wine region.	
Travel to	Wine en route (e.g. at restaurant or on airline). Airline promotional video/in-flight magazine article of destination that includes wine.	Wine on airlines or major stopping points en route. Promotional video and magazine articles.
Destination/on-site visit	Winery experience – Tasting – Education/interpretation – Service – Setting – Activities (e.g. tours) – Food	Positive winery experience.
	Wine at hotel, restaurant or café in region.	Wine in local hotels, restaurants and cafés.
Travel from	Wine en route home (e.g. at restaurant or on airline).	Wine on airlines or major stopping points en route.
Post-visit (reminiscence)	Wine from destination/winery at home, restaurant or wine club.	Distribution in main origin areas for regional tourism.
	Previous experience at winery/wine region. Previous experience of other wineries.	Positive on-site experiences (past). Promotional material that uses place attributes as well as wine attributes.
	Promotional material and advertising for winery/wine region.	
	Photos and souvenirs.	Souvenirs
	Wine purchased at cellar door.	
	Mail order/newsletter	Mail order/newsletter.

FUTURE BEHAVIOUR

relatively small (i.e. those with advanced knowledge) and this is supported by other specialist/generalist distinctions within tourism (see for example Richards 1996).

In this section we have learnt about who the winery visitor is (demographically speaking) and we have made some assertions relating to their lifestyles and motivations. However, the insights put forward thus far only go part way towards effectively describing the winery visitor and their experiences. As yet we have not been able to elicit anything of the hedonic nature of the very 'human' experience of the winery. The last part of this chapter provides an *experiential* insight into winery visitor behaviour, providing a framework for future consumer behaviour study in the area.

An experiential perspective of wine tourist behaviour

In the 1980s consumer behaviour researchers began to recognize the significance of the hedonistic nature of purchases of many goods and services (e.g. Holbrook and Hirschman 1982; Lofman 1991) and as a result the 'experiential view' emerged. In contrast to the more traditional 'information processing model', the 'experiential view' recognized the special nature of products and services that have a hedonic component, such as wine, leisure activities and pleasure travel. When purchasing these products decision-making is not always based on problem-solving, rather, decisions are often the result of 'primary process thinking': 'fun, amusement, fantasy, arousal, sensory stimulation and enjoyment in much the same way that a baby seeks immediate gratification' (Holbrook and Hirshman 1982: 135). By recognizing the significance of these primary processes, the 'experiential view' identifies the '. . . stream of consciousness or sensory, imaginal and affective complex that accompanies a tourist experience' (Lofman 1991: 729).

While much of the consumer research into wine tourism is based on elementary aspects of consumer behaviour and the 'information processing model' (largely because little or no baseline information exists), studies advocating the 'experiential view' have emerged in wine tourism literature (e.g. Dodd and Gustafson 1997; Mitchell in progress). Dodd and Gustafson (1997) have advocated the use of an experiential approach to the study of wine tourism. While their work has applied some of the principles of an experiential approach, and does provide some useful information on the attributes of the winery visitor and how the winery and its staff may influence behaviour and attitudes (see Chapter 7), it falls short of providing a thorough appraisal of the experience. In particular, Dodd and Gustafson (1997) have largely ignored the role of the individual tourist in shaping their own experiences.

Depictions of the winery experience can be found throughout popular cuisine and travel literature. Most explore not only the sensuous nature of wine, but also its romantic and lascivious nature. One illustration of this can be found in an article by Vic Williams (Bieder, Campbell and Williams 1997: 131, 132) (a wine writer for *Cuisine* magazine):

> Where there is good wine, you will find joyful people and honest food. Nowhere is this happy truism more evident than in the Barossa...
>
> In an ideal world I would devote at least six months to exploring every nook and cranny of the Barossa Valley. I would visit only one winery each week and stay until the wines and winemaker had become old friends. There would be time enough to enjoy the sunny days and cool nights of a warm Mediterranean climate, to have lazy picnics amongst the spring wildflowers that border ancient vineyards and try Barossa beef with Shiraz at boisterous evening barbecues.

Such mellifluous imagery suggests that there is more to wine and wine tourism than the simple consumption of a beverage or that this experience is limited to the senses and emotions associated with the wine alone. Wine tourism experiences (as with most tourism experiences) are much more than this, relying on the characteristics of the individual (some of which have been outlined above), the setting in which they occur, socialization with the personalities of wine, and interaction with other elements of the experience such as food, accommodation and other visitors. It is the sum of these elements, not each individually, that make up the winery experience. Exhibit 6.1 provides some quotes from a study of Central Otago wineries that are indicative of some visitor opinions of the winery experience.

Exhibit 6.1: Statements from visitors to Central Otago wineries

'I like all the vines growing down there. I've always liked going to wineries. I like the feel of the wineries. It's relaxing, for me it relates totally to relaxing, this is total relaxation. I've completely forgotten about work, I'm in another world. That's what I like doing.'

'He [the sales person] holds it, he holds the person that is there to try wine. That's always a major thing. Although I like wine, I don't know a lot about wines, so if I'm going somewhere I can say I like it. But I'd like to know also maybe if there is a reason why I liked something and if someone can tell me that, that's a really good thing too.'

'. . . the speed of the service, the pleasant smiles of the proprietor and the I don't know, its just a very pleasant place, the lavender bushes, the green grass and healthy looking vines, a bit of shade. . . . Can you think of anything better than to be sitting amongst the grapes and eating crackers and cheese . . . I know I can't. . . . There's nothing like seeing those green globes growing right there.'

'Too many New Zealand vineyards offer wine without the interaction that should go with it. It's an opportunity for the host to widen visitors' knowledge about his/her wines and hopefully ensure future sales. In my experience vineyard visits influence future purchases! This can be positive or negative.'

Richard Mitchell (all quotes taken from Mitchell, in progress)

Using a bunch of grapes as a metaphor, Figure 6.3 provides a visual representation of the winery experience – the winery attributes (at its core), the experience of the wider region and wine experiences from outside the region – each of which must be present to give the experience its unique 'flavour'. Interspersed throughout, the grapes (like naturally occurring yeast) is the 'active ingredient' of the experience (represented by the green globes) – the personal traits of the visitor.

Despite the recent proliferation of experiential research within tourism studies, there are still some areas that have not been dealt with at an empirical level. In particular, experiential studies have tended to be limited both in their temporal and spatial extent. Perhaps most significantly, while it is widely accepted that there are five stages of the tourism experience (e.g. Clawson and Knetsch 1966; Pearce 1982; Fridgen 1984; see also Table 6.4), most empirical studies of the tourism experience (perhaps with the exception of Pearce 1982) have focused on one or other of these stages. Similarly, it is recognized that the tourism experience is not limited to a particular site or attraction and that several elements of the wider experience of a region will impact on the on-site experience (Hall 1996; Johnson 1998). Most studies of on-site experiences have not addressed the linkages with other experiences within the region that may influence the individual's attitudes, perceptions and behaviour, isolating the experience to the attraction in question.

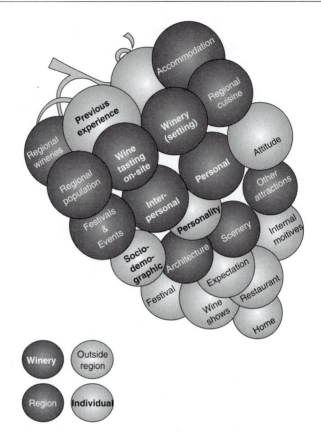

Figure 6.3 The winery experience. (*Source*: Mitchell, in progress).

The issue of the temporal and spatial scope of experiential studies is particularly pertinent to wine tourism. Wine, noted for its attachment to place (Hall 1996; Macionis 1996, 1997; Hall and Johnson 1998b; Hall and Macionis 1998; Johnson 1998), is also a tangible, transportable and durable product that can be experienced in a number of locations before, during and after the on-site winery experience (which tends to be less tangible, transportable and durable) (Table 6.4). Wine tourism, therefore, provides an excellent opportunity to study the on-site tourist experience within a wider temporal (pre- and post-visit) and spatial (the experience at home and of the wider regional tourism) context.

Some existing wine tourism studies (e.g. Maddern and Golledge 1996; Longo 1999) have provided a useful insight into the activities that winery visitors also undertake while in a wine region, but have stopped short of exploring the linkages between them. King and Morris (1999) have also made a preliminary attempt to track winery visitor consumer behaviour over time. These studies, while providing an understanding of some of the wider spatial and temporal elements of wine tourism, do not fully integrate all their findings into a comprehensive appraisal of the experience.

In order to provide a framework that might allow for a more holistic view of the winery experience, Mitchell (in progress) posits a three-dimensional model that combines the spatial (*setting*) and temporal (*stage of travel* or *time*) dimensions of the wine tourism experience with the *activity* of tourism. Figure 6.4 illustrates how these three individual elements interact to shape the overall wine tourism experience. Examples of the various types of wine tourism experience have been used to illustrate how this model can be applied to the wine tourism experience (although any tourism activity might be placed in this framework). A pre-visit experience in a familiar setting, for example drinking wine from the host region at home before the winery visit, is placed at the *familiar/past/real* end of each dimension (bottom left foreground). At the other end might be the recollection of the winery experience that takes place at another location (*post-visit/imagined/remote*).

While outwardly the elements of the experience (e.g. anticipation at home, on-site experience or reminiscence) are discrete this is not the case. Connections exist between the elements that are unique to the individual, who

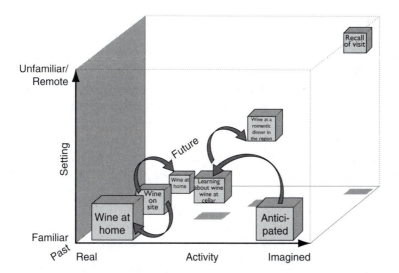

Figure 6.4 Dimensions of the wine tourism experience. (*Source*: Mitchell, in progress).

constructs a unique (subjective) experience based on their personality, values, beliefs and attitudes along with their own experience, perceptions and knowledge of the world. This phenomenological perspective of the model also suggests that a 'real world' view of the model is inappropriate as '... phenomenologists argue that there is no objective world independent of man's [sic] experience' (Holt-Jensen 1988: 80). Using the framework presented in Figure 6.4 it is possible, then, to suggest three phenomenological dimensions of the tourism experience: *phenomenal environment* (environments as perceived, and acted upon, by humans) (Holt-Jensen 1988: 137 after Kirk 1963); *human constructs of time* (concepts such as past, present, future, reminiscence and anticipation) and the *phenomenon* itself (tangible and intangible tourist activities).

Mitchell (in progress) is attempting to apply this three-dimensional framework to the study of the New Zealand (and, more specifically, the Central Otago) winery experience. This research attempts to gather information (both qualitative and quantitative) on the on-site experience, but relates it to pre-visit experiences (through expectations and previous experience), post-visit experience (through follow-up surveys of reminiscence and purchasing behaviour) and the wider regional context (through an examination of visitors' other activities in the wine region). In doing so, it is hoped that such an holistic view of the winery experience will not only allow wineries to gain a better understanding of their visitors, but also how the experience they provide can influence future behaviour and how this fits into the wider regional experience.

Conclusion

Consumer behaviour literature is beginning to recognize the importance of not only the demographics and psychographics of the consumer but also the experience of purchasing the product. Nowhere is this more important than in the on-site sale of wine. Our understanding of the winery visitor and their experience is therefore paramount in gaining an understanding of why and how wine is purchased and consumed. As Macionis and Cambourne (1998) point out

> By understanding the nature of winery tourists or visitors and recognising the broad and multifaceted motivations for engaging in wine tourism, wine regions and individual wineries will be better able to develop and market their destination and wine tourism products. Also, by examining their entire market portfolios, rather than focusing on

narrowly defined, single market profiles wine regions can take steps to cultivate new markets, facilitating their evolution through both the destination and market lifecycle, thus ensuring that their wine tourism product is both sustainable and profitable.

While wine tourism research has begun to recognize the importance of descriptions of the winery visitor, their lifestyles and motivations, there is still much to be done before we can draw conclusions about the 'human' nature of their experiences. An approach that utilizes an experiential framework, such as the one described in this section, will not only allow future research to fill many of the gaps in our understanding of the wine tourist, but may also provide a framework for the integrated management (both long and short term) of tourism in the wine region.

7

Influences on cellar door sales and determinants of wine tourism success: results from Texas wineries

Tim H. Dodd

Winery managers may have several goals when attempting to develop tourism. These goals may include educating people about the wine industry, developing a database of mail-order customers, or testing new products being considered for release in restaurants and supermarkets. However, the principal purpose in developing tourism for the majority of wineries is to generate immediate and future profitable sales.

In recent years, sales of wine and wine-related items have become an increasingly important means of distribution for wineries. Hall *et al.*, (1997) for example, noted the strong growth of winery tourism in Australia and New Zealand. Academics, and those related to tourism development, have become keenly interested in winery tourism although little research was conducted before the mid-1990s. Despite this relatively recent interest, tourism has played an important role in the wine industry for many years. This is especially so in New World wine regions, such as the United States, where, in the 1960s, winery managers were encouraging people to visit their wineries and try their wines. The major purpose for encouraging visits was an attempt to overcome consumer concerns that the wines were of poor quality, compared with wines from the more traditional regions such as Italy and France. By visiting the wineries consumers can try before they buy, thus removing the risk involved with making a bad purchase. In addition, in many United States wine regions, where the sale and distribution of alcohol is often strictly regulated, tourism provides an opportunity for wineries to circumvent the traditional retail system which may have numerous legal constraints and be dominated by large competitors and wholesale distributors. However, tourism is by no means a key strategy for all wineries to follow. Managers of many large wineries, for instance, may pay little attention to tourism (see Chapter 1). For example, in the New Zealand situation, Beverland (1998) argued that the real growth for a winery is likely to come from mass distribution channels and that too much concentration on tourism is a distraction (see also Chapter 8).

One region where there is a dichotomy between the interests of large and small winery managers towards tourism is in Texas. Cellar door sales constitute around 10 per cent of total sales within this relatively newly developed wine-producing area. The larger wineries in the state, with one or two exceptions, tend to concentrate their attention upon other distribution channels such as supermarkets and liquor stores. However, for the small wineries it is very important for them to develop tourism as the main form of distribution. Half of the wineries in the state produce less than 10,000 gallons per year, and, although they produce just 11 per cent of total sales, they account for more than 70 per cent of all tasting room sales. On average, these wineries sell more than 60 per cent of their total production directly to winery visitors.

This chapter first discusses how success is perceived with respect to winery tourism and, second, examines cellar door sales as one component or measure of that success – and the factors that may influence those sales. The results of a major study in Texas that address some of these issues is presented.

Tourism success factors for wineries

When assessing the success wineries ascribe to tourism participation and development, it is important to understand what constitutes or what is perceived as success for a particular winery. Successful wine tourism outcomes may be related to a variety of goals that a winery has and the visits by tourists may be just a small part of the winery's overall business. The interrelationship between the various antecedents of success is also potentially complex; many of these relationships remain untested. The following is a summary of some of the approaches taken by winery managers to tourism and the responses of visitors in Texas, although comparisons are drawn with other regions.

Attracting the most visitors

Some winery managers view success as simply trying to attract the largest number of visitors possible to their facility. To the winery manager that adopts this paradigm, head count can often appear more important than visitor satisfaction or future visits and customer relationships. In such circumstances the winery is adopting a sales orientation, based on a belief that there is essentially an endless supply of visitors, and efforts to develop those closer relationships with individuals are simply not worth the effort. Some wineries in California's Napa Valley, for instance, appear to have taken this approach. The region has become so overrun with visitors that on the main tourist routes some of the wineries have simply adopted a mass marketing approach with little effort to spend time showing the visitor the winery or providing wine education that focuses on the particular interests of the visitor.

Maximizing sales

Other wineries focus on maximizing sales at the winery. The provision of, and emphasis on, value-added winery attractions or activities, such as tours and presentations in the tasting room, is designed to encourage sales of wine and other items. Some wineries use very sophisticated approaches and spend time with each customer while, for others, there is more of a hard-sell approach. However, the focus is still on increasing sales.

Relationship marketing

For some wineries, sales and increasing the numbers of visitors may be the outcome of developing close relationships with customers and ensuring they have a positive attitude. This relationship approach is based upon the idea that there are a limited number of customers and each should be cultivated as much as possible. It is based on the principle that new customers cost more to find, familiarize, and develop loyalty than existing ones. These visitors provide positive word-of-mouth support and are, by far, a company's most profitable customers. In other industries, development of loyal customers has been closely linked to profitability. Although no published studies have been reported concerning this link in winery tourism, it is expected to exist, based upon the results of these other studies.

Gathering marketing information and developing long-term relationships with visitors is an important part of the activities in a winery. Visitors provide numerous opportunities for winery managers to learn more about their clientele and establish lists of customers for future contacts. Winery managers sometimes test new types of wine, new labels, and promotional approaches on people visiting the winery. This provides direct responses to planned changes that these wineries may have in view and can lead to new wines being developed. One Texas winery developed a sweet red wine after observing that new wine consumers were interested in the much publicized health benefits of red wine but liked the sweetness of some of the whites the tasting room was offering. The wine has since become one of the winery's most popular tasting room items.

Developing a list of people who visit the winery and creating a long-term relationship with these visitors through newsletters, subsequent visits, and other communications is another approach that may be a key objective for tasting room management. However, as noted by Getz (1999), the bottom line for most wineries is sales and this has been the focus of research to date.

Influences on cellar door sales at Texas wineries

Customer characteristics

Customer demographics were found to be related to purchases of wine in a variety of situations (Dodd 1994). The most strongly related variable has typically been income and education with consumption generally increasing as income and education levels increase (see also Chapters 6 and 8). The study found that visitors to wineries tended to have similar characteristics to the average wine consumer (see also King and Morris 1999).

Dodd (1994), in a study of more than 600 visitors to Texas wineries, reported that customer demographics, such as age, income and education level, can be related to wine purchasing behaviour. In this study, visitors to six different wineries in Texas were surveyed. The wineries were selected based on a geographic spread throughout the state and a variety of small and large wineries participated in the study. Visitors to the wineries were provided with a questionnaire as they were about to leave and offered a small gift for completing the questionnaire. More than 95 per cent of those approached agreed to participate and a total of 636 usable questionnaires was obtained (Dodd 1994). The Texas study found that a majority of the visitors to wineries were female (54 per cent) and this percentage was similar to a variety of other proprietary winery studies completed in other US regions. In addition, educational levels of visitors were substantially higher than the general population, with more than 60 per cent of visitors having at least a bachelor's degree.

The findings from visitors to Texas wineries suggest that age may be a useful demographic variable with respect to grouping consumers with similar characteristics. Indeed, with regard to winery visitors in Texas, a cluster analysis of visitors by Dodd and Bigotte (1997) found two distinct demographic groups. The first was a younger group with a mean age of 31, the second group had a mean age of 52. The first, younger group had significantly lower levels of income than the older group while educational levels were essentially the same.

Perceptual differences of winery visitors

Dodd and Bigotte's study (1997) found a number of differences in perceptions of winery attributes with respect to these demographic groups. Differences were found with respect to a variety of wine-purchasing behaviours, visitor perceptions of the winery and service characteristics (friendliness, courteousness, overall service, knowledge, believability, entertainment, professionalism) of winery personnel. Younger visitors tended to place more importance on the price of the wine in their decision to purchase than the older group; however, they considered the price to be at lower levels than the older group. Thus, it seems older winery visitors are more sensitive about how they perceive prices but the younger visitors indicate that wine-specific attributes are a more important factor in deciding whether to purchase wine or not. This apparent discrepancy may be related to the income and wine-purchasing experiences of the two groups. Younger wine purchasers have less experience buying wine and so are not as perceptive about wine prices, while the older group with higher income levels place less importance on that attribute and more importance on other attributes, such as taste.

Service attributes, or visitors' perception of their winery experience was also noted to have an impact on the perceptions of Texas winery visitors. The overall service of the winery personnel was considered more important for the younger people and rated lower with respect to the level of service provided for this younger group. While the younger demographic group rated the overall service they received at the winery as more important than the older demographic group, specific aspects of this service such as friendliness, courteous staff and staff knowledge were not perceived as importantly as by the older group in assessing their winery experience. Some differences were also found between the groups with respect to the components of the winery environment. Cleanliness, in particular, was seen as more important by the older group, and they rated the cleanliness of the environment higher than the younger visitors. Displays and the smells within the winery were rated better by the older group but no differences in the importance placed on these attributes were found.

Based on their spending behaviour, the older group of visitors would appear to be the more attractive market demographic group for wineries. This group spent nearly US$11 more per person on wine at the winery than the younger group. No significant difference was found in the amount spent between the groups on souvenir items. The older group also spent more money on wine per month in general, averaging nearly US$37 per month compared to nearly US$29 for the younger visitors. However, while it may seem that older winery visitors may spend more now, the younger group may be more profitable to cultivate as long-term customers!

In summary, the study found that older people seem to be less critical of the various attributes in a winery (apart from the price of the wine) and place less importance on overall service and price than the younger group. Because they tend to spend more and generally rate the wine, winery, and the service components higher, they are certainly the most attractive group of the two. However, they do seem somewhat concerned about the prices that wineries offer and this may need to be addressed directly with them.

Psychographic and behavioural characteristics

Although demographic characteristics may have some relationship with purchases and other behaviour of winery visitors, aspects such as the individual's lifestyle, attitudes, knowledge, and consumption may provide more useful information for managers. For example, product involvement – the degree to which a consumer considers a particular product to be important in their life – was found to be significantly related to both the amount spent by individual visitors and spending on souvenir items. In other words, people with a real interest and love of wine do spend more at the winery. They particularly like to buy wine accessory items such as glasses, tee-shirts and other products.

Of all the constructs examined, purchase involvement was the most closely related to consumer wine purchases. Purchase involvement attempts to determine the degree to which the purchase is important to the consumer at this particular time. Questions included in this construct are the degree to which the person cares about making the right choice of wine and the outcome of that choice. The levels of involvement may be the result of intrinsic sources of personal relevance (ISPR) or extrinsic sources (ESPR) (Celsi and Olson 1989). Thus, it may come from a visitor's existing knowledge and interest in the product or from the extrinsic aspects around them that may trigger changes in their felt involvement. The correlation between purchase involvement and product involvement was significant but quite low (0.21) indicating that other factors are involved with creating a sense by the consumer that this purchase is personally relevant at this particular time. As Celsi and Olson (1989) noted 'marketing mix factors have the potential to activate self-relevant goals and motivations. If those situational goals become linked to product attributes and functional consequences they create a state of felt involvement with the product'.

Clearly, if managers can understand these environmental components then they can try to develop strategies that will focus on the attributes that will most strongly influence this feeling of involvement. If winery managers can heighten the level of interest and concern for consumers who enter the winery this can lead to increased sales. For example, courteous winery staff, employees providing exceptional service, and an appealing environment all seem to be related to an increase in purchase involvement levels (Dodd 1994).

As assumed, consumers who consume more wine at home tend to purchase more wine when they visit wineries. This finding also relates to the product involvement construct where people who view wine as having high personal relevance consume more wine. Therefore, if wine sales is the main goal for winery tourism, then attracting consumers who have a high degree of interest in wine and who are currently the major consumers of wine will be the appropriate target. However, if other goals, such as market development via educating new wine consumers, or other such motives are important, then the frequent wine consumer may not be the most appropriate target.

Winery markers – implicit affectors of winery visitor behaviour

Markers are information signals that consumers use to gather information about the tourism area of interest (Leiper 1990). In the case of wineries, markers may include signs external to the winery on roadways or buildings

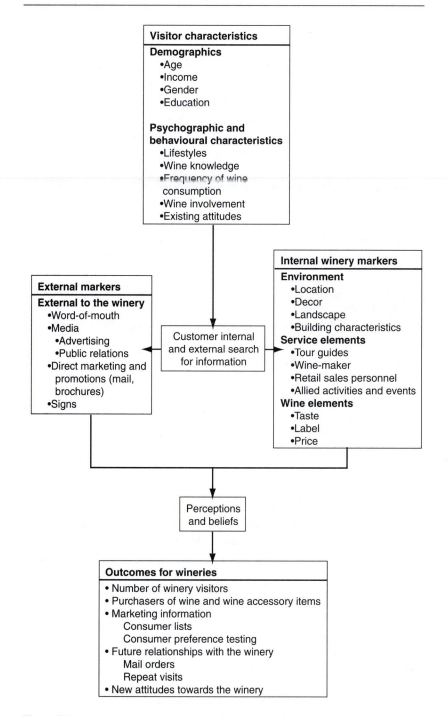

Figure 7.1 Antecedents and outcomes of winery tourism.

pointing to the winery. They may also be internal markers such as newspaper clippings, or trophies hanging on the winery's walls signalling awards achieved at wine competitions. Markers may be associated with other businesses located near the winery that can provide information and direction to people who may be interested. For example, brochures at a hotel would be markers that may provide information to travellers concerning the winery. The environment includes the building, landscaping, furnishings, and displays of retail goods, and items of educational interest. The environment also provides some tangible evidence of the winery that the service characteristics and other components of the wine tourism experience do not provide. Consumers who use these information sources gain a variety of meanings based on their own individual characteristics such as wine knowledge, demographics, and psychographics. Figure 7.1 is a model indicating the potential outcomes that may result from the various antecedents of successful winery tourism.

External markers

Winery visitors obtain information about a certain winery from a variety of sources. These sources may let them know about information such as the existence of the winery, a particular event that the winery is hosting, location, and opening hours. Depending on the buyer-readiness stage, and whether general or specific information is required, a variety of information sources may be sought. Therefore, how the winery develops and utilizes their various information sources will have an important impact on the various success factors listed in Figure 7.1. Information sources are the link between the consumer and the winery, and a clear understanding of the interaction between the two and how visitors search for information about wineries provides opportunities for winery managers to optimize their marketing abilities.

Dodd (1998) notes that 'word-of-mouth' (WOM) was found to be the most important source of information used by Texas winery visitors. This was followed by (in descending order):

- previous exposure to the winery's label;
- newspaper or magazine information;
- brochures;
- previous visits to the winery;
- billboards;
- local convention and visitor bureau.

The importance of a strong public relations programme is highlighted by the emphasis that Texas winery visitors place upon newspapers and magazines as information sources. As such, winery managers should focus considerable attention upon developing relationships with a variety of media, ensuring that key people and communicators are kept updated with relevant event information, winery promotions, and other matters of public (and hence consumer) interest. Rather than just focusing upon wine-related magazines, managers should also look to publicize the winery in newspapers and magazines which wine consumers and travellers may spend time reading.

Dodd (1998) also reported differences with respect to the distance from the winery and the type of information sources that were considered the most important by winery visitors. People living close to the winery used previous experience with the winery as their major source of information, while visitors from more than thirty miles away used brochures as a major source of information. For winery managers attempting to encourage visits from people who live a considerable distance from their winery, a strong brochure programme would thus seem to be a particularly effective way of encouraging people to stop. The brochure should provide detailed information concerning directions and hours of operation as most of these people will be first-time visitors (see also Chapter 2).

Internal markers

The research by Dodd (1994) and Dodd and Gustafson (1997) tested some of the relationships between the various antecedents and outcomes in one region. Further research is needed to continue to examine these relationships in other settings and using additional attributes. From an original list of more than 100 items, a group of 17 possible attributes were developed and used in the study.

In relation to internal winery markers, it seems there are four major attributes or groups of attributes within a winery that may influence a visitor's attitude and willingness to purchase wine. The first group is the service provided by personnel at the winery such as friendliness, courteousness, and knowledge. The people providing this service may be the owner(s) or paid employees of the winery. In some cases with small wineries, it may be that one person is the owner, wine-maker, and tasting room manager. In other cases there may be a particular employee who is the tasting room manager and several employees who act as hosts and tour guides.

Service characteristics

The findings indicate that courtesy, knowledge, and the believability of personnel influence attitude, but that this attitude does not directly translate into wine or other purchases. Only the feeling of overall service translated into direct wine purchases (Table 7.1). This should in no way indicate that winery management should not be concerned about the idea of courteousness, knowledge and being believable. Indeed, it is probably a combination of these service attributes that contributes to the visitor's overall perception of service. Additionally, individual attributes and their influence upon attitude may have many positive impacts apart from immediate sales. For example, a willingness by visitors to pass on their positive experiences to others, and perhaps subsequent sales after the visit.

The negative relationship between entertainment and wine purchases is interesting. The finding would imply that the more entertainment the winery visitor perceives as being offered the less they spend on wine. There could be a number of reasons for this relationship. For example, visitors who perceive the winery as one that is not serious about wine production and which has to provide entertainment may also view their wines as of poorer quality. Another possibility is that the winery itself may actually put their efforts into entertainment rather than focus on other things that may be more important to the consumer.

To conclude, overall service as perceived by the visitor is directly related to wine purchases. Three other items also impacted upon attitudes. A clear commitment to service quality by winery staff is critical although some care should be taken that in the enthusiasm to look after the visitor, entertainment (how does one define entertainment in this instance?) does not take

Table 7.1 Service characteristics positively and negatively related to attitudes, wine purchases, and souvenir purchases

Personnel characteristics	Attitude	Wine purchases	Accessory purchases
Overall service	●	+	●
Friendliness	●	●	●
Courteousness	+	●	●
Knowledge	+	●	●
Entertainment	●	−	●
Believable	+	●	●
Professionalism	●	●	●

Positive relationship +
Negative relationship −
No relationship found ●

precedence over the expectations that the producer can provide a quality wine. 'Serious' wine consumers, especially, may expect an environment that is at least somewhat more 'serious' about wine.

Wine characteristics

There are also a number of specifically wine-related attributes or markers that can directly affect the purchasing behaviour of winery visitors. In the Texas study, three items – taste, wine aroma, and wine quality – appeared strongly linked (Table 7.2). Both wine taste and wine quality were found to be related to both the visitor's attitude toward the wine and subsequent wine purchases. Consumer perceptions of these two attributes are linked to both outcomes and are themselves strongly correlated at about 0.50. It appears, however, that none of these specific wine-related attributes have much to do with the purchases of accessory items. It would seem that consumers purchase the accessory items for other reasons than their likes or dislikes of the actual wine. It may be that, as a gesture of courtesy, consumers feel the need to purchase something from the winery; if they do not particularly like the wines, they may purchase an item such as a tee-shirt. Therefore, those who particularly like the wines may or may not spend their money on purchasing accessories and hence this lack of a relationship is found.

Winery aesthetics

In their study Dodd and Gustafson (1997) initially assumed that the components of the winery, such as the overall environment, displays, attractiveness, and smells, would be grouped together as the overall winery

Table 7.2 **Wine characteristics positively and negatively related to attitudes, wine purchases, and souvenir purchases.**

Wine characteristics	Attitude	Wine purchases	Accessory purchases
Wine aroma	●	●	●
Wine taste	+	+	●
Wine quality	+	+	●

Positive relationship +
Negative relationship –
No relationship found ●

environment. However, when the factor analysis indicated that the wine label is also grouped with these elements, it was renamed aesthetics to indicate the overall aesthetic appeal of the winery.

There was, however, less relationship between these variables than the other groups of internal winery markers (environment and wine). In fact only the wine label was positively related to attitudes towards the winery, and 'winery displays' positively linked with accessory purchases. In Texas at least, it seems that most of the physical characteristics of the winery (such as the cleanliness, overall environment, displays, attractiveness and winery smells) have little impact on a person's actual attitude towards a winery (Table 7.3).

With respect to wine purchases, two aesthetic attributes – the 'wine label' and 'displays' – actually had a negative impact on wine purchases. There could be several explanations for these results. People who view the wine label positively may have a better attitude towards the wine but if they are not convinced it is a quality product then they are still unwilling to make significant purchases. They may also have been looking for something positive to respond to concerning the winery. The other aspects such as taste and service may not have been positive and they therefore gave a better rating to this attribute despite their unwillingness to purchase wine. The negative relationship between displays and wine purchases may also be related to the issue of consumers trying to find something to like about a winery despite not particularly enjoying the wine. These consumers may feel some obligation to make a purchase and therefore, instead of buying wine, purchase accessory items.

Table 7.3   Winery aesthetics positively and negatively related to attitudes, wine purchases, and souvenir purchases

Winery aesthetics	Attitude	Wine purchases	Accessory purchases
Wine label	+	–	●
Cleanliness	●	●	●
Environment	●	●	●
Displays	●	–	+
Winery attractiveness	●	●	●
Winery smells	●	●	●

Positive relationship +
Negative relationship –
No relationship found ●

Price

As with many other studies that investigate attributes of particular products, ranging from automobiles to restaurant meals and grocery items, price was found to be its own affective factor. Not surprisingly, there was a negative relationship between price and wine purchases. In other words, the higher the perceived price, the less wine sold. No relationship was found with respect to price and to attitudes and souvenir purchases.

Concluding comments

Many questions remain unanswered concerning winery information sources used by winery visitors and their beliefs, attitudes, and behaviours before and after their winery visit. The studies and analysis from the Texas data reported in this chapter represent a first attempt to examine some of these issues. It seems clear that winery management/managers can do a number of things within the winery to facilitate positive visitor attitudes and help boost winery sales. For example, the overall impression of service appears to have a major impact upon purchases, while courteousness, knowledge, and the believability of the tour guide seem to impact attitudes. However, there is still much to be learned about the interaction of some of these factors and how they affect a winery's market position and sales.

Replication of some of the above study in regions outside the United States would help provide additional information concerning the reactions of people to the various components involved in a winery visit. Aspects of the actual tour that many wineries provide could also be examined in greater depth. For instance, the information provided by the tour guide, and the information expected by visitors, are examples that may be helpful as winery managers make decisions concerning their wine tourism involvement and particular winery programmes.

Qualitative research efforts may go some way towards providing much needed richness to this area. In-depth interviews could be used to examine feelings of obligation that visitors may have to make purchases following a tour. For example, winery employees have spent considerable time providing free tastings, tours, and other educational assistance and visitors may feel they need to show their gratitude in some cases by making a purchase. This phenomenon could be called 'gratuity purchasing' and may explain much of purchase decisions that are made. Specific motivations such as education, relaxation, visiting the countryside, and finding unique wine items, are also research areas that could be further examined.

8

Wine tourism in New Zealand

C. Michael Hall, Anna Marie Longo,
Richard Mitchell and Gary Johnson

> I have no hesitation in saying that, were the
> industry taken up with spirit and pursued to
> only a small proportion of the available
> land, the natural advantages are such as to
> warrant a handsome reward to the grower
> and country at large (Bragato 1895: 11)

Some 100 years on from one of the first serious
appraisals of the potential for the development of
wine in New Zealand, Bragato's prediction of the
New Zealand wine industry's potential has
largely come true. The early promise of the wine
industry was thwarted by the vine louse phylloxera, prohibitionism, the Depression and two
world wars. (For the history of wine in New
Zealand see Scott (1964), Thorpy (1971), Cooper
(1993), George (1996) and Hadyn and Talmont
(1997).) Moreover, it was the broader social
changes brought on, at least in part, by greater
exposure of New Zealanders to European wine
and food traditions that provided for changes in

social attitudes towards wine and the institutional arrangements that surrounded it. For example, wine tourism only began to be feasible, let alone developed, after 1976 when it became legal to 'take wine to a cafe or call in at a winery cellar and buy its vintages by the bottle' (Hadyn and Talmont 1997: 27). In 1980, Vidals in Hastings could be considered a pioneer because it not only offered wine sales but a winery tour, a wine museum and a restaurant (Graham 1980). Indeed, Graham was (cautiously) prophetic in his statement that these services and amenities were 'perhaps a pattern for the future' (1980: 53).

The New Zealand wine industry

In Bragato's day, New Zealand wine-makers were largely enthusiastic amateurs. By 1999 the Wine Institute of New Zealand (WINZ) could boast over 300 members and a high degree of technical excellence (WINZ 1999). Moreover, New Zealand's wine industry underwent dramatic growth in the 1990s as rural areas diversified into new agricultural products and wine and winegrape production came increasingly to be seen by some smallholders as an appropriate lifestyle product (Hall and Johnson 1998b). The dramatic changes in the New Zealand wine industry are summarized in Table 8.1.

Figure 8.1 The industrial reality of large-scale wine production. Montana Winery, Marlborough, New Zealand.

Table 8.1   Summary of New Zealand wine statistics 1988–98 (Year ending June)

	1988	1989	1990	1991	1992	1993	1994	1995	1996	1997	1998
Number of wineries	112	123	131	150	166	175	190	204	238	262	293
Total vine area (hectares)	4880	5440	5800	5980	6100	6100	6680	7500	7800	8455	8720
Producing area (hectares)	4300	4370	4880	5440	5800	5980	6110	6110	6610	7410	7940
Average yield (tonnes per hectare)	12	13.8	14.4	12.1	9.3	7.1	8.8	12.2	11.2	8.1	9.9
Average grape price (NZ$ per tonne)	n/a	n/a	n/a	453	555	718	867	887	829	842	1005
Tonnes crushed	51 509	60 335	70 265	65 708	55 500	42 621	54 000	74 500	75 300	60 000	78 300
Total production (millions of litres)	39.2	45.6	54.4	49.9	41.6	32.5	41.1	56.4	57.3	45.8	*58.7
Domestic sales (millions of litres)	45	39.1	39.2	41.1	43.6	37.4	28.5	30.9	35.6	38.8	*38.0
Consumption per capita (litres NZ wine)	12.9	11.7	11.7	12.1	12.8	11	8.1	8.7	9.9	10.8	10
Export volume (millions of litres)	2.9	2.6	4	5.6	7.1	8.6	7.9	7.8	11	13.1	†15.2
Export value (millions of NZ$FOB)	11.6	11.6	18.4	25.3	34.7	48.3	41.5	40.8	60.3	75.9	97.6
Stock: Sales ratio	1.18:1	1.52:1	1.73:1	1.65:1	1.28:1	1.21:1	1.62:1	2.14:1	2.06:1	1.66:1	1.69:1

* estimate

† includes a small percentage of imported wine subsequently re-exported

Source: Wine Institute of New Zealand 1998

Despite the romantic image of wine promoted by lifestyle magazines in New Zealand such as *Cuisine*, four producers dominate current production: Corbans, Montana, Nobilos and the Villa Maria group. In 1996 they produced over 90 per cent of the country's wine (Campbell 1997). However, Campbell's declaration (1997: 2) that '[this] is the age of the micro-boutique winery' is evidenced by the fact that 244, or 93 per cent, of the then Wine Institute members made less than 22,000 cases of wine annually (WINZ 1997). The continued growth of micro-producers has also been a major driving force behind the overall growth in wineries in New Zealand (see Table 8.2).

The structure of the wine industry has important implications for wine tourism and the business strategies of individual businesses and the industry as a whole, as the strategies of the larger companies may have substantially different dimensions than those of the boutique wineries (Beverland 1998). Companies pursuing a growth strategy will typically be aiming to sell into the export market and may not perceive wine tourism to be an option in their marketing mix, while, for many of the smaller wineries, cellar door sales are an essential component of their sales and the development of their mail-order list. Nevertheless, wine tourism should not be seen as an either/or option. Instead, wine tourism needs to be recognized as one component of a range of selling options, many of which are complementary. Moreover, it needs to be recognized that not all wineries, and particularly smaller lifestyle wineries, will necessarily be pursuing the growth strategies which authors, such as

Table 8.2   Number of wineries in New Zealand

Region	1990	1998	% change
Northland	4	6	50
Waikato/Bay of Plenty	56	71	127
Auckland	10	14	40
Gisborne	5	9	80
Hawke's Bay	12	36	300
Wellington	9	35	389
Nelson	6	17	283
Marlborough	9	54	600
Canterbury	12	37	308
Otago	6	23	383
Other	2	1	−50
Total	131	303	231

Source: After New Zealand Wine Institute 1998b

Figure 8.2 The romantic image of wine is maintained by small-scale producers. Johanishoff Winery, Marlborough, New Zealand.

Beverland (1998), advocate for wineries in New Zealand. Instead of increasing production, many will seek to improve quality and/or carve out niches in the domestic and international market in terms of focusing on such factors as particular wine varieties or wine-making techniques, for example, organically produced wines.

At the national level, the development of export markets is seen as the key to the future success of the New Zealand wine industry. In 1997/98, total sales of New Zealand wine amounted to an estimated 53.8 million litres, a record despite the domestic market being constrained by economic downturn (WINZ 1998a). Exports exceeded projections, representing approximately 28 per cent of the total volume of wine sales, or NZ$97 million. The international competitiveness of New Zealand wines improved in the past year following the weakening of the New Zealand dollar in major markets. Wineries with strong brands were able to capture the benefit of the weaker currency while New Zealand's growing success internationally is also based on a vision and commitment to compete as a niche participant in the global wine market (WINZ 1998a). For example, for the six months to 31 December 1998 New Zealand wine exports grew 15 per cent in volume and 40 per cent in value according to the WINZ. Exports totalled 9 million litres in the period valued at NZ$67.7 million. This compares with exports for the six months to

December 1997 of 7.8 million litres valued at NZ$48.4 million. The average price of exports jumped to NZ$7.56 per litre compared with NZ$6.22 per litre in the corresponding six months in 1997 (WINZ 1999).

The major markets for New Zealand wine in the six months to December 1998 were the United Kingdom, the United States and Australia. Together these markets were the destination for over 75 per cent of the New Zealand exports in the period. Shipments in the United Kingdom, the largest market for New Zealand wine, grew 24 per cent in volume and 57 per cent in value compared with the same period in 1997. White wine, particularly Sauvignon Blanc, Chardonnay and blends, dominated export shipments accounting for 79 per cent of exports (by volume) in the six-month period. Red wine and sparkling wine accounted for 11 per cent and 9 per cent of exports respectively (WINZ 1999).

Given only a moderate increase in wine consumption in the price sensitive domestic market in recent years, albeit increasingly quality-orientated, there is an obvious emphasis on wine exports throughout the industry at the national level. Current projections are for international sales to exceed NZ$150 million by 2002 (WINZ 1998a). At this level wine exports will represent over one third of the industry's total sales (WINZ 1998a) (also see Table 8.1). However, in 1997/98 international growth was restricted by product shortages experienced by some wineries (WINZ 1998a). For the past five years New Zealand wineries have sold everything they have produced (Beverland 1998). Export returns are driving the focus of many wineries towards building relationships with key distributors, and placing increasing focus on quality, production, and marketing. With the drive towards quality will come the reductions of yields per hectare, which will further decrease the amount of domestically-produced wine available for the export and domestic market unless new wineries and vineyards are developed.

Several challenges therefore exist in continuing the success in export growth. New Zealand's limited production ability will most likely always be an issue in a highly competitive environment. Even with the planned expansion of producing-vineyard area, the limited availability of suitable land will always position New Zealand as a small-scale player in international markets, representing approximately 2 per cent of wine sales worldwide. In addition, the weak currency also has a downside for the export industry as major inputs such as oak barrels, corks and machinery are all imported (WINZ 1998a).

In 1998 the New Zealand wine industry's share of the domestic wine market was 64 per cent. WINZ has indicated that a reduced supply from the

1997 vintage coupled with an increase in competition from imported wines curtailed domestic performance. Greater availability of wines from the 1998 vintage and the prospect of more expensive foreign wines following the weakening of the dollar suggest New Zealand's share of the domestic market will rise in 1998/99 (WINZ 1998a). However, the growth in the number of New Zealand wineries, tariff reductions and rising production in the New World, particularly from Australia, the United States and South America, foreshadow the development of extremely competitive market conditions. It is therefore within this context that wine tourism needs to be located.

Wine tourism in New Zealand

New Zealand currently has no national or regional wine tourism associations and relatively little integration appears to exist between the wine and tourism industries (Hall and Johnson 1997; Hall *et al.* 1997). Nevertheless, at the international level, there may be some potential in marketing through Tourism Marketing Networks (TMNs). The national tourism promotion organization, the New Zealand Tourism Board (NZTB) is supporting the development of Tourism Marketing Networks and describes the concept as the fundamental pillar of their new promotional strategy, which has significant potential for increasing New Zealand's foreign exchange earnings (NZTB 1998c 1998b). TMNs are cooperative international marketing efforts amongst tourism industry members, e.g. regional tourism organizations (RTOs), the NZTB and wineries. TMNs are industry driven and designed to make it easier for New Zealand to develop specialized markets by sharing information, identifying future goals and investment objectives, and communicating productively with NZTB (NZTB 1998a). The first wine tourism TMN meeting was held in February 1999, which included members from the NZTB and RTOs from New Zealand wine regions. Johnson (1998) argued for the development of a wine and tourism industry collaborative organization along the lines of some of the Australian initiatives (see Chapters 4 and 12). The timely creation of such an organization, as well as evolution of the Food and Wine TMN, may well provide the impetus for developing a national wine tourism strategy which concentrates on both the export and domestic markets. However, any such organization or network must be developed within the framework of both the wine and tourism industries as not only wine industry involvement, but also wine industry ownership, is necessary for it to succeed.

As has been noted by various authors, and elsewhere in this book, for smaller wineries welcoming visitors is an important way of introducing wines to a wider public, and the only way of becoming known, when production is so small and under-represented on retail shelves (Aplin 1999: 32). According to American research, the most profitable way to sell wine is through a tasting room (Kendziorek 1994a, b, c, d), while Aplin (1999: 32) adds that 'cellar-door sales for smaller wineries make up a significant part of a winery's income, and just as importantly, it is income that the winery can pocket in full; there is no one in the middle taking their cut'. There is a clear reduction in average revenue as the wine gets sold further from the winery due to increased selling and distribution costs, and greater competition in the wider market (Bigsby *et al.* 1998). In their study on the economic impacts of the Marlborough wine industry, Bigsby *et al.* (1998) found that cellar door sales generate the highest revenue per litre in comparison to other market outlets. However, the question has been raised that if wine tourism offers significant benefits to wineries, why have New Zealand wineries been so slow (or even reluctant) to commit resources in this area (Hall and Johnson 1997; 1998a; Beverland 1998; Beverland *et al.* 1998a)?

The answer to this is several-fold. First, there is the market context that wineries operate in and the related opportunity costs of committing scarce resources into cellar door facilities and network building (Beverland *et al.* 1998a). For example, in the Texan context, Dodd and Bigotte (1995) note that increasing focus on cellar door activity may take winery owners' time and money away from developing more traditional distribution channels and production expansion that may also lead to greater sales in the future. Nevertheless, even large-scale wineries may have wine tourism as a component of their promotion and sales mix. Second, many wineries may have a poor understanding of their customers and of the role that the cellar door plays in sales and creating positive customer relationships through being product focused as opposed to market focused (Hall and Johnson 1997; Hall *et al.* 1997). Third, and related to the second point, there is a poor research base from which an understanding of wine tourism and its relationship to broader sales issues may be developed. Without such a knowledge base it is extremely unlikely that wineries will come to embrace wine tourism as a component of their business strategies. Nevertheless, wine tourism is important in New Zealand at both a regional and an individual winery level.

At the regional level wine tourism is a significant component of tourism in a number of wine regions (Table 8.3) as well as being a major contributing factor in the creation of regional tourism images (Table 8.4). The economic impact is also significant. Johnson (1998) estimated that the aggregate contribution measured in terms of products and services sold at wineries was approximately NZ$127 million for 1997 (also see Hall and Johnson 1998a). In

Table 8.3 Wine tourism in New Zealand's wine regions 1997–98

Region	VICs consulted	Wine in generic guide	Regional winery guide	Winery or wine festival brochure	Wine trail	Wine tour companies	Wine festivals held in 1998
Northland	Kaitaia Paihia Whangarei	Y	N	Y	Y	0	1
Auckland	Auckland Kumeu Takapuna	Y	Y	Y	Y	7	5
Waikato/Bay of Plenty	Hamilton Tauranga	N	N	Y	N	1	5
Gisborne	Gisborne	Y	Y	Y	N	1	0
Hawke's Bay	Napier Hastings	Y	Y	Y	Y	6	1
Wellington	Masterton Wellington	Y	Y	Y	Y	6	1
Nelson	Nelson	Y	Y	Y	Y	2	1
Marlborough	Blenheim Wellington	Y	Y	Y	Y	7	2
Canterbury	Christchurch Hurunui Kaikoura	Y	Y	Y	Y	2	1
Otago	Dunedin Queenstown Wanaka	Y	Y	Y	Y	1	3

Source: Visitor Information Centre requests in wine regions, Campbell, 1997).

Note: Hokitika Wildfoods Festival is not included. Gisborne winery guide is a general tourist map that shows location of wineries.

VICs consulted   The Visitor Information Centres that responded to the information request.
Wine in generic guide   Information on wineries or the region's wines is included in the generic promotional brochure for the region.
Regional winery guide   A regional guide to wineries or winery location map is included.
Winery or wine festival brochure   Either the brochure of an individual winery, or the brochure of a local wine and food festival is included.
Wine trail   A regional wine trail is reported to exist (NB a winery location map alone is not taken to constitute a trail).
Wine tour companies   The number of companies providing tours of the region's wineries or vineyards.
1998 wine festivals   The number of wine and food festivals occurring in the region for 1998.

Table 8.4   Regional wine tourism brands, images and trails

Region	Brand/Images	Trail
Northland	–	Northland Wine Trail
Auckland	'Wild West Wine Coast'	Wine and cuisine (Waitakere) Wine Makers of West Auckland
Waikato/ Bay of Plenty	–	–
Gisborne	'Chardonnay Capital of New Zealand'. Images of vine rows	–
Hawke's Bay	'Hawke's Bay – The Wine Country'. Images of wine tourists	Hawke's Bay Vintners (guide)
Wellington	'Wine Country' 'Martinborough Wine Village'	Winemakers of Martinborough (guide)
Nelson	–	Winemakers of Nelson
Marlborough	'Marlborough – Wine Country' Images of vine rows	Marlborough Winemakers Wine Trail Guide The Wine and Wineries of Marlborough
Canterbury	–	Canterbury Wine Trail
Otago	'Wines of the Wakatipu' Images of vine rows (Wanaka)	Central Otago Vineyards –

Sources: Visitor Information Centre requests in wine regions, Campbell (1997); Hawkesbury (1997).

a survey of New Zealand wineries 75 per cent of the respondents to Johnson's survey described cellar door sales as being highly or extremely important to their business, representing approximately 20 per cent of the wineries' total sales. Cellar door sales were only second in importance behind other domestic wine sales in the composition of total winery sales (Johnson 1998). Johnson's survey represents the most comprehensive picture of wine tourism in New Zealand from a supply-side perspective. A broad overview of the results is given in Table 8.5.

Published literature on wine tourism in New Zealand is relatively scarce, with the majority of studies only being published in the late 1990s (Hall 1996; Hall *et al.* 1997; Hall and Johnson 1997, 1998a, 1998b; Johnson 1997; Hall and Macionis 1998; Beverland *et al.* 1998a, 1998b; Mitchell *et al.* 1999).

Table 8.5   Overview of results of New Zealand Wineries Survey

Winery operations

- Most producers are small, employing less than six full time staff.
- The estimated annual turnover at New Zealand wineries is NZ$127.1 million.
- Cellar door sales account for 20% of winery turnover and were available at 83% of wineries.
- 75% of respondents rate cellar door sales as very or extremely important.
- Opening times for wineries show a clear seasonal dip for the winter months when vines are dormant.
- Slightly over half of the respondents charge tasting fees, most commonly for groups at NZ$2.00 per head.
- Nearly all producers have wines available in local restaurants or retailers.
- Wine tasting is the most commonly offered service.
- Accommodation at wineries is scarce with only 7% of respondents offering any type of accommodation.

Wine producers' perceptions of their winery visitors

- Producers reported that visitors tended to be middle aged with an intermediate knowledge of wine.
- Tasting and buying wines were identified as the main reasons for visitation.
- There is no significant gender imbalance, but domestic visitors predominated at 81.9% (the remainder were international visitors).
- Nearly 60% of producers reported that they counted visitor numbers systematically, though many used only informal counting methods.
- The total number of all visits to all wineries in New Zealand for the year was estimated at over three million.

Tourism and marketing

- There was a lower frequency of alliances with tourism organizations than with wine or grape organizations.
- Producers identified personalized and friendly service as the most important aspect of their winery for attracting visitors.
- The quality of wine was rated the most important regional attribute.
- Word-of-mouth was rated the most important information source to attract visitors and mailing lists the most important medium.
- Wine trails and winery-based events were regarded as the two most successful regional tourism promotions.
- Producers valued time spent with their visitors.
- They felt that the wine industry had much to offer the tourism industry and that the tourism industry was important to the wine industry as a whole.
- The primary responsibility for the promotion of wine tourism is seen to rest with the wine industry.

Sources: Hall and Johnson, 1998a; Johnson, 1998

However, significant graduate wine tourism research includes dissertations by Reid (1990); Smith (1992); Austin (1993); Pratt (1994); Johnson (1997 1998); Longo (1999) and Mitchell (in progress). Moreover, the majority of New Zealand research has often been focused on wine industry perceptions of wine tourism rather than direct studies of consumers. Such a paucity of research may have substantial implications for industry understanding of wine tourism. For example, Scenario 2010 prepared by the Wine Institute of New Zealand and the New Zealand Grape Growers' Council for the New Zealand Ministry of Research, Science and Technology stated that 'Wine tourism will expand significantly, as will the hospitality industry (restaurants etc.) to which the industry is a prime supplier. The growth in wine tourism is likely to be dominated by international tourists as New Zealand wines penetrate a greater number of international markets and become more widely known to international consumers' (*New Zealand Wine Grower* 1999: 8). However, such a statement appears to be at odds with recent research on winery visitors which clearly demonstrates the dominance of the domestic visitor in wine tourism.

Understanding the winery visitor

The size of the winery visitor market is substantial. In 1997 the University of Otago conducted a travel lifestyles study of 1703 New Zealanders (Lawson *et al.* 1997). The percentage of New Zealanders reported having visited a winery during their most recent holiday of the last ten years was 17.7, with 18.5 per cent of respondents holidaying overseas and 17.4 per cent holidaying in New Zealand having visited a winery. These results compare with those from the New Zealand International Visitors' Survey 1995/96 which found 13 per cent of international visitors had either gone on a wine trail or visited a vineyard during their stay (New Zealand Tourism Board (NZTB) 1996). The New Zealand International Visitors' Survey 1992/93 found approximately 12 per cent of international visitors had participated in wine tasting (estimated from NZTB 1993). Unfortunately, the figures from the two surveys are not directly comparable as wording of the questions was changed from 'wine tasting' in 1992/93 to 'wine trail/visited vineyard' in 1995/96 (NZTB 1993: 94; 1996: 73). The question has been reworded for a third time in the international visitors' survey for December 1997, which presents difficulties for valid comparisons across time. In summary, publicly available data on wine-related tourism in New Zealand place it as a sizeable niche activity undertaken by approximately 17 per cent of domestic tourists and 13 per cent of international visitors.

It is difficult to quantify precisely the total number of visitors to wineries each year, as counting methods are not standardized or consistently applied at all wineries. Current methods appear to be biased toward wine purchasers rather than visitors and therefore may underestimate visit numbers. However, the results of Johnson's study (1998) suggest that a sizeable wine tourist market exists. Based upon responses from a survey of New Zealand wineries, Johnson estimated that there are approximately three million visits to wineries in New Zealand per year, of which 81 per cent are by domestic visitors and 19 per cent by international visitors. These visit numbers are only indicative as they were calculated based upon a selection of respondents to the survey question and respondents did not use consistent methods to count visits; as a result they are likely to be an underestimate of winery visitation (Longo 1999).

Three surveys have been directly undertaken of winery visitation in New Zealand (Beverland et al. 1998a, b; Longo 1999; Mitchell in progress). In April 1998 a cellar door survey was conducted at a selection of wineries in the West Auckland region by Beverland et al. (1998a, b). A profile of visitors to West Auckland was developed based upon a sample size of 150 participants. Visitors were described as well-educated professionals under the age of 55. The majority were domestic residents, with 80 per cent residing in Auckland, 12 per cent coming from outside Auckland and 8 per cent international visitors. The primary sources of winery information were word-of-mouth or personal knowledge. Many respondents were repeat visitors to the region and on average they planned to visit approximately three wineries a day. Eighty-six per cent indicated an interest or high interest in wine and 57 per cent described themselves as being knowledgeable or highly knowledgeable about wines (Beverland et al. 1998a, b).

However, one of the difficulties in studying visitor surveys is the extent to which the results in one region can be translated to other areas; given regional differences in infrastructure, accessibility and location in relation to major urban areas, caution also needs to be given to such issues as sample size, survey technique and representativeness. For example, in the case of the West Auckland survey the short distance to the Auckland urban area may produce substantially different demographic and psychographic profiles compared with wine regions which are further from major urban areas (Mitchell in progress) (see below). Similarly, in her research Longo (1999) reported that of the three areas she studied Marlborough had significantly more international visitors to wineries than Hawke's Bay or Waipara, with two thirds of her respondents coming from outside of the wine regions.

Longo (1999) studied winery visitors in three different regions through a series of in-depth personal interviews, with particular attention being given to issues of motivations and brand loyalty. In Longo's study (n=103) male and female participants were almost evenly divided. Seventy-seven per cent of visitors were between 25 and 54 years of age, the largest percentage (31 per cent) being in their thirties. There was almost an even split between participants who had children and those who did not. Of the respondents who had children, the majority of their children were over the age of 18. Approximately half (49 per cent) of the participants reported their household income as over NZ$80,000, followed by 14 per cent between $60,000 and $69,999. The highest percentage (21 per cent) for individual income was $40,000–49,999, closely followed by NZ$60,000–69,999 (17 per cent). These figures indicate that winery visitors were higher than average income earners by New Zealand standards. Sixty per cent of participants had a university or postgraduate degree, with 18 per cent having attended some university. In terms of occupation 30 per cent of respondents were professionals (25 per cent) and administrators / legislators / managers (5 per cent). Another 18 per cent were self employed, 11 per cent retired, and 10 per cent working in sales and services.

Mitchell (in progress) has broadened the study of wine tourists in New Zealand to provide the first attempt to gather a nationwide sample of winery visitors. The *1999 New Zealand Winery Visitors' Survey* is a two-stage survey that gathers data on the winery visitor, their experiences and their on-site and regional travel behaviour (Mitchell, in progress), with a follow-up survey of the same sample to determine actual post-visit behaviour and reminiscence. A preliminary analysis of interim data (621 of a sample of 1104 gathered in the first stage of the study) from four of New Zealand's ten wine regions (Auckland, Wairarapa, Marlborough and Central Otago) provides us with a summary of the demographics of the regional winery visitor, their trip characteristics and intended future purchasing behaviour.

Table 8.6 illustrates that the demographic profiles for the four regions are relatively similar and that they confirm several of the characteristics found by both Beverland *et al.* (1998a, b) and Longo (1999). Once again, the gender balance was relatively even and visitors were generally well educated (around 50 to 60 per cent with some university education); high income earners (60–75 per cent earning more than NZ$40,000); aged between 30 and 60 (with the exception of Wairarapa visitors, where 30 per cent were between 18 and 24) and dominated by professionals (with at least half being professionals) or retired professionals (with at least 70 per cent of retirees stating their career as professional).

Table 8.6   Demographic profile and trip characteristics of New Zealand winery visitors

Demographic trip characteristics		Auckland (n = 104)	Central Otago (n = 334)	Marl-borough (n = 118)	Wai-rarapa (n = 65)	Mean (4 regions) (n = 621)
Gender	Male	56.3	52.3	46.6	46.2	50.8
	Female	43.7	47.7	53.4	53.8	49.2
Age	18–29	17.3	15.3	12.1	30.8	16.7
	30–39	33.6	26.7	29.3	32.3	28.9
	40–49	30.7	21.9	27.6	10.8	23.3
	50–59	10.6	23.7	19.0	20.0	20.2
	60+	7.6	11.4	12.0	6.1	10.3
Income	Less than 20,000	7.1	13.0	7.9	6.3	10.3
(NZ$)	20,000–29,999	11.1	7.4	1.5	9.4	8.8
	30,000–39,999	13.1	16.4	16.7	17.2	16.0
	40,000–49,999	23.2	15.7	14.0	18.8	17.0
	50,000–59,999	15.2	13.3	11.4	9.4	12.8
	60,000–69,999	8.1	4.9	7.9	7.8	6.3
	70,000–79,999	7.1	4.3	8.8	3.1	5.5
	80,000+	15.2	21.6	21.1	26.6	21.0
Occupation	Professionals	59.2	63.1	55.2	70.8	61.7
	Other	24.3	16.9	27.6	16.9	20.2
	Retired*	6.8	15.1	12.9	3.1	12.0
	Student	2.9	1.8	0.9	1.5	1.8
	Self-employed	2.9	0	0.9	1.5	0.8
	Home maker	1.9	2.5	0.9	4.6	2.3
	Unemployed	1.9	0.3	0	0	0.5
Education	High school	21.0	18.9	1.3	12.5	16.9
	Trade/polytechnic	23.0	17.1	22.4	17.2	19.1
	Some university	17.0	15.5	2.7	1.9	16.3
	Undergraduate	13.0	13.1	12.1	20.3	13.7
	Graduate degree	26.0	35.4	33.6	39.1	33.9
Place of	Auckland	70.2	10.2	15.4	6.2	20.8
residence	Wellington	4.8	3.6	12.0	50.8	10.3
	Christchurch	2.9	11.7	23.1	6.2	11.8
	Dunedin	0	17.1	0.9	0	9.4
Nights in	Live in region	73.9	16.4	9.9	13.3	24.4
region	Day trip	2.2	3.9	12.9	51.7	10.4
	1 or 2 nights	4.3	16.4	21.8	25.0	16.3
	3 or 4 nights	8.7	29.6	36.6	10.0	25.3
	5 or 6 nights	0	13.8	9.9	0	9.3
	1 to 2 weeks	9.8	19.4	6.9	0	13.5
	More than 2 weeks	1.1	0.3	2.0	0	0.7

Source: Mitchell (in progress), interim results only.

Note:* 76.7, 72.3, 78.5, 100 and 75.7 per cent, respectively, of retirees in each sample were retired professionals.

While the demographic characteristics of each region were relatively similar, clear differences exist in the nature of the visit to the wine region. Two indicators of this are the origin of the visitor and the length of their stay in the wine region. Table 8.6 identifies clear differences in both the origin and length of stay. The origin of visitors and length of stay in the wine region appear to be reflective of the region's proximity to major urban populations and, closely related to this, the nature of the destination. Auckland wineries, for example, were dominated by day visitors (70.2 per cent) from Auckland (73.9 per cent) (see also Beverland *et al.* 1998a, b), a number of which appeared to be treating the winery as simply another wine outlet (Mitchell, in progress). Wairarapa visitors also were largely day visitors (51.7 per cent), but were from outside the region (50.8 per cent from Wellington, 1.5–2 hours from the Wairarapa region). The Wairarapa region is also recognized as a weekend destination, which is reflected in an average stay of 2.19 nights for those who did stay overnight (Mitchell, in progress). Visitors to Marlborough and Central Otago wineries came from origins both within and outside the region, reflecting their small local populations, distance from major urban centres and resort status (domestic and international, respectively). Visitors to these regions were also more likely to stay overnight (around 80 per cent) and for longer periods, with average stays of 4.53 nights for Marlborough and 4.78 for Central Otago (Mitchell, in progress).

These differing trip characteristics (along with the differing characteristics of the wine industry within each region) need to be recognized when making inferences that relate to the New Zealand winery visitor. Different trip characteristics, for example, may lead to differences in motivation, the experience of the winery and purchasing behaviour. What may hold true for one region (or winery for that matter) may not necessarily be true for the others.

Using information from Mitchell's study, the next section examines some of the intended purchasing behaviour for New Zealand winery visitors, noting some of the regional differences and postulating reasons for this. The remaining sections review some of Longo's results (1999) in terms of sources of information of winery visitors, their motivations, and their purchasing relationships to the winery at which the interview took place.

Intended future purchasing behaviour

In the previous section we have noted that there are some differences in the nature of the trips that winery visitors make to wine regions. An examination of figures from these four New Zealand regions suggests that there may also

165

be some significant differences in the purchasing behaviour of these visitors.

Using a 5-point Likert scale of intended behaviour (1 being no intention, 3 being some intention and 5 being strong intention), Mitchell (in progress) asked winery visitors their intention to visit this and other wineries within and outside the region and to purchase wine from this or other wineries from the region. Across all regions there was a relatively strong intention for repeat visitation to the winery surveyed and others within and outside the region (with the exception of visiting the surveyed winery and wineries outside the region on the current trip). While intended purchases of wine (both from the winery surveyed and others in the region) from restaurants and wine shops were only moderate, no significant difference could be identified between the regional means (Table 8.7).

In most instances there was no significant difference in the regional mean scores; however, three means did differ: intention to visit another winery in the region; intention to purchase wine from this winery by mail order, and intention to purchase wine from another winery in this region. The first difference might be explained by the nature of the visit to the wine region. Lesser intentions for visits to another winery in Auckland, for example, tend to reflect the close proximity to the urban area and the short duration of the trip, while stronger intentions in Marlborough and Wairarapa reflect both the longer duration of the trip, short distances between clusters of wineries and the well-established wine trail infrastructures. Visits to Central Otago, while longer in duration, are less likely to result in a visit to another winery, which may be the result of a relatively new wine industry, long distances between wineries and an underdeveloped trail.

Significant regional differences in intention to purchase wine by mail order (see Table 8.7), on the other hand, might be reflective of the nature of distribution channels (or at least perceptions of these) available for wineries in each region. In particular, and perhaps not surprisingly, visitors to Auckland wineries were less likely to need to use mail order as they are able to purchase easily either directly from the winery (evidenced by 45.7 per cent visiting more than once per year compared with only 12.5 per cent visiting in Central Otago) or at other retail outlets. Visitors to Central Otago and Marlborough wineries, on the other hand, are less able to visit the winery or wine region, may not be aware of the availability of the wine in their home town and see mail order as the logical alternative.

This brief analysis of the interim results from Mitchell (in progress) provides us with a useful reminder of the need to recognize that, while visitor

Table 8.7 Intended future purchasing behaviour of winery visitors

Intended behaviour	Auckland (n = 104)	Central Otago (n = 334)	Marlborough (n = 118)	Wairarapa (n = 65)	Mean 4 regions (n = 621)
Visit this winery again (this trip)	1.56	1.51	1.65	1.22	1.52
Visit this winery again (another trip)	3.95	4.00	3.92	3.64	3.94
Visit another winery (this trip)*	3.03	3.55	4.08	4.11	3.65
Visit another winery (another trip)	3.99	4.08	4.40	4.13	4.14
Visit wineries outside region (this trip)	1.65	2.07	2.04	1.88	1.98
Visit wineries outside region (another trip)	3.96	4.10	4.20	4.25	4.12
Purchase winery's wine at a restaurant	3.26	3.17	3.31	3.09	3.20
Purchase winery's wine at a wine shop	3.23	3.28	3.4	3.13	3.28
Purchase winery's wine from mail order †	1.57	2.15	2.06	1.78	1.99
Purchase region's wine at a restaurant	3.30	3.38	3.76	3.49	3.45
Purchase region's wine at a wine shop	3.20	3.30	3.48	3.42	3.33
Purchase region's wine by mail order ‡	1.79	2.09	2.46	2.19	2.12

Source: Mitchell (in progress)

Notes: Mean score on the basis of a 5-point Likert scale (1 = no intention, 3 = some intention and 5 = strong intention). 'Don't knows' were excluded from the analysis.

* A significant difference (p<0.05) exists between the mean scores of Auckland and Marlborough, Auckland and Wairarapa and Marlborough and Central Otago.
† A significant difference (p<0.05) exists between the mean scores of Auckland and Central Otago.
‡ A significant difference (p<0.05) exists between the mean scores of Auckland and Marlborough.

profiles might be similar across several regions, a number of other variables may influence consumer behaviour. As a result, studies of wine tourists based on regional samples (e.g. Reid 1990; Austin 1993; Beverland *et al.* 1998a, b), although useful in their own right, should only be used to generalize at a national or international level with substantial caution. Further analysis of the data gathered by Mitchell (along with a qualitative analysis of in excess of 100 interviews and the follow-up survey) may reveal further regional differences that will shed light on the nature of influence of both the on-site winery and regional experience in winery visitor behaviour. The next sections review some of Longo's results in terms of sources of information of winery visitors, their motivations, and their purchasing relationships to the winery at which the interview took place.

Source of information

Visiting wineries serves an important educational purpose in improving the level of wine knowledge of consumers. Maddern and Golledge (1996) segmented Victorian winery visitors into three wine knowledge categories: advanced, intermediate and basic. Johnson's survey (1998) contained a similar question asking winery owners/managers to indicate which categories best described the majority of their visitors. The groupings were wine lovers (advanced knowledge), wine interested (intermediate knowledge) and curious tourists (basic or no knowledge of wine) (Hall 1996). Visitors to the wineries in Longo's survey were asked to describe their current knowledge of wines. Four response categories were adapted from Maddern and Golledge (1996) and Hall (1996) and were defined as follows:

- advanced – international knowledge of wines, have completed wine courses;
- intermediate – know different wine styles and can identify most of them;
- basic – know the names of most wine styles, but cannot identify differences;
- no prior knowledge of wine.

Ninety per cent of visitors expressed that they had a basic (39 per cent) or intermediate (51 per cent) knowledge of wine and only 9 per cent considered themselves as advanced. These are consistent with profiles of visitors to Victorian wineries which reported 55 per cent with intermediate knowledge, 41 per cent with basic knowledge and 4 per cent with advanced knowledge (Maddern and Golledge 1996). Similarly, most winery owners/managers in Johnson's survey (1998) felt that wine interested (intermediate knowledge) formed the majority of winery visitors, followed by curious tourists (basic or no knowledge of wine). In terms of the development of that knowledge several sources were identified. According to respondents, word-of-mouth was perceived as by far the most important source in attracting visitors (41 per cent of all respondents). Previous visits to the winery were also important and were cited by 21 per cent of respondents as the major source of information. Brochures were used by 14 per cent, while 5 per cent of visitors' decision-making process was influenced by wine reviews and road signs, respectively. The remaining 14 per cent, classified as 'other' sources of information, consisted of wine clubs, newspaper articles, visitor information centre, guidebooks and previous knowledge of wine, each individually representing 2.8 per cent. These categories may be further subdivided into proactive and passive promotional efforts by wineries. The proactive promotions would include advertisements of both visitor amenities and wine products. These consist of brochures, visitor information centres, guidebooks, road signs, wine clubs, wine reviews, and newspaper articles. While proactive promotions, aggregating 35.2 per cent, played an important role in informing and influencing visitors, it was previous exposure to the wine, winery or someone who had shared a positive experience that overwhelmingly influenced 64.8 per cent of visitors' choice. It should also be noted that certain proactive promotions, such as wine reviews or visitor information centres, may also eventuate into positive word-of-mouth advertising (Longo 1999).

Figure 8.3 Signage for Chard Farm Winery, Central Otago, New Zealand.

Visiting wineries

Friendly service was rated as the most important attribute in selecting a winery to visit (mean = 1.24). This attribute was selected as extremely important or very important by 98 per cent of respondents (Table 8.8). The significance of friendly service was also expressed in candid post-visit comments. There were instances where visitors noted that the service received in the cellar shop influenced not only their impression of the winery and its product, but also directly affected their on-site purchasing behaviour and overall experience. These remarks were expressed in both positive and negative contexts. Interestingly, winery owners/managers shared the same view as visitors; in Johnson's survey (1998), personalized and friendly service was rated as the most important attribute of their winery in attracting visitors.

Table 8.8   Importance of attributes when selecting a winery to visit

Attribute	Mean score*
Wine tasting – free of charge	1.88
Nominal cost of wine tasting	3.41
Winery/vineyard tour	3.37
Wine-making demonstrations	3.52
Meeting the wine-maker	3.42
Wine sales	1.62
Retail price of wines	2.30
Type of wines produced	2.20
Historical displays	3.71
Picnic/BBQ area	2.95
Restaurant	2.41
Conference/function facility	4.38
Accommodation	4.39
Children's playground	4.06
Live entertainment	3.63
Petanque/other games	3.60
Wheelchair access	3.33
Friendly service	1.24
Scenery	2.20
Convenient/accessible location	2.60
Region of origin of grapes	2.98
Previous experience/visit	3.05

Source: Longo 1999

* The mean score is from a Likert importance rating scale of 1 = extremely important, 2 = very important, 3 = somewhat important, 4 = not very important, 5 = not at all important. n = 103

Having wine available for sale was the second most important attribute (mean = 1.62), followed by gratis wine tastings (mean = 1.88). Perhaps not surprisingly, 87.2 per cent of visitors (mean = 1.42) responded that they would definitely or were highly likely to participate in wine tasting at the winery in question that day. Conference and function facilities and having accommodation available were rated as the least important attributes (means = 4.38 and 4.39, respectively) when selecting a winery to visit.

Purchasing wine (54 per cent) and having lunch or dinner (51 per cent) were also definite or highly likely activities for participants (means = 2.5 and 2.65, respectively) (Table 8.9). Another 30 per cent and 12 per cent, respectively, stated that these activities were possible during their visit that day. These scores indicate that over half of the winery visitors had the intention of making purchases at the cellar door during their visit. This is an interesting finding, because, as noted above, cellar door wine sales can be an important contributor to a winery's overall financial performance. In Johnson's study (1998), 75 per cent of winery owners/managers rated cellar door sales as extremely or very important to their business.

There was less interest by respondents in adding their name to the mailing list (mean = 3.85), taking a winery/vineyard tour (mean = 4.11), and purchasing winery-branded material (mean = 4.19). There is potential that these activities may become more likely if visitors encounter a positive experience during their winery visit and wish to enter a more long-term relationship with the winery, learn more about the wine-making process, or purchase memorabilia from their visit (Longo 1999; Mitchell in progress).

Table 8.9 Likely activities at this winery today

Activity	Mean score*
Purchase winery branded material	4.19
Have lunch/dinner	2.65
Purchase wine	2.5
Add name to mailing list	3.85
Winery/vineyard tour	4.11
Wine tasting	1.42

Source: Longo 1999

Notes: n = 101

* The mean score is from a Likert likelihood rating scale of: 1 = definitely, 2 = highly likely, 3 = possibly, 4 = highly unlikely, 5 = definitely not.

Figure 8.4 The development of tasting and winery facilities at Olssen's Winery, Central Otago, New Zealand.

Figure 8.5 Wine tasting and purchasing, Olssen's Winery, Central Otago, New Zealand.

Some 40.8 per cent of respondents had previously visited the winery in question. Of these 29.4 per cent had visited between two and five times previously with 20.6 per cent on more than five previous occasions, suggesting a high degree of brand loyalty and customer satisfaction. Over half, 53.5 per cent, of visitors had previously purchased the wine produced by the winery where the survey was completed. Of these, wine shops, at 51.1 per cent, were the most popular location for previous purchases of this wine. This was followed by the cellar outlet, selected by 38.3 per cent, which indicates a good percentage of repeat visitors to the winery. Supermarkets, which in recent years have become an important distribution outlet for wines in New Zealand, were chosen by 31.9 per cent of participants, while 23.4 per cent had purchased from a restaurant or café. Very few visitors, 4.2 per cent, had previously purchased wine from the winery through mail order or at a pub/tavern/wine bar.

Eighty per cent of visitors who had made a previous purchase of the wine in question also had at least one previous visit to the winery. This emphasizes the importance of having a cellar door shop available for visitors at small wineries, especially since on-site wine sales often yield a higher margin than other means of wine distribution. Sixty-five per cent of participants reported that after their winery visit that day, the likelihood of future purchases of the wine in question was definite or highly likely. Only 2 per cent stated they would be unlikely to purchase that wine in the future and there were no respondents who felt they would definitely not make future purchases of that wine. The 33 per cent of possible participants may have expressed some uncertainty as the survey was completed before their actual winery visit. The significant percentage of at least highly likely future purchases suggests the potential for developing brand-loyal wine consumers through cellar door visits.

As Table 8.10 indicates, wine tourism is an extremely important source of knowledge regarding wine, clearly being more significant than formal wine education or appreciation programmes and information provided by the media. Although further research is required the educative function of winery visits may well play a major role in improving the market's understanding of wine and lead to changes in the purchasing patterns of consumers in terms of quality and quantity of wine purchased. In addition, although the sample size is relatively small, the results do provide some preliminary evidence suggesting potential brand loyalty. Eighty-eight per cent of visitors who had previously visited the winery expressed the opinion that they would definitely or were highly likely to make future purchases of that wine. This indicates the possibility of a continuing post-visit relationship between the winery and

Table 8.10 Development of wine knowledge

Source	%
Radio/TV programmes	6.2
Formal wine education	8.2
Not applicable	12.4
Other	17.5
Wine appreciation course	18.6
Books/magazines	35.1
Friends/family	45.5
Previous wine tour/winery visit	52.6

Source: Longo 1999

Note: The percentages do not total 100% because this was a multiple response question with 190 responses received from 97 participants.

these consumers, a point taken up in the most comprehensive survey of wine tourism in New Zealand, undertaken by Mitchell, which provides a basis for comparisons of wine tourism on a national level.

Conclusion

Much of the research outlined above demonstrates that, at least in terms of demographics, New Zealand winery visitors do not differ from those in other parts of the world. However, a closer examination of some of the psychographic and lifestyle characteristics of the New Zealand winery visitor not only reveals some differences between New Zealand and other countries but also some distinct regional differences. Recognizing these differences will hopefully allow New Zealand's wine regions to draw upon their unique regional characteristics to develop wine tourism strategies that reflect the needs of the region's wineries and the demands of their visitors.

Despite scepticism from some sectors of the New Zealand wine industry (e.g. see Hall and Johnson 1997; Beverland 1998), there is also increasing recognition of the importance of winery visitation in the development of strong brands and loyal markets for many New Zealand wineries. Continuing research in this area will assist the wine industry to overcome some of this scepticism and to develop a strong and fruitful relationship with the, already strongly branded, New Zealand tourism industry.

9

Wine tourism in the United Kingdom

Michael Howley and Jetske Van Westering

The United Kingdom has a long viticultural history stretching back to the Roman invasion of AD 43, although firm evidence of growing vines does not exist until the end of the third century (Skelton 1989). The spread of Christianity gave English wine-making an impetus as many monasteries produced wine from their own vineyards, and by the time of the compilation of the Domesday Book in 1086 forty vineyards were noted to be in existence. Viticulture does not seem to have thrived in medieval England, however, with factors such as the dissolution of the monasteries by Henry VIII and also the Black Death (1348–70), which killed off many of the estate workers, contributing to a steady decline of viticultural enterprise (Howley and Van Westering 1999).

It was not until the UK joined the Common Market of the European Union (EU) in the 1970s that there was any substantial increase in the UK wine industry (Table 9.1 indicates the growth in

Table 9.1   UK wine production 1964–97

Year	Bottles produced
1964	1 500
1971	30 000
1975	60 000
1976	200 000
1978	500 000
1981	250 000
1983	2 000 000
1985	870 000
1986	1 250 000
1992	3 500 000
1995	1 978 664
1997	869 761

Source: Ministry of Agriculture, Fisheries and Food in
http://sol.brunel.ac.uk/~richards/wine/britain.htm

Table 9.2   Number of vineyards and area under vine in 1997

Area	Counties	Number of vineyards	Ha
Northern	Cheshire, Cleveland	0	0
N. East and N. Mercia	Durham, Shropshire, W. Yorks, Staffs	6	16.7
South Mercia	Glos, Hereford, Warwicks	25	55
East Midlands	Derby, Leics, Lincs, Northants, Notts	6	3.28
Anglia	Beds, Cambs, Essex, Herts, Norfolk, Suffolk	63	128.2
Wessex	Avon, Somerset, Dorset, Wilts	51	55.58
South West	Cornwall, Devon	41	49.8
Central South East	Berks, Bucks, Oxfordshire	25	49.86
Hampshire Basin	Hampshire, Isle of Wight	37	102
South East	Sussex, Kent, Surrey	116	417.29
Wales	Dyfed, Gwent, South Glamorgan	16	22.93
Total		386	900.64

Source: Ministry of Agriculture, Fisheries and Food in
http://sol.brunel.ac.uk/~richards/wine/britain.htm

Table 9.3   Wineries and production figures by region 1995 and 1997

Area	Number of wineries		Production (hectolitres)	
	1995	*1997*	*1995*	*1997*
Mercia	8	8	1 406	1 588
Anglia	16	15	2 060	938
Wessex	17	17	792	391
South West	19	14	424	170
South East	51	53	8 182	2 256
Wales	4	4	175	65

Sources: Ministry of Agriculture, Fisheries and Food in
http://sol.brunel.ac.uk/~richards/wine/britain.htm

bottle output from 1964 to 1997). Ministry of Agriculture surveys report that in 1975, 1984 and 1988 there were 196 ha, 430 ha, and 546 ha respectively of vineyards in the UK. The early 1990s saw further significant growth in the UK wine industry. According to the UK Vineyards Association, in 1996 there were some 413 vineyards in the UK, totalling around 965 ha of vines (Anon. 1996). However, there was a drop in 1997 with the figure falling to 386 vineyards and 900.64 ha of vines (Table 9.2) as vineyards were abandoned. Table 9.3 details the number of vineyards and area under vine for some of the individual regions for 1995 and 1997 (see Exhibit 9.1).

Exhibit 9.1: Is there a future for UK wine?

An article appeared in the UK *Sunday Telegraph* on 7 February 1999 entitled 'England's wine hopes wither on the vine' (Jackson 1999). In it, the writer examined two of the big vineyards in the south of England, Barkham Manor and St George's, which are closing because their elderly owners, like many who started in the early 1970s, are retiring. The writer concluded that such closures meant that the English vineyard industry was dying. Is this a valid viewpoint?

Of a sample 120 vineyards examined:

- five now only produce grapes;
- ten have closed through retirement of owners;

- five have closed for other reasons;
- eight new vineyards have opened;
- seven have changed ownership

This suggests an industry in a normal state of change. In southeast England profitability has decreased as a result of fierce competition from larger low-tax continental vineyards. However, as the examples outlined below show, in areas such as the Welsh Marches vineyards appear to be thriving.

Near Bromyard, the owner of the new 1.6 ha Frome Valley Vineyard has invested in a shop, a model vineyard to demonstrate training methods and extensive tourist-brochure advertising. Three Choirs vineyard make his wine so investment has been saved. He is confident in the strength of the tourist market.

At Bartestree near Hereford, the 2.4 ha Hagley Court (also a Three Choirs customer) has also recently invested in a new shop and café. Publicity leaflets are in all the local tourist centres and a popular monthly dinner in the café ensures local as well as tourist trade.

Three Choirs at Newent is one of the largest vineyards in Britain (26.3 ha) and one of the most visited tourist sites in the area. Investments include a smart and highly regarded restaurant, new winery, increased plantings and an Internet site (www.three-choirs-vineyard.co.uk).

They provide a contract wine-making service for nearly 20 vineyards and their own wines are sold in most supermarkets and served by British Airways. Publicity stunts included an 'Anglais Nouveau' race to Paris involving plane, train and veteran car – widely featured in national newspapers (Greaves 1996).

In order for small industries to survive, they must identify a niche in the market and create an image.

The larger producers, Denbies, Chapel Down and Three Choirs, are helping to create this image by selling large quantities of standard competitively-priced wines through the supermarkets. They are also gaining income by investing in large-scale tourist facilities selling more expensive wines from varieties that are rarer in Britain – Pinot Noir, Chardonnay and Cabernet Sauvignon.

The smaller vineyards can benefit from this image. Many save investment by having their wine made by the larger producers and can therefore concentrate on serving the local and tourist market. Some have developed successful mail-order businesses.

A third part of the 'image-jigsaw' is filled by internationally regarded producers, the best example of which is the Sussex-based Nyetimber Vineyard of Stuart and Sandy Moss. They have 20 ha of Pinot Noir, Pinot Meunier and Chardonnay on soils identical to those of Champagne. Their 1992 and 1993 sparkling wines have won International gold medals and sell in prestigious stores and by mail order (White 1999).

While the closure of a few vineyards may suggest decline, closer examination of the evidence suggests that the three sections are successfully working together to build an identity that should survive into the twenty-first century.

Oliver Richardson

Despite real growth in recent decades, the English and Welsh wine industry is characterized by its small scale. In 1996, only 20 of the 413 UK vineyards were larger than 4 ha (with the average size being around 1 ha) (Anon. 1996). In addition, Denbies in Surrey, the UK's largest vineyard, accounts for an estimated 10 per cent of all English wine production (see Exhibit 9.2).

With one or two exceptions, the amounts produced per vineyard do not permit any economies of size and, consequently, English wine is often a relatively expensive commodity. Even in the domestic market, it cannot compete on price with the wines of other countries with better climates and where larger vineyards dominate. In the context of overall industry development, it would appear that English wine can only be sold successfully on the basis of quality, image and, possibly, the novelty of its country of origin rather than price. In the past neither quality nor image have been good (Simon 1996). However, similar to other developing wine regions and countries (see Chapters 8, 12 and 13) wine tourism represents an opportunity for the UK wine industry to develop a quality image and emphasize the novelty of its appellation. In addition, approximately 65 per cent of all UK produced wine is sold via the 'farm gate' (Anon. 1996) providing wine producers with an increased profit margin and cash flow.

This chapter provides an overview of wine tourism in the UK. First, it examines some aspects of the UK wine market and discusses factors that have contributed to a growing interest in wine and wine tourism in the UK. It then examines wine tourism marketing in the UK and notes several wine tourism developmental issues. Finally, via several brief case studies, it examines the wine tourism strategies of three UK wine businesses.

The UK wine market

In contrast to traditional European wine-producing countries, the consumption of wine in the United Kingdom is increasing. Statistics (Anon. 1998a: 18) show that the percentage increase in wine consumption in the UK since 1970 is almost 400 per cent. In 1970 almost 3 litres of wine was drunk per capita; this increased to over 13 litres per capita in 1997, with the change in consumption of wine between 1996 and 1997 being 9.3 per cent. Despite such figures, wine consumption in the UK is still far behind that of traditional wine-producing countries such as Portugal, France, Italy, Greece and Spain (Anon 1998a: 17) (see Chapter 2). In the UK, wine is sold to all age groups over 18 (but mainly to those over 25), predominantly (86 per cent) of the higher socio-economic strata (AB and C1) and mainly in the London area (Public Drinks Market Survey 1997 in Anon. 1999: 105, 96).

Figure 9.1   Drink English Wine.

The tastes and preferences of UK wine drinkers are gregarious, with exports from all major New World, as well as traditional countries, except for Germany, rising. Although UK-produced wine accounts for only 0.3 per cent of all wine consumed (Anon. 1996: 14) its growing presence and reputation can be evidenced by the fact that most major supermarkets now stock several UK-produced wines on their shelves.

In recent years the quality of UK wines has undoubtedly improved. One factor contributing to this has been the 'importation' of wine-makers from established wine regions. For example, Keith Brown who was, for a time, in charge of production at Denbies, one of England's largest wineries (see Exhibit 9.2), is a graduate of Roseworthy College in Australia. There has also been a pronounced change in the production of wine styles by UK wine-makers, from Germanic to French or New World. As a consequence of extreme (for successful viticulture) northerly latitudes English vineyard owners had, historically, drawn upon the German experience with regard to grape varieties and wine-making practices. With greater experience and confidence in the industry, growers are moving away from German practices, such as the use of sweet reserve to soften the high acidity levels, and from German varieties, such as Muller-Thurgau and Reichensteiner in favour of essentially French varieties like Pinot Gris and Auxerrois.

Exhibit 9.2: Denbies Wine Estate

Denbies Estate is located in the south-east of England, close to the capital city of London, and on the North Downs, an area of chalky ridges with a soil structure similar to that of the Champagne area of France. The vines are planted in an ideal position, on south-facing slopes to attract the maximum amount of sunlight, and in a sheltered valley, allowing protection from the westerly winds.

Denbies is England's largest wine estate, producing around 400,000 bottles per annum from 265 acres of vineyards (Denbies Wine Estate 1999a, b). The remainder of the 635 acres of Denbies Estate comprises 250 acres of woodland and 125 acres of pasture land used for deer and sheep. Part of the estate has been designated an SSSI (Site of Special Scientific Interest), and, as such, is governed by strict planning permission. The Denbies management team stress that they are keen to function as an organization that is environmentally conscious and one that seeks to preserve the nature of its historic landscape.

A range of ten wines is available from the Denbies 1999 wine list, primarily white, but also featuring some red and sparkling wines. A wide range of grape types are cultivated at Denbies (18 in total) from well-known varieties such as Chardonnay and Pinot Blanc to the less well known Dornfelder, Optima and Ortega. About 30 per cent of the total wine production is retailed through supermarkets, 35 per cent sold from the Visitor Centre and the rest supplied to restaurants, off-licences and to organizations wishing to publicize English produce, such as embassies and wine associations.

Denbies is, however, not just a producer. It was the first wine estate in England to offer visitors an insight into all aspects of wine production in an innovative and novel way. Denbies market their attraction as 'The Ultimate Wine Experience', and, on arrival, visitors are given the opportunity to see two films in the audio-visual theatre. The first shows wine-making through the seasons, and the second is a 3-D lapse film which shows the growth of the vine from 'budburst' to picking in just four minutes. Visitors are then transported around the winery in an indoor 'people-mover' train which provides a commentary, in four languages, about the different stages of wine production. The tour ends with a wine tasting in the Denbies cellars, assisted by an expert guide.

Other facilities on the site include a Conservatory Restaurant which is open daily, a well-equipped conference suite which can seat up to 100 guests for a banquet, and a well-stocked wine and gift shop. A cloistered garden contains 18 planted vines, an illustration of the different varieties used in Denbies wine-making, but visitors can also see the expanse of the Denbies vineyards by walking part of the 7 miles of vineyard trails accessible to the public. The vineyard is open throughout the year and charges £5.50 entrance fee for adults and £2.50 for children (1999 rates). Discounts are available for senior citizens, students and organized groups.

Denbies employ approximately 80 staff during the winter months but this rises to 110 staff during the summer season. A comprehensive induction and training programme is in place for all their employees.

A range of different promotional tools is used to market the vineyard, including stands at trade fairs, promotional offers in regional papers and brochure distribution in local tourist offices and hotels. A loyalty card offers discounts for visitors who use the centre regularly. An ongoing research programme regularly collects market information through customer questionnaires handed out at the centre, and specific research carried out in supermarkets and town centres. The centre was awarded the English Tourist Board Visitor Attraction of the Year Award in 1994.

Liz Sharples

A third significant change is that a gap is emerging in both quality and marketing presence between the few large producers and small and medium-sized vineyards. In the view of experts there is a tendency developing for the latter to limit themselves to being grape-growers and suppliers rather than individual names (Taylor 1999).

The nature of the UK vineyard operation is also changing with wine production seen and undertaken more as a commercial operation, whereas in the past it was often characterized as enterprises operated by retired professional people as a hobby. Industry affairs are coordinated by a national body, the UK Vineyards Association, which involves itself largely in legal and political activities; organizations such as English Wine Producers, a marketing consortium that brings together four of the major UK vineyards; and a series of regional organizations, such as the South-East Vineyards Association. The problem with the latter bodies is that not all the members are equally commercially minded and, like other organizations where a large number of individuals have a say, they seem to lack a concerted marketing effort. The UK industry now even has its own tertiary wine education and training programmes at Plumpton College near Lewes in East Sussex. The College offers a number of academic courses in Wine Studies and has its own vineyard of six acres in which students can learn the practicalities of viticulture and oenology.

Wine tourism marketing in the UK

Wine tourism in the UK is still in its infancy – as such there is a general lack of information and documentation regarding UK wine tourism. For example, visitor numbers are generally not recorded (except by some of the larger wineries), and as yet no profile of visitors to UK wineries has been developed. As a consequence, UK wine tourism marketing could be considered somewhat ad hoc and 'hit-or-miss'. Despite this, several initiatives have been undertaken to promote wine tourism, especially in the south-east of England where the majority of vineyards are located. Visiting wineries and vineyards is, however, often not the primary focus of these activities. Most of these initiatives, for example *Best Places to Visit in Kent*, pair visits to vineyards with other activities such as visits to manor houses and castles, gardens and farms. Hampering the efforts to develop a wine tourism image is the fact that UK wines or vineyards are not marketed overseas, and, according to the English Tourist Board (ETB), no plans to do so currently exist (ETB, pers. comm. 1999).

Wine tourism per se is also not marketed nationally. Efforts by the South-East England Tourist Board (SEETB) to jointly promote vineyards as part of a wine route have been relatively unsuccessful so far. For example, the brochure *Vineyards of the South-East* published in 1996 has been only marginally successful due to lack of consumer interest. However, there is still signage in place which promotes wineries and wine routes.

Other UK initiatives have focused on the promotion of regional produce more than tourism. For example, vineyards in Sussex and Surrey can join 'A Taste of the South-East', a regional association of speciality food and drink producers and retail outlets. The aim of 'A Taste of the South-East' is to establish quality food and drink from these counties at a time 'when traditional standards and quality in our food and drink matter more and attract more public interest than ever before' (Anon. 1998b). A Taste of the South-East Ltd was developed and part-funded by the Ministry of Agriculture, Farming and Fisheries. Amongst the other funding bodies are Food from Britain, four county councils and the Rural Development Commission (Anon. 1998b). In addition to its promotion presence, the organization offers a range of corporate marketing, training and individual business development benefits to its members. The 1998 *Taste of the South-East* brochure, available from all tourist boards in the region, features eighty-six producers, of which eleven are vineyards, and incorporates three 'Gourmet Trails'. Typical of the UK industry, all (except for one) vineyards included in the brochure, welcome visitors. Other marketing initiatives of interest include:

- a leaflet produced by the East Anglian Winegrowers Association which provides details of twenty-four vineyards open to the public;
- a leaflet produced by the Mercian Vineyards Association that contains details of eleven vineyards that are open to the public in the Midlands and North of England;
- a map produced by the United Kingdom Vineyards Association in conjunction with Jancis Robinson. Compiled by Gerry Symons in

September 1998 it costs £2.95 and gives locations of 178 vineyards in the UK – fourteen in Wales and the rest in England. It also illustrates many of the wine labels used by wine producers;

■ as noted above, the English Wine Producers, which is an organization formed by four of England's largest wine producers – Chapel Down in Kent, Chiddingstone in Kent, Denbies in Surrey and Three Choirs in Gloucestershire – to benefit from joint marketing at key trade and consumer exhibitions and tastings, as well as other promotional activities. They are keen to pursue links with ETB and regional tourist boards (Trustram, Eve, pers. com. 1999).

Problems of wine tourism development for UK wineries

Like other emergent or developing wine industries, the UK wine tourism sector is faced with a range of developmental concerns. Foremost among these in the UK context are consumer and trade attitudes. As noted by Dodd (1995) with regard to the Texas wine industry, negative perceptions of relatively new wine industries can detrimentally impact upon their growth and development. Dodd (1995) states that many of the wineries were not at first highly respected by some of the local wine retailers and therefore they experienced considerable difficulty selling wine through this channel of distribution. Scepticism from retailers that good quality grapes and wines could be grown and made in the region and a traditional reliance upon imported wines are said to be two of the obstacles that need to be overcome. In these circumstances, and particularly to facilitate trial of their product, the Texas wineries utilized wine tourism to help their businesses grow.

While cellar door, or 'tasting room', sales can be an important source of volume, particularly to small wineries, Dodd also notes a range of possible negative aspects of wine tourism and the associated cellar door sales. Several of these, which also have implications for some English wineries are briefly discussed below.

■ *Increased costs and management time* Staff may have to be employed to run a tasting room and there is the cost of the free wine allowed for sampling. In addition, the owner or manager's time and effort may be needed to manage a tasting room and greet and entertain visitors. The problems of cost of wine for sampling and the pressures on an owner's time were voiced most forcibly by the proprietor of Breaky Bottom Vineyard in East Sussex (see the case study below).

- *Capital required* For newly-established wineries that may have recently invested extensively in wine-making equipment the added burden of establishing a tasting room may be prohibitive.
- *Inability to increase sales substantially via the cellar door* The fact that many visitors may visit a winery for a family outing rather than because they have a serious interest in wine is frequently commented on by UK vineyard proprietors. In addition, there is the distinct possibility that wine tourism activities can distract a winery proprietor from focusing on and developing other potential market opportunities.

Case studies

In an effort to illustrate the wine tourism and business strategies of some UK wine producers several case studies are provided below.

Penshurst Vineyards

This is a family-owned vineyard of approximately 5 ha. (12 acres) in the eastern part of Kent. Like many English vineyards it is situated in a beautiful location, on a slope overlooking a river valley. Its proprietor, David Westphal, is Chair of the South-East Vineyards Association and as such often takes the role of speaking for the English wine industry. This almost certainly enhances the marketing of Penshurst, thus making it better known to the public than many other vineyards of its size. Wine tourists are actively encouraged to Penshurst and about 80 per cent of the wine produced is sold at the cellar door. The proprietor is well aware that direct sales to the consumer provide a better margin than selling to the trade. In addition he notes that direct sales also confer significant cash-flow benefits. When wine is sold to the trade they take 60 days on average to pay, thus reducing liquid capital to maintain vineyard and winery operations.

The principal means of generating wine tourists to Penshurst is believed to be inclusion in tourist brochures, distributed via local tourist information centres. The key brochures for Penshurst are *Best Places to Visit in Kent* and *Vineyards of the South-East*. In addition, as previously noted, the vineyard benefits from the proprietor's public relations profile and from attendance at regional festivals and exhibitions.

Interestingly, Penshurst takes the view that an English vineyard of this size is difficult to make financially viable on its own and as such has invested in supplementary attractions to increase its tourism appeal. It also has a wildlife park, featuring wallabies and, when last visited, the proprietor was considering walnut production. Indeed, it is not uncommon for English vineyard owners to engage in some other form of farming or tourism development to supplement their income and increase their appeal, the philosophy and strategy being to offer something of interest to every member of a family group. A typical example of this approach is given by Nutbourne Vineyards in West Sussex whose entry in *Vineyards of the South-East* reads: 'Beautiful vineyard, lakes and lamas' (Anon. 1998b).

Breaky Bottom Vineyard

This small vineyard of around 2.5 ha (6 acres) is planted with approximately two thirds Seyval Blanc and one third Muller Thurgau. It is situated in a beautiful but isolated valley in East Sussex downland. The only way in or out of the valley is one rough track, deeply potholed in places, of over a mile long. While the vineyard announces in brochures that it is open to tourists, the very difficulty of reaching it means that it is never likely to receive anything near the number of wine tourists of, say, Penshurst. This isolation is in fact a deliberate business strategy of proprietor Peter Hall. Indeed, Hall does not view the innaccessibility and consequent lack of visitation to Breaky Bottom as a problem. As the vineyard is a very small operation he sees the problems of wine tourism for small wineries as outlined by Dodd (1995). In particular, as an active producer, he does not want to have to stop his own work to entertain casual visitors who arrive unexpectedly. He is also deterred from wine tourism by the cost of wine involved in tastings for other than serious buyers and cites the example of a group of six visitors to an English vineyard who tasted eight wines each and eventually purchased one bottle.

Rather than depending on casual wine tourists, Breaky Bottom's strategy is to develop high quality products, both still and sparkling, and to build their reputation by public relations and by a direct-mail campaign directed at serious customers who are also likely to be knowledgeable. Those with a genuine interest in wine are, of course, welcome at Breaky Bottom and a number of private buyers of the product become regular visitors. The success of this strategy is borne out by the fact that 50 per cent of sales are made to the trade rather than to cellar door or other private customers; and that the wine commands a relatively high price and has attracted excellent coverage by media pundits, notably in wine periodicals and on specialist television programmes.

The English Wine Centre

Despite its name the English Wine Centre is a commercial operation rather than a cultural or trade institution. It has a tiny area planted with vines

(0.25 ha), but its importance to the industry lies not in the role of producer but in providing a marketplace and publicity voice for English wine. Based not far from the coast, in East Sussex, it houses an English wine museum and, according to its own marketing literature offers 'The largest range of English wines in a wine shop'. Under the guidance of its energetic proprietor Christopher Ann, it is active in English wine wholesaling and retailing; it participates in an extensive range of promotional activities centred on English wine and in encouraging vineyard owners to become involved in wine tourism. Christopher Ann has developed literature to promote wine trails, such as the Wealden English Wine Trail, linking wine with food, and uses the Internet effectively to promote his wine tours. Recognizing the importance of distribution facilities, especially for smaller producers, his latest innovation is to set up a 'groupage' system. This saves small producers the cost of using the postal system or expensive carriers and also involves non-wine businesses.

Future developments

The future for wine tourism in the UK looks bright. Because of the current interest in wine in the UK it is anticipated that wine tourism both from and in the UK will increase. Drinking wine has become fashionable and a part of contemporary lifestyle, as evidenced by the increase in books on wine, by television programmes, and journal and magazine articles. The origins of wine are often the subject of these programmes and articles, and as such they are encouraging readers to visit wine regions and vineyards. It is unlikely that wine production will ever reach the scale of some European neighbours but, despite the obvious climatic challenges of trying to cultivate vines at such a northern latitude, the UK wine-making industry is now firmly established and continues to thrive.

Since the 1970s, the attitude towards the UK production of wines has altered and has ceased to be a 'sort of music hall joke' (Skelton 1989). Over the last twenty years the UK wine industry has grown dramatically. The resurgence of the wine-making industry can be attributed to several factors including better site selection and the cultivation of more robust grape varieties that are capable of cropping well in the northern soils, but most important has been the increased professionalism of today's wine-makers (Joseph 1998). Several influential and charismatic figures have imported knowledge from established wine-producing nations such as Germany and Australia, and their new approaches to viticulture and blending have significantly influenced both the output and quality of wines being produced.

Garden centres, herb gardens, wildlife trails, adventure playgrounds, animal sanctuaries, agricultural museums and art galleries are all 'value-added' attractions that have been incorporated into vineyard experiences within the English and Welsh counties and many vineyards now provide excellent café/restaurant facilities and gift shops that may encourage visitors to extend their stay and increase spend per head. Links are also being forged between English Wine Producers and the regional tourist boards which look encouraging for the future. In 1999, some of the English vineyards organized wine tastings in their local tourist information centres as part of the St George's Day celebrations, and the Internet is now starting to play its part by providing up-to-date information on wine trails and wine tastings throughout the country, e.g. the Wealden Wine Trail (http://village-net.co.uk/customers/englishwine/tours.html).

Vineyard owners in the UK have also started to appreciate the benefits that can be derived from marketing and managing their operations in a visitor-friendly way, firstly as a means of increasing their cellar door sales, but also as a way of educating and informing visitors about the world of viticulture. Winery owners have the choice of remaining 'small and select' as at the Breaky Bottom operation or adopting a more commercial approach to their operation such as that of Denbies. It would be inappropriate to suggest that one strategy is preferable to another; for some production is a passionate hobby, for others a serious business proposition. The strength of the UK wine industry must surely come from its rich diversity rather than its rigid conformity, but for those vineyard owners who wish to widen their appeal, the opportunities for diversification are enormous.

10

Vasse Felix winery development

Michael Whyte

These days, the Margaret River region, 280 km south of Perth in Western Australia, is well known for its fine wines, gourmet foods, original art and, of course, pristine beaches. Both local and international tourists come to sample the scenery and the produce, in particular the unique wines. Many of these wines are exported to discerning consumers worldwide and can now be found in restaurants from London to Melbourne, Sydney to New York. So it is hard to believe that, only thirty years ago, Margaret River was little more than a surfing destination. There were no vineyards and few tourists.

Perth is one of the world's most isolated cities, and in 1967, establishing a vineyard in a remote region to the south seemed a daring step into the unknown. However, this did not stop Dr Tom Cullity, the forward-thinking founder of Vasse Felix who, trusting in some preliminary viticultural research, planted the region's first grapevines. Despite a general lack of grape-growing and wine-making experience, Shiraz, Cabernet and Riesling grape varieties rose steadily from gravelly, loamy soils into a climate that would later allow them to flourish. The pioneers of this region were nurturing what would, in years to come, become the nucleus for some of the region's benchmark wines, and a world-renowned tourist destination.

A winery was built alongside the vines in 1971, and Vasse Felix released its first vintage. These first Margaret River wines were introduced to the public through cellar door sales and tastings. However, production quantities were minimal and the cellar door generally operated on an 'appointment only' basis. Indeed, tourism to the region was still in its infancy, but, throughout the decade, interest in Vasse Felix wines and the numbers of visitors to the winery and the region continued to grow. Along the way, national distribution was secured and the production of the estate's boutique wines steadily increased.

Throughout the 1980s, the region experienced substantial growth in tourism. Margaret River had been discovered as a premium holiday destination, providing a continuous flow of patrons. As tourist interest in the

Figure 10.1   Entrance to Vasse Felix Winery.

area developed, so did the demand for organized group tastings and tours. Vasse Felix accommodated these requests, and visitors enjoyed a more comprehensive winery experience.

In 1988, in response to growing public interest, a restaurant was built above the winery using local stone and recycled wood. The restaurant served to achieve two aims. Firstly, visitors to the region would be provided with a fine dining experience in the picturesque Margaret River region, excellence in service and the opportunity to enjoy the combination of premium Vasse Felix wine and regional cuisine. Secondly, and most importantly, it was also envisaged that the restaurant would significantly contribute towards the provision of a 'complete experience' at Vasse Felix, further enhancing the estate's allure as a desirable destination. The restaurant's impressive setting offered sweeping views over the region's oldest vines. Vaulted timber ceilings, original art, fine wines and exceptional food naturally embellished this breathtaking view.

At the time, establishing the restaurant was a bold initiative as the estate's location was far from even the smallest neighbouring towns, from which a restaurant would usually attract its patrons. Indeed, the restaurant's seating

Figure 10.2 Vasse Felix Winery restaurant.

capacity of 75 seemed overly optimistic and ambitious. However, the subsequent interest and growth in wine tourism has justified this optimism and proven that the potential demand for fine dining had been underestimated.

The years following the completion of the restaurant illustrated the importance of developing regional cuisine as well as wine, as the matching or pairing of food and wine seems to have become an obsession. This is reflected in the correlation between the number of patrons in the restaurant to the number of visitors to the cellar door. The current ratio is 1 to 4. Correspondingly, the generation of sales at the cellar door is proportional to the level of patronage at the restaurant. Knowledge of the association between wine and food emphasizes the importance of Vasse Felix's insistence on the provision of superior service. To further enhance the Vasse Felix wine and food experience considerable importance is placed on the creation of an essentially 'regional' and seasonal menu, by both the Executive Chef and the Chief Wine-maker.

The next exciting development for Vasse Felix is the conversion of the original winery into a high quality, multi-purpose arts centre and public facility, incorporating an auditorium, gallery, conference room and café featuring alfresco dining. This is seen as a natural progression from the establishment of the restaurant and represents a further diversification of the winery's tourism product, designed to contribute further to Vasse Felix's

Figure 10.3 Tasting cellar, Vasse Felix Winery.

'complete winery experience'. Positive word-of-mouth generated by an enjoyable cellar door visit is essential for the development of the Vasse Felix label and estate, and creating a pleasant, memorable experience for customers is vital to maintaining brand loyalty.

Whilst Vasse Felix is first and foremost a producer of fine wines and not in the business of entertainment or food they represent an important aspect of the image and marketing. It is also recognized that the promotion of wine has a strong synergy with the arts. As a member of the Heytesbury group of companies, under the chairmanship of Janet Holmes à Court, Vasse Felix is fortunate to have pieces from the Holmes à Court art collection on display at the winery. The completion of the arts centre will further emphasize the link between fine art and fine wine while at the same time heralding the beginning of the active role Vasse Felix will play in uniting artists from the region and beyond. Aimed at attracting a wide variety of visitors to the area, the centre will have a programme calendar, catering to varied interests, and is the ideal venue for performances and visual arts at every level.

Visitors to the arts centre will be invited to register their interest in Vasse Felix products and events by joining mailing and e-mail lists. The new arts facility will also provide the opportunity for customers to purchase Vasse Felix wine and merchandise, further increasing the label's exposure. During and after their stay, it is anticipated that the Vasse Felix label will be selected by customers to enjoy either at home or in a restaurant environment. Sales will also be encouraged through an expanding product range using both the cellar door and direct sales to reach established clients and new buyers. The facility's value to the Vasse Felix brand will be substantial.

The arts centre development coincides with investment in the planting of a further 180 ha of vines and establishing a new wine-making facility. The capacity of the restaurant will also be increased. These developments are expected to grow the number of tourists to Vasse Felix by almost 50 per cent. Currently, around 50,000 people visit the Vasse Felix estate each year and it is projected that, once the works are complete, these numbers will rise to an estimated 70,000 people per year. The additional patronage will help to promote the Vasse Felix brand and image, building a stronger profile and bigger public awareness of the label, an integral part of the business strategy. It is proposed that the increase in visitors will create a greater demand for the Vasse Felix label, in both the national and international marketplace.

It is important to remember that, while providing a complete experience for visitors is vital to the continued success of Vasse Felix, efforts are futile without the provision of 'service excellence'. Vasse Felix employees (indeed, any front-line winery personnel) are in a unique and influential position when communicating with customers. Ultimately, the service provided by staff has an unquantifiable impact on visitors. A positive experience at Vasse Felix has the potential to convert a one-time buyer into a passionate devotee of the Vasse Felix label.

It is for this reason that a high standard of service has been established throughout the winery, and enjoyed by all visitors. All Vasse Felix staff, whether their involvement lies in administration, vineyard, restaurant or cellar, are continually kept informed of new wine releases or events.

The training involves a comprehensive induction programme to all new staff that encompasses most procedures from welcoming visitors to bidding them farewell. Knowledge of their wines is provided in the form of tasting sessions with the Cellar Master, as well as monthly blind tastings. This introduces local, national and international wines that are formally judged alongside Vasse Felix wines. Regular morning meetings take place with front-of-house staff where all business issues are discussed and evaluated. Above all, incorporating flexibility into the duties of all personnel has provided the most important form of training, by providing a greater appreciation of all duties ranging from the vineyard to sales.

The staff's knowledge of these activities ensures they can provide valuable information and advice to visitors. Excellence in service continues to be an extremely important asset of the Vasse Felix estate, and an integral part of their overall business philosophy.

Conclusion

More than thirty years on, it is difficult to appreciate the quest of their intrepid founders, with their great vision for commercial grape-growing in geographically isolated conditions. Perhaps their only vision was to produce wine, but, regardless of their motives, they are now recognized as pioneers of the modern-day experience of enjoying fine wines, food and the arts in a naturally inspirational environment. Their decision to establish vineyards at Margaret River has also significantly altered the way wineries now cater to the needs of their visitors. Whereas once, a visit to the cellar door was sufficient, wineries are now beginning to recognize the benefits – and importance – of providing customers with service excellence and a complete winery experience.

11

Wine tourism and regional development

C. Michael Hall, Gary Johnson and
Richard Mitchell

Wine and tourism are both products which are
differentiated on the basis of regional identity.
Wine is often identified by its geographical
origin, e.g. Burgundy, Champagne, Rioja,
which, in many cases, has been formalized
through a series of appellation controls. Similarly, tourism is also promoted by the attraction
of regional or local destinations. It should
therefore be of little surprise that the relationship between wine and tourism is extremely
significant at a regional level through the contribution that regionality provides for product
branding, place promotion and, through these
mechanisms, economic development. Both the
wine and tourism industries rely on regional
branding for market leverage and promotion
(Fuller 1997; Hall and Macionis 1998; Hall *et
al.* 1998). Tourism is fundamentally about the
difference of place (Relph 1996), while wine is
'one of those rare commodities which is branded on the basis of its geographical origin'
(Merret and Whitwell 1994: 174). Hall (1996:

114) describes the importance of tourism place and wine appellation or region thus: 'there is a direct impact on tourism in the identification of wine regions because of the inter-relationships that may exist in the overlap of wine and destination region promotion and the accompanying set of economic and social linkages'.

Tourism has long been regarded as having the potential to contribute to regional development. However, in recent years, the desire to develop tourism products and attractions has had an increased sense of urgency in many countries, and in rural areas in particular, as the changing global economy has led to a range of measures of economic restructuring. Economic change is, of course, not new. For example, rural areas in Western countries have long been subject to changes in technology, rural legislation, rights of access, and farming techniques. Nevertheless, there does appear to be a perception that the rate of change is greater than ever before. Moreover, these changes have been accompanied by the perceived need to retain or attract people in rural areas, maintain aspects of 'traditional' rural lifestyles and agricultural production, and conserve aspects of the rural landscape. Wine is an important component of the complex process of regional change. Many wine regions around the world have been affected by changed patterns of demand for wine and levels of tariff protection which has meant substantial replantings of new grape varieties or, in some cases, loss of vineyard to other forms of production. Yet demand has also meant that some areas, particularly in New World wine regions, have now been planted, which had previously not been considered for wine production. Within this context, wine tourism is therefore emerging as an increasingly important component of rural diversification and development for both the wine and tourism industries, having the potential for income generation at both the regional and individual business levels.

The purpose of this chapter is to examine the interrelationships between wine and tourism at the regional level and note the manner in which greater synergies can be achieved while also acknowledging some of the potential pitfalls of wine tourism development. The chapter is broadly divided into two main sections. The first section discusses issues of regional promotion, planning and development, including the role of networks as an important contributing factor to regional development and promotion. This section will also include an exhibit on the role of the Internet in wine tourism. The last section looks at issues of regional development, resource management and sustainability and notes the effects that urbanization, lifestyle migration and tourism development can have on wine-producing areas.

Regional promotion, planning and development

Given the downturns in rural economies in many Western countries over the past three decades, it is perhaps understandable that much attention has been given to the economic benefits of diversification strategies, such as tourism, particularly in those rural areas struggling to keep pace with, and adapt to the vagaries of, a globalized economy. Tourism development has therefore received increasing recognition as a tool to encourage regional and national economic development and employment generation (e.g. Hall and Jenkins 1998; Wilson 1999). For example, the Australian Commonwealth Department of Tourism (1994: 2) argued: 'Tourism creates jobs, stimulates regional development and diversifies the regional economic base. With the decline in many traditional industries in rural and regional areas, tourism offers an opportunity to revitalize regional Australia and spread the social benefits of tourism'. However, as Hall and Jenkins (1998) noted, there is a long-standing, widespread, but erroneous, perception that tourism offers salvation from local economic crises (e.g. Clout 1972).

Optimism over the potential employment and economic benefits of tourism 'owes much to a policy climate that has been uncritical over a range of issues' (Hudson and Townsend 1992: 50). Such an observation has extremely important implications for the development of wine tourism, because, while such developments may bring benefits for the region as a whole and for many individual businesses and operators, it cannot be automatically assumed that all stakeholders will either directly benefit from wine tourism or that they will seek to include wine tourism as a component of their business strategies. Furthermore, unrealistic expectations of tourism's potential are unfortunately combined with ignorance or wilful neglect by decision-makers of the potentially adverse economic, environmental and social consequences of tourist development that threaten to curtail its benefits. Yet, as Duffield and Long (1981: 409) commented, 'Ironically, the very consequences of lack of development, the unspoilt character of the landscape and distinctive local cultures, become positive resources as far as tourism is concerned'. Duffield and Long's observation again has extremely important implications for wine tourism development as visitation is often encouraged by the characteristics of the winescape and its components, e.g. wineries and vineyards, which help convey the 'romance of the wine' to consumers (see Senese 1999).

Elements of the winescape, including vineyards, wineries and wine itself, are important components of regional promotion. Given the extent to which wine is seen as a lifestyle commodity (see Chapter 6) it should come as no surprise that wine is used as a means to promote regions in order to attract not only tourists, but also investment, as it becomes an element in making places attractive. For example, Chapter 8 on wine tourism in New Zealand commented on the extent to which vineyards are used in regional promotion brochures, noting that, in one case, there was only one vineyard but that it was still used for promotional purposes.

Growth in rural tourism, and escalating pressures on resources stemming from such forces, necessitates closer examination of planning, development and management of the tourist resource bases of rural regions. However, according to Hall and Jenkins (1998) in their discussion of rural tourism policy formulation, such pressures are only poorly understood by policy-makers. According to Craik (1991: 8), many

> governments are embracing tourism as the industry of the future and hoping that the benefits will outweigh the costs. The reality is that, as tourism becomes part of more local, regional and national economic strategies, the range and degree of impacts is increasing . . . Inevitably, changes attributable to – or coinciding with – tourist development are becoming more intense and increasing in scope. Over time, this phenomenon transforms the amenity, culture and lifestyle of destinations.

Such observations are significant (e.g. see Chapter 15 where Angela Skinner discusses problems of development control in the Napa Valley in California); as one of the few national industries concentrated outside metropolitan areas, the wine industry clearly plays a major role in rural regional development (e.g. Australian Wine Foundation 1996). As Scales *et al.* (1995: 73) observe 'one feature of the wine industry, which is not shared with most other industries, is its capacity to attract tourists and boost activity in regional tourism ventures'. Viticulture also has the capacity to provide sustainable land use in previously uneconomic areas. For example, new vine plantings were possible in Bannockburn, Central Otago, New Zealand, where rabbit infestation had thwarted other farming activity (Smith 1997). Tourism supports the viability of land diversification and maximizes the returns on existing viticulture. Wine-related tourism is therefore a significant factor in rural development, most obviously through the creation of jobs and the sale of local merchandise (Sarkadi *et al.* 1995; Morris and King 1997b). Wineries are the archetypal small business in rural economies where small-scale businesses dominate. As Hudson and Townsend (1992: 52–53) observed:

Non-tourist activities that are incompatible with one type of tourism may be perfectly compatible with another. Thus, the broader question of the relations between tourism and other economic activities could be related to segmentation of the tourist market and to policy choices to develop one sort of tourism rather than another. Exploring possible combinations of activities, relative to the specific attributes of particular places, could identify windows of opportunity to which local authority policies might respond in formulating an overall programme for local economic development and employment.

The role of tourism and recreation in rural regional development is a complex and pressing issue. However, management decisions for the allocation of related outdoor recreation resources are seldom guided by strategic policy frameworks. Decisions are typically made in a reactive manner in response to various pressures from groups competing for the same resource or lobbying for different management of a particular resource (Hall and Jenkins 1998). Even in Europe, where rural tourism, including wine tourism, has been increasingly promoted over the last decade as an important mechanism for regional economic development and European integration (see Exhibit 11.1), substantial problems have emerged with respect to policy formulation and implementation. For example, according to the LEADER II rural development programme:

> Unfortunately, there are numerous instances, particularly in Mediterranean Europe, where over-estimation of the contribution which tourism can make to the process of local development has led to stagnation, regression and even total loss of profitability of local tourism and its authenticity. This over-estimation leads to excessive creation of tourist accommodation, speculation by local people and outsiders, environmental degradation and the deadening of the human element and the personal touch which are features most sought after by real rural tourism enthusiasts.
>
> This over-estimation of tourism potential is often aggravated by a lack of the appropriate institutions at local level, the reckless and headlong rush to make a profit, a level of vocational training and management well below the requirements of a quality tourism service, on both individual and collective levels (this is particularly true of areas 'deep in the country' in Southern Europe). On top of this, there is a lack of planning and tangible objectives. All of these factors [weaken] this development model and all are possible causes of failure, even in areas with numerous natural and cultural assets. (LEADER 1995)

Exhibit 11.1: The European Union and wine tourism

Tourism is an area of great economic significance to the European Union (EU). Tourism accounts for approximately 5.5 per cent of GDP, around 5 per cent of export earnings and over 6 per cent of total jobs (Hall 1999). Although the European Parliament has been relatively slow in establishing policies for tourism relative to other economic, social and environmental concerns, the extent of EU involvement in tourism is substantial. Tourism has become a significant part of EU planning and policies for a number of reasons:

- tourism is now recognized as an important economic activity;
- the transnational character of some tourism businesses has necessitated the development of a European-wide policy framework;
- the cultural impacts of tourism have raised concerns over the retention of cultural identity while at the same time attempting to promote the concept of Europe;
- there have been increased concerns over the environmental dimensions of tourism;
- concerns over the social dimensions of poverty and unemployment, particularly in disadvantaged and rural regions, which has given impetus to the use of tourism as a tool for employment generation and economic development at a regional level (Jenkins *et al.* 1998).

The importance of tourism in relation to indirect expenditure is primarily reflected in EU funds allocated to implement regional development and social cohesion policies. As the EU has enlarged so the extent of regional disparities has also expanded. The ten most prosperous regions in the EU are three times as wealthy, and invest three times as much in their economic fabrics, as the ten poorest (Hall 2000). In response to such problems of regional disparity, the EU established a series of 'structural' funds. One of the main structural funds is the European Regional Development Fund (ERDF) which was established in 1975, following the accession of the UK, Denmark and Ireland to the then European Community. However, the development of the single market and the establishment of economic and monetary union in 1999 provided even greater impetus to encourage regional development, with a new fund, the Cohesion Fund, being established to channel financial assistance to the four poorest member states: Spain, Portugal, Greece and Ireland (Jenkins *et al.* 1998). Regional development is a collaborative effort between the EU, national, regional and local authorities, and the private sector. Areas qualifying for EU regional aid programmes are defined according to the nature of their economic problems. Four categories are identified which have regional emphasis:

- *Objective 1:* promoting the development and structural adjustment of the regions where development is lagging behind;
- *Objective 2:* converting regions or areas seriously affected by industrial decline;
- *Objective 5b:* facilitating the development and structural adjustment of rural areas;
- *Objective 6:* promoting the development and structural adjustment of regions with an extremely low population density (European Commission 1996 in Hall 2000).

The Community Support Frameworks (CSFs) for the period 1989–93 made explicit provision for tourism to the amount of ECU 2305.9 million in connection with Objectives 1, 2 and 5b. This figure represented some 4 per cent of all EU assistance. For the 1994–99 period, the EU contribution to tourism under Objectives 1, 2, 5b and 6 amounted to ECU 7284.9 million. This figure represented some 6 per cent of all assistance. In addition, direct European Investment Bank (EIB) financing (individual loans and global loans) in the 'tourism–leisure' field amounted to ECU 1014.2 million over the 1990–94 period, while other monies allocated under other objectives, initiatives and funds, although substantial, are impossible to quantify (European Union 1998 in Hall 2000).

As economic restructuring has affected many Western European wine regions (see Chapter 2), so many of these regions have come to receive assistance under the various objectives of the EU. One of the most significant European strategies for rural development is LEADER (*Liaison entre actions de développement de l'économie rurale*). LEADER is a 'Community initiative' launched in 1991 as part of the major 'cohesion' policies of the EU, by the Directorate General for Agriculture of the European Commission. As LEADER acknowledges, the 'drive among government administrations and the various ... operators to promote rural tourism – is undoubtedly a response – in some cases prompted by a guilty conscience – to economic crisis and the need to find solutions to it, to the negative effects of reforms of farm structures and to the eradication of basic structures in many rural areas' (LEADER 1995).

Four types of measures are eligible to meet the goals of LEADER:

- skills acquisition, e.g. local rural needs analysis, training programmes, and strategies;
- rural innovation programmes – model and transferable pro-grammes which are usually promoted by local action groups that can include technical support for rural development, vocational training, support for rural tourism, support for small businesses, local exploitation and marketing of agricultural, forestry and fisheries products, and preservation and improve-ment of the environment and living conditions;
- transnational cooperation, e.g. joint projects between groups from member states;
- contributions to the European network for regional develop-ment (LEADER II 1995).

There are numerous EU projects which have been designed to assist wine regions and wine tourism directly through improved tourism and viticultural developments. For example, many of the Portuguese initiatives in wine tourism are supported by European funding in an attempt to improve the infrastructure and com-petitiveness of tourism in Portugal, an important sector of its economy (http://www.inforegio.org/erdf/po/prog_9.htm). One such scheme is in the north-west of the country, the Minho region, famous for its production of the green wine – Vinho Verde. A wine tour of the region, the Rota do Vinho Verde, encompasses approximately 60 stopping places and is supported by a number of different funding organizations including the Fundo European de Desenvolvimento Regional (FEDER), Programa Operactional do Norte (PRONORTE), Associacao para o Desenvolvimento do Turismo na Regiao do Norte (ADETURN) and Centro do Informacao e Promocao do Vinho Verde (CIPVV).

An example of a collaborative wine and tourism project supported by EU European Regional Development Fund (ERDF) finance is WITRANET (ERDF, n.d.) which has been undertaken through the involvement of Greece (Attica/East Attica under Objective 1) Italy (Calabria/Provincia Di Crotone under Objective 1), Portugal (Vale Do Ave/Sol do Ave under Objective 1) and Germany (Kleinregion Feldback/Entwicklung-Sterein under Objective 5b). The total cost of the project is 830.500 ECUs of which almost two-thirds is funded by the EU. The WITRANET project aims to preserve and enhance the tradition of wine-making which forms an important part of the European culture. According to the ERDF (n.d.), 'Wine making is an important economic activity which gives a unique identity to the regions it prevails, an identity shared by vine-growing areas across Europe. The unique wine-culture may be used for strengthening regional and European identity, for developing cultural tourism and for educational purposes'.

The implementation of the project includes the following activities:

- setting up the network, including the organization of a databank;
- selecting and renovating/adapting traditional wineries to form the focus of a 'living museum' of wine-making;
- establishing a European festival for the tradition of wine-making, which will be hosted in all network countries at grape-harvesting time and will involve exchanges of cultural events and groups between regions;
- introducing a variety of events, e.g. seminars on wine-tasting and appreciation, exhibitions, and wine tours, throughout the year in each area related to interpretation and appreciation of the wine-making tradition, with a view to stimulating recreation and cultural tourism in each area;
- stimulating the economic activity centred on wine by promoting marketing activities through the network, including the production of wine appreciation guides, trans-regional exhibitions of wines, seminars and conferences.

A similar international cooperative project supported by the EU is the ECOS Ouverture Project. The project aims to provide for the integration of Moldova in the rural tourism network of the European wine-producing regions. A former region of the Soviet Union, Moldova has a long history of wine production. At one time Moldova produced one fifth of the Soviet Union's wine when the latter was the world's third-ranked country in terms of production (Johnson 1994). At its peak, the area under vineyard had reached almost 600,000 acres (235,000 ha). However, by the early 1990s, Moldova had 450,000 acres (180,000 ha) under vine. Johnson (1994: 241) described Moldova as 'politics permitting, it will become one of Europe's most exciting "new" wine regions'. A part of the new politics is the privatization of previous state-owned vineyards including the development of joint ventures with Western companies. In addition, the European Union is seeking to encourage economic development and greater integration with Western Europe through a series of aid and development programmes including the ECOS Ouverture Project. The project, which is the outcome of a cooperative agreement between Franche-Comté and Moldova, aims to:

- enable Moldova to support the efforts for the improvement of the quality of its wine production through the strengthening of the image and renown of its wines, notably through the development of tourism;
- enable Moldova to gain access, on an equal basis vis-à-vis other European regions, to the 'European Wine Routes' labelling;
- enable the European Union regions sharing the same objective (Franche-Comté, Piedmont, Rioja, Lombardy) to join in this project and share their experiences and expertise;
- study the possibilities and opportunities of further cooperation with the regions taking part in the project.

The Franche-Comté region (France) had already established a successful cooperative agreement with Moldova, in the field of vineyard renovation. However, in order to further improve their wine production and marketing, the Moldavian authorities seek to 'devote their efforts to develop the touristic potential of their wine-producing regions'. Similarly, the Franche-Comté region also intends to develop a wine route. Participation in the Ouverture project is regarded as the first step in a rural tourism development project which includes Spanish (Rioja) and Italian (Lombardy and Piedmont) partners (http://www.regione.piemonte.it/ruraltour/proj2ukf.htm).

Michael Hall and Liz Sharples

One of the other major problems of projects such as LEADER is the failure of development agencies to create appropriate networks between stakeholders so that they collaborate towards a common series of goals (Hall and Jenkins

1998; Hall 2000). Networking refers to a wide range of cooperative behaviour between otherwise competing organizations and between organizations linked through economic and social relationships and transactions (Hall *et al.* 1998). Network development is an important component of European and Australian wine tourism initiatives. For example, many of the European wine trails and routes are being developed with the assistance of the Europäische Wein-strassen (European Council of Wine Routes) based in Bordeaux. The Council is an organization which is incorporated within the European Council of Wine Regions (Assemblia das Regioes Europeias Viticolas (AREV)) which was created within the framework of the Dionysus multimedia network of European wine-producing regions. The network was established in 1992 with European Union support and now encompasses more than sixty European wine regions (Hall and Macionis 1998). According to the Europäische Weinstrassen, wine trails are, 'the best framework for cooperative work between government, private enterprises and associations, the tourism industry, wine and the local council' in encouraging regional development and job creation. In addition, from the perspective of individual producers, 'an opportunity exists for the wine-grower to establish advantageous connections and a strategically important means of obtaining trade in high quality produce which encourages the development of direct sales and levels of awareness, and consolidates the image of products as well as creating a loyal consumer market' (translated from Europäische Weinstrassen, n.d.: 1 in Hall and Macionis 1998).

Networks involve firms of all sizes in various combinations: they can be locally or internationally based, they can occur at all stages of the value chain, and they range from highly informal relationships through to contractual obligations. Network development has received enormous atten-tion in both academic and government circles in recent years (Hall *et al.* 1998). However, networking is not a new phenomenon and has long been a hallmark of innovative organizations. The innovation literature attests to 'the central importance of external collaboration with users and external sources of technical expertise [and] these empirical studies of innovation demon-strated the importance of formal and informal networks, even if the expression 'network' was less frequently used' (Freeman 1991). Networks are specific arrangements of inter-organizational cooperation and collabora-tion. Such collaboration occurs, for example, 'where firms cooperate in production and marketing, to exchange know-how and market intelligence, to jointly train their employees, to develop research capacities and new markets, to purchase raw materials in bulk, to share equipment and infrastructure, and so on. If the collaborators also compete in input and product markets – as is often the case – networks are said to encompass the cooperative elements of otherwise competitive relationships' (Bureau of Industry Economics 1991b: 5). Similarly, in a much cited work, Powell notes that in networks

> A basic assumption of network relationships is that parties are mutually dependent upon resources controlled by another, and that there are gains to be had by the pooling of resources. In network forms of resource allocation, individual units exist not by themselves, but in relation to other units. These relationships take considerable effort to establish and sustain, thus they constrain both partners' ability to adapt to changing circumstances. As networks evolve, it may become more economically sensible to exercise voice rather than exit. Benefits and burdens come to be shared ... Complementarity and accommodation are the cornerstones of successful production networks. (Powell 1990: 78)

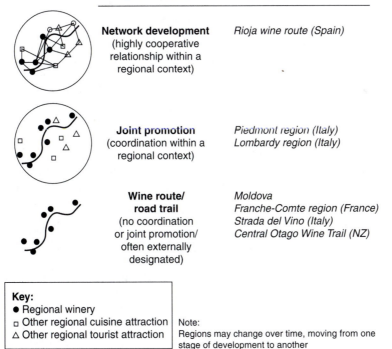

	STAGE OF DEVELOPMENT	EXAMPLES OF DEVELOPMENT
	Network development (highly cooperative relationship within a regional context)	*Rioja wine route (Spain)*
	Joint promotion (coordination within a regional context)	*Piedmont region (Italy)* *Lombardy region (Italy)*
	Wine route/ road trail (no coordination or joint promotion/ often externally designated)	*Moldova* *Franche-Comte region (France)* *Strada del Vino (Italy)* *Central Otago Wine Trail (NZ)*

Key:
● Regional winery
□ Other regional cuisine attraction
△ Other regional tourist attraction

Note:
Regions may change over time, moving from one stage of development to another

Figure 11.1 Stages of wine tourism network development.

Networks are therefore particularly important for the wine industry, e.g. wine cooperatives or regional wine associations, which may pool expertise or equipment or may engage in joint promotional activities. However, in the context of wine tourism, such networks are critical as there is a need to create linkages between businesses which have previously identified themselves as being in separate industries with separate business foci (Figure 11.1). Several different types of inter-organizational linkages can be recognized (after Harper 1993). Table 11.1 illustrates the different types of networks, with wine tourism related examples. One of the most important

Table 11.1 Network categorizations

Interorganizational relationship		Example
Dyadic linkage	formed when two organizations find it mutually beneficial to collaborate in achieving a common goal.	a joint venture between a winery and a tour company to promote winery visitation
Organization sets	interorganizational linkages that refers to the *clusters* of dyadic relations maintained by a *focal* organization.	a visitor information centre or wine tourism organization develops individual relationships with wineries so as to provide tourists with information on each winery
Action sets	a coalition of *interacting* organizations that work together in order to achieve a specific purpose.	a visitor information centre and the wineries in a region come together to produce a regional wine tourism promotional campaign
Networks	used here in a narrow formal sense, refers to a group of organizations that share common organizational ties and can be recognized as a *bounded* interorganizational system.	a federation or association of wine tourism organizations, e.g. the Movimento del Turismo del Vino; the European Council of Wine Regions (Assembleia das Regioes Europeias Viticolas (AREV)); and the Dyonisos multimedia network of European wine-producing regions

Source: Hall *et al.* 1998

aspects of all four types of networks is that not only do they represent flows of business information, e.g. research and promotion, but, from a tourism perspective, they may also represent flows of tourists on the ground. In other words, the economic and social characteristics of networks parallel the flow of goods and services, including tourists. Such flows are particularly attractive as they represent a potential enhancement of the multiplier effect of visitor spending in rural areas, thereby enhancing regional economic development. Networking is also important from the perspective of marketing as collaboration between businesses in a given region can assist in regional promotion through the pooling of scarce funds. In addition, networking is integral to using the Internet for effective regional promotion (see Exhibit 11.2) as the electronic network of websites and links should be tied with economic and social relationships. Furthermore, from a policy perspective, networking is attractive because it reflects a middle ground that 'seeks a more interactive role with firms, and rejects the two extreme cases of total reliance on the market on one hand, and the proliferation of subsidies and "hand outs" on the other' (Australian Manufacturing Council 1991: 8). However, network formation may be difficult in areas where there are information gaps about the perceived benefits of such linkages, such as in the wine tourism area (Hall and Johnson 1997; Hall *et al.* 1998). Difficulties in the development of networks and coordination between wine businesses are also discussed in Chapters 4 and 12.

Exhibit 11.2: WWW (The World Wine Web): Wine tourism and the Internet

Internet marketing and sales is a growing phenomenon and 'the popularity of on-line wine sellers is booming . . . allowing buyers to buy wines they can't find in their local stores and take advantage of the kind of information most retailers don't offer' (Dow Jones n.d.). Demand for Internet wine sales in the USA for example are fuelled by 'increased demand for premium wines, coupled with an inadequate distribution system' (Dow Jones n.d.) and has led to estimates of Internet wine sales of about US$300 million annually (Sweeney 1999). In January 1999, the Beverage Testing Institute was able to list over 700 winery and brewery websites from throughout the United States (Krummert 1999), while in a survey of 176 California vintners suggested that more than half used the Internet for wine sales (Anderson 1999).

The first Australian winery to establish a website was Jane Brook winery in Western Australia in 1995 (www.janebrook.com.au). In 1998, only 88 of 1288 (less than 7 per cent) Australasian wineries reported that they had a website (Clayton 1998: 206). In 1999, Australasian wine websites had more than doubled in number. The New Zealand Wine Online site (operated by the Wine Institute of New Zealand) has links to over sixty of New Zealand's 303 wine producers, with several other wineries having sites not linked to New Zealand Wine Online. Australian wineries, while appearing to be less eager to join the cyber-wine community, have increased their Internet presence to around 11.5 per cent (127) of the 1104 Australian wineries (Australian Wine Online 1999). While many Australian wineries do not have their own dedicated website, many have an Internet presence through regional wine tourism organizations such as the Victorian Wineries Tourism Council (VWTC) and Barossa Wine and Tourism Association (BWTA). Use of New Zealand Internet wine sites also appears to be relatively high, with New Zealand Wine Online (1999) reporting that its website 'had surpassed the 4.5 million hit mark in April [1999] . . . which translates into an average 250,000 raw hits each month [and is predicted to] reach over 5 million by the end of June [1999]' (Robins 1999).

Many of the wine websites that are being developed are from small-scale wineries eager to overcome poor distribution channels for small producers, to expand sales and increase their national and global presence (Anderson 1999, Dow Jones n.d.). Small wineries (as well as large) are not only able to offer descriptions of their wines and on-line distribution services, but are able to provide virtual tours of the winery (e.g. Grant Burge Virtual Winery Tour: http://www.wineaustralia.com.au/tour/grant_burge.html and Sequoia Grove Tour: http://www.sequoiagrove.com/index.html), something retail outlets or mail-order catalogues are not able to do. Dr Irwin Steiger of Chateau Lo Vecchio (USA) describes the significance of the Internet for his winery as follows: 'We haven't released our first wines yet and they're in demand, it's like having individual tours. We really haven't scratched the surface of what this medium can bring to the facility of customer interaction. We're working on an interactive, live motion audio-visual tour where I walk through the vineyards with an Internet guest. It's exciting' (Wine News Network 1998). Similarly, David

Atkinson, owner of Jane Brook winery, Australia's first on-line winery (www.janebrook.com.au), noted that, with 60–70 per cent of sales already being derived through the cellar door, the Internet was a natural extension in seeking low cost sales and marketing avenues. According to Atkinson, 'The real benefit of online payments is that you're often paid before your product is even dispatched', while the Internet also 'gives you credibility in a wider marketplace'. He describes the Internet as 'fantastic' from an advertising point of view, though he notes that it is 'much more a marketing tool than a direct sales medium at this stage . . . The main benefits from the web site are in raising the winery's profile, locally and internationally and attracting cutomer loyalty . . . I'm trying to give information and build relationships to make sales'. However, importantly, Atkinson also emphasizes that the web page has to be marketed (Jane Brook 1999a).

The Internet does more than provide a sales outlet for small wineries. Winters (1997) suggests that 'Large or modest, web pages share some or all of these features: Profiles of their wine and managers, stories of the winery, mail order offerings, maps to bring tourists to the tasting room, discussion groups to get customers talking about their wine concerns, surveys, information about related tourist attractions, calendars of events, links to related firms and associations, recipes matching up wine with food, tips on storing wine, educational information about health and tips on other information'. Wine websites have been established by commercial wine retailers (e.g. Virtual Vineyards: http://www.bath.ac.uk/~su3ws/home.html), individuals (e.g. James Halliday M.W.: http://www.jameshalliday.com.au/) and wine clubs (e.g. University of Bath Students Union Wine Society: http://www.bath.ac.uk/~su3ws/home.html) as a tool for sales and promotion and the education of consumers and fellow wine lovers. More importantly for this discussion, however, is the use of the Internet by wineries, wine regions (both as producers of wine and as destinations) and national wine and tourism organizations as a promotional networking tool.

Table 11.2 provides examples of various types of wine and tourism related organizations that provide websites related to wine tourism and winery visitation. Of particular importance for wine tourism is the number of links between wine and tourism websites. These links form an informal business promotion network that draws on

Table 11.2 Features of selected websites

Site type	Example (website address)	Wider regional information	Wine trails information	Maps	List of visitor facilities	List of visitor services	Links to wine sites	Links to tourism sites*	Links to wine events/festivals sites	Online purchase options
National wine organization	Wine Institute of New Zealand (http://www.nzwine.com/)	✓/L	L	L/✓	L	L	75+	15	7	L
	American Wine Institute (http://www.wineinstitute.org/)	L	x	x	x	x	60+	x	35	x
National wine tourism organizations	Movimento del Turismo del Vino (Italy) (http://www.wine.it/)	x	✓	✓	✓	✓	5+	x	1	✓/L
National tourism organizations	New Zealand Tourism Board (http://www.purenz.com)	✓	✓	L	L	L	8	450+	3	L
	French Government Tourist Office (http://www.francetourism.com/)	✓	✓	✓	x	x	1	50+	x	x
National wine website	Greek Wine (http://www.greekwine.gr/)	x	✓	✓	x	x	under construction	x	x	x
	South African Wine (http://www.wine.co.za)	x	✓	✓	x	x	x	x	1	L
Regional wine organization	Napa Valley Vintners Association (USA) (http://www.napavintners.com)	L/✓	L	✓/L	x	x	90+	2	4+	x
	Wine Council of Ontario (http://www.wineroute.com/guide.html)	L	✓	✓/L	L	L	24+	1	3	x

Regional wine tourism organizations								
Victorian Wineries Tourism Council (Aus.) (http://www.wineries.tourism.vic.gov.au/)	L	✓	✓/L	✓/L	200+	20+	own	L
Barossa Wine and Tourism Assoc. (Aus.) (http://dove.mtx.net.au/~barossa/)	x	✓	L	L	11	58+	own	L
Regional tourism organizations								
Destination Marlborough (NZ) (http://destination.co.nz/marlborough)	✓	✓	✓	✓	14	20+	2	L
Terroirs Bourguignons (France) (http://www.terroirs-b.com/)	✓	✓	x	x	100+	25+	x	L
Individual winery								
Robert Mondavi (http://www.mondavi.com/)	x	✓	x	✓	x	x	own	x
Chard Farm (NZ) (http://www.chardfarm.co.nz)	x	x	✓	✓	x	x	x	✓
Tour companies								
Avalaon Tours (http://www.avalon-tours.com/)	✓	✓	x	x	x	x	x	x
France in Your Glass (http://www.inyourglass.com/)	x	✓	x	x	4	18	x	x

* = Includes links to restaurants and cuisine sites as well as tourism-related businesses and activities.

L = Link to dedicated website. (Note: Only where there is a first level link, links from linked sites not included.)

✓ = Information included in website.

x = No information or links.

+ = At least × number of links, but exact numbers difficult to ascertain (although they are for separate businesses/activities) as some are included in the domain of the main website.

material from a number of wine and tourism businesses to provide the consumer (and winery visitor) with a comprehensive picture of the wine region and its attractions. In many instances, and perhaps not surprisingly, wine tourism organizations provide the greatest opportunities for links between the wine and tourism industries. At an individual winery level, on the other hand, competition for visitors and customers may mean that there is likely to be less of an incentive for networking between wineries or between wineries and related tourism enterprises.

A particularly good example of a website that provides a wide array of information is that of the Victorian Wineries Tourism Council (VWTC) (http://www.wineries.tourism.vic.gov.au/). This site provides descriptions of over 200 wineries throughout Victoria (Australia), giving virtual visitors access to maps, descriptions of facilities and links to winery sites that are both informative and visually stimulating. The site provides tourism links to wine tour companies and the state tourism organization which allow the virtual visitor to explore in more detail the wine regions of Victoria (refer to Table 11.2). Figures on the use of the VWTC website indicate that between 15 October 1998 and 13 May 1999 some 33,051 visits were made to the site, an average of around 24 users per day, making an average of 6.5 visits each leading to a total of around 157 visits/day (Figure 11.2). The vast majority of visits were domestic in origin, with 85.8 per cent originating from within Australia, reflecting the relative proportion of domestic to international visitation to Australian wineries (refer to Figure 11.3). Of the remaining originating countries the United States provided the largest number, some 2297 visits (6.74 per cent), while only Singapore (154) provided more than 100 visits.

While many see the use of the Internet as a positive move for wineries, there exists a large legal debate over issues associated with on-line wine sales, especially in the United States where state laws vary widely (e.g. Anderson 1999; Dow Jones n.d.; Sweeney 1999). In Australia, too, there are legal concerns over licensing, confidentiality and transactions (Clayton 1998). More widespread barriers to entry into the cyber-wine community include such things as the technical expertise and understanding necessary (including a level of techno-phobia amongst small business operators) and the time needed to establish and maintain an effective website.

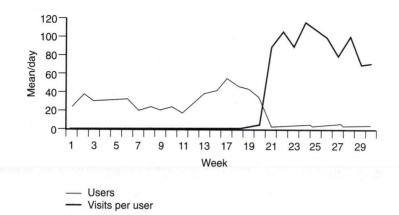

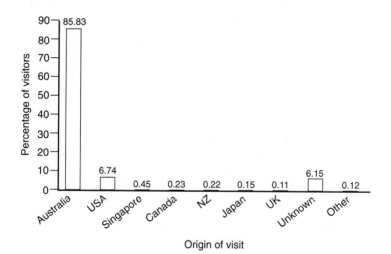

Figure 11.2 Mean daily web visits for Victorian Wineries Tourism Council site (15/10/98–13/5/99).

Figure 11.3 Country of origin of visits (n = 34,048).

Despite these barriers the benefits of the Internet for wineries, wine tourism businesses, wine regions and wine consumers are several-fold. For wineries and wine tourism businesses the biggest advantage is the relatively low cost of establishment and maintenance of a website. Winters (1997) reported an average establishment cost of US$1400 and maintenance costs of just US$92 per month. For the wine consumer and winery visitor the Internet provides an informative and stimulating tool from which they can both plan visits to wineries and wine regions and purchase wine. For both consumer and producer of wine and wine tourism products the greatest benefit is the Internet's ability to provide a network of information on a wide variety of related products and services that is interactive, cheap, effective and entertaining.

Richard Mitchell and Michael Hall

Hall and Johnson (1997) and Johnson (1998) reported on the results of a survey of New Zealand wineries which illustrated the range of perceptions that exist towards tourism and the problems which therefore arise in encouraging linkages between wine and tourism. For example, in responses to questions about their attitudes towards tourism, three Hawke's Bay wineries commented:

'Overseas tourists are not as interested in wineries, wine buying, wines. They have not, in general, come to the region because of the wines . . . This could be a pointer for the promotion of the region'.
'Do you mean overseas or local visitors?'
'Generally tourists don't buy much wine but are time-consuming for staff'

with similar reactions from two Canterbury wineries: 'Not at this stage – but more money spent on wine promotion instead of administration would be good', and 'I don't really support tourism – most countries I have travelled to which are heavily tourist orientated were ruined countries'. In a reflection of a widely-held attitude among over half of those interviewed, a Martinborough winery stated: 'As I don't consider being a tourist operator, I am in the business of selling my wine, all the rest is carried out by us to welcome people to us'. A statement supported by another local winery:

Our small business is to grow and make wine for sale to customers, whether they are 'tourists' or not. I am coordinator of group visits for the wineries that are prepared to take groups – five or six at the present date. Many groups are not interested at all in wine and groups often only buy one to six bottles between them. None of us, if truthful, consider ourselves to be tourist orientated as we are very small establishments and tourism is an extra expense just at present and time consuming without extra (unpaid!) staff.

Nevertheless, in Marlborough, a region which has some of the strongest relationships between the wine and tourism industries with a high proportion of wineries offering cellar door sales (Hall 1996), the response was much more positive (Hall and Johnson 1997). Following are two responses which are representative from the region:

'Here in Marlborough we are fortunate that most wineries and tourism operators work together well.'

'Need to look at generating greater volumes of tourists through Marlborough [and] attempt to cater all seasons. I believe most tourists are intimidated by the atmosphere of some wineries – need to bring these people into a "comfort zone" in addition EDUCATE! – people seek information constantly – need to provide professional quality, varied levels of education – improve their awareness and comfort with the wine industry.'

In an extremely supportive statement about wine tourism in the region, one winery commented:

'Although we do not undertake cellar door sales [and] tastings we still see ourselves as part of the tourism industry. Tourism promotion is important to regional wine industries [and] to all small local vineyards . . . We belong to a wine marketing group (sub group of a wine growers [association]) which produces a winery map, undertakes displays [and] could in future mount food and wine events.'

Indeed, several responses, even from those who had otherwise been negative about tourism, recognized the value of relevant cooperative relationships and networks. For a example, a Marlborough winery called for 'Relationship marketing with parallel industries – arts, music, food, etc'. Similarly, a Martinborough winery called for 'Linkage of wineries to events held in area – golf tournaments, cycle tours, flower and garden shows, music and entertainment', with another observing a 'Lack of cooperative element within the wineries of the region'. Finally, a Central Otago winery noted that New Zealand wineries were 'Just babies at wine tourism . . . [We] need local and central government financial assistance to get further down the track'.

The results of the survey by Hall and Johnson (1997) and Johnson (1998) on linkages between wine and tourism in New Zealand have important implications for the development of wine tourism and organizational linkages in New Zealand (see Exhibit 11.3) and parallel those of Macionis (1997) in Australia who had similar findings (also see Chapter 4). While positive attitudes towards wine tourism are often strong in the tourism industry, there appears to be a much lower level of support in the wine industry, at least in the Australian and New Zealand context.

Exhibit 11.3: Coordinating wine and tourism in Canterbury

Founded in the early 1980s, Canterbury's wine-producing area is still relatively young, yet is now producing internationally recognized wines. Canterbury wines make up 1.3 per cent of New Zealand-produced wines. The area is the fifth largest of New Zealand's ten grape-producing areas, both in terms of planted vineyard area, and grape-producing vintage. However, despite a period of substantial growth, 'there is an element of dissatisfaction among a number of key winemakers' (Ibbotson 1999), with problems of intra-regional coordination and a lack of support from the tourism industry and the Christchurch City Council, the region's urban centre. For example, in 1997, the City Council signed a contract with Montana Wines for pourage rights to the city's major venues, including the Convention Centre and the Town Hall. A number of local wines were included on the wine lists but only after local wineries complained.

Although some major city hotel chains have between 5 per cent and 15 per cent local wine on their lists. Alex Giesen, of Giesen Wines, believes that the perceived lack of local support is due to 'politics, purchase powers, and economic factors . . . There's no pride in Canterbury for its own industry. We have insufficient support from the local players, starting from the top level [of the City Council]' (in Ibbotson 1999). Giesen Wines currently exports 60–65 per cent of its wine. The push for coordinated local support, Giesen believes, 'has to be part of a larger drive'. Similarly, Waipara wine-growers' promotions coordinator, Ian Blowers, states, 'The Canterbury wine industry has so much marketing potential, but as yet it hasn't been happening' (in Ibbotson 1999).

In 1995 five wineries, Giesen, Sherwood, Sandihurst, Rossendale, and St Helena, formed Cellars of Canterbury in order to improve overseas marketing. St Helena Wines' managing director, Robin Mundy, said it was a reaction to the lack of local enthusiasm. 'After looking at promoting their wines in Canterbury, they found they weren't getting anywhere, so they shifted their emphasis to the export market' (in Ibbotson 1999). However, the group has recently begun to focus again on the local market and have employed a full-time representative to visit licensed hotels, restaurants, cafés, and bars in the central business district to promote inclusion of the wineries on wine lists.

Robin Mundy believes that the tourism industry and the major Canterbury wineries do not regard themselves as being connected at all, a view shared by a number of vineyard operators in the region. For example, Larcomb Vineyard's Warren Barnes spoke of a 'lack of cohesiveness among the industry in contrast to Waipara ... people should put aside differences of the past and work together like other areas such as Marlborough, Hawkes Bay, and Martinborough do' (in Ibbotson 1999). According to Brian Westwood, the Marketing Manager of the regional tourism organization Canterbury Tourism, he is aware that a number of vineyards and wineries are not involved in the tourism industry. 'Either they're focusing on their individual sales, or aren't interested . . . Some may decide it's not their core activity, so may steer away from it' (in Ibbotson 1999). However, Ian Blowers, promotions co-ordinator for Waipara wine-growers (the northern Canterbury vineyards), said that, although he had been in the position for 18 months, he had had little interaction with the Canterbury Tourism Board, while, in his former position as sales manager for Torlesse Wines, another Canterbury winery, he said that he was not approached by the Board. Blowers' mission is to promote Waipara as a 'unique' grape-growing region, and as a destination for tourists. He said the area, 65 km north of Christchurch, is 'distinctly different' from the rest of Canterbury, and building up from a small group of wineries gives a lot more control (in Ibbotson 1999).

Michael Hall

To argue, as does Morris and King (1997b), with respect to wine tourism and regional economic development that 'The opportunities abound. It is simply a matter of being sufficiently entrepreneurial to explore the options and work with others to create tourism products that are unique and provide contributing SMEs with a competitive advantage' is insufficient. As Hall et al. (1998) argued, many wineries and wine businesses, particularly in those areas which are not major tourist destinations, require substantial persuasion and information provision so as to illustrate the potential benefits of linkages between wine and tourism. In this sphere government has an appropriate role to play. Hall et al. (1998) identify three main elements which contribute to the development of wine tourism linkages and its use by wineries to maximize individual business goals and by regions to maximize overall economic benefits:

- a substantial research effort to illustrate the potential benefits or otherwise of linkages. It is here that government can play a major role through the provision of financial support for such research where individual companies may not be able or willing to make such a commitment;
- an education component which will convey research information to wineries and the wine industry in an understandable manner in order to persuade involvement and commitment to networks;
- the development of action sets and formal networks to maximize the overlap and linkages that exists between the wine and tourism industries.

Although, as Hall *et al.* (1998) also noted, there will always be people and companies who would prefer to go their own way (see Beverland 1998). Nevertheless, network arrangements and cooperation between stakeholders do provide a firm basis for sustainable business development. However, the regional environmental aspects of wine tourism also need to be considered.

Wine tourism, rural development and sustainability

Rural areas are increasingly popular 'playgrounds for urban dwellers' (Swarbrooke 1996). This presents many opportunities for wine tourism, but, perhaps somewhat paradoxically, may potentially threaten viticulture if it develops without any constraints, and thus, ultimately, wine tourism as well. Rural tourism has been a major force for change in rural regions contributing to permanent in-migration and increased second-home ownership in rural areas (Swarbrooke 1996) (see also Chapter 15 by Skinner). For example, in the Nelson area, in the north of the South Island of New Zealand, the price of suitable land for wine-growing is inflated by high demand from 'lifestylers' migrating from urban centres (Gillion 1998), with similar problems also having been recorded for the Martinborough area as well. In addition, viticultural practices may not be welcomed by second home owners who are attracted in their purchasing behaviour by tranquil images of vineyards in a pleasant rural area. For example, in order to deter birds which may peck at grapes on the vine, thereby potentially causing substantial damage, many vineyards will employ bird scarers such as loud air guns. Similarly, in order to prevent frosts from damaging tender grape buds, helicopters are sometimes employed. However, the noise from such activities has come to be opposed by a number of people in some grape-growing areas to the point where limitations have been imposed on helicopter use (Hall and Johnson 1998).

Wine-growing regions near urban centres are also being increasingly subject to urban pressures. For example, in areas as diverse as California, Auckland, and Adelaide, vineyards have been replaced by suburbs as urban regions have spread. In the case of the Swan Valley near Perth in Western Australia, current proposals by the Western Australian Ministry of Planning for further urban subdivisions are opposed by a number of organizations including Swan Valley & Regional Wine Makers Association, the Grape Growers Association of WA, the Swan Valley Tourism Council, the Midland Chamber of Commerce and Industry, the Wine Industry Association of Western Australia, the Margaret River Wine Industry Association, the Perth Hills Vignerons Association and the Swan Valley Residents and Ratepayers Association. According to Jane Brook (1999b), 'this development if it proceeds will destroy what is a major grape growing and tourism region. Many local wineries and grape growers will be destroyed by this unnecessary plan. There is an adequate supply of unproductive land outside the Swan Valley that is suitable for [u]rbanisation', and, they 'recommend that the localities of Herne Hill and Middle Swan should be reserved for viticulture, tourism and other related rural activities'. The reasons for opposition to the development proposals are further outlined in Table 11.3.

Such processes contribute to what the Wine Institute of New Zealand (WINZ) Chair has described as the 'intrusion of urban values and expectations into rural working environments' (WINZ 1997: 10). Unless the 'right to farm' is preserved and vineyards remain a part of rural life, the key resource of winery tourism is undermined, to the clear detriment of wine tourism (IGUW and GGW 1984; WINZ 1997). For example, the Wine Institute of New Zealand (WINZ 1998a: 5) perceives the 'right to farm' as 'critical to growth' and argued that vineyard investments proceed on the basis that it will be possible to farm the land according to established best practice. The 'right to farm' is a central tenet of the New Zealand wine industry's resource management strategy. Within New Zealand the Hastings District Council, the South Wairarapa District Council and others have incorporated 'right to farm' statements in District Plans with WINZ (1998a: 5) arguing that 'These provide long-term assurance to viticulture as well as to horticulture and agriculture'. Furthermore, WINZ seek promulgation, under the New Zealand 'Resource Management Act, of a National Policy Statement on the "right to farm" [as] the logical extension of these developments. Significant benefits would accrue from this initiative – agricultural producers would benefit from increased

Table 11.3   Reasons for opposing proposals for the development of urban villages within the Swan Valley, Western Australia.

1. The proposal for blanket rezoning of the entire area to residential is not in accordance with the general planning objectives of the Swan Valley Planning Act 1995. This rezoning will cause extreme difficulties for the existing vignerons who presently have approximately 64 hectares (and expanding) of productive vineyards. These vineyards produce mainly premium quality winegrapes that are desperately needed to meet the Swan Valley's expanding wine sales both within Australia and overseas.

2. The planning objective for Areas D in relation to establishing villages in a rural setting cannot be achieved without massive disruption to existing vineyards and wineries. Our water supplies will be destroyed by overuse and pollution.

3. The proposal will shatter the rapidly expanding wine tourism industry of the Swan Valley which will have an adverse flow-on effect to Midland and loss of local job opportunities within the tourism, viticulture and wine-making industries.

4. It will make it almost impossible to promote the Swan Valley as a wine region.

5. It will impact on rural activities within the rest of the Swan Valley.

6. It will raise nutrient levels in the Swan River, as the whole of the Swan Valley drains into the Swan River.

7. No allowance has been made for buffer zones around existing vineyards.

8. The suggested proposal of 500 sq.m. lot sizes is not in accordance with the general planning objectives of the Swan Valley Planning Act 1995.

9. The proposed residential area (710.9 hectares) is already needed to cater for the expansion of the grape-growing and tourism industry within the Swan Valley. Three new wineries have been established in the Swan Valley during the last four years. There are already a number of new vineyards established within the Middle Swan, Herne Hill and Caversham localities.

10. The majority of the communities in Herne Hill, Middle Swan and Caversham have always been against urbanization.

11. Local community and business organizations (Swan Valley Tourism Council, Swan Valley Ratepayers and Swan Valley & Regional Winemakers' Association) were ignored during the original planning process for the Swan Valley.

Source: Jane Brook 1999b. www.janebrook.com.au/savetheswanvalley.html

certainty, while compliance costs would reduce as the Policy Statement would be binding on regional and district plans' (1998a: 5).

However, rural holidays will impact on the everyday lifestyle of urban tourists when they return home, and this includes changes to their mindset regarding rural concerns (Swarbrooke 1996). As a Michigan tourist council director described it, agricultural tourism (including winery tourism) is an opportunity for agriculture to develop urban stakeholders in rural issues (Waldsmith 1997). Wine tourism can therefore also be an ally in retaining the 'right to farm'.

In several New World wine regions, particularly in Australia, the west coast of the United States and New Zealand, wine tourism is already a significant feature of rural development strategies (Maxwell 1991). For example, in New Zealand the formerly lucrative sheep and beef farming industry of Martinborough has largely given way to viticulture, resulting in the district becoming a leisure destination for both international and domestic visitors (Gillion 1997). However, in some instances, wine tourism must also compete with existing farming practices. For example, Seifried winery in Nelson, New Zealand reported extreme difficulty in establishing facilities such as a winery, barrel room and restaurant (Gillion 1998). The existing planning regimes were designed to protect the important horticulture industry by preventing industry encroaching on rural areas. Any sustainable development of wine tourism will thus have to balance these competing demands on resources. Similarly, concerns may sometimes be expressed over the biocide spray programmes employed on some vineyards.

Figure 11.4 Transformation of a village due to the development of wine tourism. Martinbrough Hotel, Martinborough, New Zealand.

Figure 11.5 The restored Martinborough Hotel, Martinborough, New Zealand.

Wine and wine tourism can both contribute to the local economy as well as help redefine the image of tourist destination. For example, Whangarei in New Zealand has suffered in recent decades from high unemployment and freezing work closures; it now promotes wineries as part of the regional tourism mix (WINENZ Magazine 1997). Similarly, the gastronomy and renowned wines of Languedoc-Roussillon, France were identified as having the potential to help re-image the region from a single mass-market seaside resort to a diverse destination of coast, countryside, mountains, spas and historic towns (Klemm 1996).

While heritage tourism, along with ecotourism, has often been seen as one of the cornerstones of sustainable tourism and rural development, it has the disadvantage of often being based on fossilized or even falsified traditional culture (Swarbrooke 1996). In La Rioja, Spain, the objective of the European Union and the regional tourism board is to 'manage tourists in a balanced and sustainable way in order to improve the economy and the social life' of the region (Nitsch and van Straaten 1995: 174). In the action programme developed for the region, wine and gastronomy was identified as one of five types of tourism central to stimulating sustainable tourism (Gilbert 1992). Wine tourism therefore has the advantage of being based on a working industry and a 'living' culture and thus has the potential to change and be sustained by that change.

Conclusion

This chapter has provided an overview of some of the issues associated with the relationship between wine and tourism at a regional level. It has noted that while wine tourism has the potential to make substantial contributions to regional economies there are also potential drawbacks with respect to longer-term landscape change as the attractiveness of winescapes may lead to lifestyle migration and inappropriate developments. The issues raised in this chapter also set the scene for the chapters that follow. Issues of network development and promotion are discussed in more detail in Chapter 12 by Niki Macionis and Brock Cambourne, which examines the development of a national wine tourism plan in Australia, and in Chapter 13 by David Telfer which provides a case study of wine tourism in Ontario, Canada and New York State. The role of European Union funding in wine tourism development is briefly examined in a case study by Nigel Morpeth on cycle trails and wine tourism in Europe (Chapter 14). Chapter 15, which examines issues of regional development, is a case study by Angela Skinner on the Napa Valley in California (Chapter 15). As with some of the issues raised in this chapter, Skinner provides a more cautionary note on wine tourism development and highlights the need for the development of appropriate regulatory frameworks which help ensure that regional winescapes are not subject to unsustainable regional development strategies.

12

Towards a national wine tourism plan: wine tourism organizations and development in Australia

Niki Macionis and Brock Cambourne

The country [Australia] has first-rate wines (particularly red wines) and unsurpassed beer. ANTA [Australian National Tourism Association] should launch a programme to promote the sale of these two products to tourists. .. (Clement 1961: 200).

While the quality of Australian wines and the potential synergies of the wine and tourism industries were clearly acknowledged as far back as 1961, 'wine tourism' in Australia is a relatively new tourism sector and product (Hall *et al.* 1998; Macionis and Cambourne 1998; Macionis 1997 1998). Indeed, the last few years has seen an unprecedented interest in the marketing and development of wine tourism in Australia.

In an effort to capitalize on and maximize the tourism potential of the wine industry, several Australian states have instituted specific wine tourism bodies to facilitate and coordinate the development of wine tourism. Indeed, Australia is unique in its approach to wine tourism development, with the formal establishment of such organizational structures to facilitate the development of Australian wine tourism. Significantly, in 1997 the Federal Government's Office of National Tourism (ONT) provided the Winemakers' Federation of Australia with a grant under the National Tourism Development Programme for the development of a National Wine Tourism Strategy (Office of National Tourism 1997).

This chapter examines the various approaches to wine tourism development in Australia, ranging from the activities and focus of regional associations to state organizations and the development of a national wine tourism strategy. Specifically, it examines the current nature of wine tourism and the level of tourism involvement of the Australian wine industry; wine tourism development issues in Australia; and the focus and structure of various wine tourism development organizations and associations.

A snapshot of the Australian wine industry

From the beginning of European settlement, the pursuit of viticulture and wine-making has been an important part of Australia's culture. Seeds of the claret grape and several rooted vines from the Cape of Good Hope were, in fact, featured as 'plants for the new settlement' in the inventory of the eleven ships of the First Fleet (Halliday 1985; Rankine 1989; Beeston 1994; Macionis 1997).

In a little over 200 years, the Australian wine industry has reached a healthy maturity (Rankine 1989). According to Office International de la Vigne et du Vin (OIV) figures, in 1996 Australia was the world's tenth largest wine-producing country, making 2.5 per cent of the world's wine production. In pursuing the ambitious targets of the Australian wine industry's 2025 Strategy the last few years have seen substantial further growth and development in the industry. In 1998 there were in excess of 1000 wineries in Australia (Australia and New Zealand Wine Industry 1999; Winemakers' Federation of Australia 1998). These producers are spread across more than fifty separate regions in every Australian state and territory.

Australia has a tradition of small family-owned wineries, many with an annual crush of less than twenty tonnes typically (Committee of Enquiry into the Winegrape and Wine Industry 1995). An analysis of winery size by categorizing them according to tonnage crushed, shows that the industry is dominated by two categories: very large and very small. Of the over 1000 wineries in Australia in 1998, 504 or around 50 per cent crush less than fifty tonnes of grapes, with only thirty-four wineries crushing more than 10,000 tonnes of fruit (Winemakers' Federation of Australia 1998). This dichotomy in the structure of the Australian wine industry is further emphasized by recent data from the 1999 vintage which notes that the Australian vintage looks set to have surpassed one million tonnes for the first time, and that Australia's two largest producers, Southcorp Wines and BRL Hardy, will account for almost half of the 1999 crush (AAP Reuters 1998).

In contrast to the assertions of Beverland (1998), it is precisely this structural dichotomy that has made wine tourism an important component of the business success of many small regional wineries in Australia. According to Victorian Wineries Tourism Council Chief Executive Officer, Jack Rasterhoff:

> There are a number of perspectives to wine tourism. For small wineries it provides cash flow and assists them in achieving a better sales mix at a higher price or yield. It also allows them to successfully brand their product and wineries. For larger wineries the effect is different. While wine tourism is an economic necessity for smaller wineries, large wineries often support cellar door activities as a publicity or public relations commitment. (in Fuller 1997: 35)

Current status of wine tourism in Australia

Hutchinson (1997: 115) in *Tourism: Getting it Right for the Millennium* highlights the wine tourism experience as one of Australia's 'emerging [special interest tourism] winners'. Such enthusiasm would appear to be well founded. The Bureau of Tourism Research (BTR) estimates that 390,400 international tourists visited wineries during their stay in Australia in 1996. This represents around 10 per cent of total international visitors in 1996 and is an increase of 68 per cent from 1993 figures (Robins, P. 1999). Similarly, the Victorian Wineries Tourism Council (VWTC) reports that visits to Victorian wineries have increased from 1.6 to over 2 million in the period 1995 to 1998. The VWTC also estimates that tourism expenditure in Victorian wine regions was approximately A$200 million in 1998, with cellar door sales accounting for around A$40 million and the balance expended on food, accommodation, fuel, and other goods and services. Indeed, it is estimated that for every A$1 spent at the cellar door of a Victorian winery, another A$3 to A$4 is spent regionally (King 1998; Shelmerdine 1998). Based upon these figures, the Australian Wine Foundation (1996) estimates total Australian wine tourism figures to be in the order of 5.3 million visits, and worth A $428 million nationally in 1995, and is expected to grow substantially to A$1100 million by 2025.

An indication of the extent of wine tourism development and participation in Australia can also be gauged by the proportion of wineries that offer cellar door and visitor facilities (Hall and Macionis 1998). The *Australian and New Zealand Wine Industry Journal* (1999: 7) reports, that in 1998, 79 per cent of all Australian wine producers have a cellar door tasting and sales outlet. This is in sharp contrast to data from Old World wine producers, such as Italy and France, where active wine tourism participation is reported to be only around 3 per cent (see Chapters 2 and 3).

The supply and nature of value-added tourist facilities at Australian wineries is also an index of the level of tourism participation in the Australian wine industry. A substantial number of Australian wineries possess not only cellar door and sales facilities, but also restaurants, catering, BBQ facilities and picnic areas. An analysis of tourist facilities at Australian wineries in 1997, segmented by state, is presented in Table 12.1.

Wine tourism development issues in Australia

While the above data and predictions would seem to indicate that Australian wine tourism is in good shape with a buoyant future, it is, however, a relatively new tourism sector and product. As such it is confronted by a range of critical developmental issues which have the potential to adversely affect its sustainability and profitability.

Lack of inter-industry integration

While the Australian Wine Foundation (1996: 7) states 'The wine industry and tourism industry have a common objective of capturing and presenting a unique sense of place to consumers, whether they be wine drinkers or tourists', there is currently relatively little inter-industry integration and cohesion (Macionis 1996; 1997).

This lack of integration and the divergent foci of the wine and tourism industries is apparent in a number of Australian states and regions. The *South Australian Tourism Plan 1996–2001* (South Australian Tourism Commission 1996: 139) notes that 'if the way in which the wine and tourism industries

Table 12.1 Tourist and visitor facilities at Australian wineries in 1996

Tourist/visitor facilities	NSW No.	NSW %	Vic No.	Vic %	SA No.	SA %	ACT No.	ACT %	Qld No.	Qld %	WA No.	WA %	Tas No.	Tas %
Total number of wineries	162	100	274	100	211	100	16	100	29	100	149	100	50	100
Total cellar door	142	87.6	227	82.8	170	80.6	13	81.2	29	100	117	78.5	40	80.0
BBQ	30	18.5	39	14.2	13	6.2	2	12.5	3	10.3	11	7.4	1	2.0
Tours	9	5.5	12	4.4	5	2.4	0	0	3	10.3	6	4.0	0	0
Function facilities	4	2.4	9	3.2	9	4.3	2	12.5	1	3.4	7	4.7	1	2.0
Festivals	2	1.2	1	0.4	0	0	0	0	0	0	3	2.0	0	0
Children's facilities (playground etc.)	4	2.4	8	2.9	6	2.8	0	0	1	3.4	4	2.7	0	0
Restaurant/catering facilities	25	15.4	39	14.2	26	12.3	2	12.5	4	13.8	30	20.1	6	12.0
Accommodation	8	4.9	9	3.3	10	4.7	1	6.3	1	3.4	3	2.0	8	16.0
Picnic facilities	12	7.4	31	11.3	19	9.0	3	18.8	3	10.3	9	6.0	2	4.0
Historic building/museum	14	8.6	25	9.1	35	16.6	1	6.3	0	0	5	3.4	4	8.0
Resort	1	0.6	1	0.4	0	0	0	0	0	0	0	0	0	0
Conference facilities	2	1.2	4	1.2	6	2.8	1	6.3	0	0	0	0	1	2.0
Craft/produce/gallery	11	6.7	2	0.7	18	8.5	1	6.3	0	0	13	8.7	0	0
Souvenirs	3	1.8	0	0	1	0.5	0	0	1	3.4	0	0	0	0
Other activities (golf, cricket, camel rides, fishing etc.)	2	1.2	11	4.0	2	0.9	0	0	0	0	0	0	0	0
Visitor centre	0	0	2	0.7	0	0	0	0	0	0	0	0	0	0
Other wines(mead/fruit wine)	4	2.5	6	2.2	5	2.4	1	6.3	3	10.3	4	2.7	1	2.0
Disabled facilities	0	0	1	0.4	1	0.5	0	0	0	0	1	0.7	0	0

Source: Compiled from Deves 1996.

currently operate in relative isolation to one another can be changed and a stronger working partnership forged, there will be simultaneous benefits to both industries'. The lack of effective inter-sectoral linkages and integration is also illustrated by Macionis (1997), who reports a general lack of understanding by wine-makers in the Canberra District regarding the functions and relevance of tourism organizations and associations, particularly broad-based national or membership-based tourism organizations. Hall and Johnson (1997) report similar findings in a national survey of wineries in New Zealand (see Chapter 11).

Macionis (1997) notes that this lack of inter-industry integration and cooperation arises and is compounded by a range of factors, including:

- the relative infancy of wine tourism, resulting in a paucity of information and research regarding wine tourism and wine tourists;
- the often secondary or tertiary nature of tourism as an activity in the wine industry;
- a lack of experience with regard to tourism among wine-makers.

Paucity of information

In a series of interviews with key wine tourism stakeholders including wine tourism agencies, Macionis (1997: 53) reported that wine tourism agencies and state and regional tourism associations generally believed that 'the wine industry is becoming a major visitor drawcard'. However, due to the infancy of wine tourism there was little data or information relating to wine tourism development or marketing. Regional wine industry associations also reported a paucity of information regarding wine tourism and tourism in general. One major regional wine industry association representative stated that 'the paucity of information was the major obstacle to wine industry and tourism development' (Anon. pers. comm. 1996, in Macionis 1997: 53)

As a result of the lack of information about wine tourism, there is a general lack of understanding by the wine industry of wine tourism, wine tourists and tourism in general which has led to a common wine industry perception that cooperative arrangements between the wine industry and the tourism industry benefit only the tourism industry (South Australian Tourism Commission 1996). In fact the Winemakers' Federation of Australia *Strategy 2025* document (1996: 7) states 'in the past, the economic benefits of tourism have often been captured by tourism operators and other non-wine related businesses, while wineries bear the costs of providing the experience'. Conversely, the wine industry does not feel that the tourism sector recognizes the value of the wine industry, or necessarily understands it. The Hunter Valley Vineyards Association's (HVVA) submission to the Industry Commission Inquiry into the Australian Wine Industry states that they would like to see 'the importance of the wine industry to the tourism industry in the Hunter Region recognized, by having the Federal Government focus upon the wine industry as part of its tourism promotion' (Hunter Valley Research Foundation 1994: 23).

Lack of appropriate market research

In addition to a paucity of information regarding wine tourism, there is a relative lack of basic published market research into the behaviour and characteristics of wine consumers and winery tourists or visitors (see Chapter 6). For example, Macionis (1997: 181) reports that while 60 per cent of Canberra District wine owners believe that cellar door sales are extremely important to their business, only 27 per cent strongly disagreed with the statement that 'tourism does not contribute greatly to my business success', suggesting an anomaly in the connection made by winery owners in the relationship between tourism and cellar door sales, and the often incorrect categorization of wine-tourists as 'mobile drunks' (Spawton 1986a: 57). Golledge and Maddern (1994) also note similar sentiments among wine-makers in Victoria.

Dominant product focus of wine-makers

Despite the often economic necessity of tourism, particularly for small wineries, (Australian Wine Foundation 1996), it remains essentially a secondary or tertiary activity. Compounding this is the fact that wine-makers, particularly small wine producers, are often the sole contributor to the operation, making all management decisions without the assistance of paid expertise. In defining small wineries, Edwards (1986: 3) states that 'the small wine maker is usually the supplier of capital, the viticulturalist, the mechanic and welder, the chemist, the farm labourer, the bottler, the purchasing officer, the accountant and sales person'.

As a result, wine-makers exhibit a strong product orientation, focusing predominantly on wine production and often having little understanding of tourism or tourism marketing. Indeed, the Augusta-Margaret River Tourism Association (1994: 2) in *The Cellar: Opening the Door to Tourism*, a funding proposal to the former Commonwealth Department of Tourism under the Regional Tourism Development Program, notes a general lack of cooperation between the wine and tourism industries 'because of the wineries' primary focus on producing premium wines rather than facilities and, secondly, because of the poor understanding of tourism operators about boutique wineries'.

State and regional wine tourism development initiatives in Australia

Several Australian states are proactively addressing some of these developmental issues, and through the activities of specific wine tourism agencies or strategies, are attempting to maximize the potential of wine tourism. Tables 12.2 to 12.5 outline the key approaches of these organizations and strategies. These are focused in four broad areas, including:

- marketing and promotion;
- product development and training;
- research;
- industry integration and communication.

Victoria

In 1993, Victoria became the first Australian state to explicitly recognize the potential and value of wine tourism, when the Victorian Government established the Victorian Wineries Tourism Council (VWTC). The VWTC is a ministerial advisory body established to develop and implement tourism strategies to promote Victoria's wineries and wine regions. Its specific goals include:

- to enhance Victoria's competitive advantage in wine tourism;
- to develop and implement marketing and promotional strategies to increase tourism activity and visitor numbers and yield to Victoria's wine regions;
- to promote the diversity of Victorian wine regions and the quality of Victorian wines;
- to take a leadership role in the wine tourism industry to encourage professional standards which maximize industry effectiveness;
- to develop closer links with regional wine and tourism organizations;
- to ensure that Victoria's wineries involved in wine tourism adopt customer service standards accepted as best practice in the tourism industry in the State;

Table 12.2   State wine tourism marketing and promotion activities

State	Critical issue/focus: wine industry and wine tourism marketing and promotion
Victoria	production, promotion and distribution of marketing collateral, such as *Great Victorian Winery Tours* booklet;
	development and marketing of an extensive Internet site and presence;
	development and marketing of an extensive calendar of events;
	provision of financial support for regional festivals and major wine shows and exhibitions;
	support and extension of the State Tourism Commission's Visiting Journalist Programme (VJP);
	promotion and branding of regions as wine AND food destinations.
South Australia	production, promotion and distribution of motivational marketing collateral, such as the *South Australian Wine and Food Tourism Guide*;
	further development and support of regional wine-related festivals and events;
	support and extension of the State Tourism Commission's VJP;
	support for regional marketing boards;
	hosting of an international wine expo,
	the development of a National Wine Centre in South Australia.
NSW	promotion of wine growing areas of NSW as centres for food, wine and cultural experiences;
	development, production and distribution of quality food and wine marketing collateral, such as *The Food and Wine Trails of NSW*;
	participation in international trade shows aimed at promoting NSW and Australian wine tourism;
	explore opportunities provided by major 'signature events' for promoting and integrating the culinary and wine strengths of NSW and Australia;
	feature food and wine as a major component in the packaging and promotion of Sydney's key cultural precincts.

Table 12.3   State wine tourism product development and training activities

State	Critical issue/focus: wine tourism product development and training
Victoria	development and marketing of a series of 'total experience' wine, food and accommodation packages for retail and wholesale distribution;
	development of a quality accreditation scheme for cellar door outlets which establishes basics such as possession of an answering machine outlining opening times, development of individual enterprise marketing plans and a commitment to the training of cellar door staff;
	development of quality guidelines for state sponsored festivals and events;
	the implementation of a Winery Tourism category in the State Tourism Awards structure.
South Australia	provision of educational opportunities for the wine and tourism industries;
	development of walking, cycling and driving trails linking attractions and regions;
	encouragement of investment in projects deemed to meet the demands of the wine tourism market;
	the development of wine tourism packages;
	the implementation of a Winery Tourism category in the State Tourism Awards structure.
NSW	development of incentives which encourage and recognize quality food and wine tourism products (e.g. Winery Tourism award, menu competitions);
	encourage the development of quality food and wine tourism packages for retail and wholesale distribution;
	conduct a pilot project in the Mudgee region directed at determining how best to develop and promote wine growing regions in NSW as centres for food and wine cultural experiences;
	extend this pilot project to other NSW regions to facilitate the use of local food, wine and produce and access of food and wine experiences to visitors.

Table 12.4   State wine tourism research activities

State	Critical issue/focus: wine tourism research
Victoria	undertake research into winery visitor numbers, expenditure and characteristics; monitor tourist trends to Victorian wineries and wine regions.
South Australia	undertake market research into wine tourism including; determining the benefits for linking the wine and tourism industries; identifying methods to broaden the appeal of the wine experience; and identifying wine tourism market segments.
NSW	access industry expertise and advice in the development and implementation of food and wine strategies and actions; conduct an audit of the NSW food and wine product.

■ to advise the Minister for Tourism and Tourism Victoria on major issues which impact upon tourism activity and visitor numbers to Victoria's wine regions (VWTC 1994; Shelmerdine 1998)

South Australia

Rushton (1998) reports that, between 1993 and 1996, international visitation to South Australian wineries increased by 63 per cent. Indeed, with wine becoming one of the main foci of the tourism drive in South Australia, the South Australian Government has followed Victoria's lead, with the development of a state wine tourism strategy and the formation of the South Australian Wine Tourism Council (SAWTC) in October 1995, charged with 'raising the profile of, and championing, wine tourism in South Australia' (South Australian Tourism Commission 1996: 8). Included among the activities of the SAWTC are the coordination of major food, wine and tourism events, market research, educating the wine tourism workforce and the development of the National Wine Centre in Adelaide (Fuller 1997).

New South Wales

The marketing opportunities of wine promotion are also seen as having great potential for increasing the benefits of regional tourism in New South Wales

Table 12.5   State wine tourism industry integration and communication activities

State	Critical issue/focus: wine tourism industry integration and communication
Victoria	development of a database of key wine and tourism bodies;
	communication of the objectives and strategies of the VWTC to tourism and wine industry groups;
	development of a conventions and events marketing strategy;
	encourage wine industry participation in the Victorian Tourism Awards.
South Australia	foster linkages between the tourism sector and wine industry associations;
	development of a conventions marketing strategy;
	encourage linkages between restaurants and hotels;
	prepare guidelines for development in wine regions for developers and local government;
	encourage wine industry participation in the South Australian Tourism Awards.
NSW	encourage cooperative intersectoral marketing;
	theme promotional events (e.g. NSW Tourism Conference) around NSW quality food and wine tourism experiences;
	maintain Culinary Tourism Advisory Committee as a key forum/peak body for referral;
	consult with peak regional/state/national food/drink/culinary/ tourism associations to identify opportunities;
	facilitate and promote the development of tourism industry and community awareness of culinary and wine based tourism;

(NSW), with former NSW Tourism Minister, Mr Brian Langton, stating that 'NSW will embrace food and wine as an integral part of the visitor experience, and the focus of food and wine will broaden the destinational appeal of NSW, and encourage more first time visitors to come back for seconds' (Langton 1996). While NSW has yet to institute a formal wine tourism body, Tourism NSW and the Culinary Tourism Advisory Committee released a *Food and Wine in Tourism Plan* in November 1996.

This plan states that 'this is the start of an exciting journey to better integrate the state's fine food and wine into the wider lifestyle experience of tourism' and that as an initial wine and food tourism initiative it 'simply aims to set a direction' and 'is not meant to be a catch-all strategy. Rather it is the beginning of Tourism NSW's effort to bring food and wine into the mainstream of tourism marketing by forging a closer partnership between the food and wine industries' (Tourism NSW 1996: 2). Furthermore, it notes that the primary aim of this early *Food and Wine in Tourism Plan* is 'to weave the food and wine product through every aspect of the tourism experience' (Tourism NSW 1996: 5).

Other Australian states and territories

Several other Australian states and territories have also begun both to develop wine tourism strategies and to consider the formation of wine tourism agencies. The Western Australian Wine Industry Strategic Plan, jointly developed by the Wine Industry Association of Western Australia and the Western Australian Government lists the development of 'an integrated wine tourism industry through the establishment of a Wine Tourism Council' as one of its priority actions (Western Australian Government 1997: 16). The formation of the Western Australian Wine Tourism Council (WAWTC) was formally announced at the First Australian Wine Tourism Council, held in the Margaret River Region, Western Australia in May 1998, with a tourism strategy being released in late 1999. Similarly, the development of a wine tourism strategy is also recommended in the Australian Capital Territory's Wine Industry Development Strategy (ACT Chief Minister's Department 1999), while the Queensland Wine Industry Project (see Exhibit 12.1) also has a significant wine tourism component.

Exhibit 12.1: Queensland – beautiful one day, perfect the next!

The State of Queensland is better known both domestically and internationally for its tourist image of sun, sand and beaches. Indeed, these tourist icons of Queensland and the Gold Coast make it one of Australia's premier overseas tourist destinations (McKercher 1995). The last few years, however, have seen a concerted effort to broaden Queensland's tourism image and develop new products and markets – including wine tourism and wine tourists.

Winegrapes have been grown in Queensland since the 1860s, with vineyards spread across what are today Brisbane suburbs, Ipswich and Toowoomba. The industry declined in the early part of this century but, like other Australian states, the boutique boom of the late 1960s and early 1970s (see Exhibit 2.7) witnessed a minor resurgence of wine-making in Queensland. Today, Queensland has 38 wineries, spread across six different wine regions including the Darling Downs, Bundaberg, the Sunshine Coast Hinterland, South Burnett, the D'Aguilar Ranges and the Gold Coast.

To facilitate the development of this emerging wine industry, in 1997 the Queensland Department of State Development provided funding for the Queensland Wine Project. The primary aim of this project is to double the size of the state's wine industry within three years. It is run with a whole-of-government model, with representatives from a range of government departments, including Economic Development and Trade, Department of Primary Industries, Queensland Tourist and Travel Corporation, and Liquor Licensing sitting on the project board and making a commitment to the development of the Queensland wine industry. Such representation also allows access to various areas of expertise as required (Westthorpe, pers. comm. 1999).

Since the inception of the Queensland Wine Project, A$11.2 million has been invested directly in the industry. To date the project has implemented initiatives such as the marketing of a Queensland dozen, organized the state's first wine industry forum, and sponsored the Queensland Wine Industry Training Seminar. It has also resulted in a considerably higher media and consumer profile for the wine industry as well as facilitating investor confidence and developing industry cohesion.

The project also has a significant tourism focus including the general planning and development of wine tourism in Queensland (such as the development of B&B and motel accommodation, the development of food outlets and regional wine tours); and the establishment of wine festivals and shows throughout the state. Significantly, the 'new kid on the Australian wine tourism block' made a considerable investment (via the Queensland Wine Project) and impact in showcasing Queensland as a wine tourism destination at Wine Australia 98 (the largest consumer wine show in the southern hemisphere) in October 1998 – with wines made to suit the lifestyle and food of the state served up under the umbrellas of a professional and cohesive industry.

Niki Macionis and Brock Cambourne

Regional initiatives

At a regional level in Australia, there are a number of examples of proactive wine tourism initiatives (Macionis 1997; Hall *et al.* 1998; Centre for Tourism and Leisure Policy Research 1998). One such example is the Barossa Wine and Tourism Association (BWTA). BWTA is a cooperative association, established in 1995, which comprises business operators, wineries and wine-makers, tourism operators, accommodation operators, and Vintage Festival organizers. Although it sees itself primarily as a tourism body, the Association notes that it is an amalgamation of previous Vintage Festival, Tourism and Wine-Makers' Associations. The Association receives financial support from its core business partners – SATC, other government agencies, local government (Angaston, Tanunda, and Barossa Councils), and its membership, including the local wine industry and wine-makers, business and accommodation operators and the Barossa community (Sterk 1995).

The Barossa Wine and Tourism Association's primary function is to provide a range of services and support in the broad areas of promotion of events, communication, administration and a targeted approach to marketing the whole Barossa region. It also provides the voice for tourism, wine-making and associated industries in local, state and federal bodies on matters relating to those industries. In essence, the Association sees itself as being in the business of promoting all facets of tourism, events and wine in the Barossa (Sterk 1995: 4).

Several regional wine industry groups and alliances have received assistance with regard to tourism development under the former Commonwealth Labor Government's now defunct AusIndustry Business Networks Programme. This project was designed to assist businesses to establish and develop business networks and was delivered in three stages including:

1 a feasibility study in which the network concept is defined;
2 the development of a business plan;
3 the implementation of the business plan.

The services of a trained network broker, independent from the businesses in the network, were provided during the first two stages of the project. These network brokers were either located in selected industry associations and government or regional bodies, or private consultant brokers contracted on a fee-for-service basis.

The AusIndustry Business Networks Programme meet all broker costs, up to an agreed amount, in Stage 1 of the project, while network participants were required to meet non-broker costs such as marketing and legal advice. In Stage 2 of the project, the Programme met half of the broker and other approved costs. Stage 3 of the project was in the form of financial assistance towards the network's first year of operation of which the network must at least match the funding provided by the AusIndustry Business Networks Programme.

AusIndustry (1996: 8) lists three Business Networks Programme projects involving wine regions with a specific tourism focus. However, due to the confidential nature of these projects, no details regarding their activities and strategies are publicly available. The broad objectives and nature of these projects are detailed in Table 12.6

Table 12.6   Overview of wine tourism projects funded under the AusIndustry Business Networks Programme

Region/network	Programme objectives
Wine-makers of Rutherglen	Nine participants intend to promote the Rutherglen region as a preferred source of premium table wines and as an acknowledged tourism destination.
The Name is Barossa	Ten participants intend to develop a regional image based on Barossa culture and environment (includes Barossa Wine and Tourism Association).
Yarra Valley Wines	Three participants (reported to be three of the region's more active, entrepreneurial and regional leaders) intend to increase wine sales in response to an increase in tourism in their region, by examining elements behind how other regions (internationally and nationally) have developed their reputation (including investigating events, accommodation, infrastructure and food and wine links).

Source: Macionis 1997.

Implications of these wine tourism development initiatives

The formation of specific wine tourism bodies such as the Victorian Wineries Tourism Council, South Australian Wine Tourism Council, and NSW Culinary Tourism Advisory Committee provide a basis for increasing the profile and position of the wine industry within the tourism sector. Importantly, they establish a framework for creating and developing inter-industry linkages and facilitating inter-industry understanding and integration through stakeholder involvement (Macionis 1996, 1997: Hall *et al.* 1998). The composition of wine tourism bodies and alliances such as BWTA and the AusIndustry networks, also provides an exogenous source of skills and expertise in marketing and other areas which facilitate wine tourism development, and which are all too often lacking.

The considerable emphasis placed upon the production of marketing collateral and the development and funding of regional wine festivals and events, and the development and implementation of wine region packages appears to be yielding substantial results. VWTC Chief Executive Officer, Mr Jack Rasterhoff, says that the short-break packages developed by the VWTC have made Victoria's wineries even more accessible and affordable, and have proved very beneficial to people who have little time to organize their breaks, stating that 'Nearly 40 per cent of people visiting Victorian wineries do so as part of a short break – which confirms that we're giving them what they want' (in Jones 1996: 1). In addition, the calendar of Victorian wine festivals and events has nearly doubled in the three years since the VWTC's implementation, with 34 events and festivals now listed in the VWTC Calendar of Winery Events. As a result of these initiatives and activities, winery visits now rank among the top four regional tourism experiences in Victoria (Jones 1996). The VWTC also reports an increase in attendance at festivals of around 19 per cent since its inception, while the South Australian Tourism Commission reports a 19 per cent increase in winery visitation by international visitors over the past three years (Fuller 1997; Macri 1997). More significantly perhaps, the VWTC reports that tourism expenditure in Victorian wine regions has increased from an estimated A$120 million in 1995 to approximately A$200 million in 1998 – with a considerable proportion spent at the cellar door (Shelmerdine 1998).

Hall *et al.* (1998) note, however, that the establishment of an organizational structure alone (such as a wine tourism body) is not enough to guarantee success, and that greater emphasis needs to be given to information provision and training for wine tourism practitioners. Educating both the wine and tourism sectors, and government as to the nature and operations of both sectors, would do much to identify and mitigate further obstacles to wine tourism development and profitability. The provision of wine tourism training, especially marketing and product development, would also substantially empower states, regions and individual operators with the skills to maximize the benefits of wine tourism participation.

The strategies of the VWTC, SATC and NSW *Food and Wine in Tourism Plan* also include a number of product development activities such as the provision of educational opportunities for the wine and tourism sectors; the development of cellar door quality accreditation schemes and quality guidelines for sponsored festivals and events; and the implementation of a Winery Tourism category in the State Tourism Awards structure. These activities are directed at addressing a number of wine tourism development issues – including the lack of tourism knowledge and experience; limited tourism infrastructure at Australian wineries; and emphasizing the complementary nature of the wine and tourism sectors.

The research activities of the VWTC and the SAWTC, which aim to quantify the value of wine tourism and identify the distribution of benefits arising from wine tourism, should substantially dilute the common wine industry perception that cooperative arrangements between the wine and tourism industries benefits only the tourism industry. Significantly, research commissioned by the VWTC (Golledge and Maddern 1994; Maddern and Golledge 1996), which documented the level and nature of tourism activity at Victorian wineries, has, for the first time, placed a dollar value on wine tourism. Components of these research activities, which are directed at better understanding winery visitor needs and motivations, are also important in developing and promoting the supply of quality wine tourism experiences.

Towards a national wine tourism strategy

The Australian wine industry's thirty-year development plan, Strategy 2025, identified wine tourism as a priority strategy to 'improving the profitability for Australian winemakers' (Winemakers' Federation of Australia 1996). According to Winemakers' Federation of Australia Chief Executive, Ian Sutton, 'central to this strategy is the development and implementation of a National Wine Tourism Strategy' (Sutton 1999: 107).

In 1997, the Federal Government's Office of National Tourism (ONT) provided the Winemakers' Federation of Australia with a grant of A$70,000 under the National Tourism Development Programme to develop a National

Wine Tourism Strategy (NWTS). The stated objectives of this project include:

- raising the awareness and understanding of tourism in the wine industry;
- establishing wine tourism industry standards, increasing the skill levels of wine tourism practitioners and employees;
- fostering links between wine, food and Australian lifestyle (Office of National Tourism 1997).

This initial A$70,000 funding has been increased by additional contributions from state and territory governments, the Winemakers' Federation of Australia, and the Australian Wine and Brandy Corporation. The development of the NWTS is significant in that it represents the first attempt, anywhere in the world, at enhancing the development of wine tourism on a national basis, involving both a Commonwealth government/private sector partnership and a multisectoral (wine and tourism industry) alliance. In other countries where nationally directed wine tourism development initiatives may claim to have been implemented, such as Italy's Movimento del Turismo del Vino, the efforts are primarily private sector initiatives (see Chapter 2). Where there have been significant public and private sector partnerships involved, they have largely consisted of single project activities such as transnational cooperation (see Chapter 11), rather than long-term strategic national industry development and coordination.

Development approach

To facilitate the development of the NWTS a working party consisting of representatives from state and territory wine industry associations, state wine tourism councils, state and regional tourism commissions and associations, the Australian Tourist Commission and other wine and tourism stakeholders (such as the Australian Wine and Brandy Corporation and QANTAS), and chaired by the Winemakers' Federation of Australia, was convened to assess outcomes and opportunities of the NWTS. In February 1998, a consultant was contracted to develop the NWTS in conjunction with this working group.

In an effort to identify relevant wine tourism issues and properly assess the aspirations of all wine tourism stakeholders, an extensive consultation process was implemented. This involved approximately 180 individual discussions and 68 formal recorded interviews with:

- representatives of the wine and tourism industries;
- educational institutions;

- local government authorities and municipalities;
- national, state and regional tourism authorities;
- other relevant individuals (King 1998).

A draft strategy was released for comment in July, and was reviewed and refined in a series of workshops with key wine tourism stakeholders in each state and the Australian Capital Territory. In October 1998, this draft NWTS was prepared as a Green Paper for wider industry distribution and comment. The final strategy or NWTS 'White Paper' was released in 1999.

The NWTS green paper

The NWTS Green Paper notes that, by 2008, wine tourism in Australia is expected to be

- worth around A\$1.5 billion annually;
- a major source of profits for both the wine and tourism industries;
- a key driver of economic, social and identity development in regional Australia (King 1998).

It lists as the projected strategy outcomes:

- increased development of both the wine and tourism industries;
- increased economic and social benefits for regional communities via business growth, investment and employment;
- greater dividends for local, state and national governments through increased regional economic activity, employment growth, investment in tourism and wine production, promotion of domestic and international tourism, wine sales and the associated increase in government revenues.

Reflecting a need to satisfy the aspirations of, and facilitate ownership by, both the wine and tourism industries, the NWTS Green Paper has at its core, the aims of:

1 generating greater tourist visitation to wine regions and wineries (tourism focus);
2 generating a greater yield at the cellar door via this increased visitation.

Table 12.7 Focus and activities of the National Wine Tourism Strategy 'Green Paper'

Focus	Suggested strategies and activities
Marketing and promotion	facilitate the development of complementary marketing strategies between the ATC and AWEC;
	ensure the ATC uses wine tourism imagery in international tourism promotion;
	promote wine tourism to international tourism wholesalers and inbound tourism operators;
	in conjunction with the ATC and AWEC develop an international 'sub-brand' to promote Australian wine tourism to international markets;
	ensure that wine tourism is a component of the National Domestic Tourism Initiative;
	establish a register of wine related festivals and events and encourage networking and cross regional promotion of events;
	facilitate the development and promotion of food and wine touring trails, including the linking of such trails with common symbols and signposting.
Product development and training	establish a framework for wine tourism product and service standards and refine and adapt existing State Quality Assurance programmes to create a national system of wine tourism accreditation;
	compile a national database of wine tourism related study courses and curricula;
	promote and influence the development and availability of appropriate wine tourism training programmes;
	establish minimum standards linked to 'export readiness' for inclusion in international wine tourism programmes;
	identify wine tourism product gaps and opportunities;
	encourage all state and territory tourism authorities to develop wine, or wine and food tourism strategies;
	develop a workshop programme targeted at the development of wine tourism by winery and tourism operators;
	develop a 'Successful Wine Tourism Training Manual', which identifies the necessary expertise, resources and operational requirements for the establishment and management of successful wine tourism operations;
	develop a wine tourism trade show in conjunction with the National Wine Tourism Conference.

Research	identify and eliminate barriers to wine tourism development, including the development of an inventory of wine tourism impediments and identification of case studies where barriers to development have been overcome;
	appoint a national wine tourism research manager to commission, coordinate, collate and disseminate wine tourism research;
	encourage all states and territories to conduct nationally compatible wine tourism research;
	develop and disseminate a practical guide to monitoring visitor patterns, expectations and satisfaction;
	develop sections of the 'International Visitor Survey' pertinent to wine tourism.
Inter-industry integration and communication	develop and implement a wine tourism awareness campaign in both the wine and tourism sectors to promote better mutual understanding of each industry;
	encourage the establishment of regional wine, food and tourism industry networks;
	encourage the participation of both the wine and tourism sectors in regional tourism and economic development agencies;
	undertake wine tourism industry awareness programmes at relevant state and national tourism events;
	actively seek to develop new market and product opportunities by encouraging states to develop convention and meeting industry strategies.
Lobbying	prepare and pursue a case for the elimination of taxes on wine used for tourism purposes (e.g. cellar door tastings);
	affiliate the National Wine Tourism Council with Tourism Council Australia;
	work with Government at all levels (including regional government associations and regional planning authorities to develop policies and programmes to foster wine tourism development.

Like the previously discussed state wine tourism strategies, the objectives and activities of the NWTS Green Paper are focused on the broad areas of marketing and promotion; product development and training; research; and inter-industry integration and communication. Significantly, and appropriately at a national level, the NWTS Green Paper activities also include a strong focus on industry lobbying and policy influence. Table 12.7 outlines the key activities and strategies of the NWTS Green Paper.

A key strategy in the pursuit of the ambitious visions contained in the Green Paper is the proposed establishment of a National Wine Tourism Council, comprising representatives of peak state wine industry bodies, state wine tourism councils or tourism authorities, the Australian Tourist Commission (ATC), the Australian Wine Export Council (AWEC) and the Winemakers' Federation of Australia (WFA). This National Wine Tourism Council is to be almost entirely responsible for the implementation of the NWTS.

While it may be argued that the establishment of a National Wine Tourism Council to co-ordinate the specific initiatives of the Green Paper is essential, this is perhaps its weakest link. Indeed, the substantial number of proposed actions identified in the NWTS Green Paper will require considerable funding and a significantly resourced National Wine Tourism Council. Given the importance of many of the NWTS initiatives in ensuring the sustainable growth and profitability of the wine tourism sector, putting all of the implementation eggs in the single basket of a national council is fraught with danger. With the range of wine and tourism bodies, that already exist in Australia, it may be argued that there is perhaps no requirement for such a National Wine Tourism Council, and that existing industry bodies should be examined to ascertain their capacity and appropriateness to fulfil this role.

In addition, it could also be considered that a National Wine Tourism Council has the potential to duplicate the roles, responsibilities and activities of existing state organizations. However, while the activities and objectives of the NWTS Green Paper can be categorized in the same broad, generic foci as existing state wine tourism strategies, critical examination reveals that many of the Green Paper's initiatives are differently directed and quite appropriately guided from a national context. For example, the Green Paper 'Product Development and Training' strategies in particular are initiatives that national leadership would undoubtedly enhance and reinforce. Activities such as the development of a national wine tourism accreditation scheme; identification of wine tourism product gaps and opportunities; and encouraging (if not facilitating) all state and territory tourism authorities to develop their own wine and food tourism strategies will contribute to providing the foundations for sustainable development of the wine tourism sector.

Similarly, many of the 'Marketing and Promotion' activities listed in the Green Paper, such as those relating to developing synergies between international marketing agencies like the Australian Tourist Commission (ATC) and the Australian Wine Export Council (AWEC) and the facilitation of domestic wine tourism via inclusion in the National Domestic Tourism Initiative, would also benefit from national coordination. However, while the marketing efforts of state and regional wine tourism agencies have undoubtedly yielded substantial results with regard to both increasing the profile of the wine tourism and wine industry and facilitating winery visitation, the NWTS needs to avoid succumbing to the 'glossy brochure syndrome'.

Although it may be tempting to direct the majority of resources to marketing and market development – particularly in the international arena – a national wine tourism strategy should not simply become a vehicle for inbound tourism operators or marketers to 'put bums on seats'. Some stakeholders, such as states that have already made some efforts in wine tourism product development via various wine tourism councils or agencies, could feel justified in pursuing such international tourist market development. To do so, however, at the expense of national product development requirements, would do little to ensure a sustainable wine tourism sector. Indeed, to follow such a path is akin to building the proverbial 'house of cards'. Furthermore, appropriately directed product development initiatives are essential if the wine tourism product available is to meet the expectations of the consumer. It is also essential if individual wineries and regions are to increase their wine tourism yield.

In developing and specifying a national wine tourism research agenda careful consideration must therefore be given to accessing existing structures and resources. Wine tourism in Australia is fortunate to have access to both intellectual and capital multi-disciplinary resources via the Co-operative Research Centres (CRCs) for Sustainable Tourism and Viticulture. While the research activities listed in the Green Paper are generally appropriate at a national level, they are almost entirely supply and demand focused, with little apparent consideration of wine tourism planning and development issues such as, for example:

■ urbanization and rural disenfranchisement, such as encountered in the Napa Valley (see Chapter 15);

- a risk assessment of pest and disease dispersal (such as phylloxera) via human tourist vectors.

A National Wine Tourism Strategy must also strive to foster inter-industry understanding, and cultivate effective and sustainable inter-sectoral and government linkages, in an effort both to coordinate national wine tourism policy and to deliver the wine tourism message in a unified fashion. With a coordinated and cohesive presence, a National Wine Tourism Strategy can effectively address issues such as the removal of taxes on tasting wines (that is, wine used for tourism purposes). Imposts such as the current wholesale sales tax (WST) and the proposed Goods and Services Tax (GST) plus Wine Equalization Tax (WET) undoubtedly represent a disincentive to the development of tourism and visitor infrastructure at Australian wineries by reducing already scarce development capital (see Exhibit 12.2). Appropriately, the NWTS should provide leadership in calling for the full impact of such regulatory impediments to be investigated and quantified in the context of wine tourism.

In short, evolving from the NWTS Green Paper, a final National Wine Tourism Strategy must provide the foundations for sustainable wine tourism development. While a heavily resourced National Wine Tourism Council may not be appropriate, or perhaps even supported by stakeholders who have already invested in such infrastructure, the NWTS should demonstrate leadership in that it provides a framework for the evolution of existing state and regional wine tourism agencies and alliances according to their level of interest and resources. Specifically, it should focus on alleviating the critical issues discussed previously, such as:

- the paucity of information and research regarding wine tourism and wine tourists;
- raising the awareness and understanding of tourism in the wine industry and vice versa;
- establishing wine tourism industry standards, increasing the skill levels of wine tourism practitioners and employees;
- fostering links between wine, food and Australian lifestyle (Macionis 1997; Office of National Tourism 1997).

In doing so, it will empower wine tourism participants at all levels to develop their wine tourism products. It will also facilitate the development of a product and sector that is marketable, both domestically and internationally, and, more importantly, profitable and sustainable.

Exhibit 12.2: Taxing time for the Australian wine industry

In the last few years, the Australian wine industry has become one of the most highly taxed of any major wine-producing nation in the world. Direct taxation of wine in Australia commenced with the imposition of a Wholesale Sales Tax (WST) of 2.5 per cent in 1930, which was removed in 1931. In August 1971, a A$0.50 per gallon excise applied to the industry. It was shortlived, being withdrawn by the Whitlam Labor Government in December 1972.

In 1984, the Federal Government reimposed a WST of 10 per cent on the wine industry. With the anti-alcohol lobby, government officials and federal parliamentarians arguing that governments have a responsibility for reducing alcohol consumption via taxation – as well as successive governments viewing the growing wine industry as an easy tax target – this WST gradually increased. In August 1986, it was lifted to 20 per cent, and in August 1993, to 31 per cent. Industry lobbying saw the WST quickly reduced to 22 per cent by December, but set to rise by 2 per cent a year to a cap of 26 per cent in July 1995.

On 5 August 1997, the High Court of Australia ruled that the collection of state liquor licence fees was unconstitutional, and the Commonwealth Government responded by increasing the WST by 15 per cent to accommodate the reduction of the state's revenue. As such, the wine industry's taxation base had effectively risen from 0 to 41 per cent in the space of fourteen years. Under this regime however, state governments provide a rebate of 15 per cent for wine sold from the cellar door.

Under the current review of the Australian taxation system, it is proposed to eliminate WST and a range of other indirect taxes and replace them with a Goods and Services Tax (GST) at a flat rate of 10 per cent. The conservative Howard Government also intends to place a Wine Equalization Tax (WET) of 29 per cent upon the industry so that the price of wine does not decrease. Because the GST is levied at a retail rate, the actual wine tax will, in fact, increase under this GST plus WET tax regime.

The impact of this *ad valorem* (value based) tax will be felt most dramatically by small regional wine producers, operating at the premium end of the market – that is, those most involved in, and most dependent upon, wine tourism and cellar door sales. While the proposed GST legislation clearly states that 'where goods are given away [for example, tasting samples at the cellar door] no sale has occurred [and] there will be no GST paid', it is believed that the Howard Government will impose the WET on both wine utilized for cellar door tasting samples and 'own-use' wine (consumed by the wine maker). Smaller regional wineries argue that this GST plus WET taxation regime will result in an increased tax grab by the Government of between 1.9 and 12 per cent. This, they argue, will do little to foster regional development, wine tourism or employment, noting that considerable compensatory tax dollars, generated primarily by wine tourism activity, will also be lost. Indeed, some believe that it will seriously jeopardize the survival of smaller wineries, who play such an important role in promoting regional areas as tourist destinations and promoting Australian wine as a quality product both domestically and to many overseas tourists (Vineyards Association of Tasmania 1998; ABC News 1999; Parliament of Australia 1999).

Niki Macionis and Brock Cambourne

13

The Northeast Wine Route: wine tourism in Ontario, Canada and New York State

David J. Telfer

'Winescapes' are becoming an integral part of the rural environment evolving into destinations comprising of wineries and vineyards (Peters 1997). Wineries are not only producing inputs for the tourism industry in the form of local wines, but they have also become tourist attractions as part of the complex relationship between agriculture and tourism (Telfer and Wall 1996). Wine, having an agricultural base, has the potential to play an important role in rural tourism development (Dodd and Bigotte 1997; Hall *et al.* 1998), yet wine tourism has received little attention in the literature (Hall and Macionis 1998). At a broader level, however, there has been increased understanding of the value of tourism in rural development, which has been recognized by both the public and private sectors (Page and Getz 1997; Sharpley and Sharpley 1997; Butler *et al.* 1998).

This chapter examines the role of government legislation and entrepreneurial response in the development of wine tourism along the Northeast Wine Route in Southern Ontario, Canada, and New York State, in the United States. This international trail links seven major wine regions including Ontario's Pelee Island, Lake Erie (north shore) and the Niagara Peninsula in Canada, and Lake Erie (southern shore), the Finger Lakes, the Hudson River and Long Island in New York State. The chapter will first review the nature of wine tourism and its role as a tourism product in the context of the Northeast Wine Route. In addition, the evolution of the wine industry, within the two regions, will be examined. The chapter will illustrate that government legislation has played a significant role in the establishment of wine tourism in the area and how local entrepreneurs have responded to these changes in regulations by establishing boutique wineries that are attracting increasing numbers of tourists. The major wine-producing areas of Niagara in Ontario and the Finger Lakes in New York State will be used as examples, documenting recent trends in wine tourism on both sides of the border.

Wine tourism and the Northeast Wine Route

Focusing on the role of the landscape, Peters (1997) has introduced the concept of 'winescapes' as unique agricultural landscapes shaped by three elements:

- the presence of vineyards;
- the wine-making activities;
- the wineries where wine is produced and stored.

Peters (1997) suggests that successful viticulture transforms the local landscape into a combination of agriculture, industry and tourism. This concept is related to a definition of wine tourism as the 'visitation to vineyards, wineries, wine festivals and wine shows for which grape wine tasting and/or experiencing the attributes of a grape wine region are the prime motivating factors for visitors' (Hall and Macionis 1998: 267) (also see Chapter 1). This section briefly illustrates the main components identified with wine tourism, using examples from the Northeast Wine Route

The development of wine routes throughout Europe, and increasingly in the New World, provides the link between wine and tourism (Hall and Macionis 1998). The Northeast Wine Route, created in the early 1990s, is a bilateral attempt to connect the seven wine regions that stretch from Windsor, Ontario, Canada in the west to the Long Island region of New York State in the east,

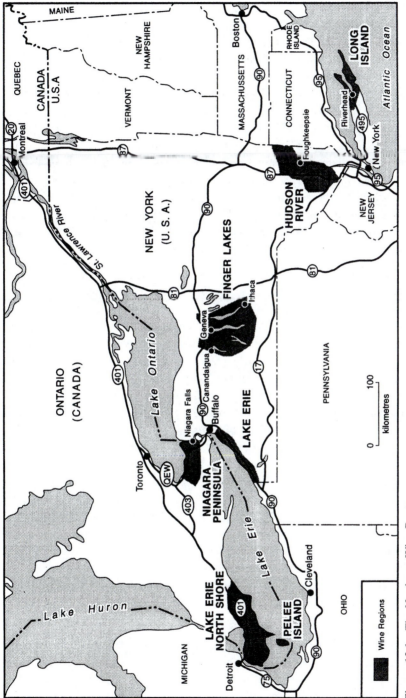

Figure 13.1 The Northeast Wine Route.

with the deliberate and specific aim of developing the rapidly growing wine tourism industry (Sharp 1996 in New York Wine and Grape Foundation 1997) (see Figure 13.1). This international wine route was proposed by entrepreneur Donald Ziraldo, one of the founders of Inninskillin Winery in Niagara, at the Fourth International Symposium on Cool Climate Viticulture and Enology in Rochester, New York. The Canadian unveiling took place at an international tasting at the Royal Canadian Yacht Club in Toronto. The New York Wine and Grape Foundation, the Wine Council of Ontario and the VQA (Vintners, Quality Alliance) of Ontario have now partnered the concept by developing and implementing cross-border marketing strategies. In addition to providing individual tourists with information on the location of wine routes, the published Northeast Wine Route brochure is aimed at independent tour operators in the hope that they will develop cross-border wine tour packages. The smaller wine routes on both sides of the border which make up the Northeast Wine Route will be highlighted later.

In the cool climate growing regions of Ontario and New York, wine-makers must take advantage of microclimates, making the role of place a determining factor in producing high quality wines (Dickenson and Salt 1982; Botos 1996). Along the Northeast Wine Route, slope and the presence of bodies of water are key variables in the production of high quality wine, thus making the relationship between land, climate, grape varieties and the commitment of the wine-makers intrinsically connected (Clarke 1995). Appellation systems for specific regions are used by wine producers who meet certain production criteria. These function as a trademark, signifying quality standards often linked with the artisan principles of craftsmanship (Bell and Valentine 1997). The Niagara region in Ontario and the Finger Lakes region in New York have both been identified under respective regional appellation systems and, as noted above, are now linked through a range of cross-border marketing initiatives. In outlining the importance of appellation systems to tourism, Bell and Valentine (1997: 17) suggest that mutual beneficial publicity occurs as 'wines are famous for coming from a particular region, the region is renowned for its wines – making wines and vineyard tours popular with tourists'. The appellation system increases customer awareness and focuses on the nature of the location by giving regional wines a place in the global marketplace (Bell and Valentine 1997). Meanwhile, appellation systems have also been referred to as an example of the regional politicization of food (Moran 1993).

As visitation increases along the wine routes, tourist facilities have become more widespread. The number of lodging facilities, spas and eateries is on the increase and, in some cases, is found to be out of proportion to the size of the local communities (Peters 1997) as wineries evolve from tourist attractions into destinations (Dodd and Bigotte 1997). Attendance at grape and wine festivals, such as those held annually in Ontario and New York, is an important element in wine tourism (Hall and Macionis 1998: 267). Peters (1997) argues that festivals or celebrations in wine country are designed more to attract tourists who bolster the local economy through the purchase of wine, food, souvenirs and accommodation. Local communities promote these events, and often wineries sponsor various functions, from concerts and picnics in the vineyards to more formal wine tastings and auctions.

Artefacts of the viticultural landscape have also come to define wine regions (Peters 1997). The architecture of the wineries ranges from functional buildings to elaborate French chateaux-like structures. Tammemagi and Tammemagi (1997) state that it is the charming boutique appearance of the wineries in the Niagara region which makes wine touring so pleasant. In Niagara, for example, Inniskillin Winery has converted a 1920s barn (thought to have been designed in the Frank Lloyd Wright style) into a retail wine boutique and tour centre (Ziraldo 1995). In 1994, Château des Charmes opened a 35 000 square foot stone chateau designed to capture the flavour of Canada's grand old railway hotels and Bordeaux estate homes (Kislenko 1994). While some buildings are more opulent, Peters (1997: 139) suggests that 'most wine owners are aware that visitors are an important source of potential revenue; well-kept grounds (often wonderfully landscaped), and cordial tasting rooms with knowledgeable personnel are more important to many visitors than ostentatious displays and expensive wines'. Older homes are also being converted into bed-and-breakfast inns appealing to wine country visitors, with everything from quiet quarters and easy access to vineyard landscapes and wine tastings (Peters 1997). Flood (1990) cautions, however, against the dilution of the product as more people enter the wine tourism market. For example, an overdevelopment of wine tourism in the Napa Valley has led to some resentment by locals (Sharp 1992).

Citing past studies in New York, Washington, Texas, and New Mexico, Dodd and Bigotte (1997) indicate that purchases by winery visitors can represent a substantial proportion of the winery's total sales and this applies especially to smaller wineries that have limited access to distribution outlets. Beamsville, located in the Niagara region, for example, saw four new boutique wineries open in 1999, all of them selling the the majority of their products on site (Waters 1999b).

The chapter now turns to examine the evolution of the wine industry and wine tourism in Ontario and New York. Legislation has been passed in both areas, paving the way for the development of these small boutique wineries, stimulating wine tourism.

The Ontario wine industry and the Vintners' Quality Alliance (VQA)

Accounting for over 80 per cent of the winegrapes grown in the country, the Niagara Peninsula has become a premier wine-growing region, sharing similar latitudes with wine-growing regions of France, Italy and Spain. Benefiting from a unique microclimate created by two of the Great Lakes (Erie and Ontario), the Niagara River, and the Niagara Escarpment, the region currently has over 20 000 acres of vines devoted to the production of wine, which are naturally protected during the cold Canadian winters (WCO 1998). However, in the development of high quality wine, both Ontario and New York wine-makers have faced numerous similar challenges. Both viticultural regions are in cool climate zones and hold the threat of phylloxera (which attacks the roots of vines), with which wine-makers have encountered difficulties for generations. To combat phylloxera, wineries have been grafting vines on to resistant rootstock (Peters 1997), and, more recently (in 1997), to combat the cold, Château des Charmes in Niagara planted the world's first transgenic grapevines, which have been genetically engineered for winter hardiness (Janke 1999).

In the development of the Northeast Wine Route, it is apparent that government legislation has played a significant role in establishing and shaping today's wine tourism. Early government involvement in the wine industry sought to control both production and consumption, and Prohibition had a direct impact on wine quality on both sides of the border. The Ontario Temperance Act of 1916 made it illegal to sell liquor, but not to manufacture it (Bramble and Darling 1992). A subsequent modification of the bill allowed manufacturers with permits to sell wines from Ontario grapes, resulting in the development of illegal shipments across the border to the United States. However, as a consequence of alcohol being considered an illegal drug in the United States, Canadian grape growers were often more concerned with supplying the market with wine in terms of quantity instead of quality (Clarke 1995).

Following the repeal of Prohibition in 1927, the Province of Ontario created the Liquor Control Board of Ontario (LCBO). This organization was formed to control the industry as well as to regulate price, and to distribute and sell alcohol (including wine) through government-run liquor stores. In 1928 the LCBO also assumed responsibility for the quality of wine. With the creation of government liquor stores, customers had a new focus for complaints and, with the government now being responsible to the customers, the first steps were taken to regulate the quality of wines. Early quality control measures stressed the importance of cleanliness, as well as limiting the amount of water and volatile acid that could be added (Aspler 1995). Over time, legislation was passed focusing on the types of grapes that are allowed in Ontario wine. The movement to loosen the controls from the government-run LCBO liquor stores, allowing wineries to sell wine directly to restaurants, has recently succeeded (*Canadian Wine News* 1999; Waters 1999a). During the early 1900s, a number of factors, including Prohibition and the switching of many vineyards to higher value (at the time) crops, such as tobacco, resulted in considerable consolidation of the Canadian wine industry (Hackett 1996). By the 1930s the number of Ontario wineries had decreased from sixty-seven to eight (Bramble and Darling 1992).

The Great Depression and the Second World War followed Prohibition, and by the 1950s, another two generations in North America had grown up with little experience of high quality wines (Clarke 1995). Indeed, right up until the 1970s, the Canadian wine industry was dominated by a few large wine producers who, aided by protective legislation which favoured the use of domestically grown *Vitis labrusca* and *Vitis riparia* grapes, made inferior bulk wines such as the fizzy Baby Duck or Gimli Goose. However, the 1960s saw a significant change in the North American wine industry with the development of the Napa Valley and a new focus on the production of high quality table wines, using classic winegrape (*Vitis vinifera*) varieties. This trend eventually reached Ontario with the establishment of Inniskillin Winery, one of Canada's first cottage or boutique wineries. On 31 July 1975, Inniskillin Winery's Karl J. Kaiser and Donald Ziraldo were granted the first winery licence in Ontario since 1929 (Ziraldo 1995). Ziraldo and others, including Paul Bosc of Château des Charmes Winery, firmly believed that the Canadian wine industry's future also lay in premium wine production and *Vitis vinifera* grape varieties. Under provincial law, all table wines must now be produced with French hybrids and *viniferas* and Ontario table wine sold through the LCBO is not allowed to contain any of the native *labrusca* grapes (Bramble and Darling 1992).

The current boom in Canadian wine tourism is closely related to the growing reputation and quality of Canadian wines in domestic and international markets. An important step in raising the quality of the wine sold in Ontario was the creation of the Vintners' Quality Alliance (VQA) in 1988. The VQA appellation systems governs the quality of the wines in both Ontario and British Columbia and has increased visitation to wineries with consumers seeking higher quality wines. The VQA has three designated viticultural areas in Ontario: Pelee Island, Lake Erie North Shore and the Niagara Peninsula. All three are situated in southern Ontario and are influenced climatically by the moderating effects of Lake Erie and Lake Ontario. Except for 1994–95, which had a harsh winter with damaged crops, the sales of VQA wines have risen by 40 per cent per year since 1989, reaching C$65 million in 1996–97 or 20 per cent of wine sales in the province. In Niagara, there were fifteen wineries in 1989 and, by 1998, there were fifty opening their doors to tourists (Chidley 1998a,b). In the Province, 36 million litres of wine were produced, generating sales of C$257 million (Wine Council of Ontario 1998a).

Changing trade practices and the impacts on the Ontario wine industry

A second important factor in the development of high quality wines in Ontario, and arguably the most important factor in wine tourism development, was the introduction of new trade laws in the late 1980s. Hackett (1996) argues that several international trade agreements forced the Canadian wine industry to restructure and become more internationally competitive. A ruling under the General Agreement on Tariffs and Trade (GATT) caused the Ontario Government to revise their Wine Content Act to allow Canadian house wines to contain 70 per cent of imported grapes, up from 30 per cent under previous regulations (Chapman 1994). In addition, a price equalization policy was established under the Canada–US Free Trade Agreement, thereby creating a framework for the elimination of the 66 per cent mark-up on foreign wines.

As a result of these decisions, the federal and provincial governments negotiated a Grape Acreage Reduction Program (GARP), where farmers were paid over a five-year period to remove up to 3300 ha (8200 acres) of grapes, representing 40 per cent of the Niagara grape acreage (Chapman 1994).

The pull-out had a huge impact on the structure of the wineries, which has ultimately benefited wine tourism. First, the majority of grapes removed consisted of inferior *Vitis labrusca* and *Vitis riparia* varieties. This and the simultaneous development of the VQA have been crucial in reforming the image and reputation of Canadian wines, with the new wave of boutique, or estate wineries, following Ziraldo's entrepreneurial vision at Inniskillin and replanting with premium *Vitis vinifera* varieties. Recognizing the importance of the smaller, high quality boutique wineries, some of the larger wineries such as Vincor have joined with the likes of Inniskillin to increase market share. Second, the GARP-induced industry rationalization provided many growers with the economic motivation to diversify into tourism. Further regulatory assistance in the development of wine tourism has come from the easing of alcohol distribution restrictions. In Ontario, estate wineries were legally allowed to accept credit cards for on-site sales in 1990, a full five years before this was permitted for liquor retailers. In addition, they are the only retail outlets licensed for Sunday wine sales. Such privileges have been a huge advantage in facilitating the development of the wine industry as tourist attractions (Hackett 1996). Recently, however, the government has allowed LCBO stores to open on Sundays and winery sales have declined (Davidson 1999). The Free Trade Agreement also froze the number of new off-site wine retail shops. The larger wineries, such as Vincor and Andres, which control the Wine Rack and the Wine Shoppe chains respectively, in order to bring in new brands legally, have been merging with some of the boutique wineries. The Vincor and Inniskillin merger is one such partnership taking advantage of the reduced tariffs allowed through the now limited off-site retail outlets.

As well as providing a regulatory framework that has encouraged and facilitated wine tourism development, the Canadian governments, both federal and provincial, have provided considerable financial support. For example, in relation to the Canada–US Free Trade Agreement, federal funding of C$6 million was provided to the Canadian Wine Institute in 1989, to assist grape growers and wine producers. The bulk of these funds, around C$5 million, went to Ontario to be administered until 31 December 2000 and has been used to help create tourist and wine routes. More significantly, since 1989, approximately C$50 million has been provided under the Canada–Ontario programme in creating the Wine Council of Ontario and in developing and implementing the Council's marketing and research programme (Hackett 1996). More recently, the Wine Council of Ontario has received substantial support from Agriculture and Agri-Food Canada's Canadian Adaptation and Rural Development Fund (CanAdapt) to develop and implement specific wine tourism initiatives. For example, in 1997 and 1998, CanAdapt funded a programme focused on 'Creating a New Wine and Culture Experience'. This project successfully developed a summer-long tour programme in the Niagara and south western Ontario regions, utilizing a trip-planning guide and cross-marketing the wine industry and cultural tourism products of the regions. The programme, which will operate until 2000, resulted in an increase in wine region visitation of 25 per cent, a 20–40 per cent increase in winery retail sales and a substantial increase in the market share for Ontario wines (CanAdapt 1999). The change in the structure of the wine industry and the orientation to boutique wineries has generated a new interest in Ontario wines and has resulted in an increase in wine tourism (Hackett 1996). Many of the new boutique wineries opening in Niagara rely heavily on cellar door sales and have opened gift shops, selling related merchandise to visitors. By keeping their operations small (many maintain jobs elsewhere), the entrepreneurial owners also avoid using the LCBO for distribution and thereby avoid loss of profits through liquor store taxes (Waters 1999b).

The following section explores the implications of these developments for wine tourism in the Niagara region.

Wine tourism in the Niagara region

Known widely for Niagara Falls, the Niagara region has expanded its tourism base by promoting regional wines and cuisine. Facing pressures to compete in the global economy through the Canada–US Free Trade Agreement and GATT, the viticultural landscape of the region has been radically altered geographically, financially and psychologically (Aspler 1995). As Lawrason and Wilson (1998: 7) suggest, there was very little in the way of wine tourism ten years ago and Canadian wine was not seen as attached to gourmet vacations, music festivals or sporting activities. Now, 'voyages of vinous discovery within Canada have become both fascinating and fashionable' (Bramble 1998). Entrepreneurs have responded to opportunities created, in part, through changes in government legislation, developing numerous innovative wine and tourism initiatives. Since 1994, 3000 acres of premium varieties of grapes have been planted at a cost of C$14 000 an acre, and independent growers have financed 80 per cent of that (Bramble 1998). There has been a move to open competitive boutique estate wineries. Based on a desire to create a wine region, the production of high quality wines on a small scale, with a critical mass of wineries, has led to the development of a wine tourism destination (WCO 1998). Total wine industry related employment is estimated at 4000, including operations, growers, retail and suppliers. The reorganization of the industry has generated record high sales of Ontario wine and achieved international acclaim with Ontario Chardonnay, Riesling, Pinot Noir, Cabernet and Icewine, the latter a product which has become very popular with Japanese tourists. In 1997, there were 20 000 acres of grapes devoted to wine in Ontario. In 1996, the value of grape purchases was C$20 million and 28 700 metric tonnes were produced (WCO 1998).

In addition to featuring as part of the Northeast Wine Route, a local wine route has been signposted connecting twenty-seven wineries in the region that offer guided tours, tastings, restaurants, and shopping. The Internet (http://www.tourismniagara.com/wineregion/vinroute.html.) is being used to promote the wineries and events, along with a wine trails newspaper. The annual 'Four Weekends in July' promotion brings in approximately 100,000 people to the region. A large number of festivals, special events and marketing strategies have been developed to promote the wines of Niagara. In 1998, the Niagara Grape and Wine Festival entered its 47th year of celebrating the grape harvest with over 100 scheduled activities. Founded by the City of St Catharines and the Ontario Grape Growers Marketing Board, the Wine County Celebration has grown into an international event, attracting over half a million people each year. Attempts have been made to extend the celebrations related to wines throughout the year. In January 1998, Xerox sponsored 'Images of Winter', an Icewine evening with over 400 attending to sample a product for which the region is becoming widely known. In the spring of 1998, Canada Trust (a financial institution) sponsored 'New Vintage Niagara' which gave guests an opportunity to taste new vintages before they went to market.

Other notable events include the 'Six Unforgettable Weekends' organized by the Wine Council of Ontario, an umbrella concept that promotes dozens of weekend events at Niagara wineries. An example of the strategic alliances which are forming between related industries is the fine dining and festival theatre package put together by Hillebrand Winery and the Shaw Festival Theatre. Other activities are diverse and range from stargazing at Stonechurch Winery to wild-west shows at Konzelmann Estates Winery.

Efforts have been made to link area wines with local food products in order to create a regional cuisine. The shift to small-scale estate boutique wineries with restaurants has helped showcase local cuisine on the wine tourism circuit. A 'Wine and Dine' programme has been set up to promote Ontario's wines in fine restaurants. 'Tastes of Niagara' is a new Quality Food Alliance of Niagara wine-makers, food producers, chefs, restaurateurs and retailers promoting the uniqueness of local produce and cuisine (Telfer, forthcoming). Vineland Estates Winery is planning to open an international culinary institute on its property, with lodging for up to seventy students, visiting chefs and agritourists. Strewn Winery hosts the Wine Country Cooking School, which presents various half-day cooking demonstrations on Saturdays and Sundays, using local Niagara ingredients and wines.

Several tour companies have responded by developing speciality wine tours in Niagara. Niagara Wine Tours International offers daily tours by van or bicycle, including a gourmet picnic lunch and stops at several wineries. Wine Country Tours offers customized tours for groups and companies including 'speciality tastings, meals at top wineries and local restaurants, wine and food matching seminars, agricultural seminars, shopping excursions in Niagara-on-the-Lake, sporting activities (golf, cycling, hiking), and a large number of cultural events' (Lawrason and Wilson 1998: 7).

Companies specializing in biking and hiking tours also operate in the region, stopping at the wineries and restaurants along the way. Finally, the local transit authority also operates wine tours on Sundays during June, July and August, costing C$40 per person. The Wine Council of Ontario (WCO 1998) has estimated that tourists spend between C$50 and $500 on wine and many turn into loyal customers of Ontario wines. It is estimated that the region's wineries receive over 300,000 visitors a year (Chidley 1998a,b) and the estimated future potential has been projected at 450,000 visitors per year (WCO 1998). Employment related to wine tourism tripled in the three years preceding 1998 (WCO 1998).

The chapter now turns to examine trends south of the border in New York along the Northeast Wine Route, using the Finger Lakes region as an example. Legislation and entrepreneurial response will continue to be the focus in the development of wine tourism. The partnership which evolved to develop the wine route itself between the Wine Council of Ontario, the VQA (Ontario) and the New York Wine and Grape Foundation was initiated by an entrepreneurial winery in Ontario in an effort to promote local wines across the border.

Evolution of the New York wine industry and the Farm Winery Act

New York was one of the first states to grow grapes and produce wine, with the Brotherhood Winery in the Hudson River Region, established in 1839, being the United States' oldest continually operating winery. Since the repeal of Prohibition, New York State has become the second largest producer of grapes and wines in the United States behind California and it is the nation's largest grape juice producer (Baxevanis 1992). The state stretches from Lakes Ontario and Erie in the west to the Atlantic in the east. Many New York wineries, such as the Brotherhood Winery, survived Prohibition (1920–33) by making sacramental wine and grape juice and selling grapes to home wine makers (Baxevanis 1992). As in Ontario, the industry has historically relied heavily on native grapes. The successful introduction of *vinifera* vines in the Finger Lakes region occurred during the 1950s, a step which was facilitated by the vision of several entrepreneurs, including Charles Fournier and Konstantin Frank, who proved that the delicate *vinifera* vines could not only be successfully cultivated, but could thrive in New York's climates. The industry enjoyed increases in production until the 1980s when it entered a depression. Vine acreage peaked in the early 1980s at 42,000 and currently stands at 31,400. During the difficult 1980s, the state government funded the development of the New York Wine and Grape Foundation, an industry organization charged with responsibility for conducting comprehensive promotion and research programmes to support the state's grape and wine industries (New York Grape and Wine Foundation 1997). The Foundation has a membership in the hundreds across related industries, including growers, producers, retailers and restaurants, and develops and promotes wine tourism through a variety of mechanisms including:

- the production of a nine-part video and pay TV series titled *New York's Wine Country*;
- the provision of a strong Internet presence;
- the production of a range of brochures and marketing collateral;
- the funding of cooperative alliances or 'wine trails' (in this context 'wine trail' refers to the grouping of geographically clustered wineries for the purpose of conducting cooperative marketing and wine tourism activities).

As in Ontario, industry restructuring was initiated by the passing of legislation facilitating the development of small, premium wineries that are now at the heart of the wine tourism circuit. The 1976 Farm Winery Act gave the New York wine industry a major impetus, helping to increase the number of wineries from sixteen in 1976 to ninety-seven by 1990. The total number of wineries in New York State is now 125. The Farm Winery Act essentially made it more economically feasible to operate a small boutique or cottage winery by allowing small farms (those operating a winery producing 50,000 gallons a year or less) to engage in direct sales to visitors at the winery and reducing previously prohibitive licensing fees (McGrath Morris 1985). In addition, prior to the introduction of this Act, wineries had been required to sell 95 per cent of their wines through distributors. The new Act encourages the establishment of small wineries with production too limited to be carried by a distributor. It has been argued that 'the New York State Farm Winery Act of 1976 changed the face of the state's wine industry' (Wiener 1990). Recognizing the impact of such enabling legislation, farm wineries are now allowed to produce up to 150,000 gallons (New York Wine and Grape Foundation 1997).

Most of the newer wineries are small, producing less than 10,000 cases; however, they have had an impressive impact, extending the premium market for the more sophisticated consumer (Baxevanis 1992). Growth areas for wineries in the state have been in the small and premium sectors concentrated in the Finger Lakes and on Long Island. These small boutique wineries have been at the forefront of quality as they have switched from American grapes to French-American and *vinifera* grapes. Similar to

Niagara, these steps have helped establish the premium wine industry and promoted the development of wine tourism. During this time, consolidation has also occurred as corporations and investment groups have bought undercapitalized wineries and the large volume producers still dominate the market (Peters 1997). Laws also allow the inclusion of wines from other states in New York wine.

The introduction of an appellation system in the United States occurred in 1983, five years earlier than the VQA in Canada and it was modelled after the system in Italy and France (Clarke 1995). As the United States began to hold its own at the international level it began to compete in export markets against wines from countries with more developed quality control methods (Clarke 1995). There came a need to introduce similar controls to other top wine nations and the US Federal Government Bureau of Alcohol, Tobacco and Firearms introduced the American Viticultural Areas (AVAs). Boundaries are based on topography, climatic zones and soil conditions; however, they do not place restrictions on grape varieties or yields and they do not guarantee quality. If a viticultural designation is used on a bottle of wine, then at least 85 per cent of the wine has to be made from grapes grown in that AVA (Peters 1997). The AVAs are designed to provide consumers with geographical information about a wine's origin. Peters (1997) suggests that AVAs may ultimately help to improve the image of US wines in foreign markets as wine exports have been increasingly steadily in recent years, especially to England, Japan and Canada. There are over a hundred AVAs in the United States and over sixty are in California. Major requirements of the labelling laws are by grape variety, region of origin and health warnings (Clarke 1995). Table 13.1 contains a list of the twenty-six AVA wine areas along the American Northeast Coast. New York State has six officially recognized viticultural areas (Lake Erie, Finger Lakes, Cayuga, Hudson River Region, the Hamptons, Long Island and the North Fork of Long Island). Similar to the VQA areas in Ontario, all the locations of the AVA areas in New York are influenced by the presence of large bodies of water, which help to create microclimates.

Sixty-five per cent of the grapes are used for grape juice, 33 per cent is used for wine and the remaining 2 per cent is used for fresh fruit. There has been a rapid expansion in the number of wineries since the mid-1970s. There are currently 125 wineries and 106 of these have opened since 1976. The four main wine regions in the State of New York are Lake Erie, Long Island, Hudson River and the Finger Lakes. The state produces 100 million bottles a year worth over US$500 million in gross sales. In addition, the industry generates US$85 million in state and local revenues and employs over 18,000 people (New York Wine and Grape Foundation n.d.).

Table 13.1 AVA wine areas along the American northeast coast

Ohio
1. Isle St George
2. Grand River Valley
3. Loramie Creek
4. Ohio River Valley (also in Kentucky, Indiana and West Virginia)

West Virginia
5. Kanawha River Valley

Virginia
6. Rocky Knob
7. North Fork of Roanoke
8. Monticello
9. Northern Neck George Washington Birthplace
10. Virginia's East Shore
11. Shenandoah Valley (also in West Virginia)

Maryland
12. Linganore
13. Catoctin
14. Cumberland Valley (also in Pennsylvania)

Pennsylvania
15. Lancaster Valley

New Jersey
16. Central Delaware Valley (also in Pennsylvania)
17. Warren Hills

New York State
18. Lake Erie (also in Pennsylvania and Ohio)
19. Finger Lakes
20. Cayuga Lake
21. Hudson River Region
22. North Fork of Long Island
23. The Hamptons

Connecticut
24. Western Connecticut Highlands
25. Southeastern New England (also Rhode Island and Massachusetts)

Massachusetts
26. Martha's Vineyard

Source: Clarke 1995

The Finger Lakes region has been at the centre of the state's wine industry since the Civil War (Baxevanis 1992). The region comprises eleven glacial lakes, covering 4000 square miles. It is influenced by sloping hillsides that increase air drainage along with the lakes. Two viticultural areas have been created: the Finger Lakes and Cayuga Lake. The Finger Lakes region in total has fifty-eight bonded wineries with 10,414 acres of vineyards producing 61,448 tons of grapes a year (New York Wine and Grape Foundation, n.d.). While the region has faced a decline in the number of growers, the number of wineries has increased, with many of the newer boutique wineries focusing on premium vines and linked to the tourist trade. Due to the high cost of growing grapes in the Finger Lakes, some of the industry growth has resulted from the importation of *vinifera* grapes and juice from the west and east coasts. The region has also been home to some of the largest commercial wine companies in the country. The speciality wines include Sparkling Riesling, Pinot Noir and Icewine (New York Wine and Grape Foundation n.d.).

Wine tourism in New York and the Finger Lakes

The New York Wine and Grape Foundation estimates that over one million tourists visit the state's wineries each year. In a study of wineries in New York, Henehan and White (1990) found that many wineries relied to a large extent on tasting rooms as a means of distribution. In each of the four wine regions of New York, groups of wineries have joined to form wine trails. Similar to events in Ontario, the wineries host tastings, wine and food pairings and seasonal festivals, which are marketed as day trips, weekend adventures or longer vacations. Each of the wine trails is defined by the surrounding geography. In the Finger Lakes, the wine trails follow the shale hillsides, which surround the lakes of Keuka, Seneca and Cayuga. In the Hudson Valley, trails drive through the Shawangunk Mountains on the west side of the Hudson River and through Dutches County on the east side of the river. On eastern Long Island, the wine route parallels the Atlantic and runs along the North and South Forks (New York Wine and Grape Foundation, n.d.). Long Island has historically been the vacation area for New Yorkers and the development of wineries has given an additional reason to visit (Peters 1997). Estimates for wine tourism expenditure in Long Island have been placed at US$30 million per annum (Moynahan 1995).

A previous study by Henehan and White (1990) examined six wine trails in New York, detailing the nature of the wine tourism activity undertaken by the wine trails/alliances and evaluating the effectiveness of these activities. The most salient points arising out of Henehan and White's 1990 study in the context of this section of the chapter relate to the nature of tourism activity undertaken by the various trails. Their study reported that wine trail members engaged in a range of wine tourism initiatives, including the production of marketing collateral such as wine trail brochures; the provision of wine route signage; the production and distribution of newsletters and press releases, and a range of events such as food and wine events, harvest festivals and special tastings (such as barrel tastings and vertical tastings). Henehan and White also reported that the production and distribution of wine trail brochures was the most important wine tourism promotional activity engaged in. The ideal customer was considered to be over thirty, lived in New York or a neighbouring state in a metropolitan area, was in the middle to upper income bracket and owned a small to medium-sized wine cellar (cited in Dodd and Bigotte 1997).

The region of the Finger Lakes has been depicted as 'an area of legendary beauty, captivating geology, spectacular waterfalls, small historic towns, outstanding glacial remains, and rolling hills. Peppering the entire region, the remaining and best vineyards rest on the hillsides that overlook the water' (Baxevanis 1992: 131). Peters (1997: 150) characterizes the winescape of the Finger Lakes viticultural region as 'visually appealing throughout the year, with seasonal changes that are more dramatic than those of the Napa Valley'. The natural attributes and man-made attractions contribute to the development of wine tourism in the area.

The region comprises two AVAs: Cayuga Lake and Finger Lakes. The Cayuga Lake Wine Trail is relatively new and presents a clear indication of the growth of the small wineries. There are ten small wineries along the shores of the Lake, none of which existed before 1980. The much broader Finger Lakes AVA refers to a cluster of eleven narrow north–south glacial lakes, the more important of these being Keuka, Canandaigua, Cayuga and Seneca. The wineries around Keuka, Seneca and Cayuga have organized smaller wine trails with their own brochures. Lake Canandaigua and Lake Keuka have both been referred to as the 'American Rhine' with Lake Canandaigua being the most tourist intensive of the Finger Lakes (Baxevanis 1992). The importance of strategic alliances in marketing wine tourism is evident in the promotional material. The Keuka Lake Wine Route brochure lists nearby bed and breakfasts, motels, restaurants, museums and attractions. The Seneca Lake Wine Trail is also an area of growth with twenty-one wineries, many of which were opened after the Farm Winery Act in 1976 (Baxevanis 1992). The Seneca wineries offer tastings, gourmet food, picnic areas, restaurants and views of the lake.

As in most wine regions, festivals are an important activity and help provide additional sources of income. Around the Finger Lakes regular festivals include the following: Wine and Flower in April, Wine and Herb in May, Pasta and Wine in June, the Finger Lakes Wine Fest in August, the Keuka Lake Harvest in September, the Wine Glass Marathon in November, the Champagne and Desert Wine Festival in November and the Christmas Cheer and Library Auction in December (New York Wine and Grape Foundation, n.d.). In the Annual Deck the Halls event along the Seneca Lake Wine Trail, visitors receive a cookbook and grapevine wreath that they use to collect ornaments as they travel the various wineries. Food and wine pairing are offered based on the cookbook distributed. Several of the wineries have opened restaurants to go along with the tours and the tastings. The region also has several museums, which highlight the wine-making history of the area.

The popularity of wine tourism is undoubtedly continuing to grow in the Finger Lakes region. As McGrath Morris (1985: 19) commented, 'each summer and fall, hundreds of thousands of tourists drive the back roads winding around the Finger Lakes to get a first hand view of the art of winemaking'. In describing wine tourism in the Finger Lakes, it is therefore not surprising that Morgan (1995) predicted a strong future for the area.

Conclusion

The continuing production of high quality, New World wines from regions such as Ontario and the Finger Lakes has considerably re-imaged both the wine industry and the region in these areas. Consequently, increasing numbers of tourists are travelling new wine routes exploring the rural environment. Attempts are being made on both sides of the Ontario–New York border through wine tastings, seminars and festivals, to make wine tourism more accessible to all and perceived less as an elite form of tourism. The development of small boutique wineries, emphasizing high quality wines in both Niagara and the Finger Lakes, has helped to create new winescapes and new tourist destinations.

Similarities in the historical development of the wine industry in Ontario and New York have led to the development of wine tourism. Both regions have been strongly influenced by legislation that has resulted in the restructuring of the wine industry, facilitating the development of small boutique wineries. New York introduced the Farm Winery Act in 1976, recognizing the importance of farm or boutique wineries and permitting increased cellar door sales, while the General Agreement on Tariffs and Trade and the Canada–US Free Trade Agreement rulings catalysed both the Ontario Government and the Ontario wine industry to reconsider the very nature and structure of their industry. In response to these international rulings, 40 per cent of the grape acreage in Ontario, consisting of *labrusca* varieties, was pulled out and has been gradually replaced, mainly by premium varieties grown by independent operators. In effect, these rulings encouraged smaller operators to enter the market with high quality wine. In addition, the introduction of advanced growing techniques and quality control measures in the form of appellation systems have also helped to raise the quality of the wine. In this regard, the development of wine tourism in both areas has also been greatly assisted by entrepreneurs with vision. Indeed, wine tourism in both the Finger Lakes and the Niagara region has been largely driven and assisted by the production of a quality product.

In addition to offering tastings and tours, many wineries are opening gift shops selling related wine and tourism merchandise, thus further diversifying their economic base. Many of the wineries have also linked with other tourism related industries and attractions such as bed and breakfasts, wine tour companies, festivals and local theatres. The development of 'Tastes of Niagara' in Ontario also reflects the emerging trend of linking wine with food to expand the tourism product. Restaurants have opened at some of the wineries on both sides of the border, further strengthening the commitment to local agricultural products.

The wineries have joined forces in the creation of local wine routes and it was the entrepreneurial spirit which led to the creation of the Northeast Wine Route. This concept is an international alliance that provides the opportunity to develop and market a considerably more diverse tourism product. Indeed, as noted by the New York Wine and Grape Foundation 'New York City, Corning, Niagara Falls, and Toronto are major international attractions for tourists. The wine regions of New York and Ontario are either close to, or on the way to, all of those places, so there's great potential synergy from working together to promote a truly international wine route' (Sharp 1996 in New York Wine and Grape Foundation 1997).

As with many wine regions, wine tourism in New York and Ontario is relatively under-researched, and reliable and accurate figures for numbers of visitors and production levels are difficult to find. As the popularity of the wine circuit develops, new wineries are opening up, presenting additional difficulties in determining accurate statistics. In many cases individual wineries do not keep statistics on visitors, and production figures are kept confidential. Nevertheless, the importance of wine tourism to the respective regions as a means of rural development is increasingly being recognized and there is a movement to improve record keeping on the number of visitors. The New York Wine and Grape Foundation, for example, is currently in the process of conducting a survey collecting a wide range of information from all of its wineries. Nevertheless, as wine tourism continues to expand, additional comparative research needs to be done to further investigate the industry, customer profiles, the response of local entrepreneurs and the resulting impacts in the destinations.

14

Diversifying wine tourism products: an evaluation of linkages between wine and cycle tourism

Nigel Morpeth

This chapter explores linkages between cycle tourism and wine tourism as special interest tourist activities that combine the distinctive quality of winescapes, as environments for cycling, and assesses the scope for cycle tourists to take advantage of hospitality, educational and commercial dimensions of wineries. Three principal aspects of linkages between cycle and wine tourism are evaluated.

The chapter initially investigates the philosophy and role of travel companies in providing cycle tourism products linked with wine growing regions, featuring three UK-based travel companies, with comparisons with New World winery bicycle tours. Secondly, the emergence of policy networks and their role in creating linkages between wine tourism and cycle tourism, particularly through the development of themed routes, is investigated. Specific attention is given to a European case study of the Wine and Gourmet Cycle Route, a proposed 3653 km route from the Atlantic Coast of Nantes in France, to Constanta on the shores of the Black Sea in Romania. Finally, there is an analysis of the tourism potential of wineries within major wine regions on the French section of the proposed Wine and Gourmet Route, evaluating the response of vignerons to wine tourists, and in particular the scope for visitation by cycle tourists.

Underpinning these three areas of investigation is the theme of cycle tourism, as a quintessentially environmentally-sustainable tourism form (Bramwell *et al.* 1996), which offers an alternative to the car or coach as a means of winery visitation. Commentators on transport issues have raised concerns about the car as an inefficient mode of transport and of the policy problem of creating parity with other transport modes (e.g. Tolley and Turton 1995; Charlton 1998). Arguably, if transport and tourism policy-makers consider the potential of promoting environmentally-based sustainable tourism in wine regions there is a burden of responsibility to consider alternatives to car-borne tourism. These would allow environmental, as well as the economic and community dimensions of sustainable tourism to emerge, including a reduction in traffic congestion which may otherwise detract from the overall wine tourism experience. This might then allow the scope for diversified tourism forms to provide a 'shift in the centre of gravity' (Hitchcock *et al.* 1993), of motorized visitation to wineries.

Cycle tourism: a reinvented tourism form?

Cycle tourism is emerging as a reinvented tourism form which has many new guises. The solid tradition of cycle tourism as a leisure activity is now augmented by other forms, such as mountain biking. Beioley describes this metamorphosis of the image of cycle tourism, as a transition with 'wicker baskets, cycle clips and plastic capes, replaced by figure hugging lycra' (1995: 17). Increasingly, cycle tourism has become the focus for policy-makers and indeed policy communities (Colebatch 1998) as an exemplar of sustainable tourism (FNNPE 1993). Whilst recent research has defined specific market segments for cycle tourism, from the casual day cyclist to the more independent cycle tourist (Beioley 1995; Lumsden 1996), there is limited research on the motivations of cycle tourists. As a special-interest tourism form, cycle tourism is clearly the hub around which tourist experiences are built; however, this core tourism experience might be augmented by other distinct interests (Hall and Weiler 1992). Gausden puts this view further into perspective by stating that

Enjoyment of nature and sight-seeing combine almost as a matter of course with cycling, and those of you who travel by car will be delighted and surprised by the amount of detail to be discovered as you travel more slowly and easily able to stop and investigate something that has caught your attention. Cycling combines well with many hobbies. (1994: 5)

Additionally, cycle tourism might conform to Fayos-Sola's notion (1996) of the super segmentation of 'new forms' of tourism, in which there is a matrix of activities with which cycle tourists might augment their central tourist activity. This clearly presents challenges to the suppliers of cycle tourist products to recognize and interpret the myriad of motivations that might underpin the choice of a cycle tourism holiday.

In the absence of data on environmental considerations as a key motivating factor for winery visitation by bicycle, it is nevertheless possible to contrast the different philosophies of travel associated with winery visitation. In a recent web page promotion of 'Vineyard crawls in Britain', advice was given to use a car

with good shock absorbers and a large boot (for cases of wine!). It also helps to have a teetotal driver or someone who has sworn off alcohol for the day. Please remember that these vineyards are commercial organizations and if you taste, it is hoped that you will buy wine. (Richardson 1999)

Similarly, New Zealand's De Luxe Travel Line offer luxury air-conditioned coach tours of wineries on the Marlborough Wine Trail. In contrast to this philosophy of winery visitation the New Zealand-based Pacific Cycle Tours promote an independent cycling and wine tasting holiday to the Marlborough Wine Region stating that 'Marlborough is renowned to be one of the world's top ten wine regions. And what better way to experience the dramatic transformation of the fruit of the vine into today's bottle of wine than on a Wine Trail tour by bicycle?' (Pacific Cycle Tours 1999).

With the sustainable credentials of tourist activities, particularly within rural areas, increasingly under greater scrutiny, there is a justification to look more critically at the characteristics of tourists visiting wineries and associated winescapes. What is the role then of travel companies in packaging cycle and wine tourism holidays, combining seemingly disparate forms of tourism and promoting broader environmental considerations within their itineraries?

The role and philosophy of the travel companies

There is a range of specialist tour companies offering products that combine walking, boating and cycle holidays, targeting wine-growing areas of Europe and the New World. Three UK-based travel companies who organize cycle holidays to wine-growing regions, and act as cultural brokers between tourist and wineries, are highlighted. Common dimensions include an enjoyment of local food and wine combined with educational and commercial dimensions of winery visitation. Underpinning these elements are the distinctive winescapes, as environments for cycle touring, either for day or longer vacation periods.

Wine Trails

Stephen Dallyn, Managing Director of Wine Trails, describes his company as providing exclusive group and independent wine holidays, touring the winescapes of eight countries in Europe, South Africa and South America. Their client base is approximately 500 people a year; in response to demand, and by Dallyn's own choice, their main focus of walking holidays has been augmented by cycling itineraries to wine regions (estimated at 5 per cent of their total holidays). The company offers tailor-made itineraries, independent and group holidays, arranging accommodation in small country hotels, with baggage transport arranged.

The philosophy of these holidays is centred on the enjoyment of local wine and food, combined with cycling and walking. In response to the question of the central motivation for holidays, Stephen Dallyn believes that clients have equal motivations related to the centrality of wine and cuisine and the activity content of the holidays – a case of the notion suggested by Smith (1992) of a 'tourist being half a pilgrim and pilgrim being half a tourist'. He also acknowledges that holidays are aimed 'at all people with a wide range of interests that may include history, art, culture, nature, comfortable living, and wine, walking, and most holidays are designed to show an area at its best on foot. There are often chances to stop and sample wines along the way, sometimes formally with a tutor, grower or other expert, sometimes just visiting a *cave* as we walk by, perhaps buying a bottle for lunch' (Wine Trails Brochure 1999/2000). There is also an emphasis on the use of local experts and guides, and their role as cultural brokers in enabling their clients to 'interact' with wine-makers is governed by the requirement of clients for 'quick tastings' or more 'involved visits'.

The Alternative Travel Group

Now with a twenty-year pedigree, the Alternative Travel Group was originally established on the 'principles of conservation and sustainable tourism'. The company has built up well-researched itineraries for cyclists and walkers on continuous routes throughout Europe and also enables travellers to create their own à la carte itineraries. As with Wine Trails, the Alternative Travel Group transports luggage between accommodation destinations, and stress their role as cultural brokers, providing invaluable local insights on the cultural facets of each location particularly focusing on local cuisine and wine.

Bike Tours

Bike Tours specialize in longer trans-European routes (e.g. Bordeaux to Barcelona, Prague to Venice) but also have itineraries with a more regional focus, incorporating two principal wine tours in France, the Loire Valley and the Bordeaux Wine Trail. The Bordeaux itinerary provides an opportunity for

> a real wine education in a week. From the flatlands of the reclaimed Medoc, this tour includes vineyards of the famous Clarets of Haut Medoc and St Emilion . . . Throughout the week you will visit several chateaux where you will have the chance to taste wines and explore the vines and the process of winemaking. The vignerons, or winemakers, really make this holiday – with luck you may get to taste from the barrel and you'll get the chance to see every step in the process from vine to 'bottled sunshine' against the wonderful backdrop of the Gironde and the Dordogne rivers. (Bike Tours Brochure 1999)

The cycle tourist products of these three companies, incorporating the special qualities of winescapes, are by no means unique; specialist cycle tours to wine regions are organized in California, New Zealand and Australia and share common philosophies with the three UK companies. Cycle tour itineraries in California include the Napa and Sonoma County Wine Country Tour, promoted as a gourmet cycling adventure based on group camping which follows existing wine trails.

Cycle Tours

Cycle Tours advertise a nineteen-day tour to twelve wineries in New Zealand's North and South Islands, and Pacific Cycle Tours offer an independent cycling and wine tasting holiday to the Marlborough Wine region extolling the advantages of cycle tourism. Each of the wine-producing regions within Australia boasts an itinerary for cycle tourism. The Wine and Wilderness Company offer tours in all the major wine regions, with itineraries including visits to up to seventeen vineyards within one holiday. Gourmet Tours of Australia offer five to six night Gourmet Cycling Tours for A$2200 including tours of vineyards in South Australia, WA, NSW and Tasmania.

Travel companies have responded to commercial opportunities and are playing a key role in providing linkages between cycle tourism and wine tourism, often combined with a range of other interests, and as cultural brokers they also interpret the extent to which tourists and wine-makers interact, stressing the importance of the regional qualities of wine-growing areas, as much as the central focus of winery visitation.

The European cycle network: The wine and gourmet route

It is clear that supply-side operators have responded to the commercial opportunities of linking tourists with wineries across a number of continents, but what is the legitimate role of public sector policy-makers in relation to the development of tourist opportunities associated with wine tourism? Hall and Macionis (1998: 220) note the key role that regional and national governments play in developing networks that stimulate greater linkages between wine and tourism (also see Chapter 11). Wine regions possess the potential cultural capital to use wine as an intrinsic part of the branding of regions for tourism and for overtly economic policy aims. Through the regional organization of *routes des vin*, France has a well-established network of promoted routes for tourists to follow in each of the wine-producing regions. Anecdotal evidence suggests that these routes are mainly used by car-borne tourists and that they are underused by cyclists. The planned Wine and Gourmet Route from Nantes in France to Constanta in Romania is a current initiative which relies on cooperative development by many stakeholders, including regional and local government, working in partnership with cycle and tourist organizations. This route is part of a broader EuroVelo initiative of twelve pan-European routes, co-developed by Sustrans (a UK-based sustainable transport charity) and the European Cyclists' Federation. The project has two principal aims, which focus on the development of utilitarian cycling and cycle tourism. Great emphasis is placed in using financial resources, including EU support and financial backing. In November 1997 in Logroño, Spain, Robert Coleman, the Transport Commissioner of the European Commission, added legitimacy to this project; he declared financial backing to bolster international cooperation

between inter-regional bodies such as cycling organizations, tourist organizations and local and regional governments, towards not only a more
sustainable form of tourism but also major themes of environmental
protection, local job creation and heritage projects. Sustrans observes that

> EuroVelo would be an important factor in uniting Europe at a human
> level. Whilst the car shields its occupants from their surroundings, the
> bicycle does just the opposite. Cyclists are very much in touch with
> everyday life of the towns and villages they pass through. They meet the
> local community in shops and cafés, in farms and at the road side.
> Travelling slowly, they avoid the culture shock of motor travel, see the
> similarities between regions as well as the differences, and become
> familiar with language and the culture. (1996: 6)

Sustrans views the ongoing development of this project as mobilizing
'campaigners, politicians, professionals and anyone in transport, tourism and
the environment [in] play[ing] a role' (1996: 6). Sustrans in conjunction with
EuroVelo has adopted the UK National Cycle Network model of branding the
twelve planned routes with a particular theme. The Wine and Gourmet Route
is designed to draw on the regional cultural identities expressed through wine
and cuisine. Le Petit *et al.* identify 'a strong cultural and physical coherence'
in favour of this choice of route which combines 'Locations of world-wide
reputation which link prestigious tourist areas such as the Loire Valley,
Burgundy, the Rhine and Danube Valleys, Vienna, Budapest, the Sub-
Carpathian hills and the Danube Delta' (n.d.: 5).

This proposed 3653 km cycle route links together ten specific sections,
combining existing cycle routes in France, Switzerland, Germany, Austria,
Hungary and Romania (with the original planned route passing through
Serbia). The impetus for route development in France is the emerging 'Loire
à Velo' 240 km route from Nantes to Mulhouse. In Austria and Germany route
development incorporates the existing 700 km transnational 'Donauradweg'
cycle route, described by Philip Insall, Sustrans' European Liaison Officer, as
'Europe's most successful long distance cycle route'. There is also 1400 km of
continuous signed cycle routes linking Basel and Budapest. The proposed
route can rely therefore on existing traffic-free sections with a developed
accommodation and tourist infrastructure and established inter-modality with
public transportation. Whilst the route concept is at an early stage of
development, it is hoped that cycle tourists will capitalize on the wine and
gourmet elements that combine to add distinct regional identity to the various
sections of the route infrastructure. Le Petit *et al.* believe that the route will

enable cyclists to take advantage of 'the famous white wines of Loire and Burgundy to the less known Stadtberger in Eglisau on the Rhine till the Hungarian Tokaj, or the Sub-Carpathian wines in Romania' (n.d.: 6). Given that this route traverses six different European countries there is a further challenge of uniting project aims in countries and regions which are at different stages of developing cycling and tourism policies (Le Petit *et al.*, n.d.: 6).

L'Association SABINE (the French equivalent of Sustrans), in conjunction with L'Association pour le Développement des Veloroutes, have acted as consultants on route selection. Philippe Coupy of L'Association SABINE indicates that the route is at an early stage of development, with the first task to persuade regional administrative authorities, initially within the various Départements, to embrace the concept of the development of an infrastructure for cycle tourism. He acknowledges that the interest shown by central government, with the Ministre de l'Environnement creating a working group on cycle routes, will help to galvanize support for the concept of cycle route development such as the Wine and Gourmet Route within France.

Philippe Coupy hopes that regional governments and tourist authorities will be impressed by the economic potential of cycle tourism. Whilst still largely in the conceptual stage, the route architects are confident that this proposed development can capitalize on the popularity of the Donauradweg route cited earlier, with Le Petit *et al.* (n.d.) estimating that 100,000 cyclists currently use this route each year. This also mirrors the success of routes such as the Noordzeeroute, a 470 km cross-border cycle route, which has united policy communities in route development in the Netherlands, Belgium and France. The Wine and Gourmet Route will be supported by interpretative materials, providing cyclists with information on the main thematic elements of wine and cuisine, of opportunities to visit historic villages and towns and to take part in a range of leisure activities. One of the key issues to address, however, is the response of wineries to visitation by tourists, and in particular by cycle tourists.

The tourist potential of wineries on the Wine and Gourmet Route

Consistent with the significance of the Wine and Gourmet Cycle Route following three major European rivers, Loire, Rhine, Danube and linking waterways, Hilary Wright (1996b) focuses on the recreational use of waterways and canals. She highlights their utility as a means of exploring some of France's greatest wine-producing regions, and identifies the role of the bicycle in augmenting water-borne travel into wine areas. Her book combines information on the major wine regions of France with guidance on cycling and walking routes to wineries, and offers the view that with 'a bike your touring range is vastly increased, making some of the prettiest regions and best winemakers in France accessible. If you are hiring a cruiser you can hire bikes from the boat company' (1996b:12).

Her accounts of visits to wine-makers are described from the perspective of cyclists searching out vineyards from their boats, capitalizing on the often spectacular countryside of the wine regions and taking advantage of local cuisine and wines. Wright states that the waterways, which initially encouraged the opening up of the rural countryside to trade, and significantly the development of wine-making, are increasingly used as corridors for water-borne tourism. She uses the example of Alsace, with the north-flowing Rhine over the ages taking wine to the non-producing regions of Northern Europe, and now there is a reverse flow of tourists travelling down to the wine regions of France. The leitmotif of Wright's book emphasizes the personal contact of the tourist arriving by boat and cycle interacting with wine-makers, who she argues positively encourage visitors.

On the basis of wineries listed by Wright as 'cyclist/boat friendly,' a faxed questionnaire was sent to 40 vignerons within the wine-growing regions of Nantes and Angers, Chablis, Sancerre and Pouilly-sur-Loire, Burgundy and Alsace. The purpose of this survey was to identify the tourism potential of wineries that will be accessible on the Wine and Gourmet Route, and particularly to assess the current visitation by cycle tourists. Of the ten responses received, nine of the vignerons organized tours of wineries either as a *visite* or *dégustation*. On average 70–95 per cent of visitors arrived by car, with between 4 and 15 per cent arriving by coach. Arrivals by bicycle ranged from 1 to 5 per cent, with an awareness that 5–10 per cent of visitors arrive by a combination of boat and bicycle. Château de la Tour in Burgundy identified four groups of American cyclists who had visited the winery in the same year, and likewise Domaine Prieur-Brunet, in Burgundy, received two cycle groups. Domaine Tinel Blondeflet in Sancerre listed fifteen to twenty cycle groups in the same year, from England, Germany and the Netherlands. Fifty per cent of respondents identified the existence of cycle tracks within their vineyard, with 60 per cent of vignerons stating that their wineries were on existing *routes des vin*, routes that are shared by motorists and cyclists alike.

Although only three wineries stated that they had a tourism business plan, all but one winery had infrastructure to receive visitors, with a combination of restaurants, accommodation, shops, picnic places and museums. Sixty per cent of wineries are part of a festival of wine, either organized by the winery or appellation. There was a mixed response to the number of visitors who buy wine, with answers ranging from 1 to 100 per cent. Vigneron Gitton Père et Fils, in Sancerre, stated that 'cyclists are not necessarily very interesting to organize tours – if they have boats or cars to back up vehicles O.K. But cyclists usually drink as much as they buy as they don't have the facility for portage. This is certainly not appreciated as wine makers also need to give of their time. This is not always recognized by cyclists'. He does receive bicycle visitors each year from boats from the local canal and clearly places great emphasis on the commercial opportunities of receiving visitors.

The evidence from this brief survey is that the majority of visitors to the wineries surveyed arrive by car, take advantage of signed *routes des vin*, and are welcomed for either a *visite* or *dégustation*. Facilities for hospitality at the wineries are well developed with accommodation, restaurants, shops, picnic places and museums, and three vignerons recognized the tourism potential of the winery through the existence of a tourism business plan. Cyclists do feature as visitors and the acknowledgement of group visits by different nationalities of cyclists indicates the potential to attract market segments beyond a domestic market. The fact that 50 per cent of wineries have cycle tracks through their vineyards provides a further dimension for cyclists to enjoy the terrain of the vineyard as well as the winery itself.

Conclusions: Future scope for linkages between cycle and wine tourism

There is compelling evidence that wineries are increasingly the focus of tourist activity. The evidence from the survey of vignerons is that wineries have a range of tourist facilities ranging from restaurants, shops, accommodation, picnic places and museums and a limited number of wineries have tourism business plans. They are hosting both independent travellers and travel companies such as Wine Trails, the Alternative Travel Company and Bike Tours, who exemplify a philosophy and a scale and pace of tourist activity that allows the tourist to appreciate both the landscape and cultural aspects of wine regions and wineries from a different perspective to car-borne visitation. The development of tourist routes specifically for the bicycle, such as the planned Wine and Gourmet Cycle Route, indicates the commitment of a combination of stakeholders to create alternatives to car-borne travel in the wine regions of Europe. This is perhaps an indication of a commitment to foster sustainable forms of tourism that embrace environmental, community and economic dimensions and provide new opportunities for tourists to enjoy wineries and the landscapes of wine-making regions from a different perspective to car-borne travellers. There is a solid foundation of route development to capitalize on with the Loire and Donauradweg sections of the route and 1400 km of continuous signed routes from Basel to Budapest offering immediate cycle tourism opportunities. However, there are operational constraints to overcome, not least the proposed section from Budapest to Constanta which is identified as having limited tourist potential and an underdeveloped accommodation infrastructure. Nevertheless there is great optimism by Le Petit *et al.* (n.d.) that by 2005 the route will provide the cycle tourist with an exposure not only to wineries en route but to a rich combination of cultural attractions and leisure activities.

The extent to which wineries recognize the significance of the cyclist in winery tours is still open to question. The indication from the survey of vignerons in the wine-growing regions of France is that there is visitation by cyclists and indeed some wineries have cycle tracks through their vineyards. Clearly if wineries are to feature increasingly as a central focus for sustainable visitation of wine-growing regions, and in particular by cycle tourists, then linkages identified in this chapter require further development. Wright's observations (1996b) about the linkages between water-borne tourism and cycling adds a further dimension to the diversification of linkages between wine and tourism, a point reiterated in the plans for the Wine and Gourmet Cycle Route. It appears from the survey responses that this linkage between water-borne tourism and cycling is acknowledged by vignerons and provides encouragement to stakeholders wanting to combine the tourist potential of cycling, waterways and wineries.

15

Napa Valley, California: a model of wine region development

Angela M. Skinner

The wine industry in California is big business. According to the Wine Institute, a California-based industry lobby group, winegrapes are grown in 45 of California's 58 counties and with more than 407,000 acres of vines wine production ranks among the state's top ten agricultural commodities. Furthermore, they note that in 1998 the wine industry contributed an estimated US$10.9 billion in economic activity to California, while around 8 million people visit Californian wine-producing areas each year. This wine tourism activity generates additional expenditure of more than US$300 million in restaurants, hotels and other associated establishments (Wine Institute 1998).

California's Napa Valley, with more than 240 wineries along its 30-mile length, is the heart and soul of the state's wine industry and its wine tourism Disneyland. The Napa Valley Vintners

Association estimate that 17,000 jobs are directly related to wineries, wine-making and wine tourism in the Napa Valley and that wineries, vineyards and the scenic open spaces of the region are Napa County's top tourist attraction, drawing 5 million visitors in 1998 (Napa Valley Vintners Association 1999).

While tourism, marketing, and wine industry experts tend to view wine tourism viability in such an economic context, very little has been written about the effects of wine tourism on destination sites, or on sustaining the natural and cultural environments on which they are based (see Chapter 11). Indeed, the development and maintenance of a sense of place is critical to both wine and tourism (Hall *et al.* 1998). What is sold is an image of uniqueness imbuing both wine and area with character. In the case of the Napa Valley, there are concerns that the grape-ification of the region and subsequent tourism development have resulted in the loss of some of the destinational characteristics of the area, such as its scenic beauty, that originally made it desirable (Boxall 1999). It has even been suggested that wine tourism has become so successful that wine-making is now a peripheral activity (Sharp 1992). The negative impacts of wine tourism not only severely limit the capacity of the wineries to provide a positive tourism experience for their patrons, but in altering the rural, pastoral landscape, they ultimately threaten to destroy the tourism product itself.

In order to maintain the distinctive character of a wine region or destination appellation, a number of important factors impacting wine tourism destination sites should be considered. This chapter examines some of these impacts within the framework of a model of wine region development and discusses the need for the implementation of sustainable wine tourism development practices in a destinational context. Applying Butler's destination evolution model (1980) to the development of a wine region, and using a case study of the Napa Valley, issues of wine tourism sustainability are discussed.

The impacts of tourism on a wine region destination

While the benefits and costs of wine tourism participation have been examined in an individual enterprise context (e.g. see Dodd 1995; Hall and Macionis 1998; Macionis and Cambourne 1998; Hall *et al.* 1998; see also Chapters 7 and 8), the impacts of wine tourism are seldom analysed in a complete destination context.

At a regional or destination level, a number of benefits may accrue from the development of wine tourism. For example, the immediate economic impact from tourist expenditure, as noted earlier in this chapter, is often cited as a wine tourism development incentive. Tourists and consumers have also become sensitive to environmental issues and, as a result, a number of grape growers and vintners have begun to recognize the economic advantages of ecosystem management (Baum 1999). Other benefits to residents of wine tourism destination sites include education and employment opportunities within the industry, better wages, working conditions and social status, as well as increases in and development of local entrepreneurial endeavours. Visitor interest in these regions can also bolster the value and esteem of local culture (Macionis and Cambourne 1998).

Yet, despite the benefits that wine tourism can offer, there are also numerous negative impacts. Environmental degradation, such as pollution and denudation, of tourism areas presents problems for residents and aesthetic eyesores for tourists (Andereck 1995; Haight and Ratha 1995). In Santa Barbara County, California, conservationists are fighting the loss of native California oak trees to viticultural development, arguing that monotonous grapescapes have replaced scenic oak-studded grazing land (Boxall 1999). Residents of Sonoma, California, actively concern themselves with maintaining wild green space, eschewing large-scale development and what they term 'Napafication' (DeTurenne 1999).

Residents of tourism sites face a range of other problems. They are often not given any control over planning or implementation of tourism development, are relegated to the lowest wage jobs within the industry, and are sometimes forced off their lands, either directly or through increases in land values (Lindberg, et al. 1996; Hall and Johnson 1998b). A rise in land values around wine regions is common as viticulture expands and tourism development grows. In Napa Valley, land values have reached six figures. Workers immigrating to the tourism site can also overload services and lead to higher levels of unemployment. Additionally, in many cases, wine tourism revenues bypass the wineries and local communities completely, remaining instead in the hands of tour operators (Hussey 1982; Cambourne 1999; Macionis 1999). Without the ability to control tourist access to their communities, local people may become increasingly marginalized, their social framework no longer having meaning or function beyond entertainment value (Greenwood 1989).

Sustainable wine tourism planning considerations

As wine regions become increasingly dependent on tourism revenues, the need to sustain tourism as a viable economic resource grows. It is important,

285

however, to make the distinction between sustaining the wine tourism industry itself and developing wine tourism according to sustainable development principles (Butler 1999). In the first case, tourism is developed in such a way so as to ensure its own success indefinitely. In the second, it is developed with the intention of sustaining all of the elements which comprise a destination site.

Of these two approaches to destination area success, unlimited growth or sustainability, the former is impossible to maintain and the latter is extremely difficult (Butler 1997). Indeed, the term sustainable development is something of a paradox in that it implies both preservation ('sustainable') and change ('development') (Aronsson 1994). The way in which sustainability is defined depends upon the context in which the term is used. There is little agreement on an exact definition. For the purposes of this chapter, however, Aronsson's definition (1994: 77) provides a basis for examining the sustainability of wine tourism:

> Sustainable tourism development should entail a long-[term] perspective for the use of resources in tourism production. A form of tourism should be developed that contributes to creating equality and economic and social welfare for the local community; tourism development should make careful use of the natural and cultural conditions, including the built environment; positive tourism development in line with the above points should not be a burden on other people and areas or on coming generations.

Essentially, for tourism to survive and prosper, the resources on which the tourism product is based must be protected (Andereck 1995). In the case of wine tourism, implementing sustainable regional development guidelines is crucial to its long-term success.

Adopting such guidelines requires planning, management, and commitment (Butler 1997). Most importantly, it also requires an understanding of the needs of local people and a commitment to improving their economic welfare, allowing them to benefit from tourism and resist unwanted changes. Indeed, an understanding of the attitudes and aspirations of wine tourists, tour operators, government, and local residents within a wine region destination area should be one of the first steps in wine tourism planning and management. Including local residents in management strategies facilitates their understanding, and thus their acceptance of those strategies, and minimizes stakeholder perceptions of their lifestyle disenfranchisement as evidenced within Napa Valley (Sharp 1992; Kaltenborn 1996).

Successful wine destination planning and development also requires a knowledge of the carrying capacity of the natural and cultural environments. Often an examination of the carrying capacity of a wine region is limited to profit distribution or the visual quality acceptable to tourists (Cambourne 1999). Carrying capacity has environmental, economic, socio-cultural, and aesthetic qualities. It is more than a matter of the maximum number of tourists a site can accommodate. The carrying capacity of a tourist site is reached when the number of tourists and their activities begin to degrade the natural environment, the quality of life desired by the resident population, and the visual quality of the site.

It is important to note that unrestrained development can drastically alter any tourism site. Even low-impact, sustainable tourism will result in change over time. The objective is to keep the changes positive and appropriate. Without a plan of action and the management infrastructure to enforce policies for sustainability, the tourism industry, in this case wine tourism, has a tendency toward uncontrolled growth. The pressure for short-term gains is strong, often outweighing long-term plans (Martin and Uysal 1990; Butler 1991, 1997; Healy 1994). This trend is most often contained by market forces, which encourage development on a basis of cost rather than on the inherent qualities of the region which make it attractive in the first place.

A commitment to common goals and objectives is critical, especially if an area is managed by more than one agency. Government intervention may be necessary. Without legislation and regulation, the control of negative impacts is exceedingly difficult (Andereck 1995).

Butler's tourism area cycle of evolution

Formal models of tourism development are difficult to present, as variables at each site can change markedly and no two sites will respond to tourism development at the same rate or in the same sequence of stages (Butler 1980; Price 1992). Not all elements need be present for an area to reach a certain stage, nor will stages be followed in a continuous fashion at each destination. Tourism development can have a number of vectors, from the presence of low-budget travellers such as backpackers causing the initiation of locally-controlled (or organic) development, to government (or induced) institution of tourism, to mixed approaches which lie between the organic and induced extremes (Cohen 1983). Butler's model (1980) of the hypothetical evolution of a tourist area provides a conceptual framework within which to analyse the development of wine regions with respect to tourism.

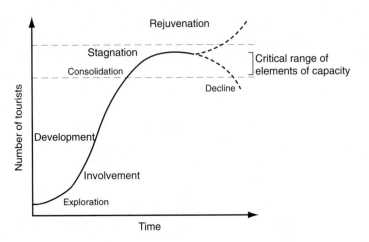

Figure 15.1 Hypothetical model of tourism evolution. (*Source*: after Butler, 1980).

Butler's model describes the evolution of a tourist area, from exploration or discovery, through growth to stabilization, and ending in a range of alternative outcomes, from rejuvenation to decline (Figure 15.1). These various evolutionary stages are described below:

- *Exploration* – In the exploration stage, a few pioneering visitors discover and visit a site despite a lack of facilities, and their arrival and departure affects little within the local community.
- *Involvement* – Once the number of visitors begins to show a significant increase, facilities are built specifically for catering to the needs of tourists. Changes in the social and economic structure of the community can be expected as the area begins to organize some of its activities around the tourist.
- *Development* – At this point, the area has made noticeable changes to the physical landscape, especially with respect to infrastructure. Marketing to the tourist is heavy, planning requires political involvement, and the seasonal cycle is pronounced. Local population may double at peak times. The pioneering tourist no longer finds the area an acceptable destination.
- *Consolidation* – Eventually, the impact of continual change is met with opposition by members of the local community. Recreational business districts, seasonally active districts catering almost exclusively to tourists, are fully developed, while older facilities begin to decline.

■ *Stagnation* – At the stagnation stage, capacity is reached, with natural and cultural attractions once found appealing by the pioneering tourist often replaced by the artificial. Organized mass tourism may be present, but is not generating enough visitation to the area to replace losses to more popular sites, and local businesses feel the effects of the decline.

From stagnation, the area may either enter the decline stage, with few tourists, dilapidating facilities, and a shift away from the tourism industry, or the rejuvenation stage, whereby a drastic change in attractions will occur, making tourism redevelopment a viable alternative to a shift away from the industry.

Application of the development model to wine tourism sites

Application of Butler's development model (1980) to wine tourism destinations permits wine regions to identify their position in the evolutionary continuum and to recognize changes occurring in the destination. In Table 15.1, the evolution of a wine tourism destination is divided into Butler's evolutionary stages. This wine tourism development model also includes two alternatives to stagnation and decline.

While the model offers suggestions for identification of a site's characteristics, it is not exhaustive. It should also be recognized that any wine tourism site or destination will need to be analysed individually, as the divisions between stages are often fuzzy and the sequence of development may be interrupted or shortened. For example, viticulture may become an area hallmark (Stage IV – Consolidation) without a substantial investment in tourism, as in the Burgundy region of France, where only 260 of 5000 wine-growers actively seek tourist dollars (Choisy 1996; see also Chapters 2 and 3). Alternatively, a region may experience the beginnings of industry growth (Stage II), then be overtaken by urbanization, as is the case in parts of San Bernardino County, California, in and around the city of Fontana (Peters 1997 1998b); or as in the Swan Valley in Western Australia (see Chapter 11).

In the early stages of wine region evolution, rural viticultural areas may have only very basic tourism infrastructure, such as a small inn or run-down motel, or perhaps nothing in the immediate surrounding area (Stage I). Gradually, with the increase in visitors comes an expansion of tourism infrastructure, such as tasting rooms and more adequate and upscale accommodation, as well as a greater level of destination promotion (Stages II and III). Increasing numbers of tourists reduce the enjoyment of the pastoral

Table 15.1   Descriptions of the stages of wine tourism development

STAGE I – Exploration	■ Viticulture introduced. Appellation established. Rural residence. Little or no tourism. ■ Three to five years to crop viability. Wineries may buy grapes from other vineyards to make wine in the interim. ■ Wineries built on site. Production begins. Pioneering wine enthusiasts begin making contact to taste wines.
STAGE II – Involvement	■ Successful production. Slow growth of viticultural ventures. ■ Wine writers take note. Award-winning wines bring recognition. ■ Number of tourists showing a significant increase. Addition of tasting facilities to some wineries. ■ Outsiders looking for rural, wine country lifestyle begin purchasing vineyards and building homes.
STAGE III – Development	■ Increased growth of viticulture. ■ Area included in most guidebooks and wine maps. Pronounced seasonal tourism cycle. ■ Attempts to attract tourists successful. Number of accommodations marketing the wine country experience increase. ■ Tasting rooms, whether on-site, off-site, or collectives, now part of all wineries. ■ Immigration of workers and entrepreneurs increases as tourism infrastructure and economic opportunities improve. ■ Pioneer tourists avoid the area.
STAGE IV – Consolidation	■ Viticulture becomes area hallmark. Streets and businesses take on wine country names. ■ Guidebooks published exclusively about the area. Introduction of mass tourism. ■ Established wineries grow, planting new acreage and increasing tourism development. Some smaller ventures sell out to larger wineries or developers. ■ Tourism brings in substantial revenue. Tourists overwhelming infrastructure. Locals frustrated with traffic, noise, pollution, crowding. Some locals move away. City council holds hearings for solutions.

STAGE V – Stagnation	■ Tourism development and subdivisions removing agricultural lands from production. ■ Land prices increase such that only wealthy individuals can afford to buy homes or new land for vineyards.
	■ Viticulture loses ground to urban development, pushed to outer fringes of region. ■ Tourism still substantial, but moving to alternative attractions. Infrastructure improvements ease ingress. ■ Corporate ventures look for cheaper areas to farm. More locals move away to escape urban sprawl.
STAGE VI – Decline	■ Decline of wine tourism. Shift to new industry or tourism attraction. ■ Area character now completely urban. Viticulture no longer practised. ■ Some wineries may still produce wines with grapes purchased from other regions. ■ Wine tourism may continue on a small scale if some wineries or tasting rooms remain in the urban area. ■ Names of streets and local businesses may be the only remaining indications of former industry.
STAGE V (alternative) – Cooperation	■ Agricultural preserves established. Viticulture maintained. Development curtailed by city planners. ■ Wineries develop collective tourism plan to deal with substantial numbers of tourists. ■ Infrastructure improvements and alternative wine routes ease the pressures of tourist traffic. ■ Resident/visitor conflicts reduced through communication links between residents, tourism industry, and local government. Some locals may still move away.
STAGE VI (alternative) – Conservation	■ Viticulture in equilibrium with urban area, maintaining positive association with tourist trade. ■ Viticultural region recognized internationally. Wine region cultural traditions preserved over time.

landscape by others. They may interfere with the proper functioning of the working environment, slowing the movement of grapes from vineyard to winery with their traffic. Development is spurred on by tourism growth and the price of land increases. Frequently the land becomes so valuable that even the most successful farmers feel that holding on to it is no longer in their own best interests (Stage IV). Eventually the viticultural region becomes threatened. As agricultural interests in the area lessen, suppliers and other supporting businesses relocate, increasing production costs. Wineries move as the vineyards which supported them disappear (Stage V). Soon the wine region is subsumed by urban or suburban growth, remembered only in street names and historical accounts (Peters 1997, 1998a). Santa Clara, California, also called Silicon Valley, is a good example of Stage VI – Decline. Once highly praised for its award-winning wines, it is now better known for its thriving technology industry.

Providing a sustainable wine tourism product depends upon the survival of the local wine industry. In this wine tourism application of Butler's model, the alternative to stagnation, cooperation, requires a commitment to slow growth and the partnership of all parties affected by any policy changes. For example, agricultural preserves like those found in Napa and Santa Ynez Valleys and the Buck Mesa area of Temecula may be established to slow the growth of housing and tourism development (Conaway 1990; Gillette 1998; Peters 1998a, 1998b). However, these preserves are largely voluntary and subject to periodic renewal. Indeed, residents, farmers, wine industry professionals, and a number of other dedicated interests have fought to maintain Napa Valley's agricultural preserves, dragging the region partially into this alternate Stage V. Because the cooperation stage is difficult to achieve, the next stage, conservation, is not known at this time to be exhibited by any wine region in California.

The case of Napa Valley, California

As American land speculators moved westward in the country's early days, they began selling the idea of the California lifestyle, an eclectic combination of the cosmopolitan life and the country, where small farms, specializing mostly in cash crops such as squashes, fruits and nuts, provided the pastoral backdrop to a simpler life outside the big city. The Napa Valley was just one such area. In 1965, it had a distinctively rural character, especially in the upper valley, with cattle ranches, prune farms, and a growing number of vineyards. A few wealthy San Francisco families had summer homes there, but there were very few tourists. At that point in its development, the Napa Valley was clearly in the exploration stage of its wine country evolution.

Even at this early point, residents and growers were concerned that the area might turn into another bedroom community for San Franciscans and so passed a measure in 1968 to create agricultural preserves. These preserves were agreements between growers and local government to maintain the practice of viticulture for a contracted period of time (generally in the order of ten years or so), thus removing their lands from subdivision and speculation. The preserves supported viticulture as the Valley's trademark, and thus ensured the profits associated with wine tourism, which later grew rapidly as the Valley moved through the involvement, development and consolidation stages. While wine tourism had been promoted by wineries since the late 1940s, it was not until the early 1970s and 1980s that wine suddenly became a part of the ideal California lifestyle and interest in wine tourism grew. As a result, life in the Valley began to change:

> The children of these 'vintners' would grow up . . . accustomed to . . . the pleasures of life far from the raucous cities and suburbs their parents had left behind . . . Some would seek to turn the land into tourist attractions, increasingly urged to exploit the place. Finally, the Valley would take on a gloss that had more to do with money than with the product for which it became famous; it would be transformed into a paradigm of material ambition and dissent, threatened by the very brilliance of the imprint it left on the world. (Conaway 1990: 3–4)

Napa Valley had been made famous by its recently-acquired international status as a world-class wine-making region. And the success of the television drama *Falcon Crest*, which used the Valley as the setting for its greedy intrigues, brought tourists from far and wide looking for the real thing (Conaway 1990). Developers, eager to cash in on their new image, began pushing for development. At the same time, vintners were fighting against additional 'slow-growth' proposals which aimed to define and limit the activities of the wineries and the ways in which they catered to tourists. Growers were also concerned that the wineries were developing tourism too quickly, threatening the agricultural preserves and the whole trade of the Valley. In order to raise the price of their product, they lobbied for a law requiring all new wineries to make their wines from at least 75 per cent Napa Valley grapes.

By 1988, in an area comprising little over 100,000 residents, the number of tourists yearly visiting the Valley reached 4 million (Conaway 1990). Visitor numbers have continued to increase, reaching almost 5 million by 1998. Slow-growth initiatives reduced strip development along Highway 29, the main route and scenic corridor through wine country, but Valley vintners and entrepreneurs continue to pressure the Napa County Planning Commission and Board of Supervisors for variances.

Today, tourists crawl along the two-lane roads from winery to winery, through bumper-to-bumper traffic on summer weekends. During the grape harvest, or crush, tourist traffic also interferes with the movement of grapes from vineyard to winery. Marketed to tourists as an alternative to suffering traffic congestion, the Napa Valley Wine Train carries passengers from one end of the Valley to the other, serving wine and meals along the way, without passengers ever alighting to actually experience the Valley. Adapted from an older, disused line, the rail criss-crosses the main highway in numerous places, stopping traffic at crossings and further delaying the movement of grapes and supplies. The train's piercing whistle, which by law must be blasted at every crossing, can be heard throughout the Valley, further diminishing rural tranquillity.

There is an invisible line that separates the powerful development interests from the growers and residents who don't want to see the area subsumed by urban sprawl. While Napa County businesses fight for access to wine tourist dollars, there is an ambivalence on the part of Napa residents toward tourism. The traffic, noise, and overwhelming presence of outsiders often causes anger and frustration for those living within the confines of the narrow Valley. Cooperation and diligence on the part of those opposed to development is critical. All it takes to end Napa's agricultural preserves is a majority vote of the County Board of Supervisors (Conaway 1990).

Based on the discussion above, the Napa wine region appears to be in the consolidation stage. It also contains some of the elements necessary for cooperation, manifested by the existence of agricultural preserves and slow-growth regulations. However, despite the existence of organizations such as the Napa Valley Vintners Association, the wineries have yet to implement a collective plan to limit the effects their patrons have on the region's environment and social structure. Solutions need to be devised for problems such as the press of traffic along country routes. The needs and wants of local residents also require attention, as their voices are often subsumed beneath the din of the wine industry's money clanking in the local coffers. Again, it should be noted that this model is suggestive and the boundaries between stages are mutable, but its application can assist researchers in devising an appropriate methodology for the study of wine tourism.

Conclusions

The examination and application of this wine tourism development model raises several important questions regarding the concept of sustainable development in wine regions. How can tourism in these areas be made sustainable in terms of the physical and cultural environment? While more and more tourists are exploring alternative forms of tourism in line with sustainable ideals, mass tourism continues to grow (Butler 1999). This being the case, can sustainable practices be applied to mass tourism in wine regions? Should new and existing tourism operations be regulated by outside agencies? How can the wine tourism product be maintained in the long term?

Presenting appropriate limits to wine tourism development requires detailed studies of all the elements of carrying capacity within and around a wine region. It requires careful planning and management which incorporates all interested parties, including local, regional, and national governments; tourism operators; vintners and viticulturists; other local business operators; and most especially the residents who will be forced to bear the environmental, social, economic, political, and aesthetic burdens of tourism. Enforcement of management policies is also critical. Smaller wineries and tour operations should be regulated as closely as any corporate giant. The presence of several small, uncoordinated ventures can be as destructive as one large development.

Agricultural preserves appear to provide advantages for growers and residents, and serve to remove vineyards from development pressures. A number of California wine regions have instituted similar preserves. In Santa Barbara County, for example, the terms of the contract are for ten years, renewable at the end of each year. However, all that is required to end the contract in any one year is agreement by all parties or a majority vote by local government. As such, this would seem to make the contract somewhat tenuous. In Napa County, problems have arisen as shifts in political ideology have occurred. However, because they were employed early on, the preserves reduced urban and tourism expansion at a critical juncture in the area's history, and the Napa Valley continues to thrive, both agriculturally and in terms of numbers of tourists.

The idea that wineries and tour operators can regulate their own tourism activities is naive. Without outside control, there is a tendency to focus on short-term profits at the expense of long-term goals. Allowing wine tourism to develop along similar lines to the Napa Valley has serious consequences that cannot be ignored. Indeed, perhaps limiting the growth of wine tourism is necessary in order to preserve the viticultural backbone of the tourism product and the rural nature of wine regions. Just what those limits should be can be specifically tailored to the individual region.

Not all of the questions posed above can be answered succinctly, due in part to the youth of both the concept of sustainable development and formal wine tourism development. As Butler (1999: 20) points out, 'In the absence of accurate and reliable indicators and monitoring, one cannot comment on the sustainability of any enterprise until many years after its establishment, and only then, after comparing its operation and effects, to the state of the environment at the time of its establishment'. However, by examining their own product within the framework of this wine tourism development model, wine regions and future researchers can identify appropriate levels of tourism development that will be environmentally and socially sustainable within their destinations.

16

The future of wine tourism

Brock Cambourne, Niki Macionis,
C. Michael Hall and Liz Sharples

As suggested in the introductory chapter and in the various chapters and case studies throughout this book, wine tourism is a developing field of interest to a number of industry stakeholders, communities and regions. However, the range of economic, social and environmental impacts associated with wine tourism and the broad scope of issues associated with its development also suggest that the analyses undertaken in this book raise almost as many questions as they answer. The purpose of this final chapter is to highlight some of the key issues that need to be addressed when examining the potential future of wine tourism around the world, including the research needs of the organizations involved in wine tourism at both a business and a regional level.

Utilizing the material presented in this book and supplementary opinions and insights of a number of the contributors, this chapter discusses the future of wine tourism. Keeping within the structure of the book it examines the future of wine tourism around the world in terms of both products (supply) and markets (demand) and the inter-relationships between wine, tourism and regional development, including a separate exhibit by Stephen Page, which discusses wine tourism and rural development in the new millennium. As we have seen throughout the preceding chapters, exhibits and case studies, tourism and the wine industry are inexorably linked. Indeed, both wine and tourism are identified more by location than anything else (Dickenson and Salt 1982). It is obvious that wine tourism is an important business component and activity for individual wineries, tourism operations and regions. It is also clear that wine tourism is conceptualized and manifested in a variety of ways in different cultural, regional and developmental contexts. As such, it is perhaps appropriate that we begin looking at the future of wine tourism around the world by looking at how it is characterized and manifested and, in doing so, re-examine a definition for wine tourism.

A future wine tourism definition

Chapter 1 presented two wine tourism definitions – Macionis (1996) and Hall (1996). These, combined as *'visitation to vineyards, wineries, wine festivals and wine shows for which grape wine tasting and/or experiencing the attributes of a grape wine region are the prime motivating factors for visitors'*, identify key locations in which wine tourism occurs and clearly distinguish that visitation may be motivated by 'grape wine' specifically or, more generally, 'the attributes of a grape wine region'. Arguing that the motivations and expectations of winery visitors can be quite diverse Johnson (1998) broadens the demand focus of a wine tourism definition to encompass *'visitation to vineyards, wineries, wine festivals and wine shows for the purpose of recreation'*.

While extensive in their application neither of these definitions, however, accommodates an extension of wine tourism to the broader context of the region or 'tourism appellation' versus simple *visitation to vineyards, wineries, wine festivals and wine shows*. Wine tourism can and does occur away from vineyards, wineries and the cellar door or tasting room. For example, dining out at restaurants and trying different foods and wines consistently ranks among one of the top holiday activities in Australia, while 89 per cent of international visitors dine in restaurants (South Australian Tourism Commission 1996). Indeed, Macionis and Cambourne (forthcoming) report that the first (and sometimes only) wine tourism experience of many tourists (both domestic and international) at a destination is often at their hotel or at a restaurant. This extension of the wine tourism experience, both spatially and temporally, is also supported by data presented in Table 8.7 which notes that

New Zealand winery visitors indicate at least some intention to purchase and consume either a particular winery's wine or a specific regional wine in both a restaurant or retail context after visiting. Travelling to a winery or a tasting room to experience wine is therefore a part of a broad set of experiences. These should lead us to ask a wider set of questions about the role of previous experiences, in consumer decisions regarding wine-related travel, the role of recollection, and travel to and from on-site wine tourism experiences; and how these experiences influence the supply of wine tourism products.

While wine, or attributes of the wine region, are often important if not central in identifying the wine tourist, wine tourism activity often occurs in a non-wine specific setting or context. For example, Isabelle Frochot (see Chapter 3) notes that while wine is a strong destinational asset in France, other destination attributes such as heritage and culture dominate tourist motivations. Consequently, while wine is often an important component of a packaged tour, it is often linked with historical or cultural attractions of a region (e.g. see Chapter 14, by Nigel Morpeth). Similarly, Robert Preston-Whyte (Chapter 5) states that while tasting wine may be the *raison d'être* of many of South Africa's Wine Routes, this feature alone is unlikely to sustain tourist growth. Furthermore, he notes that the idea of exploration and discovery of a diverse range of attributes including scenic beauty, regional cuisine, heritage and architecture are crucial to the success of South African Wine Routes.

This broader conceptualization of wine tourism, including its setting and range of participants, would appear to be at least implicitly recognized by the Assemblia das Regioes Europeias Viticolas (AREV) in their *Methodological Guide to Wine Roads*, which identifies the roles, responsibilities and training needs of a range of wine road 'Actors', including wineries, restaurateurs, tour operators and tourist, recreational, cultural, environmental, sports, nature and gastronomy associations, to name just a few (see Exhibit 2.1).

When asked to consider how wine tourism would be characterized or manifested in their study areas in the future, contributors to this book predict very similar developmental outcomes. While several authors believe that wine tourism will remain essentially a niche market special interest product, there was unanimous agreement that it will also extend its market appeal and broaden its market base by increasingly developing explicit strategic links with other tourism products and activities such as festivals, restaurants, accommodation providers, craft and produce suppliers and via the development of routes and trails that incorporate wine, heritage, gastronomy and nature. These responses are presented in Table 16.1

Table 16.1 How will wine tourism be manifested in the future?

Author	Study area	Nature of future wine tourism development
Nigel Morpeth	Europe	– will remain essentially a special interest product; – specialist operators will utilize wine as a primary focus and combine it with an activity type holiday such as cycling/walking to create a broad spectrum of special interest tourism.
Robert Preston-White	South Africa	– re-energized post-apartheid South African wine industry will develop hitherto unconsidered wine routes which combine a varied natural environment, cultural heritage and outdoor leisure pursuits.
Dave Telfer	Canada/NY State	– will remain a special interest tourism product, centred on boutique or cottage wineries; – it will, however, become a less elite form of tourism; – wineries will continue to utilize festivals, concerts, craft and antique shows to attract a broader range of visitors; – there will be an increasing link with regional cuisine, with some wineries opening cooking schools and restaurants.
Angela Skinner	California	– increasing recognition of the importance of maintaining and sustaining the local environment, hence while wine tourism will remain a mainstream product in places like the Napa Valley and Sonoma County, it may also remain essentially a niche market product in developing Californian regions.
Tim Dodd	Texas	– will become a more mainstream tourism product; – increasing development of wine tourism hospitality centres offering a variety of activities such as accommodation, special events, wedding facilities to broaden the market.

Liz Sharples	UK	– incorporation of value-added vineyard/winery experiences such as garden centres, art galleries, wildlife trails, animal sanctuaries and adventure playgrounds.
Niki Macionis and Brock Cambourne	Australia	– will become a mainstream national and regional tourism icon and identifier; – integration of the wine tourism product will occur via linking of thematic regional products in trails and routes such as 'heritage and wine', the creation of culinary tourism loops and trails will become increasingly important.
Michael Hall	Australasia/Europe	– increasing links with local cuisine and the promotion of healthy lifestyles; – small wineries will continue to focus on cellar door sales, while both large and small wineries will become increasingly aware of the opportunities wine tourism provides for branding, consumer education and establishing positive customer relationships; – continued use as a tool for regional development. However, there will be increasing conflict between the desire to produce wine and lifestyle migrants in certain regions which will require regulatory planning solutions; – growth in wine consumption as a component of Western middle-class lifestyles will lead to further growth in wine tourism although there will be significant regional variability in the supply of product and the nature of demand.
Richard Mitchell	NZ/Europe	– wine tourism will continue to add value to wine and tourism products depending on region.

As also noted in Chapter 1, some travel specifically motivated by wine, such as wine shows or wine and food festivals, occurs in an urban environment, away from the cellar door. Significantly, there would appear to be an acceleration in the urbanization of wine tourism with development of mega-complexes such as Bordeaux's Vinostar (which comprises a museum, observatory, information centre, tourism facilities, wine club, exhibition halls, and restaurants and shops), and wine tourism theme parks such as Disney's California Adventure (see Exhibit 16.1).

Exhibit 16.1: Mickey picks grapes at Vinopolis!

California wine giant, Robert Mondavi is teaming with Disneyland Resort to create a US$ 10 million California wine country experience. Due to open in 2001, this will be part of a new theme park 'Disney's California Adventure', being constructed adjacent to Disneyland in Anaheim, California (Light 1998; New World Wine Communications 1998).

Drawing on the 'edutainment' expertise of Disney theme parks, the California wine country experience comes complete with demonstration vineyards, a film featuring Californian wine-making history, several wine tasting areas, a special reserve tasting area for more in-depth food and wine experiences, a gourmet food and retail area, and a restaurant modelled after the 'Vineyard Room' – the private dining room at the Robert Mondavi winery in the Napa Valley.

On the other side of the Atlantic, 'Vinopolis', Britain's answer to 'Wineworld' and described by the *Economist* as 'the most dramatic testament yet to Britain's growing taste for wine' opened to the public on 22 July 1999 (Vinopolis – City of Wine 1999). Built under the Victorian arches of Cannon Street railway bridge and covering 2.25 acres of Central London this 'City of Wine' is expected to attract more than 500,000 visitors a year for the first four years (see http://www.vinopolis-cityofwine.com/). The potential of Vinopolis to attract a mass audience has convinced over 300 investors to fund the £23 million project (Hallstead 1998).

For £10 Vinopolis visitors can partake in a multimedia 'Wine Odyssey' tour through the history of viniculture and wine regions of the world, including a virtual Roman Holiday tour of Italian wine from the saddle of a Vespa motor scooter! Visitors are also able to taste up to five wines (from a range of around 240) in the 'Grand Tasting Halls' at the end of the tour, eat at one of four restaurants or purchase wine in the 4000 sq ft retail centre.

Brock Cambourne, Niki Macionis and Liz Sharples

In the light of such theme park developments and the extended cast of wine tourism 'actors' emphasized by the predictions of our expert contributors, it is perhaps appropriate to extend the definition of wine tourism beyond the location of vineyards and wineries, to encompass tourism activity influenced by and occurring within the regional terroir or appellation. That is, wine tourism becomes *tourism activity influenced by the physical, social and cultural dimensions of the winescape and its components*. This definition also takes into account the holistic 3D wine tourism framework postulated by Mitchell *et al.* in Chapter 6. Conceptualizing wine tourism in a non-wine specific context, such as simply purchasing a bottle of regional wine in a restaurant, cycling or walking through wine country, or eating regional cuisine, broadens both the market and wine tourism practitioner base. In doing so, it not only expands backward economic linkages, but also recognizes the importance of social and environmental linkages thereby implicitly encouraging stakeholders/actors to identify their roles, responsibilities and opportunities for further development.

From a wine tourist's perspective weaving the food and wine product through every aspect of the tourism experience (Tourism NSW 1996; see also Chapter 6) permits the tourist 'participation in the consumption and celebration of a series of local rites ... allowing the social and cultural integration' into the destination (Bessiere 1998: 26).

Future winery tourists – who are they and what do they want?

A number of chapters in this book have attempted to identify and develop demographic and psychographic profiles for winery visitors (see Chapters 4, 6, 7 and 8). Chapter 6, on wine tourism and consumer behaviour by Mitchell *et al.*, compares and aggregates a range of information about winery visitors (see Table 6.1), noting that 'the wine tourist is usually 30–50 years of age, in the moderate to high income bracket and comes from within or in close proximity to the wine region itself'. Furthermore, and perhaps not surprisingly they note, 'winery visitors also tend to be regular consumers of wine and have at least an intermediate knowledge of the product'. However, as the chapter also notes, from a wine tourism research, management and marketing perspective it is important to realize that winery visitor profiles from one region or country do not necessarily transpose to another. This lack of 'blanket' applicability is due to a range of factors, including:

- the developmental and marketing history of the region;
- differences in infrastructure and facilities;
- location in relation to major urban areas;
- the nature/type of potential tourists (Macionis and Cambourne 1998; Longo 1999; Mitchell in progress; see also Chapters 6 and 7).

Similarly, wine tourism researchers also report a multiplicity of motivations for engaging in wine tourism. Mitchell *et al.* (see Chapter 6) discuss in detail a range of wine tourism motivations noting that they are rooted in the values, beliefs and attitudes of the visitor. For example, motivations such as *tasting* and *learning about wine* can reflect a desire to minimize the risk associated with purchasing wine, while *meeting the wine-maker* indicates a concern with believability and authenticity, and enjoying a *day out* or *relaxation* reveals a need to escape from city life (Mitchell in progress). Furthermore, and in keeping with our revised wine tourism definition, Mitchell *et al.* (Chapter 6) note that there is much more to wine tourism than the simple consumption of a beverage, stating that it is dependent upon a range of experiential factors including the setting in which the experience occurs; socialization with the personalities of the wine; and interaction with other elements of the experience such as food, accommodation and other visitors.

Interestingly, the overall winery experience, and in particular educative (tasting and/or learning about wine) and experiential components of the wine tourism experience, were unanimously nominated as essential components of the future wine tourism experience by contributors to this book (see also Exhibit 16.2). These data are presented in Table 16.2. It is also interesting to note that all the contributors also believe that one of the major changes to the wine tourism market of today will be an increase in the appeal of wine and wine tourism to the younger generation.

Understanding winery visitor characteristics, motivations and their effect on consumer behaviour, and applying them appropriately has important implications for wine tourism product development and marketing. Indeed, as noted in Chapter 1, the perceptions of the wine tourist can be influenced by past experiences, perceptions, and supplementary information. That is, a poor winery experience, or poor service may result in a visitor not returning to a particular winery (perhaps even the entire region) or purchasing that winery's product at another location. Tim Dodd, in Chapter 7, and Hall *et al.* in Chapter 8 highlight the importance of such factors, reporting that friendly and knowledgable service are extremely important to the winery tourist in both choosing a winery to visit and in purchasing wine.

Such findings assume particular importance when one considers the information presented in Table 16.2, noting that experiential and educative components of the wine tourism experience are expected to become more important to an increasingly sophisticated market. Viewed in this light, initiatives such as Burgundy's *Bourgogne découverte. de vignes en caves* 'welcome charter' (see Chapter 3), the Movimento del Turismo del Vino's 'merit requirements' (see Chapter 2) and the proposed development of cellar door Quality Assurance schemes in Australia (see Chapter 12) would appear to be very good investments in the future of wine tourism. If properly constructed and embraced, such schemes will ensure that the expectations of wine tourists, today and in the future, are met, ensuring tourist satisfaction and facilitating increased yield to wine tourism stakeholders.

Exhibit 16.2: Should you swirl, dump, gurgle or spit?

With the experiential and educative aspects of the wine tourism experience becoming increasingly important to wine tourists and visitors, some wineries are beginning to meet the demand by supplementing wine tasting with wine education. As noted in Exhibit 1.1, Sonoma County based Kendall-Jackson has developed an interactive culinary garden and demonstration vineyard to provide an educative hook for winery visitors. In the Napa Valley, St Supery Vineyards and Winery educates entry-level wine drinkers with a self-guided tour of the wine-making process and a display of wine aromas via their trademarked 'Smella Vision' exhibit, while the Robert Mondavi Winery regularly hosts food and wine seminars.

In an effort to educate both customers and the community about wine, every weekend Napa Valley 'micro-winery' Goosecross Cellars (n.d. 1997) hosts a free 'crash course' in the basics of wine tasting. According to Goosecross Director of Public Relations and course creator, Colleen Topper, the 'Wine Basics' Class is an excellent starting place for anyone intimidated by wine and the tasting room jargon. The course takes participants through the basics of wine tasting, explaining in plain English about oak, wine

Table 16.2 How will wine tourism markets change in the future and what will future wine tourists want?

Expert/author	Study area	Wine tourism markets, motivations and expectations
Nigel Morpeth	Europe	– the wine tourist will be an experiential traveller seeking educative and experiential components;
Robert Preston-Whyte	South Africa	– broadening of market base by integration of wine product with complementary tourism; providers such as B&Bs, restaurants, horse riding, cycling; – essential components will include wine plus an integrated range of leisure activities.
Dave Telfer	Canada	– wine tourists will become more educated; – wineries will incorporate festivals, concerts and events into their product to attract a younger market, while the creation and promotion of regional cuisine and the development of cooking schools by wineries will further broaden the market base; – essential components of the wine tourism experience will include education and experiential aspects, such as experiencing the wine-making process.
Angela Skinner	California	– there will be a broadening of the market base, particularly the younger Generation X, who will be influenced by cyber marketing;
Tim Dodd	Texas	– there will be a broadening of interest in wine and wine tourism, which will relate to more international visits to wine regions, a greater use of wineries by the corporate sector for retreats and participation in wine tourism by middle income earners as a form of entertainment; – the wine tourism experience will be made up of a range of components including basic information provision, more in-depth educative aspects/demands and activities such as grape stomps and festivals – all of which will serve to reduce the intimidation factor associated with wine.

Liz Sharples	UK	– there will be a shift towards attracting a younger market, who are keen to experiment; – good food and attractions such as craft/art galleries will play an important role in reinforcing the image of wine as a lifestyle product;
Niki Macionis and Brock Cambourne	Australia	– growing interest in wine as a lifestyle product will vastly increase the wine tourism market potential, attracting both a younger wine interested and curious market, as well as the 'baby boomer' market segment curious to understand the fuss; – wine tourists will become more sophisticated and demanding as their general wine knowledge and experience develops; – they will seek humanistic, experiential and educative experiences that contribute to both their ego-enhancement and general life experiences.
Michael Hall	Australasia/Europe	– there will be growing interest in wine tourism as a lifestyle product in the middle classes of Europe, North America and Australasia and, increasingly, Asia; – the wine tourist market will become increasingly global as middle-class consumers increasingly travel to experience places and consume food and wines from particular regions, which they will have already experienced vicariously through consuming food and wine in their own country or locale; – wine tourism will contribute to the overall development of a better educated wine market.
Richard Mitchell	NZ/Europe	– there will be a growing trend for added value winery experiences, with restaurants, cafés, tours, accommodation, events and education becoming more widespread; – there will an increasing demand for food and wine toursim experiences.

aromas, how to store your wine, and how to enjoy tasting wines and visiting wineries. It's also a perfect introduction to the Napa Valley and its wines. Topper (pers. comm), notes that approximately 20 per cent of weekend winery visitors go to Goosecross specifically for the class, before embarking on the rest of their Napa experience. She acknowledges that 'the class has never been a great revenue generator, the class is more of a marketing tool, where we get label recognition and word of mouth referrals'. Furthermore, she notes that 'the relationships we establish with our visitors are unsurpassed . . . they tell everyone they know what a great experience it was at Goosecross. Friends refer friends, who then also come to buy'. In addition, it has also been instrumental in developing strategic and mutually beneficial relationships with associated tourism operations and the community, with Topper reporting that 'the class has been a smashing success with B&Bs, hotels, inns and the local community, where most of our guests are referred from'.

To increase the longevity and relevance of their 'Wine Basics' class, Goosecross has also introduced the 'Goosecross Cellars University' (GCU). The GCU concept extends the knowledge gained via the 'Wine Basics' class by offering short courses on 'Advanced Wine Tasting', 'Napa Valley Varietals', 'Food and Wine Pairing' and 'Building the Perfect Cellar'.

Brock Cambourne

Issues affecting wine tourism – now and in the future

As a relatively recent tourism phenomenon and product, the wine tourism industry has been faced by a range of developmental issues and problems. For example, in Old World wine-producing countries, with a significant historical wine culture, such as Italy and France, one of the significant impediments to wine tourism development is convincing the domestic population to acknowledge wine tourism as a legitimate form of recreation and self-discovery – as opposed to simply a staple food component (see Chapters 2 and 3). In New World wine-producing countries wine tourism development is impacted by a variety of issues including a lack of effective inter-industry linkages, tourism participation costs, and land use issues. The range of wine tourism development issues reported in this book is detailed in Table 16.3.

Table 16.3   Wine tourism development issues

Issue	Effect/implications
Facilitating demand	In traditional wine-producing countries, wine tourism and creating supply is not yet seen as a legitimate form of recreation or tourism e.g. Old World wine-producing countries such as Italy and France
Lack of information and understanding about wine tourism by the wine industry	Results in a lack of inter-industry integration and cooperation e.g. USA, Australia, NZ
Lack of information and understanding of the wine industry by the tourism industry	Results in exploitative relationships and inappropriate product development and marketing e.g. Australia, New Zealand
Lack of tourism industry understanding by the wine industry	Inappropriate product development and lack of inter-industry understanding and cooperation e.g. Australia, New Zealand
Land use issues	Urbanization of scarce viticultural land or urbanization and/or vitification of rural landscapes due to inappropriate wine tourism development e.g. USA, Canada
Cellar door costs	Time, resource and capital costs of tourism participation can be a deterrent and impediment to wine tourism development e.g. USA, Australia, New Zealand
Tax	Regressive and inappropriate taxation regimes can adversely affect wine tourism development e.g. Australia

It should be noted that the existence of these issues is not restricted to the destinations noted in this table, merely that they have been reported in this book by various contributors. Undoubtedly, these and other wine tourism developmental problems and issues occur and are manifested in some form or another in other wine-producing and wine tourism regions throughout the world.

Table 16.4 details developmental issues, nominated by contributors to this book as potentially impacting upon the future of wine tourism development in their study area(s). Significantly, a number of the concerns and impediments

Table 16.4 Issues influencing future wine tourism development

Author	Study area	Wine tourism development issues
Nigel Morpeth	Europe	– primary developmental issues centre around securing initial European Union funding in conjunction with local and regional financial commitment to developing wine routes.
Robert Preston-Whyte	South Africa	– South African wine tourism development is affected and constrained by a number of general wine industry development issues including a shortage of planting material and limited access to new grapevine rootstocks, clones etc. and the uplift and empowerment of wine industry workers and considerations such as equity, gain sharing and access to land; – from a purely tourism perspective violent crime is an issue that damages South Africa's tourism image.
Dave Telfer	Canada/NY State	– lack of understanding of and recognition of the potential of wine tourism; – lack of appropriate information about wine tourism; – in some areas, such as Niagara, wine industry and wine tourism development is threatened by the loss of agricultural land to urbanization.
Angela Skinner	California	– unrestricted growth of the wine industry and wine tourism can lead to the loss of the destination's inherently attractive values; – conflict between competing interests of growers, vintners and residents can adversely affect future wine tourism prospects.
Tim Dodd	Texas	– while the wine industry is becoming much more sophisticated in understanding tourism, many wineries and entire regions remain isolated and subsequently unwilling to commit resources to tourism participation.

Liz Sharples	UK	– there is a continuing lack of information and data regarding wine tourism impacts, as well as a general lack of data concerning the requirements of winery tourists; – there is a concern about the standardization of the wine tourism product.
Niki Macionis and Brock Cambourne	Australia	– future wine tourism development and sustainability hinges on ensuring that wineries see a tangible return on their investment (including time, infrastructure, and human resources) in tourism. This in turn affects the wine tourism industry's willingness to invest in product development initiatives that ensure a rewarding winery experience and keep wine tourists coming back for seconds; – inappropriate taxation regimes act as a disincentive for investment in wine tourism.
Michael Hall	Australasia/Europe	– there will be ongoing difficulties in establishing network relationships between the wine and tourism industries in part because of the nature of the industries but also because of a lack of emphasis on soft infrastructure such as the research and knowledge base; – due to wider issues of genetic modification and the use of biocides there will be greater consumer concern over of the environment credentials of wine tourism products; – need to manage and regulate the impacts of urbanization and lifestyle migration on wine regions;
Richard Mitchell	NZ/Europe	– difficulties in network establishment between the wine and tourism sectors will be a major impediment.

noted in Table 16.3 are expected to adversely impact upon wine tourism into the future. For example, Telfer notes that a continuing lack of understanding and recognition of the potential of wine tourism as well as a lack of appropriate information about wine tourism will be a continuing wine tourism developmental issue in Canada and in New York State, in the USA. Similarly, Dodd notes a continuing lack of inter-sectoral integration and isolation as impediments to future wine tourism development in Texas, USA.

In addition, Macionis and Cambourne state that minimizing the perception of tourism exploitation by ensuring a financial return to wineries is crucial to the future development of wine tourism in Australia (Chapter 12). The Australian wine tourism industry, it would appear, is well aware of this, with a central objective of the National Wine Tourism Strategy focusing on delivering greater yields to wineries through their participation in tourism.

Wine tourism development issues concerning the loss of prime viticultural land to urbanization (noted by Telfer in Chapter 13), and the 'vitification' and subsequent tourism development of rural destinations (noted by Skinner in Chapter 15; see also Chapter 11) assume particular importance to the future of wine tourism if one considers the definition of wine tourism as *tourism activity influenced by the physical, social and cultural dimensions of the winescape and its components*. In this context, any changes to the physical (reduction in vineyard acreage), social (overcrowding at wine tourism destinations, or wineries) and cultural (transformation of the wine tourism experience due to commercial pressures) aspects of the winescape can substantially impact upon the wine tourism potential of a destination. While in wine tourism destinations such as the Napa Valley slow-growth policies and agricultural reserves have been implemented to minimize wine tourism impacts, in Italy the Movimento del Turismo del Vino (1995) states that its mission includes significant attention to the preservation and active restoration of the winescape. In doing so the Movimento del Turismo del Vino facilitates the protection of the ancient cultural traditions of rural villages and wine-producing areas.

Who will/should develop and promote wine tourism in the future?

With wineries, communities and national and regional governments the world over considering wine tourism as a means of improving their own business position or as a regional development tool, it is appropriate to examine the future roles and responsibilities of wine tourism stakeholders. A variety of approaches to wine tourism development have been highlighted, discussed and analysed throughout this book. These have involved either private sector leadership and entrepreneurial activity or government and public sector involvement via legislative facilitation or pump priming – or a combination of both (see also Exhibit 16.3). For example, at an individual enterprise level, Michael Whyte (Chapter 10) describes private sector infrastructure and human resource investement in wine tourism development at Vasse Felix winery in Western Australia. At an organizational level wine tourism in Italy has been largely driven by the Movimento del Turismo del Vino, a non-profit private sector association consisting of wine tourism stakeholders (Chapter 2). The initiatives of organizations such as Movimento del Turismo del Vino are also assisted, however, by specific wine tourism projects funded by European Union agencies such as WITRANET or ECOS-Ouverture (see Chapter 11).

Exhibit 16.3: Wine tourism and rural development in the new millennium

The 1990s have witnessed the emergence of niche tourism products in the marketplace which might be interpreted as a postmodernist focus on consumption, with increasing amounts of leisure time activities based on the enjoyment of eating out to consume quality food and drink. If New Zealand is typical of other developed societies, household expenditure surveys have consistently shown that eating out is a popular way of spending disposable income. This is also translating into tourist experiences, where urban destinations (e.g. the Mediterranean, cities such as Melbourne, Wellington and Auckland) have developed a café culture and fostered higher expectations of quality food. Therefore, the evolution of wine tourism and the potential for developing a distinctiveness for countries, regions and particular places, is part of the trend towards how places position themselves to nurture tourism.

It is no longer the case that places can rely on icons and attractions that are not complemented by opportunities for local cuisine and wine to be consumed as part of the tourist experience. Yet one notable feature of the research reported in this book is the relative absence of authoritative studies of wine and food tourism published in the tourism literature. It is ironic that practitioners and marketers have emphasized these new themes in the postmodern city and also in rural areas due to the potential for expenditure and employment generation, but researchers have not focused a great deal of attention on what they might view as a frivolous area of study.

One consequence is that much of the research has been action-orientated, undertaken for individual enterprises, organizations or areas and not widely disseminated beyond a limited professional audience. All too often, notions of tourism, tourists and the potential impact of tourism have been narrowly conceived and unable to recognize the diversity of views and responses to developing this niche market. As research by Hall and Johnson (1997) has shown, individual entrepreneurs vary significantly in terms of their predisposition towards integrating tourism in the business plans for vineyard operation. The implications are significant: what does this mean for rural development, product development and the tourism industry in regions and areas?

To start with, regional tourism organizations and individual wine interest groups need to cooperate and decide on whether there is sufficient support for leveraging additional tourist visitation and expenditure from this niche market. It is also worth emphasizing a point frequently overlooked in economic analyses: the amount of expenditure individuals and groups of tourists already visiting an area will spend is not infinite. Consequently, if organizations seek to develop wine tourism as a niche market it may be to the detriment of existing markets in a region. Thus, new markets have to be identified, targeted and attracted to a region as a tailor-made wine tourism product or on the back of a strong brand in existence (e.g. an urban tourist product with a wine tourism experience or short break integrated into the regional tourism product to spread urban tourists to rural areas). This is essential if the wine tourist is to be harnessed, given their discerning qualities, potential for higher than average levels of expenditure and for acquiring a long-term taste for particular wines. The example of Auckland, New Zealand, is interesting because it displays many of these attributes in a theoretical context but has failed to develop a strong brand or themed tourist experience. Whilst a number of individual vineyards have taken the initiative to develop visitor tasting centres and an environment conducive to relaxed tourist spending, only a couple have attempted to pioneer an embryonic festival concept. Clearly, individual areas (e.g. Devonport, see Figure 16.1) have an established wine and food festival, largely targeted at the domestic

Figure 16.1   ANZ Devonport Food and Wine Festival.

market. In recent studies of tourist activity patterns in the region, wine tourism features hardly at all although one or two operators have developed small wine tour operations.

Therefore, in areas seeking to develop wine tourism in the urban fringe (e.g. Auckland) or in rural areas (e.g. Otago, New Zealand and Kent, England), a number of pump-priming roles need to be initiated by regional tourism organizations, local councils and rural funding agencies. First, the appropriate infrastructure needs to be identified and developed to make vineyards accessible including good signage. Second, tourist circuits need identification and marketing for the daytrip markets in major urban destinations. Third, for the short-stay visitor, appropriate planning guidelines need to be developed to take account of accommodation and hospitality needs. Here, planning agencies need to harmonize development plans with the natural environment so that the town is not brought to the countryside, and an authentic rural experience results. Fourth, the development of any wine tourism theme in a region needs to be underpinned by initial research to understand the market and ongoing monitoring to ensure the market needs are being met. The latter is essential because service

Table 16.5 Who should be responsible for wine tourism development in the future?

Author	Study area	Wine tourism development roles and responsibilities
Nigel Morpeth	Europe	– there is a public sector responsibility to develop infrastructure; however, the wine and travel industry should package and market wine tourism.
Robert Preston-Whyte	South Africa	– South African wine tourism has traditionally been developed and marketed around the wine routes. Wine route organizers are becoming increasingly sophisticated in their structure with various committees undertaking developmental initiatives.
Dave Telfer	Canada/NY State	– governments have in the past, either directly (e.g. funding wine marketing boards) or indirectly (implementing wine tourism friendly legislation) assisted the development of wine tourism. A combination of government and private sector Wine Council initiatives will continue to be important. Strategic partnerships with associated sectors (B&Bs, hotels, tour operators etc.) will become increasingly important.
Angela Skinner	California	– governments and private sector interests need to cooperate more effectively with regard to wine tourism planning and development and sustainability issues.
Tim Dodd	Texas	– winery owners are often relatively independent people, as such it is sometimes difficult to forge alliances. Additionally, networking efforts often require a critical mass of stakeholders so that there is pressure to work together. Cooperative partnerships will be assisted by a strong stick (legislative threats) or carrots (federal or state funding).

Liz Sharples	UK	– an integrated approach at both a regional and national level to viticultural land use management is required to facilitate sustainability; – a coordinated approach by both public and private sector to marketing and promotion is also necessary.
Niki Macionis and Brock Cambourne	Australia	– governments and regulators have a number of both immediately important and future roles in wine tourism development. These lie in the development of facilitating or enabling policies with regard to signposting, land and water use, licensing and taxation; – public and private sector networks such as winery tourism councils and state tourism commissions need to provide the necessary product development and marketing tools that assist the wine tourism industry to develop itself. Wine tourism stakeholders/participants need to develop strategic networks and alliances in order to develop future markets.
Michael Hall	Australasia/Europe	– all stakeholders should be involved; this will primarily be the wine and tourism industries along with government and the community. However, it is essential that wineries be the primary owners of the product.
Richard Mitchell	NZ/Europe	– wineries should be responsible for their own product and experience development. This should, however, be assisted via partnerships and the establishment of regional marketing networks.

provision and tourist expectations of wine and food are extremely discerning and volatile, so that poor signage, inability to find vineyards, inhospitable service, poor quality accommodation and average levels of food production and service will not satisfy this market. In other words, planners, business interests and their representatives will need to move away from a functional attitude which has emphasized production. This will need to recognize fully that in a postmodern society, where consumption and expenditure culminate in very judgemental experiences of quality, the tourist needs to be high on the agenda in rural areas. This is vital if rural areas have not embraced the urban ethic of service and hospitality to naturally blend in with the warmth, friendliness and welcome that has traditionally been associated with the countryside as a landscape of consumption. If rural areas can harness this market, however, it has a long-term potential for regional brand recognition and rural development as the primary sector restructures, often adding a supplementary form of income.

Stephen J. Page

In Chapter 4, Cambourne and Macionis report how the initiatives and activities of wine tourism entrepreneurs are assisted and boosted by public sector marketing assistance. Similarly, Telfer, in Chapter 13, notes how the vision and leadership of individual wineries such as Inniskillin and enabling legislation such as the Farm Winery Act catalysed the rebirth of the wine industries in Canada and New York State. Chapters 11 and 12 also highlight the role of public and private sector partnerships.

When asked about the roles and responsibilities of wine tourism stakeholders in future wine tourism development, contributors also emphasized the importance of public and private sector partnerships and networks. These data are presented in Table 16.5. Such networks lie at the heart of wine tourism. A winescape is not just a static artefact – it is the representation of a particular set of social, environmental and economic relationships that adapt and change over time according to both internal and external factors. To make wine tourism work, not just for the customer, but also for the businesses and individuals which contribute to the development and production of the winescape, these relationships have to be encouraged and nurtured over time. Where these networks break down, for example, because of the onset of urbanization or lifestyle migration in a wine region, wine tourism and wine production is threatened. Hence, the desire for

'Right to Farm' legislation and regulation in order to be able to maintain winescapes and the wine culture which underlies them. Similarly, threats also occur when a single private producer comes to dominate production and acreage in a given area. A landscape full of grapevines is not a winescape if the complexity of production is lost along with the living culture which comes from the existence of numerous small or 'boutique' wineries and the relationships which exist between them and larger producers. Therefore, wine tourism is both a contributor to and a result of winescapes and their components.

Conclusions

As this book has noted, wine tourism is particularly important to smaller wineries around the world because of the opportunity it provides for direct sales. In many cases it is wine tourism which helps sustain innovation and the developments which keeps wine regions alive. This is not to romanticize wine tourism as, like any other kind of product, there are both advantages and disadvantages in its development depending on the overall goals for individual businesses and regions. Nevertheless, the fact that wine businesses of all sizes are using visitation and direct customer contact as a way of building stronger customer relationships, educating the consumer, testing new products, building stronger brands and images and, of course, selling wine, indicates just how important it is.

This book has provided a range of chapters, case studies and examples which illustrate the complexity and diversity of wine tourism and what it offers the wine and tourism industries as well as their communities and consumers. One of the most significant underlying themes is the way in which wine tourism contributes to the 'life' of wine regions and wine producers. As much wine and tourism marketing and promotion would seem to testify, when people purchase wine they are buying much more than a physical product, they are consuming images, lifestyles, experiences and places, what we would more prosaically describe as the 'romance of the vine'. When people visit winescapes, and interact with their components, such as the wineries, and purchase wine, they are taking their memories home in a bottle – and they can keep doing so for many years to come every time they purchase, even though they may never come into physical contact with that place again. Therefore, it is vital that the wine and tourism industries work together to understand the motivations of the visitor and what they bring to wine regions as well as gaining a better understanding of their product and the relationship that they have with their customers.

As noted at the outset, despite its increasingly recognized economic and social importance, until now there has been relatively little systematic study of the development of wine tourism, the manner in which it is managed and marketed, and the people who visit wine regions and experience the wine tourism product. As has also been stressed throughout, these issues are not just of academic interest as they are important contributions to the sustained development of wine and the places and regions on which it is based. Perhaps if we were writing as viticulturalists or oenologists we would not have to make such a justification, but it is only recently that the contribution of a wider, more integrated knowledge of the connection of the social and cultural aspects of wine to its physical properties has come to be acknowledged as being of value. Nevertheless, we hope that this book does make a positive contribution to a field in which we hold both a scientific and a personal interest and provide a basis from which further research and business development can be undertaken. But perhaps, just as importantly, we are wanting to put people more at the centre of our understanding of wine. As many wineries and cellars will testify, visitors want to learn about the grape, wines, wine-making, the people behind it and the social and cultural dimensions of wine – the terroir of wine – whether such visitors are newcomers or experienced gourmets. Similarly, the editors are happy to have shared some of the fruits of their own explorations and experiences. We hope that your future travels in wine will be as rewarding and enriching as ours have been.

Bibliography

ABC News (1999). Vigneron Predicts Bottom of Barrel Under New Tax Package. ABC Online http://www.abcnet.au/news/state/nsw/archive/metnsw-23apr1999–14.htm (accessed 27/4/99).

ACT Chief Minister's Department (1999). Draft Canberra District Wine Industry Development Strategy, unpublished discussion paper. ACT Government.

Ali-Knight, J. and Charters, S. (1999). The business of tourism and hospitality: The attraction and benefit of wine education to the wine tourist and Western Australian wineries. In *Tourism & Hospitality: Delighting the Senses 1999, Part Two. Proceedings of the Ninth Australian Tourism Hospitality and Tourism Research Conference, Council of the Australian University Tourism and Hospitality Education (CAUTHE), 10–13 February 1999, Adelaide, South Australia* (J. Molloy and J. Davies; eds) p. 95, Bureau of Tourism Research.

Alkalaj, M. (1996). *Wines of Slovenia: Sampling and Buying Wines.* http://www.ijs.si/slo/country/food/ wine/sampling/index.html.

AMC (1999). *Hungarian Collective Agricultural Marketing Centre: Wine Roads in Hungary.* AMC, Hungary.

Andereck, K. (1995). Environmental consequences of tourism: A review of recent research. In *Linking Tourism, the Environment, and Sustainability. National Recreation and Park Association Meeting Papers (Minneapolis, Mn, Oct. 12–14 1994).* Compiled by S. McCool and A. Watson, Intermountain Research Station: Report INT-GTR-323, pp. 77–81, National Recreation and Park Association.

Anderson, N. (1999). Online battle brews: Battle brews over online sales of alcohol. *Los Angeles Times*, reprinted *BeverageNet* http://www.beveragenet.net/daily/news.asp?a=909 (accessed 18/6/99).

Anon. (1996). *Viticulture in the UK.* United Kingdom Vineyards Association.

Anon. (1998a). *World Drink Trends*. NTC Publications.

Anon. (1998b). *A Taste of the South East, Guide to Food and Drink in Sussex and Surrey*. A Taste of the South East Ltd.

Anon. (1999). *The Drink Pocket Book*. NTC Publications.

Aplin, J. (1999). Winery Tourism. *WineNZ*, **32**.

Arblaster and Clarke (1999). *Wine Tours Brochure*. Arblaster and Clarke.

AREV (Assemblia das Regioes Europeias Viticolas) (1997). Minutes of the Meeting of the European Council of the Roads of Wine/A Methodological Guide to Wine Roads. http://www.regione.piemonte.it/arev/lang/ted/cerv.htm (accessed 17/03/99).

Aronsson, L. (1994). Sustainable Tourism Systems: The example of sustainable rural tourism in Sweden. In *Rural Tourism and Sustainable Rural Development* (B. Bramwell and B. Lane, eds) pp. 72–92, Channel View Publications.

Aspler, T. (1995). *Tony Aspler's Vintage Canada: The Complete Reference to Canadian Wines* (2nd ed.) McGraw-Hill Ryerson.

Augusta-Margaret River Tourism Association (1994). *The Cellar: Opening the Door to Tourism*. Unpublished Funding Proposal to Commonwealth Department of Tourism (Regional Tourism Development Programme 1995/96). Augusta-Margaret River Tourism Association.

AusIndustry (1996). *Network News: AusIndustry Business Networks Programme*, **6**, 8.

Austin, P. (1993). The Central Otago vineyard industry: A supply side view of one of Otago's newest attractions, unpublished Dip. Tour. dissertation. Dunedin: University of Otago.

Australia and New Zealand Wine Industry (1990). A new Australian winery every 84 hours. *Australia and New Zealand Wine Industry*, **14**(1), 7.

Australian Commonwealth Department of Tourism (1994). *National Rural Tourism Strategy*. Australian Commonwealth Department of Tourism.

Australian Manufacturing Council (1991). *Networking Seminar Program: A Report on a Nationwide Series of Seminars*. Australian Manufacturing Council.

Australian Wine Foundation (1996). *Strategy 2025: The Australian Wine Industry*. Winemakers' Federation of Australia.

Australian Wine Online (1999). A New Australian Winery Every 84 Hours. http: //www.winetitles.com.au/auswine/news/99_2_23.html (accessed 18/6/99).

Baranyi, J. (1990). A turizmus ès az osztrákábor. [Tourism and Austrian wine]. *Gazdálkodás*, **34**(5), 73–76.

Bassler, C. (1998). Doluca: World Famous Turkish Wines. http://www.export-online.com/wines/doluca/index.htm.

Baum, M.M. (1999). Measuring and enhancing sustainability in California vineyards and wineries. *Vineyard & Winery Management*, **25**(1), 41–5, 55.

Baxevanis, J.J. (1992). *The Wine Regions of America, Geographical Reflections and Appraisals*. Vinifera Wine Growers Journal.

Beeston, J. (1994). *A Concise History of Australian Wine*. Allen & Unwin.

Beioley, (1995). On yer bike – cycling and tourism. *Insights*, September, B17–B31.

Bell, D. and Valentine, G. (1997). *Consuming Geographies: We Are Where We Eat*. Routledge.

Bessiere, J. (1998). Local development and heritage: Traditional food and cuisine as tourist attractions in rural areas. *Sociologica Ruralis*, **38**(1), 21–34.

Beverland, M. (1998). Wine tourism in New Zealand – maybe the industry has got it right. *International Journal of Wine Marketing*, **10**(2), 24–33.

Beverland, M., James, K., James, M., Porter, C. and Stace, G. (1998a). Wine tourists – a missed opportunity or a misplaced priority? In *Advances in Research, New Zealand Tourism and Hospitality Conference Proceedings* (J. Kandampully, ed.). Lincoln University.

Beverland, M., James, K., James, M., Porter, C. and Stace, G. (1998b). Wine tourists – missed opportunities in West Auckland. *Australian and New Zealand Wine Industry Journal*, **13**(4), 403–407.

Bigsby, H., Trought, M., Lambie, R. and Bicknell, K. (1998). *An Economic Analysis of the Wine Industry in Marlborough. A Report to The Marlborough Winemakers, The Marlborough Grape Growers Association, The Wine Institute of New Zealand and The Marlborough District Council*. Agribusiness and Economics Research Unit.

Bieder, P., Campbell, B. and Williams, V. (1997). The wine state. *Cuisine* (65) November, 130–8.

Blanton, D. (1981). Tourism training in developing countries: the social and cultural dimension. *Annals of Tourism Research*, **8**(1), 116–33.

Botos, P. (1996). Marketing cool climate wines, In *Proceedings for the Fourth International Symposium on Cool Climate Enology & Viticulture* (T. Henick-Kling, T.E. Wolf, and E.M Harkness, eds) pp. IX1–IX7. Communication Services, New York State Agricultural Experiment Station.

Boxall, B. (1999). Vineyard neighbors see only wrath from grapes. *The Los Angeles Times*, 18 February, A1, A21.

Bracken, C. (1994). Mudgee wine: a case study. *Australasian Agribusiness Review*, **2**(1), 41–57.

Bradley, K. (1982). *Australian and New Zealand Wine Vintages* (9th edn). Nepthene Publications Pty Ltd.

Bragato, R. (1895). *Report on the Prospects of Viticulture in New Zealand, Together With Instructions for Planting and Pruning.* New Zealand Department of Agriculture.

Bramble, L. (1998). Crunching numbers, crushing grapes, Ontario wine sales reach record highs. *Winetidings*, **191**, 12–7.

Bramble, L. and Darling, S. (1992). *Discovering Ontario's Wine Country.* Stoddart.

Bramwell, B., Henry, I., Jackson, G., Prat, A.G., Richards, G. and van der Straaten. J. (eds) (1996). *Sustainable Tourism Management: Principles and Practice.* Tilburg University Press

Broom, D. (1998a). Where spicy forces rule. *Decanter*, **24**(4), 86–90.

Broom, D. (1998b). Secret gardens. *Decanter*, **23**(6), 50–52.

Brown, R. (1981). Direct selling: The role and importance of producer outlets, promotion and advertising at the producer level. In *The Promotion and Marketing of Wine in Western Australia*. Seminar Proceedings. University of Western Australia.

Bureau of Industry Economics (1991b). Networks: A third form of organisation. *Bulletin of Industry Economics*, **10**, 5–9.

Butler, R.W. (1980). The concept of a tourist area cycle of evolution: Implications for management of resources. *The Canadian Geographer*, **24**(1), 5–12.

Butler, R.W. (1991). Tourism, environment and sustainable development. *Environmental Conservation*, **18**(3), 201–9.

Butler, R.W. (1997). Modelling tourism development: evolution, growth and decline. In *Tourism, Development and Growth* (S. Wahab and J. Pigram, eds) pp. 109–25, Routledge.

Butler, R.W. (1999). Sustainable tourism: A state-of-the-art review. *Tourism Geographies*, **1**(1), 7–25.

Butler, R.W., Hall, C.M. and Jenkins, J.M. (eds) (1998). *Rural Tourism and Recreation*. John Wiley.

Cambourne, B. (1999). Wine tourism in the Canberra district. In *Wine Tourism: Perfect Partners. Proceedings of the First Australian Wine Tourism Conference, Margaret River, Western Australia, May 1998* (R. Dowling and J. Carlsen, eds) pp. 171–84. Bureau of Tourism Research.

Campbell, B. (1997). *New Zealand Wine Annual 1998*. Cuisine Publications.

CanAdapt (1999). Approved Marketing Projects (accessed 10/03/99).

Canadian Wine News (1999). Ontario growers call for direct sales to restaurants. *Wine Access*, **10**, 51.

Canberra Tourism (1996). *ACT Tourism Development Strategy*. Canberra Tourism.

Carlsen, J., Getz, D. and Dowling, R. (1999). The wine tourism industry. In *Wine Tourism: Perfect Partners. Proceedings of the First Australian Wine Tourism Conference, Margaret River, Western Australia, May 1998* (R. Dowling and J. Carlsen, eds) pp. 267–76. Bureau of Tourism Research.

Cartiere, M. (1997). Kendall-Jackson's sensory garden: transformation of a food and wine education programme. Wine Enthusiast Online. http://www.winemag.com/globalwinenews/us-garden.html. (Accessed 30 January 1998.

Celsi, R.L. and Olson, J. (1989). The effects of felt involvement on consumers' attention and comprehension processes. *Marketing Science Institute Working Paper 1–43*.

Centre for Tourism and Leisure Policy Research (1998). Canberra District Wine Industry Feasibility Study, Unpublished consultant's report. University of Canberra.

Chambre de Commerce et d'Industrie de Bordeaux (1992). *Etude Tourisme Viti-Vinicole*. Departement Commerce et Industrie, Service Commerce Tourism Etudes.

Chapman, P. (1994). Agriculture in Niagara: an overview. In *Niagara's Changing Landscapes* (H. Gayler, ed.) pp. 279–300. Carleton University Press.

Charlton, C. (1998). Public transport and sustainable tourism: the case of Devon and Cornwall Rail Partnership. In *Sustainable Tourism: A Geographical Perspective* (C.M. Hall and A. Lew, eds) pp. 132–45. Addison Wesley Longman.

Charvet, N. and Desplats B.L. (1995). *Tourisme et Vin: Réflexion autour du Concept de Tourisme Viti-vinicole*, Dossier de Synthèse no. 18, CNTER, December.

Chidley, J. (1998a). Grape white north Canada is now a producer of exquisite prize winning wines. *Macleans*, **111**, 42–3.

Chidley, J. (1998b). Haute Canuck Canadian cuisine and wine come of age. *Macleans*, **111**, 34, 36–40.

Choisy, C. (1996) Le poids du tourisme viti-vinicole [The significance of viticultural tourism]. *Espaces*, **140**, 30–3.

Cinelli Colombini, D. (1996). Le cantine idonee alle strade del vino. *Il Sommelier*, September–October, 14–15.

Clancy, P. (1998). There's a rumbling on the pad. *Australian and New Zealand Wine Industry Journal*, **13**(1), 4.

Clarke, J. (1996). Farm accommodation and the communication mix. *Tourism Management*, **17**(8), 611–16.

Clarke, O. (1995). *Oz Clarke's Wine Atlas: Wines & Wine Regions of the World*. Little, Brown and Company.

Clawson, M. and Knetsch, J. (1966). *Economics of Outdoor Recreation*. John Hopkins Press.

Clayton, M. (1998). Legal issues in selling wine on the Internet. *The Australian and New Zealand Wine Industry Journal*, **13**(2), 202–7

Clement, H.G. (1961). Australia. In *The Future of Tourism in the Pacific and Far East*. US Government Printing Office.

Clout, H.D. (1972). *Rural Geography: An Introductory Survey*. Pergammon Press.

Cohen, E. (1983). Insiders and outsiders: The dynamics of development of bungalow tourism on the islands of Southern Thailand. *Human Organization*, **42**(2), 158–62.

Colebatch, H.K. (1998). *Policy*. Open University Press.

Comissio Vitivinicola Regional do Dão (1999). *Dão*, publicity leaflet, Viseu, Portugal.

Comité Régional du Tourisme de Bourgogne (1997). *Le Tourisme autour des Sites du Vin en Bourgogne*. Dijon Comité Régional du Tourisme de Bourgogne.

Comité Régional du Tourisme de Languedoc-Roussillon Prodexport (1994). *Route des vins en Languedoc-Roussillon: projet de valorisation du patrimone viticole par le tourisme*. Comité Régional du Tourisme de Languedoc-Roussillon Prodexport.

Committee of Inquiry into the Winegrape and Wine Industry (1995). *Winegrape and Wine Industry in Australia* (Final Report). AGPS.

Conaway, J. (1990). *Napa*. Avon Books.

Cooper, M. (1993). *The Wine and Vineyards of New Zealand* (4th ed.) Hodder & Stoughton.

Corigliano, M.A. (1996). *Caratteristiche della domanda strategie di offerta e aspetti territoriali e ambientali*. Franco Angeli.

Craik, J. (1991). *Government Promotion of Tourism: The Role of the Queensland Tourist and Travel Corporation*. The Centre for Australian Public Sector Management, Griffith University.

Crompton, J.L. and McKay, S.L. (1997). Motives of visitors attending festival events. *Annals of Tourism Research*, **24**(2), 425–39.

Cruise Club Holidays n.d. Wines & Cusine. http://www.cruiseclub.gr/tours/index1.htm.

Daniel, V. (1994). Le tourisme en espace rural. *Travaux et Innovations*, **6**, 37–40.

Davidson, J. (1999). LCBOs Sunday openings irk pro-winery councillor. *The Standard*, 29 April, D7.

Day, L. (1996). In the name of a better cause. *Winestate*, **18**(3), 26–7.

de Blij, H.J. (1983). *Wine: A Geographic Appreciation*. Rowman and Allanheld.

Decanter (1997). *Rioja Revisited*, A Supplement to Decanter Magazine in association with the Rioja Wine Exporters. Link House Magazines.

Denbies Wine Estate (1999a). Promotional Brochure, Denbies Wine Estate.

Denbies Wine Estate (1999b). Student Information Pack, Denbies Wine Estate.

Desplats, B.L. (1996). Un tourisme valorisé ou valorisant? Exemples comparée de l'armagnac et du cognac [A developed or developing tourism? Comparing the examples of armagnac and cognac]. *Espaces*, **140**, 34–42.

DeTurenne, V. (1999). They're passionate about keeping Sonoma pastoral. *The Los Angeles Times*, 3 April.

Deutsches Weininstitut (1996/97). *Vintners to Visit/Resen zum Winzer*. Deutsches Weininstitut.

Deutsches Weininstitut (1999). *Deutsches Winzerfeste/German Wine Festivals*. Deutsches Weininstitut.

Deves, M. (ed.) (1996). *The Australian and New Zealand Wine Industry Directory*, 14th ed. Winetitles.

Dickenson, J. and Salt, J. (1982). In vino veritas: an introduction to the geography of wine. *Progress in Human Geography*, **6**, 159–89.

Dodd, T.H. (1994). Influences of consumer attitudes and involvement on purchase behavior in an industrial tourism context. Unpublished Dissertation. Texas Tech University.

Dodd, T. (1995). Opportunities and pitfalls of tourism in a developing wine industry. *International Journal of Wine Marketing*, **7**, 5–16.

Dodd, T.H. (1997). Factors that influence the adoption and diffusion of new wine products. *Hospitality Research Journal*, **20**(3), 123–36.

Dodd, T.H. (1998). Influences on search behaviour of industrial tourists. *Journal of Hospitality and Leisure Marketing*, **5**(2/3), 77–94.

Dodd, T.H. and Bigotte, V. (1995). *Visitors to Texas Wineries: Their Demographic Characteristics and Purchasing Behavior*. Texas Wine Marketing Research Institute.

Dodd, T.H. and Bigotte, V. (1997). Perceptual differences among visitor groups to wineries. *Journal of Travel Research*, **35**(3), 46–51.

Dodd, T.H. and Gustafson, A.W. (1997). Product, environment, and service attributes that influence consumer attitudes and purchases at wineries. *Journal of Food Products Marketing*, **4**(3), 41–59.

Dow Jones (n.d.). Special report: internet wine sales: web wine sales under fire. *BeverageNet*, http://www.beveragenet.net/sreport/intewine.asp (accessed 18/6/99).

Dower, M (n.d.). Special Report: WITRANET European Conference on Adding Value to Wine and Wine Related Culture in Rural Europe, 10–11 September 1998, Marathon. http://www.ecovast.org/witran51e.htm (accessed 31/05/99).

Duffield, B.S. and Long, J. (1981). Tourism in the highlands and islands of Scotland: rewards and conflicts, *Annals of Tourism Research*, **8**(3), 403–31.

ECOS-OUVERTURE (1998) *ECOS OUVERTURE Project: The Integration of Moldova in the Rural Tourism Network of the European Wine Producing Regions*. http://www.regione.piemonte.it/ruraltour/proj2uk.htm (accessed 2/10/98).

Edwards, F. (1986). The Marketing of Wine From Small Wineries, unpublished Masters Thesis. Faculty of Commerce and Economics, University of Queensland.

Edwards, F. (1989). The marketing of wine from small wineries: managing the intangibles. *International Journal of Wine Marketing*, **1**(1), 14–17.

European Regional Development Fund (n.d.) ERDG Article 10, Project No. 126, WITRANET. http://www.aeidl.be/art10/culture/126.htm.

Flood, J. (1990). Napa Valley: blending tourists and grapes. In *The Proceedings of The Tourism Connection: Linking Research and Marketing, Travel and Tourism Research Association Twenty-First Annual Conference*, pp. 141–2. University of Utah.

FNNPE (Federation of Nature and National Parks of Europe) (1993). *Loving Them To Death*. FNNPE.

Focus Multimedia (1997). Focus on Greece – Cuisine. http://www.vicnet.net.au/~focus/greece/gr_coumn.htm.

Folwell, R.J. and Grassel, M.A. (1995). How tasting rooms can help sell wine. In *Direct Farm Marketing and Tourism Handbook*, pp. 11–15. Cooperative Extension College of Agriculture, University of Arizona.

France in Your Glass (1998). France in Your Glass. http://www.inyourglass.com/index.html.

Freeman, C. (1991). Networks of innovators: a synthesis of research issues. *Research Policy*, **20**, 499–514.

Fridgen, J.D. (1984). Environmental psychology and tourism. *Annals of Tourism Research*, **11**, 19–39.

Frochot. I.V. (1991). *Enquête sur les Clienteles Touristiques de Dijon*. OTSI.

Fuller, P. (1997). Value adding the regional wine experience. *The Australian and New Zealand Wine Industry Journal*, **12**(1), 35–9.

Gausden, C. (1994). *Weekend Cycling*. The Promotional Reprint Company.

Geographical (1994). Globalising the Grape. *Geographical*, November, 14–17.

George, R. (1996). *The Wines of New Zealand*. Faber and Faber.

German National Tourist Board (1999). DZT's new marketing concept: culinary Germany. http://www.germany-tourism.de/news/presse_e (accessed 17/5/99).

Getz, D. (1999). Wine tourism: global overview and perspective on its development. In *Wine Tourism: Perfect Partners. Proceedings of the First Australian Wine Tourism Conference, Margaret River, Western Australia, May 1998* (R. Dowling and J. Carlsen, eds) pp. 13–33. Bureau of Tourism Research.

Giddens, A. (1984). *The Constitution of Society*. Polity Press.

Gilbert, D.C. (1992). Touristic development of a viticultural region of Spain. *International Journal of Wine Marketing*, **4**(2), 25–32.

Gillion, M. (1997). Martinborough: then and now (a classic wine village in the making?). *WINENZ Magazine*, October/November, 18–21.

Gillion, M. (1998). Nelson Notables. *WINENZ Magazine*, April/May, 8–14.

Golledge, S. and Maddern, C. (1994). *A Survey of Tourism Activity at Victorian Wineries*. Victorian Wineries Tourism Council.

Goodall, B. (1988). How tourists choose their holidays: an analytical framework. In *Marketing in the Tourism Industry: The Promotion of Destination Regions* (B. Goodall and G. Ashworth, eds) pp. 1–17, Routledge.

Goosecross Cellars (n.d.). Wine Crash Course: Have a good time and learn about wine. http://www.goosecross.com/Plan/class.html (accessed 25/06/99).

Graca, A.V. (1999). *Rota do Vinho do Dão*. Cabinete da Rota do Vinho do Dão, Visev, Portugal.

Graham, J.C. (1980). *Know Your New Zealand Wines*. Collins.

Greaves G. (1996). What a jolly beau jest – French get taste of le English plonk nouveau. *Daily Express*, 22 November.

Grecotel n.d. Grecotel resorts' promotional brochure, Greece.

Green, K. (1999). South Africa's export wines sales growing. *SA Wine Industry News*, 12 June.

Greene, J. (1999). Portuguese varietal wine. *Wines and Spirits* (June), San Francisco.

Greenwood, D. (1989). Culture by the pound: An anthropological perspective on tourism as cultural commoditization. In *Hosts and Guests* (V. Smith, ed.) pp. 172–85. University of Pennsylvania Press.

Habermas, J. (1962). *The Structural Transformation of the Public Sphere*. Polity Press.

Hackett, N.C. (1996). Surprise success: wine tourists and the woes of free trade. Paper presented at the annual meeting of the Travel and Tourism Research Association. Simon Fraser University, British Columbia.

Hackett, N.C. (1997). Surprise success: wine tourists and the woes of free trade, unpublished research report. Simon Fraser University, British Columbia.

Hadyn, J. and Talmont, R. (1997). Our love affair with wine. *New Zealand Geographic*, **35** (July-September), 18–42.

Haight, M.E. and Ratha, M. (1995). Wastes: issues and opportunities. In *Bali: Balancing Environment, Economy and Culture* (S. Martopo and B. Mitchell, eds) pp. 215–36. University of Waterloo, Department of Geography.

Hall, C.M. (1996). Wine tourism in New Zealand. In *Proceedings of Tourism Down Under II: A Tourism Research Conference*, pp. 109–19. University of Otago.

Hall, C.M. (1998). *Introduction to Tourism* (3rd edn). Addison-Wesley Longman

Hall, C.M. (2000). *Tourism Planning*. Prentice Hall.

Hall, C.M. and Jenkins, J. (1998). The policy dimensions of rural tourism and recreation. In *Tourism and Recreation in Rural Areas* (R.W. Butler, C.M. Hall and J.M. Jenkins, eds) pp. 19–42. John Wiley & Sons.

Hall, C.M. and Johnson, G. (1997). Wine tourism in New Zealand: larger bottles or better relationships? In *Trails, Tourism and Regional Development Conference Proceedings* (J. Higham, ed.) pp. 73–86. Centre for Tourism, University of Otago.

Hall, C.M. and Johnson, G. (1998a). Wine tourism: an imbalanced partnership. In *Wine Tourism: Perfect Partners. Proceedings of the First Australian Wine Tourism Conference, Margaret River, Western Australia, May 1998* (R. Dowling and J. Carlsen, eds) pp. 51–72. Bureau of Tourism Research.

Hall, C.M. and Johnson, G. (1998b). Wine and food tourism in New Zealand: difficulties in the creation of sustainable tourism business networks. In *Rural Tourism Management: Sustainable Options, Conference Proceedings, 9–12 Sept. 1998* (D. Hall and L. O'Hanlon, eds) pp. 21–38. Scottish Agricultural College.

Hall, C.M. and Macionis, N. (1998). Wine tourism in Australia and New Zealand. In *Tourism and Recreation in Rural Areas* (R.W. Butler, C.M. Hall and J.M. Jenkins, eds) pp. 267–98. John Wiley & Sons.

Hall, C.M. and Weiler, B. (1992). Introduction: What's special about special interest tourism? In *Special Interest Tourism* (B. Weiler and C.M. Hall, eds) pp. 1–13. Belhaven Press.

Hall, C.M., Cambourne, B., Macionis, N., and Johnson, G. (1997). Wine tourism and network development in Australia and New Zealand: Review, establishment, and prospects. *International Journal of Wine Marketing*, **9**(2/3), 5–31.

Hall, C.M., Cambourne, B., Macionis, N. and Johnson, G. (1998), Wine tourism and network development in Australia and New Zealand: Review, establishment and prospects. *International Journal of Wine Marketing* (special Australasian edition), **9**(2/3), 5–31.

Halliday, J. (1985). *The Australian Wine Compendium*. Angus & Robertson.

Halliday, J. (1994). *A History of the Australian Wine Industry (1949–1994)*. The Australian Wine & Brandy Corporation/ Winetitles.

Halliday, J. (1995). *The Australian Wine Compendium*. Angus & Robertson.

Hallstead, R. (1998). Wine theme park planned in London, *Knight-Ridder/ Tribune Business News*. http://www.hotel-on-line.com/Neo/News/1998 Sep 21/k.1ti.906486530.html (accessed 23/09/98).

Hands, P. and Hughes, D. (1997). *Wines and Brandies of the Cape of Good Hope: The Definitive Guide to the South African Wine Industry*. Stephen Phillips.

Harper, D.A. (1993). *An Analysis of Interfirm Networks*. NZ Institute of Economic Research.

Harvey, D. (1989). *The Condition of Postmodernity*. Blackwell.

Hawkesbury (1997). *The Wines and Wineries of Marlborough. Wine Trail Map*. Hawkesbury Map Publishers.

Healy, R.G. (1994). The 'common pool' problem in tourism in Lancaster County. *Annals of Tourism Research*, **9**(3), 565–83.

Henehan, B. and White, G.B. (1990). *Evaluation of Wine Trails in New York State*. Research Report A.E. Res. 90–13. Agriculture and Life Sciences Department, New York State College.

Hills, C. (1998). Quenching the thirst for knowledge. *Australian and New Zealand Wine Industry Journal*, **13**(1), 66–7.

Hilltop Neszmely Ltd (1999). Publicity brochures, Budapest, Hungary.

Hitchcock, M.J., King, V.T. and Parnwell, M.J.G. (eds) (1993). *Tourism in South East Asia*. Routledge

Holbrook, M.B. and Hirschman, E.C. (1982). The experiential aspects of consumption: consumer fantasies, feelings, and fun. *The Journal of Consumer Research*, **9**, 132–40.

Holt-Jensen, A. (1988). *Geography: History and Concepts: A Student's Guide*. Paul Chapman.

Hooke, H. (1997). *Words on Wine*. Sydney Morning Herald Books.

Howley, M. and Van Westering, J. (1999). Wine tourism in the United Kingdom. In *Wine Tourism: Perfect Partners. Proceedings of the First Australian Wine Tourism Conference, Margaret River, Western Australia, May 1998* (R. Dowling and J. Carlsen, eds) pp. 73–80. Bureau of Tourism Research.

http://www.regione.piemonte.it/ruraltour/metoduk.htm#marketing (accessed 2/10/98).

http://www.veronafiere.it/winegate/news/8_3_en/turism.html.

http://www.fetedesvignerons.ch (accessed January 1999).

Hudson, R. and Townsend, A. (1992). Tourism employment and policy choices for local government. In *Perspectives on Tourism Policy* (P. Johnson and B. Thomas, eds) pp. 49–68. Mansell.

Hungarian Food and Wine Bureau (1999). *Update from Hungary.* Hungarian Food and Wine Bureau, Sussex.

Hunt, J.D. (1975). Image as a factor in tourist development. *Journal of Travel Research*, **13**(3), 1–7.

Hunter Valley Research Foundation (1994). *Submission to the Industry Commission Inquiry into the Australian Wine Industry.* Hunter Valley Vineyard Association.

Hussey, A. (1982). Tourist destination areas in Bali. *Contemporary Southeast Asia*, **3**(4), 36–85.

Hutchinson, J. (1997). *Tourism: Getting it Right for the Millenium.* Office of National Tourism.

Ibbotson, S. (1999). Winegrowers soured by civic apathy, *The Press*, 29 April. http://www.press.co.nz/17/990429f5.htm.

Indiana Wine Grape Council (IWGC) (1998a). The Indiana Wine Grape Council. http://info.aes.purdue.edu/agresearch/IN_winewww.html.

Indiana Wine Grape council (IWGC) (1998b). Who is the Indian Wine Grape Council? http://info.aes.purdue.edu/agresearch/winegrape/IN_Wine Grape Council.html.

Indiana Wine Grape Council (IWGC) (1998c). Seven Tips for Touring Indiana Wineries. http://info.aes.purdue.edu/agresearch.winegrape/Seven_Tips_Indiana_Wine.html.

Infotour (1997). Infotour Database, Israel. Ministry of Tourism. (Information provided by Israeli Embassy, Wellington, August.)

IGUW and GGW (Institut für Geographie der Universitat Würzburg and Geographische Gesellschaft Würzburg (1984). *Die Verflechtung von Fremdenverkehr und Weinbau in Mainfranken* [The link between tourism and wine growing in Mainfranken]. Institut für Geographie, Universitat Würzburg.

Innes, S. (1995). Pacesetting SA wineries, the toast of tourism. *SA Advertiser*, 6 March, 5.

Iso-Ahola, S.E. (1980). *The Social Psychology of Leisure and Recreation.* Wm. C. Brown.

Jackson. L. (1999). England's wine hopes wither on the vine. *The Sunday Telegraph*, 7 February.

Jaladis, S. and Facomprez, F. (1997). Dossier Gastronomie. *Décision Tourisme*, September, 17.

Jane Brook (1999b). Swan Valley, Western Australia – 'The birthplace of the Western Australian Wine Industry' – Under threat! http://www.jane brook.com.au/savetheswanvalley.html.

Jenkins, J., Hall, C.M. and Troughton, M. (1998). The restructuring of rural economies: rural tourism and recreation as a government response. In *Tourism and Recreation in Rural Areas* (R.W. Butler, C.M. Hall and J. Jenkins, eds) pp. 43–68. John Wiley.

Jennings, D. and Wood, C. (1992). Czechoslovakian wine: strategy on a liberalized economy. *International Journal of Wine Marketing*, **4**(3), 16–25.

Johnson, G. (1997). Surveying wine tourism in New Zealand. In *Quality Tourism: Beyond the Masses. Proceedings of the First National Tourism Students' Conference*, ed. G. Johnson, pp. 61–6. Tourism Club.

Johnson, G. (1998). Wine tourism in New Zealand – a national survey of wineries, unpublished Dip. Tour. Dissertation. University of Otago.

Johnson, H. (1986). *The Atlas of German Wines and Traveller's Guide to the Vineyards*. Mitchell Beazley.

Johnson, H. (1989). *The Story of Wine*. Mitchell Beazley.

Johnson, H. (1991). *Hugh Johnson's Wine Companion* (3rd ed.) Mitchell Beazley.

Johnson, H. (1994). *The World Atlas of Wine* (4th ed.) Mitchell Beazley.

Jones, C. (1996). A vine romance in Victoria. *The Australian Magazine*, 30 November–1 December.

Joseph, R. (1998). Drink: Robert Joseph raises a glass . . . *Sunday Telegraph Magazine*, 4 October.

Kaltenborn, B. (1996). Tourism in Svalbard: planned management or the art of stumbling through? In *People and Tourism in Fragile Environments*, (Martin Price, ed.) pp. 109–22. John Wiley and Sons.

Kendziorek, M. (1994a). Making your tasting room profitable, Part I, Ten commandments of the tasting room. *Wine Marketing*, July/August, 75–6.

Kendziorek, M. (1994b). Making your tasting room profitable, Part II, Debunking ten myths. *Wine Marketing*, July/August, 28–9.

Kendziorek, M. (1994c). Making your tasting room profitable, Part III, Low-key approach increases sales. *Wine Marketing*, July/August, 75–6.

Kendziorek, M. (1994d). Making your tasting room profitable, Part IV, Non-wine sales boost profits, *Wine Marketing*, July/August, 75–6.

King, C. and Morris, R. (1997). Wine tourism: a Western Australian case study. *Australian and New Zealand Wine Industry Journal*, **12**(3), 246–9.

King, C. and Morris, R. (1999). Wine tourism: costs and returns. In *Wine Tourism: Perfect Partners. Proceedings of the First Australian Wine Tourism Conference, Margaret River, Western Australia, May 1998* (R. Dowling and J. Carlsen, eds) pp. 233–45. Bureau of Tourism Research.

King, J. (1998). *National Wine Tourism Strategy Green Paper.* Unpublished discussion paper. National Wine Tourism Strategy Task Force.

Kirk, W. (1963). Problems of geography. *Geography*, 48, 357–71.

Kislenko, D. (1994). New Château des Charmes is the only castle around. *Hamilton Spectator*, 28 May.

Klemm, M. (1996). Languedoc–Roussillon: adapting the strategy. *Tourism Management*, **17**(2), 133–47.

Kolpan, S., Smith, B., Wiess, M. (1996). *Exploring Wine.* Wiley Press.

Kosher Wines (1997). *Kosher Wines*, B'nei Shaare Zion Congregation. http://www.spacelab.net/~david/wine.htm.

Krummert, B. (1999), Point and click wine shopping. *Restaurant Hospitality*, **83**(1), 36.

Langton, B. (1996). *News. Tourism New South Wales Newsletter*, Spring, 3.

Lawrason, D. and Wilson, K. (1998). Canadian wine getaways. *Wine Access*, **8**(4), 7–9.

Lawson, R., Thyne, M. and Young, T. (1997). *New Zealand Holidays*: A *travel lifestyles study.* Department of Marketing, University of Otago.

LEADER (1995). Marketing quality rural tourism: rural tourism and local development, harmful effects of too much tourism. In *LEADER technical dossier*, LEADER II library.

Lefebvre, A. (1991). *The Production of Space.* Blackwell.

Leibowitz, N. (1998). Background of Israel Wine. http://www.sngchicago.com/general/wine/backgrnd.htm.

Leiper, N. (1989). *Tourism and Tourism Systems.* Occasional Paper No. 1. Department of Management Systems, Massey University.

Leiper, N. (1990). Tourist attraction systems. *Annals of Tourism Research*, **17**, 367–83.

Le Petit, J-P, Murat, R. and Coupy, P. (eds) (n.d.) *The European Cycle Route Network: EuroVelo Cycle Route no 4.* EuroVelo

Light, N. (1998). Robert Mondavi to develop wine country experience with Disney's California Adventure Opening in 2001, *Robert Mondavi Press Releases.* http://www.byronwinery.com.pressreleases/dca.html (accessed 09/03/99).

Lindberg, C.S., Enriquez, J. and Sproule, K. (1996). Ecotourism questioned: case studies from Belize. *Annals of Tourism Research*, **23**(1), 543–62.

Lofman, B. (1991). Elements of experiential consumption: an exploratory study. *Advances in Consumer Research*, **18**, 729–34.

Long Island Wine Council. n.d. *Long Island Wine Country* (brochure).

Longo, A.M. (1999). Wine Tourism in New Zealand: An exploration of the characteristics and motivations of winery visitors, unpublished Dip. Tour. Dissertation. University of Otago.

Lumsden, L. (1996). Cycle tourism in Britain. *Insights*, March, D27–D32.

MacCannell, D. (1989). *The Tourist: a New Theory of the Leisure Class*. Shocken Books.

Macionis, N. (1994). Marketing the Canberra District Wineries, unpublished research report. University of Canberra.

Macionis, N. (1996). Wine tourism in Australia. In *Tourism Down Under II Conference – Towards a More Sustainable Tourism, Conference Proceedings*, pp. 264–86. Centre for Tourism, University of Otago.

Macionis, N. (1997). Wine Tourism in Australia: Emergence, Development and Critical Issues, unpublished Masters Thesis. University of Canberra.

Macionis, N. (1998). Wine Tourism: making it work for the long term. *The Australian and New Zealand Wine Industry Journal*, **13**(2), 127–31.

Macionis, N. (1999). Wineries and tourism: perfect partners or dangerous Liaisons. In *Proceedings of the First Australian Wine Tourism Conference*, Margaret River, Western Australia, 5–9 May 1998 pp. 35–50. Bureau of Tourism Research.

Macionis, N. and Cambourne, B. (1998). Wine tourism: Just what is it all about? *The Australian and New Zealand Wine Industry Journal*, **13**(1), 41–7.

Macionis, N. and Cambourne, B. (forthcoming). Food and wine tourism in the ACT: exploring the links. *International Journal of Wine Marketing*.

Macri, G. (1997). South Australia – top tourist attraction. http://www.wine-mag.com.globalwinenews/au-briefs11–29.html (accessed 30/1/98).

Maddern C. and Golledge, S. (1996). *Victorian Wineries Tourism Council Cellar Door Survey*. Victorian Wineries Tourism Council.

Mallon, P. (1996). Vin et tourisme: un développement dans la diversité [Wine and tourism: development in diversity]. *Espaces*, **140**, 29–48.

Marcus, K. (1999). Israel: Not a land for the shy. *Wine Spectator*, March. http://www.winespectator.com/Wine/Spectator/Postcards/israel1.

Market Attitude Research Services (1996). *Opportunities for Canberra in Cultural Tourism. Final Report*. Market Attitude Research Services.

Market Attitude Research Services (1999). Canberra Arts Marketing Final Report. Unpublished Research Report. Canberra: ACT Facilities Corporation.

Martin, B.S. and Uysal, M. (1990). An examination of the relationship between carrying capacity and the tourism life cycle: management and policy implications. *Journal of Environmental Management*, **31**, 327–33.

Massey, D. (1994). *Space, Place and Gender*. Polity Press.

Mayson, R. (1998). Chipping at port's pedestal. *Decanter*, **24**(3), 54–8.

Mayson. R. (1997). The Douro dream ticket. *Decanter*, May, 60–3.

McGrath Morris, J. (1985). *Wineries of the Finger Lakes*. Isidore Stephanus Sons.

McKercher. B. (1995). The destination-market matrix: a tourism market portfolio analysis model. *Journal of Travel and Tourism Marketing*, **4**(2), 23–40.

McKinna, D. (1987). *Developing Marketing Strategies for Wines*. David McKinna.

Merret, D. and Whitwell, G. (1994). The empire strikes back: marketing Australian beer and wine in the United Kingdom. In *Adding Value: Brands and Marketing in Food and Drink* (G. Jones and N.J. Morgan, eds) pp. 162–8. Routledge.

Millon, M. and K. (1989). *The Wine Roads of France*. Grafton Books.

Mitchell, D. (1996). Introduction: public space and the city. *Urban Geography*, **17**, 127–131.

Mitchell, R., Hall, M., McIntosh, A. and Johnson, G. (1999). Getting to know the winery visitor. *New Zealand Wine Grower*, **2**(3), 25.

Mitchell, R.D. in progress. 'Scenery and Chardonnay': A Visitor Perspective of the New Zealand Winery Experience, unpublished Doctoral Thesis. University of Otago.

Mitchell, R.D. and McIntosh, A.J. (1999). Investigating the Sensory and Affective Nature of the Wine Tourism Experience. In *Tourism & Hospitality: Delighting the Senses 1999, Part Two. Proceedings of the Ninth Australian Tourism Hospitality and Tourism Research Conference, Council of the Australian University Tourism and Hospitality Education (CAUTHE) 10–13 February 1999, Adelaide, South Australia* (J. Molloy and J. Davies, eds) p. 96. Bureau of Tourism Research.

Mollo, R. (1999). The Wine Roads: Circuits combining art, culture and wine. http://www.italianstyle.it/london/tourism/Wine_Roads.htm.

Montgomery, C. (1988). The role of marketing research in management decision making: the Biltmore Estate case. In *Hospitality and Tourism Invitational Proceedings* (R.J. Howell, ed), pp. 110–16, Recreation, Travel and Tourism Institute, Clemson University.

Moran, W. (1993). Rural space as intellectual property. *Political Geography*, **12**, 263–77.

Morgan, J. (1995). Touring the Finger Lakes. *Wine Spectator*, **20**(9), 80–4.

Morris, R. and King, C. (1997a). *The Cellar Door Report: Margaret River Region Winery Tourism Research*. Edith Cowan University: Churchlands Campus.

Morris, R. and King, C. (1997b). Cooperative marketing for small business growth and regional economic development: A case study in wine tourism entrepreneurship. In The Engine of Global Economic Development, 42nd World Conference International Council for Small Business, San Francisco, June 1997, Conference Proceedings, ed. S.W. Kunkel and M.D. Meeks, http:/

/www.icsb.org/conferences/w97/papers/FullPapers/index.htm   (accessed 8/1/98).

Morris, R. and King, C. (1999). Delighting the wine tourist. In *Wine Tourism: Perfect Partners. Proceedings of the First Australian Wine Tourism Conference, Margaret River, Western Australia, May 1998* (R. Dowling and J. Carlsen, eds) pp. 219–28. Bureau of Tourism Research.

Moynahan, M. (1995). East End wineries boost Long Island tourism. *Long Island Business News*, 7 August, 17.

MTV (Movimento del Turismo del Vino) (1995). http://ulysses.ulysse.s.it/mtv/.

MTV (Movimento del Turismo del Vino) (1999). The Wineday 1999. http://www.wineday.org/guest/news/mewsl/oneeng.html.

Murphy, P.E. (1985). *Tourism: A Community Approach*. Methuen.

Napa Valley Vintners Association (1999). How Does the Wine Industry Contribute to Napa County? http://napavintners.com/facts.html (accessed 24/03/99).

New World Wine Communications (1998). Mickey picks grapes: Mondavi teaming with Disneyland for wine country theme park. *Smart Wine Online*. http://smartwine.com.news/nws9804/swapr30a.html (accessed 09/03/99).

New York Wine and Grape Foundation (1997). *Uncork New York, New York Wine Industry – The Renaissance* (media kit).

New York Wine and Grape Foundation (n.d.). *Uncork New York, Welcome to the New World of World-Class Wine* (Brochure).

New Zealand Wine Grower (1999). Winegrowers foresight: New Zealand to lead world of wine by year 2010. *New Zealand Wine Grower*, **2**(3), 7–9.

New Zealand Wines Online (1999). New Zealand Wines Online: Your virtual, tour of New Zealand wines. http://www.nzwine.com/.

Nitsch, B. and van Straaten, J. (1995). Rural tourism development: Using a sustainable tourism development approach. In *Sustainable Tourism Development* (H. Coccossis and P. Nukamp, eds) pp. 169–85. Avebury.

Nixon, B. (1999). The changing face of the winery tourist. In *Wine Tourism: Perfect Partners. Proceedings of the First Australian Wine Tourism Conference, Margaret River, Western Australia, May 1998* (R. Dowling and J. Carlsen, eds) pp. 209–17. Bureau of Tourism Research.

NZTB (New Zealand Tourism Board) (1993). *New Zealand International Visitors Survey 1992/93*. New Zealand Tourism Board.

NZTB (New Zealand Tourism Board) (1996). *1995/1996 New Zealand International Visitors Survey*. New Zealand Tourism Board.

NZTB (New Zealand Tourism Board) (1998a). Increasing focus on destination marketing. *Tourism News*, August, 6–7.

NZTB (New Zealand Tourism Board) (1998b). Tourism marketing networks – huge potential for foreign exchange growth. *Tourism News*, December, 1.

NZTB (New Zealand Tourism Board) (1998c). Tourism marketing networks. *Tourism News*, September, 4.

Office des Vins Vaudois (1998a). *Vaud: The Vineyard Guide*. Office des Vins Vaudois.

Office des Vins Vaudois (1998b). *L'Hospitalite Vigneronne Vaudoise*, Office des Vins Vaudois.

Office of National Tourism (1997). *Information Sheet: National Tourism Development Program Category D: National Industry Development and Coordination*. Office of National Tourism.

Oregon Wine Advisory Board (1995). *History and Character of the Oregon Wine Industry*. Oregon Wine Advisory Board.

Pacific Cycle Tours (1999). Tour Dates. Http://www.bike-nz.com/tours.htm (accessed 30/3/99).

Page, S. and Getz, D. (1997). *The Business of Rural Tourism: International Perspectives*. International Thomson Business Press.

Paradice, W. and Krumpe, E. (1989). *The Sydney-Sider: Day Visits to the Hunter: An Evaluation of day visitation to the Hunter Region*. Hunter Valley Research Foundation.

Parliament of Australia (1999). A New Tax System (Wine Equalisation Tax) Bill 1999. http://www.aph.gov.au/library/pubs/bd/1998-99/99bd151.htm (accessed 18/5/99).

Pavan, D. (1994a). L'enoturismo tra fantasia e metodo [Wine tourism: between fact and fantasy]. *Vignevini*, **21**(1), 6–7.

Pavan, D. (1994b). Se Moametto non va alla montagna [If Mohamet doesn't go to the mountain]. *Vignevini*, **21**(5), 18–19.

Pearce, P.L. (1982). Perceived changes in holiday destinations. *Annals of Tourism Research*, **9**, 145–64.

Peters, G.L. (1997). *American Winescapes: The Cultural Landscapes of America's Wine Country*. Westview Press.

Peters, G.L. (1998). The economics of festivals: wines and vines on the metropolitan fringe. *Focus*, **45**(2), 33–6.

Platter, J. (1997). *South African Wines*. J. & E. Platter.

Platter, J. (1992). *South African Wines*. J. & E. Platter.

Platter, J. (1999). *South African Wines*. J. & E. Platter.

Powell, W. (1990). Neither market nor hierarchy: network forms of organization. In *Research in Organizational Behaviour*, vol. 12 (B. Straw and L. Cummings, eds) pp. 74–9, JAI Press.

Pratt, S.J. (1994). *Special Event Tourism: An analysis of food and wine festivals in New Zealand*, unpublished Dip. Tour. dissertation. University of Otago.

Price, M. (1992). Patterns of the development of tourism in mountain environments. *GeoJournal*, **27**(1), 87–96.

Rankine, B. (1989). *Making Good Wine – A Manual of Practice for Australia and New Zealand*. Pan Macmillan Publishers.

Ranner, G. (1997). Ein urlaub bei weinbauern hat hohen stellenwert [A holiday on a vineyard is good value.] *Fürderungdienst*, **45**(4), 31–2.

Reid, A.L. (1990). *Grape Expectations? An Exploratory Evaluation of the Tourist Potential of the New Zealand Wine Industry*, unpublished Dip. Tour. dissertation. University of Otago.

Relph, E. (1996). Place. In *Companion Encyclopedia of Geography: The Environment and Humankind* (I. Douglas, R. Huggett and M. Robinson, eds). Routledge.

Renwick, C. (1977). *A Study of Wine in the Hunter Region of New South Wales*. Hunter Valley Research Foundation Monograph No. 39. Hunter Valley Research Foundation.

Richards, G. (1996). Production and consumption of European cultural tourism. *Annals of Tourism Research*, **23**(2), 261–83.

Richardson, O. (1999). Vineyard Crawls in Britain. Http://sol.brunel.ac.uk/~richards/wine/trips.htm (accessed 23/3/99).

Robertson, R. (1995). Globalization: time-space and homogeneity-heterogenity. In *Global Modernities* (M. Featherstone, S. Lash and R. Robertson, eds) pp. 25–44. Sage.

Robins, P. (1999). Potential research into wine tourism. In *Wine Tourism: Perfect Partners. Proceedings of the First Australian Wine Tourism Conference, Margaret River, Western Australia, May 1998* (R. Dowling and J. Carlsen, eds) pp. 81–91. Canberra: Bureau of Tourism Research.

Robinson, J. (1994). Tourism. In *The Oxford Companion to Wine* (J. Robinson, ed) pp. 980–1. Oxford University Press.

Rogov, D. (1995). A vintage turnaround. *Link Israel Food Focus*, Winter 19–20.

Roy Morgan Holiday Tracking Research (1996). *Roy Morgan Value Segments*. Roy Morgan.

Rushton, A. (1999). The National Wine Centre – an icon for the next millennium. In *Proceedings of the First Australian Wine Tourism Conference*, Margaret River, Western Australia, 5–9 May 1998, pp. 119–23, Bureau of Tourism Research.

Sarkadi, E., Szμcs, J. and Urbμn, A. (1995). Role of vine and viticulture in regional development. *Falu*, **11**(1), 55–9.

Scales, W.I. Croser, B.J. and Freebairn, J.W. (1995). *Winegrape and Wine Industry in Australia: A Report by the Committee of Inquiry into the Winegrape and Wine Industry*. Australian Government Publishing Service.

Schiffman, L.G. and Kanuk, L.L. (1987). *Consumer Behavior*, 3rd ed. Prentice-Hall International.

Schroder, P. (1997). Hardy's wine plan could turn Canberra into new Coonawarra. *Canberra Times*, 30 May, 1.

Scott, A., Mentink, K. and Donnelly, D. (1994). *Canberra Advertising Evaluation. A Market Research Presentation*. Frank Small & Associates.

Scott, D. (1964). *Winemakers of New Zealand*. Southern Cross Books.

Seferiades, C. (1998). Greek Wine Routes. http://www.greekwine.gr/frames/routes.

Senese, D. (1999). Wine tourism and the evolution of cultural landscapes of the Okanagan. Paper presented at the Western Division Canadian Association of Geographers Annual Meeting 11–13 March, (1999), Kelowna, British Columbia. http://www.geog.ouc.bc.ca/wcag/oral/Senese_Donna.html.

Sharp, K. (1992). Sour grapes over tourist boom. *Los Angeles Times*, 3 December, A3.

Sharpley, R. and Sharpley J. (1997). *Rural Tourism*. International Thompson Business Press.

Shelmerdine, S. (1999). The Victorian Wineries Tourism Council. In *Wine Tourism: Perfect Partners. Proceedings of the First Australian Wine Tourism Conference, Margaret River, Western Australia, May 1998* (R. Dowling and J. Carlsen, eds) pp. 159–62. Canberra: Bureau of Tourism Research.

Sher, H. (1997). Vintage personalities. The *Jerusalem* Report, 6 March, 36–8.

Shields, R. (1981). *Places on the Margin – Alternative Geographies of Modernity*. Routledge.

Simon, J. (1996). The rise of grape Britain. *The Sunday Times Magazine*, 29 September, 24.

Skelton, S. (1989). *The Vineyards of England*. S.P. & L. Skelton.

Skinner, P.A.L. (1993). Cyprus wine: another perspective – a product-based marketing analysis. *International Journal of Wine Marketing*, **5**(1), 75–88.

Smith, C. (1992). New Zealand Cuisine as a Tourist Attraction, unpublished Dip. Tour. dissertation. University of Otago.

Smith, D. (1997). New Winery praised for diverse land use. *Otago Daily Times*, 31 March, 9.

Smith Kostyrko Cohen (1998). BRL Hardy Proposed Wine Tourism Complex, Preliminary Assessment Planning and Land Management, Canberra. http://www.palm.act.gov.au/pas/wine/brlwine.htm (accessed 25/3/99).

Snow, C. (1997). Getting a drop of the action at exhibitions. *Australia and New Zealand Wine Industry Journal*, **12**(4), 377–80.

Soja, E. (1989). *Postmodern Geographies: the Reassertion of Space in Critical Social Theory*. Verso.

South African Wine Directory (1999). Klein Karroo Wine Route. http://www.wine.co.za (accessed 22/1/99).

South Australian Tourism Commission (1996). *South Australian Tourism Plan 1996–2001*. South Australian Tourism Commission.

Spawton, T. (1986a). Understanding wine purchasing: knowing how the wine buyer behaves can increase sales. *The Australian and New Zealand Wine Industry Journal*, **1**(2), 54–7.

Spawton, T. (1986b). Marketing planning for small winemakers. *Australian and New Zealand Wine Industry Journal*, **1**(3), 89–91.

Stellenbosch Wine Route (1992). Press release.

Stellenbosch Wine Route (1996). Press release.

Sterk, C. (1995). *Tourism Business Plan*. Unpublished Tourism Business Plan. Barossa Wine and Tourism Association Incorporation.

Stratemeyer, A. (1998). Strat's Place: The Wine Label Collectors Club of America. http://www.stratsplace.com/wine_label.html.

Sustrans (1996). *LF1 Nordzeeroute: Cycling between Den Helder and Boulogne-sur-Mer*. Sustrans

Sutton, I. (1999). National Wine Tourism Strategy – introduction and overview. In *Wine Tourism: Perfect Partners. Proceedings of the First Australian Wine Tourism Conference, Margaret River, Western Australia, May 1998* (R. Dowling and J. Carlsen, eds) pp. 267–76. Canberra: Bureau of Tourism Research.

Swarbrooke, J. (1996). Culture, tourism and the sustainability of rural areas in Europe. In *Managing Cultural Resources for Tourism – Proceedings of the Tourism and Culture: Towards the 21st Century Conference*, vol. 2 (Callaghan, Long and Robinson, eds) Centre for Travel and Tourism, University of Northumbria, pp. 447–70.

Swarbrooke, J. and Horner, S. (1999). *Consumer Behaviour in Tourism*. Butterworth-Heinemann.

Sweeney, J.W. (1999). Thompson seeks ruling for Internet wine sales: tax collection among problems. *Winetoday.com*.http://www.winetoday.com/story/storyprnt.asp?id=424 (accessed 17/6/99).

Swiss Wine Exporters Association. (1996). *Swiss Wines*: A World of Difference. Swiss Wine Exporters Association.

Tammemagi, H. and Tammemagi, A. (1997). *Exploring Niagara*. Oakhill Publications.

Taylor M. (1999). Wider vision for English wines. *Harpers*, 15 January, 27–8.

Telfer, D.J. (forthcoming). Tastes of Niagara: building strategic alliances between tourism and agriculture. *Journal of International Hospitality, Leisure and Tourism Management*.

Telfer, D.J. and Wall. G. (1996). Linkages between tourism and food production. *Annals of Tourism Research*, **23**(3), 635–53.

The Australian. (1995). *The Australian*, 16 September, 4–5.

Thorpy, F. (1971). *Wine in New Zealand*. Collins.

Thèvenin, C. (1996). Quand les vignerons font du tourisme [When the wine growers practise tourism]. *Espaces*, **140**, 43–8.

Three Choirs http://sol.brunel.ac.uk/~richards/vineyards/threec.htm (accessed 16/6/99).

Three Choirs http://www.theaa.co.uk/region8/95493.html (accessed 16/6/99).

Three Choirs wysiwyg://main.20/http://www.three-choirs-vineyards.co.uk/index.htm (accessed 16/6/99).

Tolley, R. and Turton, B. (1995). *Transport Systems, Policy and Planning: A Geographical Approach*, Longman.

Tourinform Baranya n.d. *The Villány Siklós Wine Road* (brochure). Tourinform Baranya.

Tourism New South Wales (1996). *Food and Wine in Tourism – A Plan*. Tourism New South Wales.

Tourism South Australia (1991). *Barossa Valley Vintage Festival Visitor Survey, April 1991*. Tourism South Australia.

Vineyards Association of Tasmania (1998). *Submission to the Senate Select Committee on a New Tax System* Unpublished position paper. Vineyards Association of Tasmania.

Vinopolis – City of Wine (1999). Information Kit. Wineworld London.

VWTC (Victorian Wineries Tourism Council) (1994). Terms of Reference, unpublished internal document. Victorian Wineries Tourism Council.

Vysniauskus, J. (1998). Canadian wine industry rebounds after free trade scare. *Wine Business Monthly*, June (accessed 10/03/99).

Waldsmith, L. (1997). Councils view agricultural tourism as untapped mine. *The Detroit News*, 12 October. http://www.detnews.com/1997/612/9710/13/1012 0016.htm.

Waters, C. (1999a). Wineries win right to sell direct. *The Standard*, 1 May, C1.

Waters, C. (1999b). New Vintners on the block. *The Standard*, 1 March, B1.

WCO (Wine Council of Ontario) (1998). *The Ontario Wine Industry: An Overview of Recent History* (brochure). WCO.

Weekend Australian (1996). Slab hut to vintage success. *Weekend Australian*, 26 May, 28.

Weekly Times (1995). Wine tour push. *Weekly Times* (Victoria), 1 November, 22.

Welsh, A.J. (1994). An Analysis of Marketing Factors Contributing to Success Amongst Geographically Clustered Small Businesses in the Australian Wine Industry, unpublished Masters thesis. University of South Australia.

Western Australian Government (1997). *Western Australian Wine Industry Strategic Plan*. Western Australian Government.

Weston, H. (1999). Land of the Andes. *Hospitality Magazine*, May, 21.

Whitaker, N. (1999). Viva Argentina. *Food Illustrated* (February), John Brown Publishing, 36–45.

White. R. (1999). England's great Champagne-style story. *The Grape Press – Magazine of the UKVA*, 116th ed., Spring.

Wiener, S. (1990). *Finger Lakes Wineries: A Complete Touring Guide to Central New York's Acclaimed Wine Country*. McBooks Press.

Wilson, W. (1999). Okanagan agritourism. Unpublished paper presented at the Western Division Canadian Association of Geographers Annual Meeting 11–13 March 1999, Kelowna, British Columbia.

Wine Institute (1998). Wine's Importance to California. http://www.wine-institute.org/communications/statistics/wineimportant cal.htm (accessed 29/03/99).

Wine News (1999). The economic potential of wine tourism. *Wine News*.

Wine News Network (1998). Editorial: Internet wineries. http://www. napawine.com/news/Editorial1998.html (accessed 18/6/99).

Winemakers' Federation of Australia (1996), Strategy 2025. *Australian and New Zealand Wine Industry Journal*, **11**(3) 196–211.

Winemakers' Federation of Australia (1998). *Australian Wine Industry Fact Sheet: Wine Industry at a Glance – 1998*. Winemakers' Federation of Australia.

Wine Producers Association of the Macedonian Vineyard. (1999). *Wine Roads of Macedonia*. Wine Producers Association of the Macedonian Vineyard.

WINENZ Magazine (1997). Whangarei and beyond (advertisement). *WINENZ Magazine*, August/September, 12–13.

Winters, M. (1997). Web marketing hits its stride: Wineries hurry to open virtual storefronts. *Wine Business Monthly*, March 1997, reprinted *Smartwine.com*.http://smartwine.com/wbm/1997/9703/bmc9713.htm (accessed 18/6/99).

WINZ (Wine Institute of New Zealand) (1997). *Annual Report: Year End June 1997*. Wine Institute of New Zealand.

WINZ (Wine Institute of New Zealand) (1998a). 1998 Annual Report, Year Ending 30 June. http://www.nzwine.com/winz/98annual/summary.htm.

WINZ (Wine Institute of New Zealand) (1998b). Number of Winemakers Tops 300 (Press release). http://www.nzwine.com/winz/press/25sep98. htm.

WINZ (Wine Institute of New Zealand) (1999). Value of Wine Exports Up 40% in Six Months (Press release). http://www.nzwine.com/winz/press/ 5mar99.htm.

Wright, H. (1996a). On the Greek wine road. *Decanter*, July, 68–70.

Wright, H. (1996b). *Water into Wine: A Wine Lover's Cruise Through the Vineyards of France*. Kyle Cathie.

Yates, J. (1997). Touring Napa Valley's makers of sparkling wine. http://studio.bpe.com/drinks/wine/tbar/sparkling/index.html.

Ziraldo, D. (1995). *Anatomy of a Winery: The Art of Wine at Inniskillin*. Key Porter Books.

Zukin, S. (1995). *The Cultures of Cities*. Blackwell.

Personal communications

Anon. pers. comm. (1996). In Macionis 1997, 53.

Byrne, Bernadette (1997). *Mendocino Wine Growers Alliance*.

Chandler, Mark (1997). Executive Director, *Lodi-Woodbridge Winegrape Commission*.

Colombini, Donatella Cinelli (1997). Chair, *Movimento del Turismo del Vino*.

Day, C. (1997), (1999). Group Manager Strategic Planning, BRL Hardy.

English Tourism Board (ETB) (1999). Unpublished personal interview, Guildford

Gillette, W. (1998). Agricultural Commissioner (member Agricultural Preserve Advisory Committee), 10 November.

Helm, K. (1997). Director, Helm Wines.

Hook, E. (1996). Research Analyst, Department of Tourism, California Trade and Commerce Agency, USA.

Jane Brook (1999a). Cellar door notes recorded by Michael Hall on visit to winery, 7 July.

Janke, S. (1999), April, Personal interview, Hospitality Director, Château des Charmes Wines Limited.

Joshua, B. (1997). Chair ACT and Southern Highlands Viticultural Society.

March, H. (1998). Personal communication with H. March, *Winery Guide*, Martinborough, 6 February.

Montefiore, Adam (1999). International Marketing Manager, *Golan Heights Winery*. Peters, G.L. 1998b. 14–16 December.

Topper, Colleen (1998). Director of Public Relations, *Goosecross Cellars*.

Trustram Eve, J. (1999). Personal letter from Julia Trustram Eve, English Wine Producers.

Westthorpe, D. (1999). Project Manager, Queensland Wine Project.

Index